CRITICAL SURVEY OF POETRY
Spanish Poets

Editor

Rosemary M. Canfield Reisman
Charleston Southern University

SALEM PRESS
A Division of EBSCO Publishing, Ipswich, Massachusetts

Cover photo:
Jorge Guillén (© Colita/Corbis)

Copyright © 2012, by Salem Press, A Division of EBSCO Publishing, Inc. All rights in this book are reserved. No part of this work may be used or reproduced in any manner whatsoever or transmitted in any form or by any means, electronic or mechanical, including photocopy, recording, or any information storage and retrieval system, without written permission from the copyright owner except in the case of brief quotations embodied in critical articles and reviews or in the copying of images deemed to be freely licensed or in the public domain. For information address the publisher, Salem Press, at csr@salempress.com.

ISBN: 978-1-42983-666-1

CONTENTS

Contributors iv

Spanish Poetry to 1400 1
Spanish Poetry Since 1400 14

Rafael Alberti 30
Vicente Aleixandre 39
Gustavo Adolfo Bécquer 48
Pedro Calderón de la Barca 57
Rosalía de Castro 65
Luis Cernuda 75
J. V. Foix 84
Federico García Lorca 93
Garcilaso de la Vega 104
Luis de Góngora y Argote 113
Jorge Guillén 120
Juan Ramón Jiménez 128
Saint John of the Cross 139
Judah ha-Levi 152
Luis de León 159
Lucan 167
Antonio Machado 176
Jorge Manrique 185
Martial 191
Blas de Otero 196
Pedro Salinas 206
Miguel de Unamuno y Jugo 215
César Vallejo 224
Lope de Vega Carpio 237

Checklist for Explicating a Poem 248
Bibliography 251
Guide to Online Resources 254
Category Index 257
Subject Index 259

CONTRIBUTORS

Francisco J. Cevallos
Orono, Maine

Carole A. Champagne
University of Maryland-Eastern Shore

Peter Cocozzella
State University of New York at Binghamton

Mark DeStephano
Saint Peter's College

Lee Hunt Dowling
University of Houston

Desiree Dreeuws
Sunland, California

Clara Estow
University of Massachusetts

Jack Ewing
Boise, Idaho

Katherine Gyékényesi Gatto
Richmond Heights, Ohio

Shelley P. Haley
Howard University

Sarah Hilbert
Pasadena, California

Juan Fernández Jiménez
Pennsylvania State University

Theodore L. Kassier
University of Texas-San Antonio

Richard Keenan
University of Maryland-Eastern Shore

Philip Krummrich
University of Georgia

Rebecca Kuzins
Pasadena, California

John Richard Law
Auburn University

Richard A. Mazzara
Oakland University

Susan G. Polansky
Carnegie Mellon University

Norman Roth
University of Wisconsin

Jack Shreve
Allegany Community College

Kenneth A. Stackhouse
Virginia Commonwealth University

Rogelio A. de la Torre
Indiana University at South Bend

David Allen White
United States Naval Academy

SPANISH POETRY TO 1400

The development of Spanish poetry through the fourteenth century is a facet of what Ramón Menéndez Pidal, the preeminent Spanish medievalist, called *frutos tardios* (late fruits). Extant manuscripts from this period are few in number, and their condition is generally poor, but their literary quality is very high. Although this essay will focus on poetry written in Spanish, it is important to note that, during this rich period in the cultural history of Spain, significant poetry was written in other languages as well—notably the Arabic-Hebraic *jarchas*, the Galician *cantigas de amigo*, and Catalan lyric verse. Just as many consider modern Spain a quilt of five distinct national patterns (Galacian, Basque, Catalan, Andalusian, and Castilian), so medieval Spain was a mosaic of regional political entities—Asturian, Galician, Leonese, Castilian, Navarrese, Aragonese, and Catalonian, to name a few—as well as racial and religious patterns: Christian, Jewish, and Muslim.

EIGHTH THROUGH TENTH CENTURIES

The Moorish invasion of 711 and the virtual conquest of the Iberian Peninsula by the year 718 left the Hispano-Visigothic kingdom in disarray. Many of the conquered Visigoths were absorbed into Islamic culture (they became known as *mozarabes*), while others retreated into the protective mountain ranges of the northern Cantabrian coastline. From the latter came the Reconquest, a seven-century-long effort to recapture the Peninsula. Isolated pockets of resistance to Moorish domination grew into kingdoms with competing priorities and interests involving territory, preeminence of power, and collection of taxes as well as the cultural variables, such as language and literature, that made each of them distinct. Intriguingly, Galicia, Castile, León, Navarre, Aragon, and Catalonia all developed separate linguistic traditions, but only Galicia, Castile, and Catalonia produced literatures that have survived. While much medieval knowledge was hoarded and hidden to benefit a specific interest, language and literature were much more democratic; every bard, *juglar* or *jongleur*, needed to keep his material fresh, and the subsequent give-and-take of poetic style and vocabulary crossed from one language to another and from one culture to another. Medieval Spanish poetry is the product of these many influences.

The development of the Spanish language followed a path distinct from that of other languages of the Iberian Peninsula. With a tendency toward simplification of sounds and forms, Castilian standardized its grammar and vocabulary very early, making possible, for example, the reading of eleventh and twelfth century documents by an untrained twentieth century eye. (By comparison, the fourteenth century English of Geoffrey Chaucer's *The Canterbury Tales* [1387-1400] is resistant to the untrained modern reader.) The early formation of Spanish clearly had an effect on Spanish literature, as did the pioneer environment of its origin. Artificial attempts have been made to differentiate Castilian from Spanish. In the purest of senses, Castilian can be distinguished as a dialect with its marked peculiarities, but it exerted its dominion over an entire peninsula and subsequently, the New World, thereby becoming the language of Spain.

Eleventh century: Beginnings

The extraordinary and controversial beginning of Spanish verse must be assigned to the *kharjas*. Written in Arabic and Hebrew script—hence the controversy concerning their "Spanishness"—these refrains served as transitional passages between longer classical Arab stanzas known as *muwassahas*. When one transliterates *kharjas* into Roman characters and adds the missing vowels, the resulting text is clearly an archaic form of Spanish. Thus, according to Alan Deyermond, the refrain

> tnt' m'ry tnt' m'ry hbyb tnt'
> m'ry
> 'nfrmyrwn wlyws gyds(?) ydwln tn m'ly

becomes

> Tant' amare, tant' amare habib, tant'
> amare
> enfermiron welyos nidios e dolen tan male.

> My love is so great, my love is so great
> Lover, my love is so great
> My healthy eyes have sickened
> And hurt so badly

In a 1948 article that constituted the first systematic study of the *kharjas*, S. M. Stern demonstrated that a Spanish vocabulary lies hidden in the Arabic and Hebrew script of these refrains. Stern's discovery revolutionized critical understanding of the origins of Spanish verse—and, indeed, of European lyric verse. Dámaso Alonso, the distinguished Spanish poet and critic, refers to these verses as the "early spring" of the European lyric, for they predate by a century the earliest poems written in Provence.

The content of the *kharjas* is almost invariably love-oriented. Like the example quoted above, many of these refrains express the pain of separation, the sense of hurt as a result of a lover's absence or infidelity; others employ "love" as a metaphor for the relationship between a poet and his patron. Since these verses were written as transitional passages between longer texts and rarely can stand on their own as expressions of a complete sentiment, their acceptance as the earliest form of the European lyric has been questioned. On the other hand, their beauty and compactness of expression reflect the existence of a tradition of popular song or cultured verse, or both, in the Spanish eleventh century.

Twelfth Century: Textual Desert

Study of Spanish poetry in the twelfth century is hampered by a scarcity of texts. Despite the lack of texts, however, it is clear that lyric traditions were well established by the twelfth century. This is confirmed not only by the *kharjas* but also by two other verse forms which appeared in this century: the Galician-Portuguese *cantigas* and the Castilian *villancicos*. The *cantigas*, which have survived in three *cancioneros* (songbooks), of the fifteenth century, fall into three categories: a woman's lament for her lover (*cantigas de amigo*); a man's lament (*cantigas de amor*); and invective verse (*cantigas d'escarnho*). The similarity of content (lament for a lover) and speaker (a woman) between the *cantigas de amigo* and the *kharjas* suggests a connection, though none has been established.

Villancicos, multiverse refrains, repeated before and after every stanza, were not written down until the fifteenth century but are generally considered to date from the twelfth century. Their similarity to the *kharjas* is striking: They share a similar structure (refrain), content (lament for a lover), and speaker (a woman).

Thirteenth Century: Poets and Monks

Thirteenth century Spanish poetry is notable for the genesis of native epic verse; unfortunately, scholars of the thirteenth century Spanish epic have barely five thousand lines of text with which to work, in comparison to the million lines of verse available to French medieval scholars. Adducing plot summaries in later chronicles, some critics postulate the existence of lost epics, while others suggest that many poems of epic nature were never written down because of their oral means of transmission. In any case, Spanish scholarship has been left with four national epic poems: *Cantar de mío Cid* (early thirteenth century; *Chronicle of the Cid*, 1846; better known as *Poem of the Cid*), *Las mocedades de Rodrigo* (fourteenth century), and *Cantar de Roncesvalles* (thirteenth century; *Song of Roland*), composed in traditional epic meter (assonant lines of fourteen to sixteen syllables), and *Poema de Fernán Gonzalez* (c. 1260), composed in *cuaderna vía*, a syllabic meter distinguished by its rigidity of form.

The single most important epic composition of the thirteenth century was *Poem of the Cid*. Like the other epics of its period, *Poem of the Cid* is the subject of ongoing critical debate concerning the nature of its composition. Traditionalist critics argue that the Spanish epic originated in popular culture, in the songs of traveling entertainers or *juglares*. The most popular of these traditional songs, so the theory goes, were set down in manuscript and preserved for future generations. In contrast, the individualist critics believe that the great epics of medieval Spain were the work of individual poets, shaped by individual genius. Finally, the oralist critics argue that the epics of this period were transmitted exclusively by oral performance and were not committed to writing until a later date.

A manuscript of *Poem of the Cid* does exist, yet a gap in the transcription of the date, "MCC VII," has convinced the traditionalists that the date of composition was actually

1307. The individualists see the gap as typical of scribal transcription and build an argument for a date of 1207. Traditionalists argue that Per Abad, the name appearing at the end of the manuscript, refers to a copyist, while the individualists suggest that he was the actual author of the epic. In *The Making of the "Poema de mío Cid"* (1983), a book C. C. Smith calls "bold," Smith affirms that his work

> ... is the first in which the following proposition is argued: that the *Poema de mío Cid*, composed in or shortly before 1207, was the first epic to be composed in Castilian; that it was in consequence an innovatory and experimental work, in ways apparent in the surviving text; and that it did not depend on any precedents or existing tradition of epic verse in Castilian or other Peninsular language or dialect.

Smith goes on to assert that Per Abad was the actual author of the poem, not merely the copyist. Regardless of the exact method of composition of *Poem of the Cid*, however, it seems reasonable to assume that *juglares* sang verse narratives of this type, commemorating historical events and following a general, though loose, metric pattern.

Composed in traditional Spanish epic meter, *Poem of the Cid* is the story of a nobleman who is banished from the kingdom of Castile, survives the rigors of exile by defeating Moorish forces and fending off Christian encroachments on his territories, and finally achieves renown by conquering the Caliphate of Valencia. The work is divided into three *cantares*, or "tales," which highlight the rise and fall of the Cid's fortunes.

A powerful noble, the Cid is banished when King Alfonso VI of Castile heeds the insidious rumors of the Cid's enemies. Feudal relationships in the poem are not clear, and the reader is left with the impression that the two hundred men who join the Cid in exile do so of their own free will. The Cid leaves his wife, Jimena, and his two daughters, Sol and Blanca, in the monastery of San Pedro de Cardeña for safekeeping.

The second division of the poem, the *Cantar de Bodas*, relates the Cid's triumph in his struggle to survive. Fighting Moor and Christian alike, he multiplies his fortune and his prestige. With the conquest of Valencia and the betrothal of his daughters to the sons of the Count de Carrión, a match specifically arranged by the King of Castile, it appears that the Cid's achievements are complete.

In a masterful juxtaposition of villainy and nobility, however, the third division of the poem, the *Cantar de Corpes*, plays havoc with the Cid's world prior to a resolution in the final verses. The engagement of the Cid's daughters to future counts is an extraordinary achievement, given his status as a middle-line noble, yet the *Cantar de Corpes* reveals the cowardice, egotism, and greed of the de Carrión brothers. The brothers, known as the Infantes, decide that their wives are not worthy of them; but they do not want to lose their dowries. Convincing the Cid that it is time to return to Carrión, the Infantes, once well away from Valencia, take their wives into a secluded glade, beat and strip them, and leave them to die. Fortunately, a retainer, disobeying the Infantes' orders to stay away from the area, rescues them.

The conclusion of the poem celebrates the triumph of civilizing order over brutality justified by birth. Instead of pursuing and punishing the Infantes, the Cid appeals to Alfonso VI, who by this time has come to consider the Cid an equal, to summon a convocation of nobles to judge his accusations against the Infantes. In the trial, the arrogant brothers are stripped of honor: First, the Cid demands that his swords be returned by the Infantes, then the dowry of his daughters; finally, the Cid accuses the brothers of *menosvaler*, or "less worthiness." The Infantes, enraged at this affront, call for a duel and subsequently lose to the Cid's champions. As the crowning glory to the Cid's success and the triumph of judicial process, emissaries from Navarre and Aragon appear, requesting the hands of the Cid's daughters for their kings.

Poem of the Cid is a monument to the individual whose dedication to right values is ultimately rewarded and whose salient qualities are protection of his family, generosity to all, religious devotion, and loyalty to the established order. The Cid's concern for his family is presented early in the poem as he leaves them in the care of the monks at San Pedro de Cardeña, promising to reward them richly. Parting causes such anguish in him that the poet observes that "parten unos d'otros como la uña de la carne" (they part like a fingernail pulling away from the skin).

The oldest manuscript of the poem signed by the enigmatic Per Abad is missing the first folio and two others within the work. The meter, as has been noted, is traditional to Spanish epics: mono-rhymic assonanced lines divided into half by a caesura and normally totaling fourteen syllables, though the irregularity of the meter, as shown in the third line of the following passage, is a puzzle to critics.

> Dezidle al Campeador, que en buen hora nasco,
> que destas siet sedmanas adobes con sos vassallos,
> vengam a Toledo, estol do de plazdo
> Por amor de mío Cid esta cort yo fago.
>
> Say to the Campeador he who was born in good hour
> to be ready with his vassals seven weeks from now
> and come to Toledo; that is the term I set for him
> Out of love for My Cid I call this court together.

The verse of *Poem of the Cid* is characterized by the oral qualities of the *mester de juglaría* (minstrel's meter, the meter of the *juglares*). It is instructive to compare this form with the *mester de clerecía* (clergy's meter), an almost exclusively thirteenth century verse form. While the *mester de juglaría* allows, along with its oral formulas, considerable freedom, resulting in verse with a tentative, experimental flavor, the *mester de clerecía* is highly formalized. The term *mester de clerecía* is often used interchangeably with the name of the meter in which verse so designated was generally written, *cuaderna vía*. A rigidly structured syllabic verse form, *cuaderna vía* is composed of four-line stanzas; each line must be fourteen syllables long, with a caesura exactly in the middle and a full rhyme of *aaaa*. The demanding rigidity of the form is evident in the following example, as presented by Germán Bleiberg (1915-1990), from the *Libro de Alexandre* (c. 1240; book of Alexander):

> Mester traigo fermoso, non es de juglaría
> mester es sin pecado ca es de clerecía
> fablar curso rimado por la cuaderna vía,
> a sílabas contadas que es de gran maestría

> A beautiful skill I bring, it is not of the singers:
> a skill without sin since it comes from churchmen.
> To follow a rhymed course using the four verse way
> by counted syllables that requires great mastery.

Another example of the *mester de clerecía* is a work in the hagiographic tradition, the *Vida de Santa María Egipcíaca* (thirteenth century; life of Saint Maria the Egyptian), but curiously enough, it is not composed in *cuaderna vía*. The poem is a rendition of the legend of an Egyptian prostitute who, after a lifetime of dissipation, converts to Christianity when two angels deny her entrance to the temple at Jerusalem. While artistically the poem does not represent a significant advance, the clear expression of the craft of the *mester de clerecía* makes worthwhile reading. The author was able to adapt a Latin source to Spanish in a learned yet popular style; numerous learned words are integrated into the text without disturbing the poet's rapport with his audience.

The first major poet to use *cuaderna vía* as a distinguishing characteristic of his work was Gonzalo de Berceo (c. 1190-after 1250), a secular priest. Born around the end of the twelfth century, his name probably reflects his birthplace, the village of Berceo in the province of La Rioja. Information about his death is equally sketchy, and internal evidence in his poetry suggests that he died after 1250.

Gonzalo de Berceo's work can be categorized into three groups: hagiographic poems commemorating the Spanish saints Millán, Domingo, and Oria; devotional poems dedicated to the Virgin Mary; and doctrinal works related to apocalyptic material and the symbolism of the Mass; in addition, three hymns are attributed to him. His best-known works, however, are his poems about the Virgin Mary, particularly the *Milagros de Nuestra Señora* (c. 1252; the miracles of Our Lady).

The relationship between man and the Virgin Mary in the *Milagros de Nuestra Señora* could be described as maternal vassalage. The theme of the work is not obscure; those who show devotion and loyalty to the Virgin Mary will be rewarded, saved from peril or death, and even have their souls rescued from Hell. The poem relates twenty-five miracles performed by the Virgin Mary, adapted from a Latin manuscript collection. The opening lines describe an allegorical *locus amoenus*. After calling on his "amigos e vasallos de Dios" ("friends and vassals of God") to listen, he writes:

> Yo maestro Gonçalvo de Verçeo nomnado
> Idendo en romeria caeçi en un prado
> Verde e bien sençido, de flores bien poblado,
> Logar cobdiçieduero pora omne cansado.
>
> I, master Gonzalo of Berceo by name
> While out walking I lay down in a field
> Green and lush, with abundant flowers
> A comforting place for a tired man.

The story of the second miracle presents a good example of Berceo's art. Presented in a simple, straightforward progression of events, the narrative deals with a monk who demonstrated his devotion to the Virgin Mary by kneeling in front of her statue and reciting an "Ave Maria" every time he passed. A demon, "a vicar of Beelzebub," corrupted him with lust at night, and the monk began to wander, though every time he passed the statue of the Virgin, he would kneel and pray. One night, after an escapade, he fell into a river and drowned.

At this point, the story becomes a metaphysical dispute between devils and angels for the wayward monk's soul. The Virgin Mary intervenes, citing his devotion to her statue, but she is challenged by the chief devil, who reminds her that dogma decrees that whatever state of grace exists at death determines a man's life after death. The Virgin refuses to argue and calls upon Jesus to resolve the problem; the solution is the revival of the monk, who dies much later after a long life of devotion to the Virgin.

Stylistically, Berceo's verse is measured, consistent, and reminiscent of several traits of the *mester de juglaría:* direct address, enjambment, and popular vocabulary. Indeed, the poem's diction is remarkably non-Latinate, even though the topic is religious; for example, Berceo uses the word *beneito*, a vulgarized form of *benedictino*, for the term "Benedictine."

Berceo's authorship has also been claimed for the *Libro de Alexandre*, a poem of 2,675 lines composed in *cuaderna vía* around 1240. The importance of the *Libro de Alexandre* cannot be dismissed; it is the longest epic poem of the thirteenth century, in addition to being the only survivor of Spanish verse epics about antiquity. Its artistic merit is substantial as well. In his 1934 edition, Raymond S. Willis notes that

> ... the poem is not an artless assemblage, but a well contrived and coherent whole. The poetic gift and charm of its author, even though distorted by our present corrupt manuscripts, can be discerned as considerable. And, finally, this epic is a symposium of much of the erudition of the period and a mirror of contemporary life, thought, and language.

The *Libro de Alexandre* is a pageant of figures of antiquity across an epic stage. The poem begins with the birth and childhood of Alexander, with Aristotle playing a major role as adviser, councillor, and teacher. When his father, Philip, dies, Alexander's succession is challenged in Athens and Thebes, and, immediately after his coronation, he is forced to put down rebellions in those cities.

The core of the story is the conflict between Alexander and another great figure of antiquity, his rival Darius of Persia. Alexander's success in Macedonia and Greece moves him to challenge the persistent Persian threat, and he crosses the Hellespont to invade Asia Minor. The ensuing battles cast Alexander more and more in the role of a demigod. He creates the Twelve Peers, cuts the Gordian Knot, defeats Darius twice, captures Persepolis, and presides at Darius's funeral. The steady encroachment of the pathos of power on Alexander's character is developed in this central part of the epic, preparing the reader or listener for the conclusion.

Alexander cannot stop his conquests. Even though the pressure to return home is ever-growing, he alternately harangues and leads his men to defeat the Hyrcanians and the Scythians and to conquer the subcontinent of India. The element of fantasy also grows in the narrative: Alexander is visited by the Amazons; there is a detailed description of the wonders of the Orient (such as the flight of a griffon); and Alexander descends into the sea in a submarine-like vessel. Only metaphysical forces, Nature and Satan, can play a causative role in Alexander's death. The world has surrendered to him, but at the moment of his greatest achievement, he is poisoned by a trusted lieutenant, Jobas.

The interweaving of the fantastic, the allegorical, and the moral threads in the frame of the Alexander lore that had accumulated over the previous thousand years makes the *Libro de Alexandre* a notable monument in medieval Spanish verse for the modern scholar; indeed, its merits were recognized in its own day, for it is now accepted that the author of the *Poema de Fernán González* closely imitated the *Libro de Alexandre*.

The *Poema de Fernán González* (poem of Fernán González), written around 1260, is the second great epic of the thirteenth century. Though its topic is local—the deeds of a Castilian nobleman—and thus characteristic of the *mester de juglaría*, the poem is clearly a product of the *mester de clerecía* tradition. The meter is *cuaderna vía*, and the details of the story reveal a dependence on Latin historical sources, the poems of Berceo, and the *Libro de Alexandre*, all of which leads modern scholars to believe that a cleric was the author. Another clue to authorship, reinforcing the attribution to a churchman, is a mythical-biblical pattern that J. P. Keller, in his article, "The Structure of the *Poema de Fernán González*," classifies as "rise, treachery, and fall," though ultimately the hero achieves a state of prominence. Fernán González is present as a divinely chosen figure in the mold of biblical heroes.

The poem consists of three parts. The first sets the overall dimensions of the three significant episodes in Spanish history until that time: the Visigothic Empire, the Arab invasion, and the beginning of the Reconquest. The second and third parts reflect the rise of Castile: The small, frontier region gains prominence with the victories over the Moors won by its heroic leader, Fernán González, who subsequently is seated in the *cortes* (parliament) of the kingdom of León. Ambushed and imprisoned by Leonese jealous of his success, he escapes to lead the Castilians to independence from León and supremacy over the kingdom of Navarre.

In contrast to the pragmatic religious devotion of the Cid, Fernán González is carefully characterized as a God-chosen leader who reciprocates with Christlike behavior. He prays continuously, has dreams in which spirits visit, and hears voices of saints during battle that tell him how to direct his troops, and he encourages his men with the promise that those who die on the battlefield will rejoice with him in paradise.

The anonymous *Libro de Apolonio* (book of Apolonio, c. 1240) and the *Castigos y ejemplos de Catón* (the punishments and examples of Catón, c. 1280) are two other significant verse compositions. The first descends from the tradition of late classical Greek romance, full of plot mechanisms turning on storms, pirates, separations, misfortunes, and, finally, a happy ending in which virtue and trust in God are rewarded. The second is notable for its popularity in the sixteenth century but is distinct from other poems of the *cuaderna vía* style. It has no story line and is more similar to wisdom literature than to the hagiography and classical and historical epics typical of the *mester de clerecía*.

Fourteenth century: Diversification

In his classic study, *European Literature and the Latin Middle Ages* (1953), Ernst Curtius describes the impact of the *Libro de buen amor* (c. 1330; *The Book of Good Love*, 1933), the most poetically and artistically diverse composition of the Spanish Middle Ages:

> Then about 1330 Juan Ruiz (1283?-1350?) makes a bold innovation with his *Libro de buen amor*. He imports Ovid's eroticism and its medieval derivatives. To a free rendition of the *Ars amandi* . . . he added a recasting of the extremely popular medieval comedy *Pamphilus de amore*, which in turn goes back to an elegy of Ovid's (*Amores* I, 8). . . . There are critics who rank the *Libro de buen amor*, the *Celestina*, and *Don Quijote* together as the three peaks of Spanish literature.

Curtius's description, though, is only the half of it. As a peak, *The Book of Good Love* has yet to be scaled. Its structural diversity, thematic multiplicity, and rich characterization make it one of the most intriguing works of European literature.

The author, like the work itself, is a mystery. Little is known about Juan Ruiz, the archpriest of Hita, a small town north of Madrid. This lack of biographical data has given rise to the notion that perhaps "Juan Ruiz" was not the actual author but rather a persona through which the author represented himself.

In the poem, there are tidbits of biographical information about Juan Ruiz, such as a plea for mercy in response to an unjust incarceration and constant reminders that he has not been a very successful lover. Critics have sought to extrapolate information about the author from his work. They have concluded, for example, that he was almost certainly a priest, since he reveals great familiarity with ecclesiastical terminology; indeed, it is likely that he was an archpriest—that is, a priest with administrative responsibility over several dioceses. His education, however, was not confined to scripture and religious literature: He paraphrased the *Pamphilus de amore* (twelfth century), a medieval Latin love farce, and composed his verse in a variety of meters.

The Book of Good Love is a tour de force. Opening with an invocation to God or the Virgin Mary, the poet pleads for help in his present trouble, which seems to be an imprisonment. A sermon, based on the scripture "I will give understanding" (Psalms 31:8), states the purpose of the work, ostensibly to instruct the audience in the forms of "bad" (that is, sexual) love in order that they might avoid it and practice "good" love—that is, the love of God. This is followed by a series of *loores* (praises) extolling the virtue and power of the Virgin Mary. Scattered throughout are fables, illustrating a moral through tales of animals characterized as humans, and fabliaux, often of a ribald nature. The poet then begins his autobiography and follows it with a *cazurro* verse, a coarse, often humorous love story—though in this case, Juan Ruiz flirts with sacrilege as he compares forlorn lovers with the Crucifixion of Christ. A panegyric arguing that love changes men completely leads into a vision, an allegorical narrative of the poet's three-time failure at seduction.

After his failures, a debate ensues between the poet and Don Amor (Sir Love) concerning the joys and dangers of love; this is followed by invective verse condemning love. A scriptural parody, based on sexual allusions in the canonical hours, is concluded by an Ovidian *ars amandi*.

The source of the longest verse narrative in *The Book of Good Love* is the *Pamphilus de amore*, a popular twelfth century Latin comedy. Notable is the poet's introduction of the character Trotaconventos, an old go-between destined to become a type in Spanish literature. Her intervention into his love life does not provide satisfactory results, and the poet, in a counsel, warns women about the wickedness of love and suggests that men not use negative epithets for their go-betweens. He finishes the section with an enumeration of the various comments gentlemen have been known to make.

The *cantigas de serrana* are bawdy verses telling how mountain women jump unsuspecting travelers, such as the poet; these verses are followed by a collection of devotional poems concerning the Passion of Christ. Another baffling shift in tone follows, as the poet introduces a satirical mock-epic contest between Don Carnal (Lord Flesh) and Doña Cuaresma (Lady Lent), terminating in the triumphal procession of Don Carnal's forces.

A "book of hours" with allegorized seasons of the year prepares the reader for an extended reappearance of Trotaconventos, the procuress, who attempts (unsuccessfully) to woo a nun for the poet. Her rhetorical portrait of the nun provides an intriguing insight into the concept of beauty in the Spanish Middle Ages. When Trotaconventos dies, the poet delivers an impassioned lament and subsequently writes her epitaph.

Juan Ruiz's irreverence resurfaces in a mock sermon on the virtues of little women, and the poem concludes with a summation in which the poet suggests how his work should be understood. A postscript follows with a collection of *cantares de ciegos* (beggars' songs), a complaint, and goliardic verses attacking the Church.

The metric patterns in *The Book of Good Love* reveal a conscious manipulation of verse length to combat monotony and to enhance the content. While most of the narrative sections of the poem are in *cuaderna vía*, the poet often shifts between lines of fourteen and sixteen syllables. The rhyme is virtually perfect. The lyric sections of the poem present a dazzling array of verse forms, ranging from the *zéjel* (a Moorish composition with stanzas and a refrain) to the *pie quebrado*, in which four-syllable lines and eight-syllable lines are used in a single stanza.

The diversification of Spanish verse in the fourteenth century continued with the appearance of lyric poetry. Setting aside the disputed nature of the *kharjas*, Rafael Lapesa, the noted Spanish critic and linguist, suggests that lyric verse of a learned nature did not appear until 1300, with the composition of the *Razón de amor*. This earliest extant lyric poem survives in a confusing manuscript in which the first part narrates the visitation of a young man in a *locus amoenus* by a young woman who has prepared a glass of wine and another of water for them. Their lyric conversation is reminiscent of the *cantigas de amor* and *cantigas de amigo*, in which the lovers complain about love. Suddenly, the young woman leaves, and a white dove appears, spilling the vessel of water into the wine. The rest of the poem, called the "Denuestos del agua y del vino," is of the debate genre: The personified wine and water argue their respective strengths and defects; for water, wine is too sentimental; for wine, the water is too coldly rational. In *A Literary History of Spain: The Middle Ages* (1971), Alan Deyermond accurately sums up the *Razón de amor* as "the best and most puzzling" of poems. The dramatic change midway through the poem has generated considerable critical debate, some scholars arguing that the work is in fact a single poem while others contend that it comprises two distinct poems rudely joined.

It is appropriate that a survey of Spanish verse through the fourteenth century should end on the note with which it began: the dichotomy between popular and learned verse. The early contrast between the *mester de juglaría* and the *mester de clerecía* repeats itself at the end of the Middle Ages. There are, on the one hand, the predecessors of the popular *romanceros* (collections devoted exclusively to romances or ballads), and, on the other, the philosophical verse of Rabbi Sem Tob and the early Spanish Humanism reflected in Pero López de Ayala.

The diversity of medieval Spanish literature is exemplified by the *Proverbios morales* (fourteenth century) of Rabbi Sem Tov (or Santob), born in Carrión de los Condes around 1290. The distinguished Spanish historian Claudio Sánchez Albornoz referred to Sem Tob as the first Spanish intellectual. The *Proverbios morales* entries are almost exclusively composed in Alexandrine verse and—oddly, for a medieval composition—

contain virtually no exempla relating the content to everyday life. The poet is a philosopher, observing life through the prism of classical and Hebraic thought, never losing sight of the reality of being a Jew in an ever-hostile environment. His poetry is a celebration of learning and knowledge, tempered with the reservations of a skeptic.

Spanish Humanism begins with Pedro López de Ayala, courtier, knight, and man of letters. As an adult, he lived through the cataclysms of fourteenth century Spain: the plague, the Trastámaran usurpation of the Castilian throne, international wars, and the Great Schism of the Roman Catholic Church. As a man of letters, he translated or was connected with the translations into Spanish of works by Livy, Boethius, Gregory the Great, and Giovanni Boccaccio. His great poetic work, the *Rimado de palaçio* (fourteenth century), stands alongside his chronicle of the reign of Peter I of Castile as a significant contribution to Spanish literature.

The *Rimado de palacio*, an extensive poem of 8,200 lines composed over several years, provides a serious counterpoint to the frivolity of Juan Ruiz's *The Book of Good Love*. The poem is divided into three sections. The first is a scathing satire of the secular and ecclesiastical society of the day. The second part is composed of lyric *loores* and prayers to the virgins of Monserrat, Guadalupe, and Rocamador and to other religious icons, invoking their favors. It is believed that this portion was written during an imprisonment, while the third and final part was set down in the last years of Ayala's life. This last section is a compendium of religious and ethical reflections based on the Book of Job and Saint Gregory's *Moralia* (c. 6 C.E.).

In contrast to the learned verse of Ayala and Sem Tob, the late fourteenth century saw the first appearance of the *romanceros*, or romances. It is generally accepted that the composition of these popular ballads began as the longer epic poems (their probable source) were forgotten or lost their relevance. The romances are written in the same sixteen-syllable assonant line that characterizes Spanish epic verse and are generally categorized as historical (based on a recent event), literary (derived from a previous chronicle or epic), or adventurous (a miscellaneous grouping of diverse themes such as love, revenge, mystery, or simply adventure).

The quilt of Spanish culture is at once a social, political, religious, and literary phenomenon. The interplay between learned and popular, Galician and Castilian, Moor, Jew, and Christian created a poetic tradition as multifaceted as any found in Western Europe, a tradition enriched and deepened by its diversity.

BIBLIOGRAPHY
Florit, Eugenio. *Introduction to Spanish Poetry*. Mineola, N.Y.: Dover, 1991. Offers works ranging from the twelfth century *Poema de mío Cid* to twentieth century poets. Full Spanish texts with expert literal English translations on facing pages. Also contains a wealth of biographical information and critical commentary. Illustrated.
Gies, David T., ed. *The Cambridge History of Spanish Literature*. New York: Cam-

bridge University Press, 2009. A comprehensive English-language work, prepared by Gies in collaboration with forty-six other eminent scholars. Includes chronology and index.

Merwin, W. S., ed. and trans. *Spanish Ballads*. Port Townsend, Wash.: Copper Canyon Press, 2008. A reissue of the volume first published in 1961, early in the career of the translator, who became one of America's most admired poets. Includes ballads from the late Middle Ages to the twentieth century, arranged by type and in chronological order.

Schippers, Arie. *Spanish Hebrew Literature and the Arab Literary Tradition: Arabic Themes in Hebrew Andalusian Poetry*. New York: Brill Academic, 1993. An introduction to the Arabic poetry of eleventh century Muslim Spain and to the major Hebrew poets of the same period. Demonstrates how Arabic themes appear in Hebrew Anadalusian poetry.

Simpson, Lesley B., trans. *The Poem of the Cid*. 2d ed. Berkeley: University of California Press, 2007. A classic translation of the great Spanish epic.

Smith, Colin C. *The Making of the "Poema de mío Cid."* New York: Cambridge University Press, 1983. The well-known scholar and editor of the Collins English-Spanish dictionaries traces the development of the Spanish epic. Bibliography, index.

_____, ed. *Spanish Ballads*. 2d ed. London: Bristol Classical Press, 1996. Originally published in 1964, this collection is accompanied by a useful introduction and notes by Smith.

Walters, Gareth. *The Cambridge Introduction to Spanish Poetry*. New York: Cambridge University Press, 2003. Bilingual edition. A survey of Iberian and Latin American writing from the Middle Ages to the present. Conveniently arranged by genres and themes. Bibliography and index.

John Richard Law

SPANISH POETRY SINCE 1400

During the fifteenth century, Spain's mercurial transformation into a world power was the direct result of having achieved national unification (1492)—a reality that took more than seven centuries of armed conflict between the various Christian principalities scattered throughout the northern half of the Iberian Peninsula and the powerful Muslim caliphates that dominated virtually all of Spain for several centuries following the Moors' initial invasion in 711. As Spain found itself emerging into a modern state whose strong central government was busy removing the last medieval vestiges from its newly created empire (thus ushering in an era of unsurpassed economic prosperity), so, too, in the field of art and literature, a new awareness of the ancient Greek and Latin masters was taking root.

FIFTEENTH AND SIXTEENTH CENTURIES

The two men most responsible for introducing Spain to a new spirit of Humanism via Greek, Latin, and Italian literary traditions were Juan Boscán (c. 1490-1542) and Garcilaso de la Vega (1501-1536).

Whereas 1492 marked the political birth of modern Spain, the year 1543 may be said to have marked Spain's cultural rebirth into the Humanistic tradition that had been eclipsed until its rediscovery a century earlier by the great fifteenth century Italian poets. With the publication of *Las obras de Boscán y algunas de Garcilasso de la Vega repartidas en quatro libros* (1543; the works of Boscán and some of Garcilaso de la Vega), a wholly new poetic vision was introduced into Spanish literature. To appreciate the magnitude of change that Boscán and Garcilaso brought to sixteenth century Spanish poetry, both in its form and in its content, one must recall the tradition from which their revolutionary poetics were born.

Not until the fifteenth century did the Spanish literary lyric first appear as an independent written work of art. Prior to that time, Castilian verse was dominated, for the most part, by the fourteenth century romance (ballad) and the thirteenth century *villancico*. While traveling troubadours sang of the joys and woes associated with courtly love, clerics were creating their own tradition, focused on more spiritual themes, such as the many miracles of the Blessed Virgin. In 1445, the first important collection of Castilian verse was published, the *Cancionero de Baena* (songbook of Baena). Here were recorded numerous *canciones de amor* (love songs) which echoed the earlier ballads in both theme and form.

Two exceptions to these traditions were the marquis of Santillana and Juan de Mena. They transcended the traditional compositions that were recorded in the *Cancionero general* (1511; general songbook), a collection of fifteenth century verse filled with *villancicos* and ballads that reflected the love songs of the earlier troubadour tradition.

Santillana is credited with the first sonnets written in a language other than Italian, while Mena's allegorical and philosophical poems are sprinkled with frequent classical allusions and a Latinized vocabulary.

The poetic revolution that was to characterize sixteenth century Spain, however, did not truly begin until 1526, when the Spanish poet Boscán met with the Venetian ambassador to the court of Charles V, Andreas Navagero. It was at this time that Boscán was first introduced to the new Italianate forms with their classical focus on humans and nature. Although it would be another seventeen years before Navagero's revolutionary seeds would bear Spanish fruit, the poetic manifesto contained within *Las obras de Boscán y algunas de Garcilasso de la Vega repartidas en quatro libros* heralded a radical change in the exterior form of poetic expression and promised a vibrantly new vision of humankind.

Boscán found that the Italian hendecasyllable created a cadence much less emphatic than that of the traditional Castilian octosyllable, allowing the poet to express subtleties of rhythm and rhyme previously unattainable. The flexibility afforded by this new meter complemented the new aesthetic sensibility that Boscán and Garcilaso brought to Castilian verse. For example, in Boscán's *Canzoniere* (songbook), which consists of ninety love sonnets and ten *canzones* (songs), the theme of human love is explored in all its splendor. Unchecked by reason, it is a passion fraught with pain and suffering; when properly expressed, this same love brings peace and joy to the human spirit.

Garcilaso, too, reflects this newfound faith in humanity's ultimate worth and goodness. Innovative in form (he introduced into Spanish verse, among other meters, the five-line stanza known as the *lira*), his poetry evokes a landscape whose sensuously bucolic images and mythological allusions have forever changed the course of Spanish poetry. Indeed, Garcilaso might be considered the cornerstone on which modern Spanish verse has been built.

Following Garcilaso's lead, two schools of Castilian poets developed—one centered in Salamanca, and the other in Seville. Whereas the Salamancan group (known as El Broncense), headed by Francisco Sánchez, was known for moralistic and philosophical perspectives exemplified in the work of its most renowned poet, Luis de León, the Sevillan poets, whose outstanding figure was Fernando de Herrera, were known for their sensuous musicality and erudite knowledge of classical mythology. Both groups put unwavering faith in Aristotelian poetics: Art was to imitate nature, not the ephemeral happenings associated with the senses but the ideals and principles that lay hidden beneath the surface. Masters such as Horace, Vergil, and Petrarch served as models for the expression of universal themes.

Distinct from the schools of Salamanca and Seville but of equal quality was a specialized tradition, that of mystical verse. The Carmelite monk Saint John of the Cross (1542-1591) represents the zenith of this uniquely Spanish poetic expression. In his masterpiece, *Cántico espiritual* (c. 1577-1586; *A Spiritual Canticle of the Soul*, 1864,

1909), based on the Bible's Song of Solomon, he expressed with erotic intensity the soul's passionate quest for God. One can detect in the sensuous pastoral imagery produced by Saint John of the Cross the presence of Garcilaso's eclogues: Even the most religious of poets found himself enveloped within the growing Humanism of the Renaissance spirit.

The Renaissance not only reawakened an interest in classical mythology but also engendered a renewed sense of national identity. Unlike its neighbors to the west, Spain did not produce an epic comparable to Portugal's *Os Lusíadas* (1572; *The Lusiads*, 1655), by Luís de Camões. One of Spain's native sons, however, did record the heroic events involving the conquest of Chile. Alonso de Ercilla's *La Araucana* (1569-1590; English translation, 1945) sings the praises of both the conqueror and the vanquished. His vivid account of the heroic deeds accomplished by his Spanish comrades and the valiant defense of the proud Araucanian people places Ercilla y Zúñiga's poem alongside the other great epics of Western civilization.

SEVENTEENTH CENTURY

During the seventeenth century, as Spain's political and economic prowess began to show the first signs of vulnerability, the stylistic innovations first introduced into Spanish literature by Boscán and Garcilaso were embellished and brought to their ultimate poetic fruition—to the point of excess. The simplicity and clarity of the Renaissance gradually gave way to the complexity and obscurity of the Baroque.

Encouraged by literary academies and an ever-increasing number of literary competitions, poets began to create newer and more unusual images, to experiment with traditional word order, and to search for subtler allusions. In particular, two main currents came to dominate seventeenth century poetic expression: *culteranismo* and *conceptismo*. The former is characterized by its emphasis on ornate and complex images, its revolutionary syntax, and its obscure mythological allusions; the latter is characterized by its intellectual and philosophical sophistication. The many puns and double entendres which one encounters in this poetry reveal the *conceptistas'* fundamental cynicism and disillusionment with life. For the *culteranistas*, beauty was to be found in the most complex of metaphors, whereas for the *conceptistas* truth was to be expressed in satire and wit.

Of the many poets associated with these two literary tendencies, four overshadow the others because of the quality and depth of their work. The driving force behind the *culterano* style of poetry was Luis de Góngora y Argote (1561-1627); his very name has become synonymous with intricately complex metaphors and tantalizingly obscure images. Góngora's influence on seventeenth century Spanish verse was monumental; like Garcilaso de la Vega a century earlier, Góngora was imitated by virtually all of his fellow poets, even those who were most vocal in their criticism of his stylistic intricacies.

Although the term Gongorism is frequently used today to describe a type of poetry characterized by excessive ornamentation and artificially complex syntax, Góngora himself was not guilty of such literary failings. The negative connotations associated with his name more accurately describe the many less gifted poets who attempted to emulate the master's unique gift for expressing beauty in startling metaphors that both dazzled and amazed the sensitive reader. His ability to juxtapose vibrant, concrete images in a world of poetic illusion makes his verse the high point of the Spanish Baroque.

In his two masterpieces, *Fábula de Polifemo y Galatea* (wr. 1613, pb. 1627; *Fable of Polyphemus and Galatea*, 1961) and *Soledades* (wr. 1613, pb. 1627; *The Solitudes*, 1964)—a projected series of four poems only one of which, written in 1613, was completed—Góngora contrasted human mutability with nature's lasting beauty and grandeur. His fable about Polyphemus and Galatea is based on a story found in Ovid's *Metamorphoses* (c. 8 C.E.; English translation, 1567), which recounts the love affair between Acis and Galatea. Acis is eventually killed by the jealous Cyclops, Polyphemus, but, through the intercession of the gods, the slain Acis is transformed into a stream. Góngora's version, although true to the original, is much more a celebration of nature's inherent dynamism and beauty than is Ovid's.

Góngora intended to write four *Solitudes* but died before completing his second. The first one describes a love-smitten youth, who, as he travels through the countryside, comes upon a pastoral wedding celebration. In the fragmentary second poem of the series, the young man is seen visiting with a seafaring family. Although their plot is a simple one, *The Solitudes* are rich in subtle allusions and bewildering syntax, which, once properly contemplated, lead the reader to a greater sense of nature's overpowering majesty.

If Góngora is remembered today because of the sheer perfection of his poetic technique, Lope de Vega Carpio (1562-1635) is remembered for his prodigious creative output. The great lyrical playwright of Spain's Golden Age, he also managed to compose more than sixteen hundred sonnets, several literary epics, ballads, and several volumes of miscellaneous verse. Vega Carpio's poetry is not as polished as Góngora's refined verse, but what it lacks in erudition and technical skill, it more than adequately possesses in spontaneity and flowing grace.

Still further removed from the ornate images of *culteranismo* was the epigrammatic style of Francisco Gómez de Quevedo y Villegas (1580-1645). Indeed, Quevedo was one of Góngora's most caustic critics. Unlike his rival, who tried to capture in words the beauty and dynamism of nature, Quevedo was fascinated by humanity's ugliness and corruption. Rejecting the sensuous style of the *culteranistas*, he preferred a more austere and elliptical mode of expression, filled with tersely worded puns, that reflected his cynical view of life. The satirical observations and witty wordplay that characterize his poetry exemplify the mode of poetic expression known as *conceptismo*. Quevedo's stoicism led him to employ poetry as an effective way to teach his fellow man about the ugly reality of life. If there is one principal theme running through Quevedo's poetry, it is *disengaño* (disillusionment): a total disenchantment with the things of this world.

Ironically, the poet who encompassed most fully the complexity and obscurity of seventeenth century Spanish verse did not live in Spain, but in New Spain (Mexico). Her name was Sor Juana Inés de la Cruz (1651-1695). In a society that favored men, Sor Juana was regarded as one of the New World's finest examples of seventeenth century Humanism. She explored the wonders of science, the mysteries of philosophy, and the marvels of art and literature. Nevertheless, she saw the highest achievements of Renaissance Humanism as ultimately futile. In her major poem, "Primer sueño" (first dream), she expressed, in true *culterano* style, the human mind's inability to grasp life's purpose by means of purely intellectual or aesthetic activity. Ultimately, for Sor Juana, the things of this world led to disillusionment. What began in the sixteenth century as a optimistic quest for truth and beauty, ended, at the close of the seventeenth century, with man's faith in himself deeply shaken if not shattered.

Eighteenth century

As the eighteenth century approached, Spanish poetry, like the other major literary genres of the time, was in a state of decline. Poets, for the most part, attempted to imitate dominant styles of the seventeenth century. Just as political decline ultimately led to a change of royal families (the House of Bourbon inherited the Spanish throne in 1700), so, too, the decadence to which Spanish literature had fallen led to serious attempts at literary reform. For example, in 1713, the Royal Academy was founded with the responsibility of protecting and guiding the Spanish language, and was commissioned to produce an authoritative dictionary and grammar.

In 1732, there appeared a journal titled *Diario de los literatos de España* (diary of the writers of Spain), which, until its demise in 1742, attempted to review and to evaluate the literary merit of all the books being printed in Spain at that time. In one of its last editions, it published a work titled *Sátira contra los malos escritores de este siglo* (satire against the poor writers of this century), which condemned the Baroque excesses associated with the poetry of the day. The inclusion of French terms in this critical diatribe suggests a knowledge of the French neoclassical critic, Nicolas Boileau-Despréaux.

The most significant evidence of literary reform, however, appeared in 1737 with the publication of Ignacio de Luzán's *La poética o reglas de la poesía* (poetics or rules of poetry). In it are criticized the inordinate use of artificially contrived metaphors, unnecessarily complex syntax, and unusually difficult puns characteristic of many contemporary poets. Rejecting the sophisticated cynicism of Gabriel Alvarez de Toledo (1662-1714) and the bitterly satirical language of Diego de Torres Villarroel (1694-1770), Luzán advocated a clear and concise language. Literature, besides pleasing and entertaining the reader, should instruct him. Above all, a literary work should exhibit good taste. Exaggeration, either in form or in content, was to be avoided, since order and symmetry best reflected the natural harmony existing within the universe.

Luzán's poetics, like those of his French counterpart, Boileau, were an attempt to return to the clear and measured writing which had characterized the ancient Greek and Latin poets. Whereas France looked more toward classical antiquity for its models, Spain rediscovered its own classical writers such as Garcilaso de la Vega and Luis de León.

The neoclassical reformation championed by Luzán did not begin to bear fruit until the second half of the eighteenth century. Of the many poets who followed the dictates of neoclassical good taste, Nicolás Fernández de Moratín Leandro Fernández de Moratín (1737-1780) was the most respected and influential. Known primarily for his innovative ideas and techniques in the field of drama, Moratín was a key figure in the popularization of Luzán's poetic theory. Moratín formed a group of writers known as the Tertulia de la fonda de San Sebastián, among whom were such leading literary figures as José Cadalso and Tomás de Iriarte. From their literary soirées came some of the most important critical essays in support of the neoclassical style of writing.

Perhaps the most appropriate genre for expressing the neoclassical ideal of instructing while entertaining was the fable. At any rate, the second half of the eighteenth century saw the publication of two collections of fables, the second of which was a direct defense of Luzán's poetics. From 1781 to 1784, Félix María de Samaniego (1745-1801) published his *Fábulas morales* (moral fables), in which he imitated both classical and modern fabulists. In 1782, Tomás de Iriarte published his highly original *Fábulas literarias* (literary fables), in which he expressed his ideas on literature. In his fables focusing on poetry, he satirized those poets who disregarded the neoclassical call for clarity, order, and balance.

The eighteenth century neoclassical emphasis on order and sobriety clearly reflected the spirit of the times. The political and civil reforms instituted by the newly installed House of Bourbon established an atmosphere of well-being throughout the country. In particular, the highly progressive reign of Charles III (1759-1788), whose economic and social reforms helped instill within the Spanish people a newfound feeling of prosperity and stability based on intelligent planning and careful implementation of programs, supported the neoclassicists' demand for clear and orderly writing. Poetry, it was thought, like all meaningful elements of society, should not only amuse and distract but also provide the utilitarian function of instructing its citizenry. To the neoclassicists' chagrin, however, Charles III's well-ordered society soon found itself beset once again by turmoil and confusion. As the eighteenth century came to a close, the winds of change began to blow from within and without the Spanish borders, giving birth to a new literary mentality.

Nineteenth Century

The first two decades of the nineteenth century saw the total collapse of Spain's traditional political system, which is perhaps best described as a form of enlightened despotism. There followed an onslaught of radical political and social changes that combined to undermine the many years of apparent prosperity and stability associated with eighteenth century Bourbon Spain.

In 1807, heeding the unwise advice of his prime minister, Manuel de Godoy, Bourbon monarch Charles IV allowed Napoleon's forces to enter Spain (Napoleon's ostensible target was Portugal). Six years of foreign rule and a brutalizing civilian-led revolution followed Napoleon's entry into Spain. Once having ousted the foreign monarch (Joseph Bonaparte) and having restored the legitimate Bourbon heir (Ferdinand VII) to the Spanish throne, Spain experienced even greater political turmoil. Ferdinand ruled with the absolutism of his predecessors but lacked their vision and dedication. The liberal revolutionary groups that had fought so valiantly for restoration felt betrayed by their conservative monarch. After six years of absolutist rule, a coup d'état in 1820 ushered in three years of liberal reforms. With France's help, Ferdinand managed to regain his throne and ruled uncompromisingly until his death in 1833. After his death, although the pendulum was to swing in favor of the liberals, Spain suffered no less than three civil wars (the Carlist Wars) over royal succession. What was once a well-organized and well-integrated society soon found itself polarized into opposing camps: *afrancesados* (French supporters) versus those in favor of restoration, absolutists versus constitutionalists, conservatives versus liberals. The resulting chaos found its intellectual and aesthetic expression in the Romantic movement, which reflected both in its form and in its content the turbulent reality of early nineteenth century Spain.

In the field of Spanish poetry, two men in particular foreshadowed the literary revolution of the nineteenth century. Manuel José Quintana (1772-1857) and Juan Nicasio Gallego (1777-1853), although trained in the rigors of neoclassicism, infused new vigor into their verse by unabashedly singing the praises of their homeland. Quintana, in his "A España" ("Ode to Spain"), and Gallego, in his "Al dos de Mayo" (to the second of May), took the first steps in the transition from a poetics dominated by reason to one that was primarily an expression of deep emotion.

Not until Ferdinand VII's death, however, did Spanish poetry begin to free itself in earnest from the artificial bonds imposed on it by the neoclassical demand for moderation in the name of good taste. With Isabel II's accession to the throne in 1833, many of the liberals who were formerly living in exile in England, France, and Germany returned to Spain, bringing with them a radically uninhibited style of poetry.

Nineteenth century Romanticism was unquestionably a love affair with freedom. It was a direct response to and rejection of the literary norms of the day. Like most reactions, however, it frequently defined itself in terms of what it rejected. Since eighteenth century neoclassicism produced a poetry refined by reason, Romanticism strived to express a poetry unshackled by reason's tyranny. In its place, the Romantics exalted human feelings, emotions, instincts, intuition, and imagination—all of those qualities that had waited so long to be liberated. The freedom of the Romantics, therefore, was a freedom from the established rules of society, be they political, social, or aesthetic. Like

Ferdinand VII's political tyranny, which ultimately coerced the majority of liberals to search for a means of escape via self-imposed exile, so, too, reason's tyranny over free poetic expression ultimately led the young Romantics to seek refuge by escaping into private worlds, unencumbered by the demands and responsibilities that society exacts from its members.

Although the Romantic movement, which dominated the first half of the nineteenth century in Spain, produced many fine poets, three are of major literary importance: Ángel de Saavedra (better known by his title, Duque de Rivas, 1791-1865), José de Espronceda (1803-1842), and José Zorrilla y Moral (1817-1893). These three men revolutionized both the form and content of nineteenth century Spanish poetry.

Ángel de Saavedra, in his *Romances históricos* (1841; historical ballads), turned the focus of Spanish verse from the ancient Greek and Latin myths to Spain's own heroic past. Rejecting the artificial syntax and latinized vocabulary of previous generations, he captured his country's customs in a lively language that complemented its exciting history.

Accompanying their interest in Spain's glorious past was the Romantics' fondness for expressing intimately personal feelings. One of Spain's greatest lyric poets, José de Espronceda expressed more vividly than most his deepest emotions. One notes immediately, both in his disregard for traditional forms and in his rebellious themes and motifs, his unbounded love of freedom and spontaneity. Five poems in particular manifest his almost adolescent contempt for any form of coercion. In his "Canción del pirata" ("Song of the Pirate"), "Canto del cosaco" ("cossack's song), "El mendigo" ("The Beggar"), "El reo de muerte" ("The Condemned to Die"), and "El Verdugo" ("The Headsman"), he expressed a deep desire to be freed from society's dominion over the individual. In his later work, "A Jarifa en una orgía" ("To Harifa, in an Orgy"), one of the most pessimistic poems ever composed in the Spanish language, he views death as the only path to freedom.

From Zorrilla, known today principally for his dramatic reworking of Tirso de Molina's *El burlador de Sevilla* (1630; *The Trickster of Seville*, 1923), titled *Don Juan Tenorio* (1844; English translation, 1944), Spain received not only some of its most beautiful lyric poetry but also a series of legends that recorded many of the memorable deeds associated with Spain's colorful and turbulent past.

As the political turmoil of the first half of the nineteenth century gradually subsided and Spanish society once again began to experience relative stability, poetic expression showed signs of losing much of its revolutionary fervor. During the latter half of the nineteenth century, poetry became less lyrical as it attempted to involve itself with philosophical, political, and social questions being discussed in the novel, the recently rediscovered genre whose popularity was rapidly increasing. In an effort to be more relevant, poets such as Ramón de Campoamor (1817-1901) and Gaspar Núñez de Arce (1832-1903) began to focus on philosophical and social issues.

Two notable exceptions to that trend were the Andalusian poet Gustavo Adolfo

Bécquer (1836-1870) and the Galician poet Rosalía de Castro (1837-1885). In many ways, their delicate lyricism bridged the high-spirited and spontaneous verse of Romanticism with the subtler subjectivism associated with Symbolism and the measured plasticity of Parnassianism.

In particular, Bécquer might be considered the culmination of the Romantic movement, inasmuch as his *Rimas* (1871; *Poems*, 1891; better known as *The Rhymes*, 1898) expressed the most intimate of feelings. In a sense, Bécquer's verse is Romanticism come of age. Whereas Espronceda's raison d'être as a poet lay in his puerile attempt to escape the harsher realities of life by vicariously experiencing, through his verse, the imagined lives of such exotic personalities as a gun-toting pirate, an arrogant beggar, and a defiant prisoner, Bécquer drew from the springs of his own soul to express a precise, melodic language that ultimately transcended words—Beauty, Love, Poetic Creation. With delicate nuances of light and color, sound and rhythm, he created some of the most beautiful images in Spanish poetry.

Twentieth century: 1898-1936

European Romanticism during the latter part of the nineteenth century had been dominated by Bécquer. During his reign, Romanticism attained a particularly Spanish style. Current European literary trends, including French liberalism, had influenced Spanish Romantic poets. Bécquer's style eventually gave way to *costumbrismo*, the depiction of customs and manners, and realism replaced Romanticism as prose began to become the dominant form. Realism characterized Spanish prose fiction during the early twentieth century.

The literary movements of the *fin de siglo* passage from the nineteenth to the twentieth century were marked by political, philosophical, and artistic turbulence. In 1898, Spain lost its last colonies. Since the seventeenth century, Spain's expansionism had been in decline. The *generación del 98*, or Generation of '98, rose as both a literary and a philosophical movement of writers who referred to 1898 as a turning point in Spanish society. They searched for causes of its decline and ways to regain their nation's past glories. Together, the Generation of '98 and the *generación del 27*, or Generation of '27, created a kind of Silver Age that approached the literary and artistic excellence of the masters of the Spanish Golden Age. This era of literary brilliance and prolific creative activity reigned until 1936, stifled by the onset of the Spanish Civil War.

Literary influences shifted from *costumbrismo* and realism to *Modernismo*, similar to French Symbolism, and artistic and musical impressionism. A group of young writers at the turn of the century proclaimed a moral and cultural rebirth for their defeated homeland. Through studying the simplicity and austerity of Castilian life, these writers found the essence of Spain. They sought to portray it through a direct and compact style. The literary association rejected most European literary and aesthetic trends, but embraced political liberalism.

The Basque poet and prose writer Miguel de Unamuno y Jugo (1864-1936) anticipated the essential themes of existentialism. Unamuno believed that the personal aspects of history were eternal because they sustain the temporal events of public history. This concept of *intrahistoria* permeates his poems. Their symbolic elements acquire universal relevance as they relate to the Spanish experience between 1898 and 1936. After a spiritual crisis reflected in *En torno al casticismo* (1902), Unamuno sought to identify a popular protagonist. This "intrahistorical" way of life defined the Spanish spirit for his literary as well as spiritual generation.

Azorín (José Martínez Ruiz, 1873-1967) coined the phrase *generación del 98*. In his overriding goal to define the eternal qualities of Spanish life, he depicted the Castilian people and countryside with impressionistic sensitivity that captured the beauty of ordinary life. His poetry acquired an original musicality rooted in folk songs. His poetry's lyrical quality results from an adept application of rhyme and meter. Azorín is best known for his novels, but he promoted the works of poets whose idealism rebelled against bourgeois styles and themes.

Antonio Machado (1875-1939) founded modern Spanish poetry by blending symbolism with profound meditations on time and place and concern for the nation's future. His original voice paved the way for the poets of the Generation of '27 to experiment with rhyme and meter in order to express their particular voice. His poems are lucid meditations that evoke a harsh yet sharply defined Spanish landscape. *Campos de Castilla* (1912; *The Castilian Camp*, 1982) was inspired by his wife. The transition from lyricism to reflection is evident in the 1924 publication of *Nuevas canciones* (new songs), which followed *Soledades, galerías, y otros poemas* (1907; *Solitudes, Galleries, and Other Poems*, 1987). Together, they paint the Castilian landscape with clarity and sonority. He also wrote plays and translated French literature with his brother, the poet Manuel Machado (1874-1947). Tragedy marked his later works: Machado's wife died after five years of marriage from a sudden illness. Antonio died in 1939 while fleeing from the Spanish Civil War with his brother and mother, all exiled loyalists and victims of the national tragedy.

Juan Ramón Jiménez (1881-1958) wrote symbolic poetry. Over time, he developed an abstract and complex lyricism. He expanded the limits of language to convey truth through nature's images. A later stage of his work evidences his images whittled away to their essence. In *Platero y yo* (*Platero and I*, 1956), published to popular acclaim in 1914, a young poet is followed by a donkey during his reveries and idyllic journeys. Other works demonstrate the transformation and maturity of his style and structure. *Eternidades* in 1918 and *Belleza* in 1923 contemplated the changing face of beauty. He did not publish new works until the outbreak of the Spanish Civil War, when General Francisco Franco sent him to the United States as a cultural attaché. He taught at the University of Maryland and University of Puerto Rico until his wife's death in 1956, soon after he had won the Nobel Prize. His last major work, *Dios deseando y deseante*

(1964), identifies with a universal consciousness that seeks beauty in nature.

The Generation of '98 initiated a cultural revival, an ongoing literary movement that gained momentum as it was energized by the new wave of writers after 1927 until the outbreak of civil war in 1936. As literary revisionists, they were responsible for the renewal of Spanish themes and traditions as they exposed their nation to European modernity.

The transition to the twentieth century inevitably led to European cultural influences, despite Iberian isolationism. José Ortega y Gasset (1883-1955) criticized the "Europeanization" of Spain with a landmark essay, *La deshumanización del arte* (1925; *The Dehumanization of Art*, 1948), which criticizes literary realism. According to Ortega y Gasset, the Industrial Revolution of the early nineteenth century led to the confusion of life with art so that art represented reality. Through the method of dehumanization, the narrative and descriptive elements of literature are removed and devalued. This approached the avant-garde European movements such as Futurism, creating a marginal literature that gained popularity during the first decades of the twentieth century. Spanish translations of works by James Joyce, Maxim Gorky, André Gide, and Marcel Proust were popular.

The tercentenary of the death of the Golden Age master poet Góngora began a new poetic age. Literary as well as artistic genius coincided in Madrid during the second decade of the new era. The surrealist Catalonian artist Salvador Dalí (1904-1989) lived and worked with Zaragozan Luis Buñuel (1900-1983) and Federico García Lorca in the Residencia de Estudiantes (student residence) area in Madrid. The intellectual atmosphere was fed by the creative geniuses of several more residents in this neighborhood. The group of poets known as the Generation of '27 was founded in this creative community. Not since the seventeenth century's Golden Age had such a preeminent group of poets come together. Jorge Guillén (1893-1984), García Lorca (1898-1936), Pedro Salinas (1891-1951), Rafael Alberti (1902-1999), Vicente Aleixandre (1898-1984), Dámaso Alonso (1898-1990), Luis Cernuda (1902-1963), and Gerardo Diego (1896-1987) were among the major poets.

Several literary movements characterized this generation. The European avant-garde and cinematographic realism inspired them stylistically. French Symbolism and Eastern European Dadaism influenced their approaches to art and its role in society. The concept of art for art's sake gained acceptance. As a result, art was dehumanized. The role of the symbol or metaphor was not transcendent, but ephemeral. The metaphor was elevated to serve a central temporal function in poetry. This symbolic impact had political implications. During the first phase of the movement, from 1920 to 1927, the poets distinguished themselves from their predecessors with their new poetic vision. During the second phase, from 1927 to 1936, their poems were politically motivated. The creation of the Second Republic and weakening of the bourgeoisie inspired them politically to envision a societal and aesthetic revolution in which art was the patrimony of the people.

The most emblematic poet and dramatist with enduring international prominence is García Lorca. From 1919 until his death, García Lorca devoted himself to creative activity in the Residencia de Estudiantes. *Flamenco andaluz* and the Gypsy culture influenced his poetry. His publication of *Romancero gitano, 1924-1927* (1928; *The Gypsy Ballads of García Lorca*, 1951, 1953) gained for him international fame. A few years later he visited New York and related the similarities between the spirituals of Harlem and the *cante jondo*, or deep song of the Gypsy culture. The collections *Poema del cante jondo* (1931; *Poem of the Gypsy Seguidilla*, 1967) and *Poeta en Nueva York* (1940; *Poet in New York*, 1940, 1955) resulted from his American experience. He established the theater company La Barraca, which toured throughout Spain. At the outbreak of the Spanish Civil War, Franquista soldiers tortured and murdered García Lorca soon after assassinating his brother-in-law, the mayor of Granada. His poems and plays were burned and banned until the end of Franco's reign.

The Spanish Civil War destroyed many of these poets' utopian dreams as well as their lives. García Lorca's assassination by the Franquistas came to symbolize the destruction of the creative hopes of the nation. Alberti, Cernuda, Salinas, Guillén, Rosa Chacel, and María Zambrano were forced into exile. The nation torn apart by Franco's brutal and intolerant fascist regime was gradually regenerated after almost fifty years of *franquismo*. Despite the domestic tragedies, the nation's banished intellectuals were extraordinarily prolific in exile.

Vicente Aleixandre, winner of the Nobel Prize in 1977, was the lone member of the Generation of '27 to remain in Spain during *franquismo*. He served as mentor and spiritual guide for the succeeding postwar generation. In 1933, he won Spain's national prize for literature. His greatest work, which led to his nomination for the Nobel Prize, was *Sombra del paraíso* (1944; *Shadow of Paradise*, 1987). Aleixandre's imagery of human pain and horror contrasts with that of the immutable power and harsh reality of nature. Loss, sorrow, and despair characterize this stage of poetic production. Without overtly political imagery, the Spanish Civil War experience was acutely portrayed. Aleixandre's later works revealed elements of Surrealism. This technique enabled him to escape from the desolation of a paradise lost and envision a peaceful and whole Spain.

Alonso developed the concept of "poetry for the people." He communicated with the reader by abandoning the ivory tower and humanizing his poetry. Alonso used free verse, lexical variation, and rationalism that countered the trend toward Surrealist poetry. His major works include *Poemas puros: Poemillas de la ciudad* (1921) influenced by the work of Jiménez and Machado, and *Hijos de la ira* (1944), an intellectual inquiry into the role of humans in society and into their relationship to God. In his final work, *Duda de amor sobre el Ser Supremo* (1985), Alonso reflects upon his imminent death and the eternal nature of the soul.

The poetry of Salinas can be divided into three stages. His early work includes *Presagios* (1923), influenced by Jiménez. *Fábula y signo* (1931) begins the reference to the "beloved" in order to continue a quest toward attaining higher goals through his poetic voice. His second phase is characterized by love poetry: *La voz a tí debida* (1933; *My Voice Because of You*, 1976) and *Razón de amor* (1936), in which love is reinvented. The concept of "I" and "you" is redefined by the interplay of words. For Salinas, to love was to live within each other. During the third stage of his poetic evolution, Salinas was concerned with the role of the poet and the philosophical search for permanence through art. In *El contemplado* (1946; *The Sea of San Juan: A Contemplation*, 1950), he contemplated the sea through a series of philosophical reflections. In *Todo más claro y otros poemas* (1949), Salinas conducted a dialogue with nature and, in "Cero," contemplated the horrors of human nature.

Guillén wrote a series of poetry in five sections collected over thirty years as *Cántico: Fe de vida* (1928, 1936, 1945, 1950; *Canticle*, 1997). The series reflects his faith in a life centered in nature. *Clamor: Tiempo de historia* (1957-1963; includes *Maremágnum*, 1957; *Que van a dar en el mar*, 1960; and *A la altura de las circunstancias*, 1963), translated in 1997 as *Clamor*, reflects on human history and the fall of humanity into chaos. *Homenaje* (1967; *Homage*, 1997) reflects on the generous nature of art to forgive and eventually conquer human frailties.

The poetry of Cernuda serves as a biography of his lifelong spiritual journey. In *Perfil del aire* (1927) he follows the model of Bécquer as he expresses internal and external realities. *Un río, un amor* (1929) displays Surrealist characteristics, and here he laments the absence of love. The pessimistic tone of *Donde habite el olvido* (1934) reflects the predominant theme, the death of love. Cernuda's *Invocaciones* (1935) seeks to evade reality; here the poet's pessimism leads him to fall into the depths of despair.

Diego developed his own style of creationist poetry. Creationist techniques dominate in *Imagen* (1922). He won the Premio Nacional de Literatura after publishing *Versos humanos* (1925; human verses). In honor of his poetic icon Góngora, Diego published *Antología poética en honor de Góngora* (1927). Góngora's influence is evident in Diego's postwar work *Alondra de verdad* (1941; lark of truth). These later sonnets paid homage to their Golden Age models as they followed traditional patterns of rhyme and meter rather than the creationist forms and syntax of Diego's early poems.

Mid-twentieth century onward

Miguel Hernández (1910-1942) represents the transition from the Generation of '27 to the succeeding generation. His poetry was influenced by the Golden Age genius Góngora. Henández blended formal structure with surreal imagery. He befriended García Lorca, Aleixandre, and the Chilean poet Pablo Neruda, among others. After serving with the losing army of the Republicanos during the Spanish Civil War, Hernández fled to Portugal. He was captured and imprisoned until his death. When offered his freedom only if he would be exiled forever from Spain, Hernández refused. His most original poetry, written while in prison, reveals unwavering compassion and faith in the human spirit. It was published posthumously as *Cancionero y romancero de ausencias* (1958; *Songbook of Absences*, 1972).

Writers within Spain during *franquismo* either went along with Franco's political policies or devoted their creative energy to resistance. Luis Rosales (1910-1992) and Leopoldo Panero (1909-1962) wrote insular poetry with aesthetic objectives. Blas de Otero (1916-1979), Gabriel Celaya (1911-1991), and José Hierro (born 1922) were influenced by Social Realism.

Salvador Espriu (1910-1992) was stylistically influenced by the avant-garde in his prose poems characterized by nationalist themes. The group of *Novísimos* ("very recent ones") experimented with avant-garde poetry and developed a particular style. This regional literary and philosophical movement was led by José María Castellet, a Catalonian critic. The *Novísimo* phenomenon represents the politicized literary milieu of the postwar generation. Major poets were Catalonian Socialists who considered Barcelona the center of avant-garde creativity. The Editorial Seix Barral supported their efforts by publishing and distributing their poetry and prose.

Spain lacks a literary tradition for women writers. Some twentieth century women poets and prose writers have distinguished themselves, despite the success of their male counterparts. The philosopher, essayist, and poet María Zambrano (1904-1991) and novelist and poet Rosa Chacel (1898-1994) have distinguished themselves among their male literary peers with many national honors.

The women writers during the Republic include Chacel and Mercè Rodoreda (born 1908). Women who wrote during *franquismo* include Carmen Laforet (born 1921), Ana María Matute (born 1926), Elena Quiroga (1921-1995), and Carmen Martín Gaite (born 1925). In her essay "Hipótesis sobre una escritura diferente" (hypothesis about a different writing), Marta Traba finds a textual difference between the works of male and female writers. She finds that feminine poetics link images rather than endow them with symbolic value. Their poetry is more concerned with explanations rather than with interpretations of the universe. Feminine text depends on the impetus of detail to convey meaning. Another feminist critic, Carme Riera, finds stylistic and thematic tendencies in feminine writing. The interplay between subject and object, syntactic repetition, greater lexical variance, and thematic commonalities is addressed by female poets.

Since 1979, the definitive end of the Franco era, poetry production has been more identified with cultural and linguistic groups than by nationalist interests. Catalonia, Galicia, and the Basque provinces have created poetry with regional rather than centralized national identities.

BIBLIOGRAPHY

Bellver, Catherine G. *Absence and Presence: Spanish Women Poets of the Twenties and Thirties*. Lewisburg, Pa.: Bucknell University Press, 2001. The reception of major women poets of Spain is examined from a feminist perspective. The work and literary status of Concha Méndez, Josefina de la Torre, Rosa Chacel, Carmen Conde, Ernestina de Champourcin, Blanca Andréu, and others are analyzed within their social and historical contexts.

Davis, Elizabeth B. *Myth and Identity in the Epic of Imperial Spain*. Columbia: University of Missouri Press, 2000. Davis discusses the cultural role of the epic poem during the era of Spanish Imperialism. The political implications of the genre as well as the transition into the Baroque literary styles and cultural values are explored.

Flitter, Derek. *Spanish Romantic Literary Theory and Criticism*. New York: Cambridge University Press, 1992. Uses detailed summaries of articles by nineteenth century critics to prove that Spanish Romantic writers were inspired by traditional, Christian elements in German Romantic thought.

Florit, Eugenio, ed. *Introduction to Spanish Poetry*. New York: Dover, 1991. Contains thirty-seven poems in Spanish with English translation on facing pages, along with biographical and critical commentary. Illustrated.

Fox, Gwyn. *Subtle Subversions: Reading Golden Age Sonnets by Iberian Women*. Washington, D.C.: Catholic University of America Press, 2008. In their sonnets, five seventeenth century women in Spain and Portugal were able to voice their feelings about the patriarchal system that denied them education and the most basic rights.

Gies, David T., ed. *The Cambridge History of Spanish Literature*. New York: Cambridge University Press, 2009. A comprehensive English-language work, prepared by Gies in collaboration with forty-six other eminent scholars. Includes chronology and index.

Glendinning, Nigel. "The Eighteenth Century." In *A Literary History of Spain*. New York: Barnes & Noble, 1972. Discusses the eighteenth century and literature in Spain at length; includes information on poetry.

Griffin, Nigel, et al., eds. *The Spanish Ballad in the Golden Age: Essays for David Pattison*. Rochester, N.Y.: Tamesis, 2008. Nine poems are analyzed in detail in order to demonstrate how a knowledge of contemporary references and allusions aids in understanding such works.

Mudrovic, W. Michael. *Mirror, Mirror on the Page: Identity and Subjectivity in Spanish Women's Poetry, 1975-2000*. Bethlehem, Pa.: Lehigh University Press, 2009. Analyses of eight poems by Spanish women, showing how each writer identifies with and differs from a female figure in the text. A revealing study, focusing as it does on works produced in the new, democratic era that followed the fall of Franco.

St. Martin, Hardie, ed. *Roots and Wings: Poetry from Spain, 1900-1975*. Buffalo, N.Y.: White Pine Press, 2004. A reissue of a landmark bilingual anthology, containing works by thirty major Spanish poets, translated by highly acclaimed American poets.

Soufas, C. Christopher. *The Subject in Question: Early Contemporary Spanish Litera-

ture and Modernism. Washington, D.C.: Catholic University of America Press, 2007. The first systematic study of Spanish modernism, arguing that Spanish thinkers had adopted modernist theories long before the movement reached the rest of Europe. The poetry of Jorge Guillén, Vicente Aleixandre, Luis Cernuda, and Rafael Alberti is discussed at length.

Walters, Gareth. *The Cambridge Introduction to Spanish Poetry.* New York: Cambridge University Press, 2003. Bilingual edition. A survey of Iberian and Latin American writing from the Middle Ages to the present. Conveniently arranged by genres and themes. Bibliography and index.

West-Settle, Cecile, and Sylvia Sherno, eds. *Contemporary Spanish Poetry: The Word and the World.* Madison, N.J.: Fairleigh Dickinson University Press, 2005. A collection of essays on the theory and practice of various contemporary poets. Bibliographical references and index.

Wilcox, John. *Women Poets of Spain, 1860-1990: Toward a Gynocentric Vision.* Urbana: University of Illinois Press, 1997. This study focuses on often-overlooked women poets who have contributed to literary movements as well as developed original poetic voices. Poets include Rosalía de Castro, Francisca Aguirre, Carmen Conde, and Clara Janés. Contemporary poets include Amparo Amorós, Ana Rosetti, and Blanca Andréu.

Richard Keenan
Updated by Carole A. Champagne

RAFAEL ALBERTI

Born: Puerto de Santa María, Spain; December 16, 1902
Died: Puerto de Santa María, Spain; October 28, 1999

PRINCIPAL POETRY

Marinero en tierra, 1925
La amante, 1926
El alba del alhelí, 1927
Cal y canto, 1929
Sobre los ángeles, 1929 (*Concerning the Angels*, 1967)
Consignas, 1933
Verte y no verte, 1935 (*To See You and Not to See You*, 1946)
Poesía, 1924-1938, 1940
Entre el clavel y la espada, 1941
Pleamar, 1944
A la pintura, 1945 (*To Painting*, 1997)
Retornos de lo vivo lejano, 1952
Baladas y canciones del Paraná, 1954 (*Ballads and Songs of the Parana*, 1988)
Poesías completas, 1961
Rafael Alberti: Selected Poems, 1966 (Ben Belitt, translator)
The Owl's Insomnia, 1973
Alberti tal cual, 1978

OTHER LITERARY FORMS

Although Rafael Alberti (ol-BEHR-tee) established his reputation almost entirely on the basis of his poetry, he became involved in drama after emigrating to Argentina, writing plays of his own and adapting Miguel de Cervantes' *El cerco de Numancia* (wr. 1585, pb. 1784; *Numantia: A Tragedy*, 1870) for the modern stage in 1944.

Alberti's most notable achievement in prose, a work of considerable interest for the student of his poetry, was his autobiography, *La arboleda perdida* (1942; *The Lost Grove*, 1976). In addition, he was a talented painter and supplied illustrations for some of his later volumes.

ACHIEVEMENTS

Rafael Alberti had at once the ill luck and the singular good fortune to flourish during Spain's second great literary boom. Despite his acknowledged worth, he was overshadowed by several of his contemporaries—in particular, by Federico García Lorca. Although Alberti's name is likely to come up in any discussion of the famous *generación del 27*, or Generation of '27, he generally languishes near the end of the list. On the other hand, the extraordinary atmosphere of the times did much to foster his talents; even among the giants, he earned acceptance and respect. He may occasionally have been lost in the crowd, but it was a worthy crowd.

His *Marinero en tierra* (sailor on dry land) won Spain's National Prize for Literature in 1925, and throughout his long career, his virtuosity never faltered. Always a difficult poet, he never gave the impression that his obscurity stemmed from incompetence. His political ideology—Alberti was the first of his circle to embrace communism openly—led him to covet the role of "poet of the streets," but Alberti will be remembered more for his poems of exile, which capture better than any others the poignant aftermath of the Spanish Civil War.

Ultimately, Alberti stands out as a survivor. Many of his great contemporaries died in the civil war or simply lapsed into a prolonged silence. Despite his wholehearted involvement in the conflict, Alberti managed to persevere after his side lost and to renew his career. He continued to publish at an imposing rate, took up new activities, and became a force in the burgeoning literary life of Latin America, as evidenced by his winning of the Cervantes Prize, the Spanish-speaking world's highest literary honor, in 1983. Consistent in his adherence to communism, he received the Lenin Prize for his political verse in 1965. Oddly enough, then, Alberti emerges as a constant—an enduring figure in a world of flux, a practicing poet of consistent excellence during six decades.

Biography

Rafael Alberti was born near Cádiz in Andalusia, and his nostalgia for that region pervades much of his work. His genteel family had fallen on hard times, and Alberti's schoolmates made him painfully aware of his inferior status. In 1917, the family moved to Madrid, where Alberti devoted himself to painting in the cubist manner, attaining some recognition. Illness forced him to retire to a sanatorium in the mountains—a stroke of luck, as it happened, for there he subsequently met such luminaries as García Lorca, Salvador Dalí, and Luis Buñuel and began seriously to write poetry. He won the National Prize for *Marinero en tierra* and thereby gained acceptance into the elite artistic circles of the day. Personal difficulties and an increasing awareness of the plight of his country moved Alberti to embrace communism. In 1930, he married María Teresa León, also a writer, and together they founded the revolutionary journal *Octubre* in 1934.

Alberti's new political credo enabled him to travel extensively and to encounter writers and artists from all parts of Europe and the Americas. After participating actively in the civil war, he emigrated to Argentina in 1940. There, he began to write for the theater, gave numerous readings, and resumed painting. Hard work and fatherhood—his daughter Aitana was born in 1941—preserved Alberti from embittered paralysis, and his production of poetry never slackened. Indeed, many of his readers believe that he reached his peak in the late 1940's.

In 1964, Alberti moved to Rome, where he lived until 1977, when he was finally able to return to Spain, after almost thirty-eight years in exile. He was welcomed by more than three hundred communists carrying red flags as he stepped off the airliner. "I'm not coming with a clenched fist," he said, "but with an open hand." He enjoyed a resurgence of popularity after his return and proceeded to run for the Cortes, giving poetry readings instead of speeches, and won. Alberti resigned his seat after three months to devote himself to his art. He became a well-respected literary figure in his last two decades in Spain; the lost Andalusian had returned home. He died there on October 28, 1999, from a lung ailment; he was ninety-six years old.

Analysis

Throughout his long career, Rafael Alberti proved to be a remarkably versatile poet. His facility of composition enabled him to shift smoothly from fixed forms to free verse, even within the confines of a single poem. Whether composing neomedieval lyrics, Baroque sonnets, or Surreal free verse, he always managed to be authentic. His deep emotions, sometimes obscured by his sheer virtuosity, found expression in all modes. His technical skill did not allow him to stagnate: Commentators on Alberti agree in their praise of his astonishing technical mastery. He might continue in the same vein for three volumes, but he would invariably break new ground in the fourth. His massive corpus of poetry comprises a remarkable array of styles, themes, and moods.

Although he was a natural poet with little formal training, Alberti always kept abreast of current developments in his art—indeed, he kept himself in the vanguard. He associated with the best and brightest of his time and participated in their movements. When the luminaries of Spain reevaluated Luis de Góngora y Argote, Alberti wrote accomplished neo-Baroque poetry; when Dalí and Buñuel were introducing Surrealism in Spanish art and film, Alberti adapted its principles to Spanish poetry; when most of the intellectuals of Spain were resisting General Franciso Franco and embracing communism, Alberti was the "poet of the streets." He remained withal a genuine and unique lyric voice. Even his political verses are not without poetic merit—an exception, to be sure. Alberti changed by adding and growing, never by discarding and replacing; thus, he became a richer talent with each new phase of his creative development.

Alberti's poetry is suffused with nostalgia. The circumstances of his life decreed that he should continually find himself longing for another time, a distant place, or a lost friend, and in his finest poems, he achieves an elegiac purity free of the obscurity and self-pity that mar his lesser works. From first to last, the sadness for things lost remains Alberti's great theme, one he explored more fully than any other poet of his generation.

Alberti was a poet who could grow without discarding his past. The youthful poet who composed marvelous lyrics persisted in the nostalgia of exile; the angry poet of the streets reasserted himself in diatribes against Yankee imperialism in Latin America. At ease in all forms and idioms, forever the Andalusian in exile, always growing in his art and his thought, Alberti wrote a staggering number of excellent poems. In the vast treasure trove of twentieth century Spanish poetry, he left a hoard of pearls and sapphires—hidden at times by the rubies and the emeralds, but worthy nevertheless.

Marinero en tierra

The doyens of Spanish letters received *Marinero en tierra* with immediate enthusiasm, and the young Alberti found himself a de facto member of the Generation of '27, eligible to rub elbows with all the significant writers of the day. Although Alberti seems to have been happy in the mid-1920's, his early volumes glow with poignant nostalgia for the sea and the coasts of his native Andalusia. He expresses his longing in exquisite lyrics in the medieval tradition. Ben Belitt, introducing his translations collected in *Selected Poems*, confesses that he could find no way to render these lyrics in English. They depend entirely on a native tradition, the vast trove of popular verses from Spain's turbulent Middle Ages. Alberti's genius is such that the poems have no savor of pedantry or preciosity. Luis Monguió, in his introduction to Belitt's translations, suggests that "it is far from unlikely that they are being sung in the provinces today by many in complete ignorance of their debt to Rafael Alberti." The notion is a tribute both to the poet and to the tradition he understood so well.

The verses themselves may seem enigmatic, but only because the modern reader is accustomed to probe so far beneath the surface. One of the best of them, "Gimiendo" ("Groaning"), presents the plaint of a sailor who remembers that his shirt used to puff up in the wind whenever he saw the shore. The entire poem consists of only six brief lines; there is only one image, and only one point. That single image conveys a feeling close to the hearts of those born within smell of the sea—a need unfulfilled for Alberti. He speaks for all seafarers who are marooned inland, the sailors on land.

"Pradoluengo," an aubade in the same style, is only seven lines long and conveys an equally simple message. The beloved to whom the poem is addressed is told that the cocks are crowing, that "we need cross only river waters, not the sea," and is urged to get up and come along. With all the richness of the genre, Alberti hints at a wealth of erotic possibilities and natural splendors. Only William Butler Yeats, in modern English poetry, matches this exquisite simplicity and feeling for tradition.

Cal y canto

As noted above, Alberti took a leading role in the Góngora tricentennial of 1927, and many of the poems in *Cal y canto* owe much to the Baroque model. Here, Alberti reveals a new facet of his technical mastery, particularly in his handling of the sonnet, perhaps the most difficult of forms. "Amaranta," a sonnet that frequently appears in anthologies, shows how completely Alberti was able to assimilate the poetics of Góngora and to adapt them to the twentieth century. The octave describes, in ornate and lavish terms, the beauty of Amaranta; as with Góngora, the very exuberance of the description disquiets the reader. Her breasts, for example, are polished "as with the tongue of a greyhound." The sestet conceals the scorpion sting so often found in Góngora's conclusions: Solitude, personified, settles like a glowing coal between Amaranta and her lover. In this poem, Alberti displays his affinity with Góngora in two respects: an absolute control of his idiom and an obscurity that has deprived both poets of numerous readers. As Alberti himself remarked in his autobiography, "this was painterly poetry—plastic, linear, profiled, confined."

CONCERNING THE ANGELS

Concerning the Angels differs sharply from Alberti's previous work. Bouts of depression and a loss of faith in his former ideals drove him to abandon nostalgia and to confront despair. Suddenly, all the joy and tender sorrow of his early work is gone, replaced by anguish and self-pity. The revolution in content corresponds to a rebellion in form: Free verse prevails as more appropriate to the poet's state of mind than any traditional order. Alberti does not despair utterly, as Monguió indicates, but the overall tone of the collection is negative.

"Tres recuerdos del cielo" ("Three Memories of Heaven"), a tribute to the great Romantic poet Gustavo Adolfo Bécquer, constitutes a noteworthy exception to the depressing tone of the volume. Here, Alberti displays the subtlety and tenderness that characterize his work at its most appealing. Evoking a condition of being before time existed, Alberti recaptures the tenuous delicacy of Bécquer, the sense of the ineffable. The meeting between the lovers, for example, takes place in a world of clouds and moonlight: "When you, seeing me in nothingness/ Invented the first word." Alberti imitates Bécquer masterfully, at the same time finding a new way to express his own nostalgia.

"Three Memories of Heaven," however, is atypical of the collection. Virtually all the other poems treat of "angels" and ultimately of a world turned to wormwood and gall. "El ángel desengañado" ("The Angel Undeceived") debunks the ideals of the younger Alberti, particularly in its desolate conclusion: "I'm going to sleep./ No one is waiting for me." "El ángel de carbón" ("Angel of Coals") ends no less grimly: "And that octopus, love, in the shadow:/ evil, so evil." Several of the poems offer a kind of hope, but it is a wan hope, scarcely better than despair. Like the T. S. Eliot of "The Hollow Men," however, Alberti maintains his poetic control, even with the world withering away around him.

TO SEE YOU AND NOT TO SEE YOU

Two pivotal events in Alberti's life helped him out of this quagmire: meeting his future wife and becoming a communist. The political commitment, while it did little to benefit his poetry, provided him with a set of beliefs to fill the void within. Of his proletarian verse, one can say only that it is no worse than most political poetry. Like his friend and contemporary Pablo Neruda, Alberti mistook a sincere political commitment for an artistic imperative; like Neruda, he eventually returned to more personal themes, although he never wholly abandoned doctrinaire verse.

Even at the height of his political activism, however, Alberti was capable of devoting his gifts to the elegy; the death of Ignacio Sánchez Mejías in the bullring moved him to write the sonnet series that makes up *To See You and Not to See You* in 1935. The same tragedy also inspired Federico García Lorca to compose one of the most famous poems in the Spanish language, "Llanto por Ignacio Sánchez Mejías" ("Lament for Ignacio Sánchez Mejías"). A comparison of the two poems reveals the radical differences between these two superficially similar poets. García Lorca chants compellingly, "At five in the afternoon," evoking the drama of the moment and the awful immediacy of the bull. Alberti reflects on the bull's calfhood, its callow charges as it grew into the engine of destruction that destroyed Sánchez Mejías. García Lorca goes on to convey, in muted tones, his sense of loss. Alberti expresses that sense of loss in terms of distance: As his friend dies in the bullring, Alberti is sailing toward Romania on the Black Sea. The memory of the journey becomes permanently associated with the loss of the friend and thus a redoubled source of nostalgia.

IN GARCÍA LORCA'S SHADOW

As usual, García Lorca enjoys the fame, and Alberti is lost in his shadow. No doubt García Lorca's elegy speaks more clearly and more movingly; it probably *is* better than its counterpart. Alberti himself admired the "Lament for Ignacio Sánchez Mejías" without reservation. The pattern, however, is only too familiar: Alberti, so like García Lorca in some ways, found himself outmatched at every turn while his friend and rival was still alive. Alberti wrote exquisite medieval lyrics, but García Lorca outdid him with the *Romancero gitano* (1928; *The Gypsy Ballads*, 1953). Alberti captured the essence of Andalusia, but the public identified Andalusia with García Lorca. Alberti wrote a noble and moving elegy for Ignacio Sánchez Mejías, but his rival composed such a marvelous lament that Alberti's has been neglected.

All this is not to imply conscious enmity between the two poets. Alberti had cause to envy his contemporary's fame, and his bitterness at playing a secondary role may have been reflected in *Concerning the Angels*. Indeed, although Alberti gave many indications, in verse and prose, of his profound regard for García Lorca, his relationship with the poet of Granada represents an analogue to the dilemma of his literary life. The competition must have stimulated him, but, because his poetry was less accessible and less dramatic in its impact, he tended to be eclipsed. After the Spanish Civil War, Alberti emigrated to Argentina, mourning his slain and dispersed comrades, including García Lorca, who was senselessly gunned down at the outset of the hostilities. The war poems in the Alberti canon compare favorably with any on that subject, not least because his lively imagination enabled him to look beyond the slaughter.

ENTRE EL CLAVEL Y LA ESPADA

For all his faith, the poet soon found himself across the Atlantic, listening to reports of World War II, picking up the pieces. Somehow he managed to recover and to emerge greater than ever. A poem from his first collection published outside Spain, *Entre el clavel y la espada* (between sword and carnation), sounds the keynote of his renewed art:

> After this willful derangement, this harassed
> and necessitous grammar by whose haste I must live,
> let the virginal word come back to me whole and
>   meticulous,
> and the virginal verb, justly placed with its rigorous
>   adjective.

The poem, written in Spain, anticipates the purity of Alberti's poetry in exile. The poet forgot neither the horrors he had seen nor his love for his homeland.

Another elegy deserves mention in this context. Written after news of the death of the great poet Antonio Machado, "De los álamos y los sauces" (from poplar and willow) captures the plight of Alberti and his fellow exiles in but a few lines. The man in the poem is caught up "in the life of his distant dead and hears them in the air." Thus, Alberti returns grimly to his leitmotif, nostalgia.

RETORNOS DE LO VIVO LEJANO

With his return to his nostalgic leitmotif, Alberti reached his full potential as a poet during the 1940's and 1950's. He poured forth volume after volume of consistently high quality. *Retornos de lo vivo lejano* (returns of the far and the living), a book wholly devoted to his most serviceable theme, may well be the finest volume of his career. The poems are at once accessible and mysterious, full of meaning on the surface and suggestive of unfathomed depths.

"Retornos del amor en una noche de verano" ("Returns: A Summer Night's Love") recalls in wondrous imagery the breathlessness of a time long past. For example, two pairs of lips, as they press together, become a silent carnation. "Retornos de Chopin a través de unas manos ya idas" ("Returns: Chopin by Way of Hands Now Gone") evokes some of the poet's earliest memories of his family. After many years, the poet is reunited with his brothers by an act of imagination, supported by the memory of Frédéric Chopin's music as played by the poet's mother. This is the quintessential Alberti, the master craftsman and the longing man in one.

To Painting

Amid the melancholy splendor of his poems of exile, Alberti distilled a curious volume entitled *To Painting*. In contrast to all that Alberti lost in exile, painting stands as a rediscovered treasure, and the Alberti of the early 1920's comes face to face with the middle-aged émigré. The collection includes sonnets on the tools of painting, both human and inanimate; free-verse meditations on the primary colors; and poems on various painters, each in a style reminiscent of the artist's own. Beyond its intrinsic value, the volume reveals much about the mutual attraction of the two arts.

"Ballad of the Lost Andalusian"

A poem from *Ballads and Songs of the Parana*, deserves special mention. "Balada del Andaluz perdido" ("Ballad of the Lost Andalusian"), as much as any single poem, reflects Alberti's self-image as a poet in exile. Written in terse, unrhymed couplets, it tells of a wandering Andalusian who watches the olives grow "by the banks of a different river." Sitting alone, he provokes curious questions from the Argentine onlookers on the opposite bank of the river, but he remains a mystery to them. Not so to the reader, who understands the pathos of the riderless horses, the memory of hatred, the loneliness. The final question admits of no answer and in fact needs none: "What will he do there, what is left to be done/ on the opposite side of the river, alone?"

Other major works

PLAYS: *El hombre deshabitado*, pb. 1930; *El trébol floride*, pb. 1940; *El adefesio*, pb. 1944; *El cerco de Numancia*, pr. 1944 (adaptation of Miguel de Cervantes' play).
NONFICTION: *La arboleda perdida*, 1942 (*The Lost Grove*, 1976).

Bibliography

Gagen, Derek. "*Marinero en tierra* : Alberti's first 'Libro organico de poemas'?" *Modern Language Review* 88, no. 1 (January, 1993): 91. Alberti's *Marinero en tierra* is examined in detail.

Havard, Robert. *The Crucified Mind: Rafael Alberti and the Surrealist Ethos in Spain*. London: Tamesis Books, 2001. A biographical and historical study of the life and works of Alberti.

Herrmann, Gina. *Written in Red: The Communist Memoir in Spain*. Urbana: University of Illinois Press, 2009. This work examining memoirs of Communists in Spain contains a chapter on Maria Teresa León and Alberti.

Jiménez-Fajardo, Salvador. *Multiple Spaces: The Poetry of Rafael Alberti*. London: Tamesis Books, 1985. A critical analysis. Includes bibliographic references.

Manteiga, Robert C. *Poetry of Rafael Alberti: A Visual Approach*. London: Tamesis Books, 1978. A study of Alberti's literary style. Text is in English with poems in original Spanish. Includes bibliographic references.

Nantell, Judith. *Rafael Alberti's Poetry of the Thirties*. Athens: University of Georgia Press, 1986. This study puts Alberti's work in historical and social context by analyzing the influences from a turbulent decade in which civil war erupts, ignites a European conflagration, and ends in societal crises. The author discusses political poems that are not as memorable as his earlier works but deserve recognition for their artistic as well as social value.

Soufas, C. Christopher. *The Subject in Question: Early Contemporary Spanish Literature and Modernism*. Washington, D.C.: Catholic University of America Press, 2007. This overview of Spanish literature and modernism contains a chapter examining the poetry of Alberti and Luis Cernuda.

Ugarte, Michael. *Shifting Ground: Spanish Civil War Exile Literature*. Durham, N.C.: Duke University Press, 1989. Examination of the importance of Spanish exile literature during and after the civil war. The second section of the book explores the intellectual diaspora of the civil war, and an analysis of Alberti's *The Lost Grove* is featured prominently.

Philip Krummrich
Updated by Carole A. Champagne and Sarah Hilbert

VICENTE ALEIXANDRE

Born: Seville, Spain; April 26, 1898
Died: Madrid, Spain; December 14, 1984

PRINCIPAL POETRY
Ámbito, 1928
Espadas como labios, 1932 (*Swords as if Lips*, 1989)
La destrucción o el amor, 1935 (*Destruction or Love: A Selection*, 1976)
Pasión de la tierra, 1935, 1946
Sombra del paraíso, 1944 (*Shadow of Paradise*, 1987)
Mundo a solas, 1950 (*World Alone*, 1982)
Nacimiento último, 1953
Historia del corazón, 1954
Mis poemas mejores, 1956
Poesías completas, 1960
Picasso, 1961
En un vasto dominio, 1962
Presencias, 1965
Retratos con nombre, 1965
Poemas de la consumación, 1968
Poems, 1969
Poesía superrealista, 1971
Sonido de la guerra, 1972
Diálogos del conocimiento, 1974
The Caves of Night: Poems, 1976
Twenty Poems, 1977
A Longing for Light: Selected Poems of Vicente Aleixandre, 1979
A Bird of Paper: Poems of Vicente Aleixandre, 1981
Primeros poemas, 1985
Nuevos poemas varios, 1987
El mar negro, 1991
En gran noche: Últimos poemas, 1991
Noche cerrada, 1998

OTHER LITERARY FORMS

Vicente Aleixandre (o-lehk-SON-dreh) published a great number of prologues, critical letters, memoirs, and evocations of friends and literary figures, many of them later included or rewritten for his major prose work, *Los encuentros* (1958; "the encounters"). Aleixandre also made several speeches on poetry and poets, later published in pamphlet or book form.

Achievements

After receiving the Nobel Prize in Literature in 1977, Vicente Aleixandre stated that the prize was "a response symbolic of the relation of a poet with all other men." In Aleixandre's own estimation, winning the Nobel was his only worthy achievement. All other influences on the development of poetry were insignificant compared with the poet's call to speak for his fellow humans.

The extent of Aleixandre's influence is considerable, however, even if he denied its importance. He was a member of the Royal Spanish Academy (1949), the Hispanic Society of America, the Academy of the Latin World, Paris, the Royal Academy of Fine Arts of San Telmo, Málaga, the Spanish American Academy of Bogotá, and the Academy of Arts and Sciences of Puerto Rico, and, as of 1972, an honorary fellow of the American Association of Spanish and Portuguese.

All these honors recognize Aleixandre's lifelong devotion to the production of a unified body of poetry. A member of the celebrated Generation of '27, which included Jorge Guillén, Pedro Salinas, Federico García Lorca, Rafael Alberti, and Gerardo Diego, Aleixandre was one of the central figures of Spanish Surrealism. Although influenced by André Breton and his circle, the Spanish Surrealists developed to a great extent independently of their French counterparts. While French Surrealism is significant for its worldwide impact on the arts, it produced a surprisingly small amount of lasting poetry. In contrast, Spanish Surrealism—both in Spain and, with notable local variations, in Latin America—constitutes one of the richest poetic traditions of the twentieth century, a tradition in which Aleixandre played a vital role.

Biography

Vicente Aleixandre Merlo was born on April 26, 1898, in Seville, Spain, the son of Cirilo Aleixandre Ballester, a railway engineer, and Elvira Merlo García de Pruneda, daughter of an upper-middle-class Andalusian family. Married in Madrid, Aleixandre's parents moved to Seville, the base for his father's travels with the Andalusian railway network. Four years after Aleixandre's birth, the family moved to Málaga, remaining there for seven years, spending their summers in a cottage on the beach at Pedregalejo a few miles from the city.

Aleixandre seems to have been very happy as a boy in Málaga, where he attended school, frequented the movie theater across the street from his house (he particularly liked the films of Max Linder), and read the Brothers Grimm and Hans Christian Andersen. Happy memories of Málaga and the nearby sea appear frequently in Aleixandre's poetry: He calls them "ciudad del paraíso" (city of paradise) and "mar del paraíso" (sea of paradise), respectively.

In 1911, the family moved to Madrid, where Aleixandre continued his studies at Teresiano School, but he found the strict requirements for the bachelor's degree tedious and preferred reading the books in his grandfather's library: classical and Romantic works and detective novels, especially those by Sir Arthur Conan Doyle. Aleixandre frequently visited the National Library, where he read novels and drama from Spain's Golden Age to the Generation of '98. During the summer of 1917, his friend Dámaso Alonso loaned him a volume by Rubén Darío, a book that, Aleixandre said, revealed to him the passion of his life—poetry. The next year, he discovered the works of Antonio Machado and Juan Ramón Jiménez, as well as the Romantic world of Gustavo Adolfo Bécquer, and his interest in poetry was firmly established.

At the age of fifteen, Aleixandre began to study law and business administration, finishing the two programs in 1920. He became an assistant professor at the School of Commerce of Madrid and worked at night editing a journal of economics in which he published several articles on railroads. In 1921, he left his teaching post to work for the railway company, but when, in 1925, he suffered an attack of renal tuberculosis, he dropped all professional and social activities, dedicating himself to his poetry, reading, and traveling with his family through Portugal, France, England, and diverse regions of Spain.

Aleixandre's first poems appeared in *Revista de occidente* (journal of the West) in 1926, and two years later his first collection, *Ámbito* (ambit) was published. In 1929, he discovered Sigmund Freud, James Joyce, and Arthur Rimbaud, and, although he suffered a relapse into his tubercular condition in 1932, this period of his life was very productive, resulting in three collections published between 1932 and 1935.

After the removal of a diseased kidney in 1932, Aleixandre retired to Miraflores de la Sierra to convalesce, but in 1933, he returned to Madrid. Carlos Bousoño reports that during this year, Aleixandre read French translations of the German Romantic writers Ludwig Tieck and Novalis, as well as *Les Romantiques allemands* (1933; a translation of Ricarda Huch's *Blüthezeit der Romantik*, 1899; "the German Romantics"). He completed this new spiritual phase with the lyric poetry of William Shakespeare, John Keats, Percy Bysshe Shelley, and William Wordsworth. In 1934, Aleixandre's mother died, and he again traveled through England, France, and Switzerland. During the years of the Spanish Civil War (1936-1939), Aleixandre was isolated from political turmoil, spending much of the time in convalescence after renewed bouts of illness. The death of his father in 1939 brought him even closer to his sister Concepción.

Aleixandre's work reflects his psychological and physiological state as vitally passionate and chronically sick, and as a calm, patient, and creative man. His poetic production was sustained over a lifetime, although a great many years passed between his published collections. In his own words, "The poet dies only when the man dies. And then, his poetry lives forever."

Analysis

In the work of Vicente Aleixandre's first period, the poet is interested primarily in terrible mythic elements of nature without people; he is chaotic, delirious, and grotesque. His is a kind of rebellion against the middle class that hems him in, but he is not yet aware that to save himself from its oppression he must transform his blind, ineffective rebellion into a conscious, efficient one. In his middle period, although Aleixandre continues to take refuge in myth to escape the horrible realities of the day, he faces them as he recalls his family and past, realizing that he cannot remain aloof from history, politics, and other realities when people believe in him. Finally, in his later work, the poet becomes academic, literary, cultured, and decorative. Gradually, finding historical and telluric man and his own dialectical reality, Aleixandre identifies with the public, and the amorous solidarity of the man and poet with all creation is complete.

The idea that love equals death is the leitmotif of almost all of Aleixandre's poetry; it appears most clearly in his recurring images of the sea. In addition to repressed sexuality, a neurotic and somewhat limited group of fantasies recur throughout his oeuvre, many of them associated with the sea. His early years in Málaga impressed the sea on his consciousness, so that it became for him a symbol of youth, equated in turn with innocence, happiness, and his mother (in psychoanalytic dream interpretation, the sea often symbolizes the mother). His desire to return and merge with that happiness and all it represents implies his death as an individual, as he is absorbed by a larger unit. Intrauterine life, being premortal (except to the Roman Catholic Church), is easily equated with postmortal life—life before birth equals life after death.

The sea occupies a high place in Aleixandre's poetic scale of values. Among the 336 poems of his *Poesías completas*, the sea appears 182 times; moreover, it is used as a central theme in sixteen poems. The sea, a recurring symbol or archetype that integrates all of Aleixandre's characteristic themes, represents primitive, instinctive life, true values lost by modern civilized humans and maintained by simple sea creatures, a constant interplay between Thanatos and Eros, and a variety of sensual, erotic states involving repressed sexuality. Often Aleixandre juxtaposes the sea with images of forest, beach, teeth, tongue, birds, sun, moon, and breast. The sea in Aleixandre's poetry is pathognomonic in its psychological connotations, rooted in the painful dynamic of Aleixandre's own life, although at times it evokes a happy, innocent childhood, much as the gypsy symbolized the childhood of Federico García Lorca. Aleixandre disguises the relationship between the symbol and its meaning at unconscious levels; he distorts and represses it so that the symbols may lend themselves to many interpretations, which only psychoanalysis can fully reveal.

Indeed, a catharsis comparable to psychological analysis is accomplished by Aleixandre's poetry, except that here the patient ministers to himself; for example, unconscious forces account for the breast motif associated with the sea, one of Aleixandre's most constant neurotic projections. Throughout his poems, Aleixandre uses the sea as a surface on which to project his images, according to which it takes on various hues, colors, and attributes. It can be an "unstable sea," an "imperious sea," or a "contained sea," and it serves as the principal, though not the exclusive, vehicle for the projection of neurotic fantasies in which the poet employs symbols to convey meaning he might consciously wish to suppress. Aleixandre's sea imagery irrationally yet imaginatively challenges the reader's preconceptions, as the poet attempts deliberately or otherwise to recapture an unconscious knowledge and create a unity of perception.

Aleixandre's interest in Freudian analysis made him particularly receptive to Surrealism, yet he never accepted the "pure" Surrealism of Breton. Breton defined Surrealism as a psychic automatism through which he proposed to express the real functioning of thought without control by reason and beyond all aesthetic or moral norms, revealing the relationship between the real and the imaginary. For Breton, perception and representation are products of the dissociation of a single original faculty which the eidetic image recognizes and which is to be found in the primitive and the child. The distinction between the subjective and the objective lost its value as the poet sought to engage in a kind of automatic writing. Aleixandre rejected the notion of automatic writing, but in his preoccupation with the subconscious and his powerful, irrational imagery, he introduced Surrealism to Spanish poetry, where it found extremely fertile soil.

ÁMBITO

Ámbito, Aleixandre's first collection, is related to the much later volume, *Shadow of Paradise*. *Ámbito*, composed of seven sections and eight "Nights" (including an initial and final "Night" and one "Sea"), contains classical and Gongoristic forms—not unexpected at the time, since the collection was composed partly during the tercentenary of Luis de Góngora y Argote, when Baroque formalism ruled the day. Nature is everywhere; although there is a faint reflection of the cosmic force, the poet is largely descriptive and objective in a somewhat traditional way. Here, he contemplates nature, while in later works he would seek to possess it and be one with it. Written during his first serious illness, the book sensually examines the fleeting aspects of time. Within his own boundary—the limits of his sickroom, where he lived a solitary existence—he waxed both tender and uncontrollably passionate. However, *Ámbito*'s formal beauty, pleasure in the contemplation of nature, desire for perfection, and joy in life reflect both Juan Ramón Jiménez and Jorge Guillén more than the later Aleixandre. The poetry deals with the world of the senses, classic and cold at times but also warm and romantic. The elusive imagery resembles the reverberations of a musical instrument. The poet employs traditional ballad form instead of the free verse that he later came to use almost exclusively, and his ten- and six-syllable lines reveal his great sense of rhythm. In this volume of youthful love, Aleixandre delicately renders his love affair with nature, a love whose equations frequently resist logical interpretation.

Swords as if Lips

Begun in the summer of 1929, Aleixandre's second collection, *Swords as if Lips*, concerns the central themes of life, death, and love—themes that the poet, in his moment of inspiration and suffering, views from a new perspective. An epigraph from Lord Byron, to the effect that the poet is "a babbler," serves notice that the volume eschews conventional "meaning." The work as originally presented was filled with poetic transpositions and capriciously arranged punctuation to help Aleixandre release what he considered his "interior fire." His intention was not to induce a Surrealistic trance but to create a voluntary pattern of unusual images. Aleixandre, in his somewhat illogically and incoherently developed poetic structures, does not know exactly what theme he will develop. The diffuse emotion he creates in this confused and disturbed work gives rise to apparent indecision for the poet, which transfers to the reader. His liberty of form allows Aleixandre to cover a variety of subjects in a dream atmosphere that hovers between sensation and thought. *Swords as if Lips*, in its examination of reality, petrifies it—or, as one critic phrases it, indulges in the immobilization of the moment. Aleixandre's bittersweet imagery of dead roses, coals of silence (because they lack life-giving flame), and other signs of loss and decay suggests a desire to embrace the reality of death.

Destruction or Love

If *Swords as if Lips*, despite its striking images, lacks imaginative coherence, Aleixandre's third collection, *Destruction or Love*, is an undisputed masterpiece. Here, in fifty-four poems divided into six parts, the poet offers a visionary transfiguration of the world in flux, a world of mystery and darkness whose basic fabric is erotic love. Aleixandre's universe is a place of cosmic and human passion, of frustrated and desperate clamor, and of unchained telluric forces that often prove fatal to humans, absorbing them and destroying them. In Aleixandre's vision, people can obtain love only by destroying themselves and fusing with the cosmos, for human love is fleeting, and a final fusion with the earth will prove to be the most enduring love of all. Aleixandre excludes the life beyond and salvation. Absorbed in the living unity of nature, he acclaims a love without religious connotations. Aleixandre stresses the idea that the unity of the world includes humanity's works and its civilization, but they remain peripheral to the primary, instinctive life. Perhaps love can save people from society's mask—for love fuses all things, animal, vegetable, and mineral, into one substance—but to achieve fusion, people must give up their limiting structures. Thus, the title of the volume is intended to signify not a choice between mutually exclusive alternatives (either destruction or love) but rather an identification (as when the subtitle of a book is introduced by the word "or").

In *Destruction or Love*, the animal and the vegetable worlds constantly interact with the thoughts and feelings of the poet. In virgin forests, ferocious beasts surround "man," who seeks fruitlessly to find himself, half glimpsing his salvation in an identification with nature in all its forms and thus affirming rather than denying love for all creation. Animals, the forest, and the sea live in intimate union with elementary forces of nature, and tender, small animals exist with large, destructive ones: the beetle and the scorpion with the cobra, the eagle, lions, and tigers. Thus, the tiger is an elastic fire of the forest, and the eagles resemble the ocean. Like other aspects of nature, such as the ocean, the moon, or the heavens, these animals may be virginal and innocent or terrible and destructive. In this vision of nature as a physical whole in which violence and love are complementary forces, everything attacks, destroys, and loves everything and, in so doing, loves, attacks, and destroys itself. Life is death. The limits between flora and fauna dissolve into a new unity; the sea's fish appear to be birds; foam is hair; a body becomes an ocean; a heart becomes a mountain; man may be metal or a lion. Like the mystic poets of old—who had to die in order to find eternal life—Aleixandre offers a mystic fusion or death with the sea and the maternal earth.

SHADOW OF PARADISE

Shadow of Paradise, begun in 1939 and finished in November, 1943, created a sensation among young poets even before its publication in book form; when it finally appeared in 1944, it won a wide and enthusiastic readership among the literary youth of the day. Here, Aleixandre returns to the innocent world of infancy, to a paradise beyond Original Sin and knowledge, to be one with the heavens and the creatures of the dawn. He evokes a Garden of Eden where he may find lost happiness to escape the evil world of humanity, its folly and malignity. The poet narcissistically reinvents his own reality, remembers it, or perhaps imaginatively re-creates the world of childhood before the horrifying and inevitable loss of innocence. In his universe of serenity, order, and beauty, however, Aleixandre implies an awareness of the historical world, in which humans must play their role. The tension between paradise and history is always just beneath the surface.

Shadow of Paradise is divided into six parts. Of its fifty-two poems, only a dozen have a definite metric form, but through them all there are patterns of association among rhythms of different kinds. The verse lines are of varying length, including hendecasyllables, pentasyllables, hexameters, exciting combinations of anapestic lines, and irregular meters. Avoiding monotony in his rhythmical movements by means of this prodigality of expression, Aleixandre uses exclamations, interrogatives, and an almost musical progression of scales to form a polyphonic richness. His fetish for rhythmic simplicity extends to his use of adjectives, which he occasionally employs adverbially and, rarely, in double or triple combination. Often his naked nouns convey his precise tone or mood; on other occasions, for special effect, he ends a poetic line with a verb; infrequently, he employs gerundives experimentally.

HISTORIA DEL CORAZÓN

Of Aleixandre's later collections, the most important is *Historia del corazón* (history of the heart). Many underlying crosscurrents of thought and emotion can be found in this volume, but its central theme is the need for human solidarity and compassion for the victims of injustice. *Historia del corazón* reveals a dramatic change in Aleixandre's conception of humanity. Here, no longer creatures of telluric forces, humans are defined by the dolorous round of daily experience. Likewise, Aleixandre's conception of poetry has changed: The poet, a man, becomes all humans, destined to live and die, without the assurance of paradise or eternal life, in a world where death is always present. Nevertheless, the poet proclaims, it is not necessary to live desperate, solitary lives; he sings for all humankind of fleeting time, social love, and human solidarity. The poet recognizes that he is aging, but without despair, and empathizes with his neighbor, who must also stoically face the end.

OTHER MAJOR WORKS

SHORT FICTION: *Prosas completas*, 2002.
NONFICTION: *Los encuentros*, 1958; *Epistolario*, 1986 (with José Luis Cano).
CHILDREN'S LITERATURE: *Vicente Aleixandre para niños*, 1984 (illustrated by Concha Martinez).
MISCELLANEOUS: *Obras completas*, 1977 (2 volumes).

BIBLIOGRAPHY

Cabrera, Vicente, and Harriet Boyer, eds. *Critical Views on Vicente Aleixandre's Poetry*. Lincoln, Nebr.: Society of Spanish and Spanish-American Studies, 1979. Criticism and interpretation of Aleixandre's addresses, essays, lectures, and poetry. Includes selected poems in English translation.

Daydí-Tolson, Santiago. "Light in the Eyes: Visionary Poetry in Vicente Aleixandre." In *Contemporary Spanish Poetry: The Word and the World*, edited by Cecile West-Settle and Sylvia Sherno. Madison, N.J.: Fairleigh Dickinson University Press, 2005. Notes that the poet's work was filled with light and sensual descriptions of what he had observed, and that the poet's blindness in the 1970's severely affected his work.

_____, ed. *Vicente Aleixandre: A Critical Appraisal*. Ypsilanti, Mich.: Bilingual Press, 1981. A critical study of Aleixandre's work with a biographical introduction, extensively annotated bibliography, index, and Aleixandre's Nobel Prize acceptance lecture.

Harris, Derek. *Metal Butterflies and Poisonous Lights: The Language of Surrealism in Lorca, Alberti, Cernuda, and Aleixandre*. Anstruther, Fife, Scotland: La Sirena, 1998. History and criticism of Surrealism in Spanish literature, including the works of Aleixandre. Includes bibliography.

———. "Prophet, Medium, Babbler: Voice and Identity in Vicente Aleixandre's Surrealist Poetry." In *Companion to Spanish Surrealism*, edited by Robert Havard. Rochester, N.Y.: Tamesis, 2004. Discusses Surrealism in Aleixandre's poems.

Ilie, P. *The Surrealist Mode in Spanish Literature*. Ann Arbor: University of Michigan Press, 1968. A study of Surrealism in Spanish literature. Includes bibliographic references.

Murphy, Daniel. *Vicente Aleixandre's Stream of Lyric Consciousness*. Lewisburg, Pa.: Bucknell University Press, 2001. Criticism and interpretation of Aleixandre's poetics, with bibliographical citations and index.

Schwartz, Kessel. *Vicente Aleixandre*. New York: Twayne, 1970. An introductory biography and critical analysis of selected works by Aleixandre.

Soufas, C. Christopher. *The Subject in Question: Early Contemporary Spanish Literature and Modernism*. Washington, D.C.: Catholic University of America Press, 2007. One chapter examines the geographies of presence in the poetry of Aleixandre and Jorge Guillén. Information on modernism in Spanish literature provides a context for understanding Aleixandre's works.

Richard A. Mazzara

GUSTAVO ADOLFO BÉCQUER

Born: Seville, Spain; February 17, 1836
Died: Madrid, Spain; December 22, 1870

PRINCIPAL POETRY
Rimas, 1871 (*Poems*, 1891; better known as *The Rhymes*, 1898)

OTHER LITERARY FORMS

Although the fame of Gustavo Adolfo Bécquer (BEHK-ur) rests mainly on his only volume of poetry, *The Rhymes*, he was also a notable prose writer. Bécquer demonstrated his talent at an early age with the publication of *Historia de los templos de España* (1857; a history of Spain's temples), an ambitious project of which only the first volume, a study of the churches of Toledo, was completed. Posterity has recognized the greater value of a variety of prose works that appeared in Madrid's newspapers and magazines during Bécquer's lifetime. Outstanding among these works are the newspaper letters published under the heading *Cartas desde mi celda* (1864; *From My Cell*, 1924). They were written from Veruela's monastery in Aragón, where the author had gone to seek relief for his failing health. In these "letters," Bécquer pours out his moral biography, revealing himself to be a religious man who is both aware of the problems of his surroundings and sensitive to the legends and traditions he hears from shepherds and rovers in the northeast of Spain.

Also of great importance among Bécquer's prose works are the four *Cartas literarias a una mujer* (1860-1861; *Letters to an Unknown Woman*, 1924) and the prologue to the book *La Soledad* (1861) by his friend Augusto Ferrán. In these works, Bécquer expresses his ideas about love, literature in general, and, above all, poetry. In his prologue to Ferrán's book, Bécquer categorizes his own poetic production as the kind that is "natural, brief, dry, that which germinates in the soul like an electric spark, touches the feelings with a word and flees. . . ."

Bécquer's most celebrated prose works were his more than twenty legends, *Leyendas* (1858-1864; partial translation in *Terrible Tales: Spanish*, 1891; also in *Romantic Legends of Spain*, 1909). The themes of these prose tales do not differ substantially from those of the tales in verse typical of the Romantic movement in Spain and throughout Europe; they reveal a taste for the macabre, medieval settings, and exotic lore. What differentiates Bécquer's legends from the verse narratives and plays of the Duque de Rivas and José Zorrilla y Moral is their greater emphasis on the mysterious, the uncanny, and the supernatural.

Achievements

Gustavo Adolfo Bécquer achieved fame only after his death. Although in his last years he was beginning to be recognized as a good journalist and an excellent prose writer, he was virtually unknown as a poet; only a handful of his poems were published during his lifetime.

Bécquer's recognition as a poet began with the publication of *The Rhymes* one year after his death. By 1881, when the third edition of his poems was published, Bécquer was acknowledged as an important poet, and his fame was spreading throughout the Hispanic world. Since that time, Bécquer's reputation has grown steadily; his verse has achieved both critical acclaim and an extraordinary popular appeal. Indeed, after Miguel de Cervantes's *El ingenioso hidalgo don Quixote de la Mancha* (1605, 1615; *The History of the Valorous and Wittie Knight-Errant, Don Quixote of the Mancha*, 1612-1620; better known as *Don Quixote de la Mancha*), no literary work has had as many editions in Spanish as Bécquer's *The Rhymes*. Since the poet's death, no Spanish poem has touched as many hearts or has been recited and memorized as often as "Rime of the Swallows" and no poet has surpassed Bécquer's influence on Hispanic poetry. All the movements, groups, and poetic generations that have come after Bécquer in Hispanic literature have been indebted, directly or indirectly, to his innovations.

Biography

Gustavo Adolfo Bécquer was born in Seville, in the south of Spain, on February 17, 1836, the son of José María Domínguez Insausti, a painter, and Joaquina Bastida Vargas. The surname Bécquer had come to Spain from Flanders during the seventeenth century as Becker. Although the direct line of the name had ended with the poet's great-grandmother, the whole family was still known as the Bécquers. One month before young Bécquer turned five, his father died, and four years later his mother also died, leaving Bécquer and his seven brothers to the responsibility of their surviving relatives. While under the care of his mother's uncle, Don Juan de Vargas, Bécquer began to study at the Colegio de San Telmo in Seville to become a sea pilot. When this school was closed a short time later, he went to live with his godmother, Doña Manuela Monchay. It was decided that Bécquer should take up his late father's profession, and he began to study painting at the school of the Sevillian artist Antonio Cabral Bajarano. Bécquer devoted his free time to reading in his godmother's library, where he developed his preference for Horace and for the Spanish Romantic Zorrilla and where he became fond of literary studies in general.

Bécquer also studied painting with his uncle Joaquín Domínguez Bécquer. Nevertheless, his interest in literature had continued to grow, and when his uncle expressed doubts about Bécquer's potential to become a great artist, Bécquer decided, in 1854—against his godmother's advice—to go to Madrid and seek his fortune as a writer.

If in Seville Bécquer had found little happiness, he found even less in Madrid, where he always had economic difficulties and where he was soon diagnosed as having tuberculosis, the sickness that would take him to an early grave. Bécquer quickly ran out of the little money he had brought from Seville, and when he could no longer pay rent in the boardinghouse of Doña Soledad, she generously allowed him to continue residing there anyway. During his early years in Madrid, he worked in collaboration with various friends, turning out translations from French and writing original dramas and *zarzuelas* (musicals). These pieces for the stage, largely hackwork, did not command good payment, and some were not even produced. Needing to find another source of income, Bécquer obtained an insignificant position as a public servant, but he was soon fired, after being caught during working hours drawing a picture of William Shakespeare's Ophelia. In those days, he also contributed to a number of Madrid's newspapers and magazines, and he even tried, unsuccessfully, to found some new ones. These activities neither produced sufficient income for a comfortable life nor contributed to Bécquer's fame, since his works were often published without his name.

In the year 1858, Bécquer began to publish his "legends" in the newspapers of Madrid; in the same year, he met Julia Espín, a beautiful girl who later became an opera singer. It is said that, although Bécquer's love for this girl was unrequited, she inspired many of the entries in *The Rhymes*. It was at this time that Bécquer experienced his first health crisis. In 1859, a poem later included in *The Rhymes* was published under the title "Imitación de Byron" ("Imitation of Byron"); it was the first of fifteen of *The Rhymes* that appeared in Madrid periodicals during Bécquer's lifetime.

In 1860, Bécquer began publishing *Letters to an Unknown Woman* in serial form and met Casta Esteban Navarro, his doctor's daughter, whom Bécquer married the following year; the marriage would eventually produce two sons. In that same year, Bécquer's brother, Valeriano, a notable painter, came with his two children to live in Madrid and soon moved in with the poet and his wife. Throughout his married life, the poet and his wife spent several periods near Soria, where his father-in-law had a house. Between 1863 and 1864, Bécquer spent eight months living in the monastery of Veruela, where he wrote the letters in *From My Cell*. On several occasions, Bécquer and his brother Valeriano took long trips to various parts of Spain, during which the artist would paint typical local scenes while the writer would take notes for his own works or would write articles for newspapers.

The year 1864 marked a change in Bécquer's life. He was appointed to a higher civil-service position with a better salary, but a change in the government caused him to lose the job a year later. Soon, however, yet another change in the government resulted in his reappointment to the job, where he worked until 1868, when the revolution that dethroned Isabella II took place. In the same year, Bécquer separated from his wife. Taking his two children, he went to live with his brother Valeriano in Toledo, where he supposedly wrote the last poems for *The Rhymes*. A year later, they all returned to Madrid, and Bécquer resumed his journalistic work for the newspaper *La ilustración de Madrid*, where he was appointed editor in 1870. In September of that year, Valeriano died, and almost immediately Bécquer's wife repentantly returned to live with him and their children. Soon, the poet's health declined, and he died on December 22, 1870, at the age of thirty-four.

After Bécquer's death, his friend appointed a committee to publish his works. The committee collected his prose works that had appeared in the periodicals of Madrid and published them with the seventy-six poems from the manuscript of *The Rhymes*. This first edition of Bécquer's works was published in 1871, one year after his death.

ANALYSIS

The poems that made Gustavo Adolfo Bécquer famous, and that make up practically his entire production, are those included in *The Rhymes*. Only eight or ten other poems have been found, almost all juvenilia and not of high quality. When Bécquer's friends published the first edition of his works in 1871, *The Rhymes* consisted of seventy-six untitled poems as well as the previously published prose works. Another manuscript of the collection was later found, containing three more poems, for a total of seventy-nine. The discovery and publication of other poems raised the number to ninety-four, but later it was proved that many of the new poems actually had been written by Bécquer's contemporaries or had been fraudulently attributed to him.

The single most important influence on Bécquer's poetry was Heinrich Heine, whose impact on Bécquer is universally acknowledged. In addition, critics have pointed out a wide variety of other influences, ranging from Lord Byron and Edgar Allan Poe to the German poets Johann Wolfgang von Goethe, Friedrich Schiller, and Anastasius Grün (pseudonym of Anton Alexander, count of Auersperg) and the Spanish poets Eulogio Florentino Sanz (the translator of Heine into Spanish), José María de Larrea, and his friend Ferrán. Nevertheless, Bécquer's poetic genius was so powerful that he was capable of fusing these influences with that of the popular Andalusian tradition to create his own distinctive style.

The most important characteristics of Bécquer's poetry are its simplicity and its suggestive, ethereal inwardness. It should be noted that the great majority of his poems are very short; his verse lines are generally short as well, and he prefers assonance to rhyme. Bécquer's language is elegant but simple, lacking exotic and high-sounding words, and he uses a minimum of rhetorical techniques. His preference for suggestion rather than explicit statement is reflected in his frequent use of incorporeal motifs such as waves of light, the vibration of air, murmurs, thoughts, clouds, and sounds. Anecdotes are absent from his poetry, except for some extremely short ones that are indispensable to the communication of emotions. Nature appears in his poems impressionistically, mirroring the poet's interior drama. Above all, Bécquer is an eminently subjective poet who uses his poetry to express his inner feelings with almost complete indifference to the objective reality of the world.

The above-mentioned characteristics, as well as others, place Bécquer as a precursor of the Symbolist movement. Traditionally, he has been considered a late Romantic, and to a certain extent this classification is correct. In Bécquer's poetry, it is easy to observe the cult of the individual, the exaggerated sensitivity, the centering of the world on the subjectivity of the poet—all typical of the Romantic movement. Nevertheless, these characteristics appear in Bécquer in conjunction with others that typify the Symbolism of Stéphane Mallarmé, Paul Verlaine, and Arthur Rimbaud. For Bécquer, emotions or feelings are the true object of poetry. Feelings cannot be expressed with exact and precise words, and to represent his interior world, the poet must rely on suggestion and evocative symbolism. In the first poem in *The Rhymes*, Bécquer says that he would like to express the "gigantic and strange hymnal" that he knows, by "taming the rebel, and miserly language,/ with words that are at the same time/ sighs and laughs, colors and notes." In these lines, it can be seen that Bécquer conceived of the possibility of the correspondence of sensations, also typical of Symbolism. For him, as for the Symbolists, there is an ideal, absolute, and perfect world, of which the familiar physical world is an imperfect representation, significant not for itself but only for the impressions of a higher reality that it conveys. Finally, Bécquer, like the Symbolists, made frequent allusions to music and struggled to make his language as musical as possible.

THE RHYMES

In the manuscript of *The Rhymes*, the poems do not follow a chronological order; indeed, they seem to follow no logical order at all. The most widely accepted critical opinion is that, having lost the original manuscript (which he gave to a friend for publication right before the revolution of 1868), Bécquer had to reconstruct the collection from memory, adding some new poems. It is speculated that in the new copy, the majority of the poems appear in the order in which the poet remembered them, interspersed with those newly created. In any case, when Bécquer's friends decided to publish his works, they rearranged the poems, placing them in the order in which they have appeared in all their subsequent publications.

The sequence imposed on the poems, justifiably or not, gives the collection a "plot." Early poems in the sequence reflect the enthusiasm of a young poet who seeks to explain the mystery of his art and who discovers the mysterious connections between poetry and love. In later poems, however, celebration of love gives way to disillusionment with the beloved. In the final poems in the sequence, the poet is increasingly preoccupied with death.

Thus, with few exceptions, the poems collected in *The Rhymes* can be divided into four sequential groups. The first group consists of poems that consider the poet per se and the nature of poetry; the second, of poems dealing with love; the third, of poems expressing disillusionment with love; and the fourth, of poems dealing with anguish and death.

Included in the first group are poems 1 through 8—except for poem 6 (a pathetic description of Shakespeare's Ophelia)—and poem 21. In poems 2 and 5, Bécquer focuses his attention on the poet per se, trying to explain what it means to be a poet and to describe the intimate nature of the poetic spirit. In the first of these two poems, Bécquer employs a series of similes to define himself both as a poet and as a human being. To suggest the narrow limits of humans' control over their own destiny, Bécquer imagines himself to be an arrow, a dry leaf, a wave, and a ray of light, saying in the last stanza that he is crossing the world "by accident," "without thinking/ where I am coming from nor where/ my steps will take me." In poem 5, Bécquer portrays the poet as a vase containing the poetic spirit, described as an "unknown essence," a "mysterious perfume." Throughout the poem, Bécquer tries to determine the nature of that spirit. He identifies it in another series of beautiful similes in which the objects of comparison are almost always immaterial and vague, with the clouds, the waking of a star, the blue of the sea, a note from a lute, and so on. This poem introduces an important idea in Bécquer's poetics: Poetry is the marvelous reduction of ideas and feelings to words and verbal forms. The poetic spirit is described as the "bridge that crosses the abyss," as "the unknown stair/ that connects heaven and earth," and as "the invisible/ ring that holds together/ the world of forms with the world of ideas."

The remaining poems of the first group attempt to explain the mystery of poetry. Poem 1 declares that poetry is "a hymn" that cannot be confined by words and that the poet can communicate fully only with his beloved. Here again, one notes the identification of poetry with feelings and the insistence that feelings cannot be explained but can be communicated only emotionally. These same notions lie behind the succinct affirmation of poem 21, repeated by countless lovers of the Hispanic world since it was first published: Bécquer answers his beloved's question, "What is poetry?" with the simple statement, "Poetry is you."

The second group of poems, those dealing with love, includes poems 9 through 29, except for 21 (already placed in the first group) and 26 (which is closely related to the poems in the third group). Some of these poems can be considered as a series of gallant phrases forming beautiful madrigals appropriate for address to young ladies. Among them are poem 12, written to a green-eyed girl; poem 13 (the first of Bécquer's poems to have appeared in a newspaper, titled "Imitation of Byron"), composed for a blue-eyed girl; and poem 19, addressed to a girl who has the purity of a white lily. Some of the poems in this group have the charm, brevity, and sparkling shine of the *coplas* (ballads) from the Andalusian region; among these are poems 17 and 20.

In almost all the remaining poems of the second group, Bécquer appears as the poet of love, but of love as a superior and absolute feeling. Poems 9 and 10 show the universality of love. The former attempts to present all of nature as loving, and the latter describes how everything is transformed when love passes by. In poems 11 and 15, Bécquer realizes that love and the beloved for whom he searches are ideal entities of an absolute perfection and beauty that cannot exist in tangible reality. In the first of these two poems, two girls appear, one brunette and the other blond, and each in turn asks the poet if it is she for whom he is looking, to which he answers no. Then comes an unreal girl, "a vague ghost made of mist and light," incorporeal and intangible, who is incapable of loving him; immediately, the poet shows his preference for this ethereal figure, crying "Oh come, come you!" In poem 15, the ideal beloved is a "curled ribbon of light foam," a "sonorous rumor/ of a golden harp," and the poet runs madly after her, "after a shadow/ after the fervent daughter/ of a vision."

The beloved becomes corporeal in only a few poems of the second group. In poem 14, the poet sees "two eyes, yours, nothing else," and he feels that they irresistibly attract him. In poem 18, the entire physical woman appears "fatigued by the dancing" and "leaning on my arm," and in poem 29, the poet and his beloved are reading the episode of Paolo and Francesca in Dante's *La divina commedia* (c. 1320; *The Divine Comedy*, 1802) when suddenly they turn their heads at the same time: "our eyes met/ and a kiss was heard." Finally, in this second group, there is a poem that expresses the realization of love. In a typical series of incorporeal images, Bécquer says that his and his beloved's souls are "two red tongues of fire" that reunite and "form only one flame," "two notes that the hand pulls at the same time from the lute," "two streams of vapor" that join to form only "one white cloud," "two ideas born at the same time," and "two echoes that fuse with one another."

The third group of poems in *The Rhymes*, those expressing disillusionment with love, includes poems 30 through 51 as well as poem 26. Although in these poems Bécquer continues talking about love, the ideal and sublime love of the poet has decayed, ending in failure and producing great disappointment, disenchantment, and sorrow. Bécquer speaks scornfully of feminine inconstancy in a few poems, but without the note of sarcasm characteristic of Heine. In Bécquer, sorrow produces only a fine irony, which at times leads him to insinuate that women are valuable only for their physical beauty. In poem 34, after describing in detail the beauty of a woman, the poet faces the fact that she is "stupid." Bécquer resolves this conflict by saying that, as long as she stays quiet, her intelligence is of no concern to him, since "what she does not say, will always be of greater value/ than what any other woman could tell me." Similarly, in poem 39, the poet enumerates the character flaws of a woman, only to end up stressing his preference for physical beauty by saying, "but . . ./ she is so beautiful!"

The most interesting and intense poems of this third group are those in which the poet expresses his sorrow at the failure of his love. Some of them also seem to be the most autobiographical, although the impression given by the poems of *The Rhymes* is that all of them were the result of experiences lived by their author. Poem 41 appears to allude to the incompatibility between Bécquer and his wife, although it could refer to another woman. Its three brief stanzas present the poet and his beloved as opposing forces: the hurricane and the tower, the ocean and the rock, the beautiful girl and the haughty man. In each instance, the conclusion is the desolate phrase, "it could not be." The next poem, number 42, describes the moment when "a loyal friend" tells the poet a piece of "news" not mentioned in the poem. The last lines, in which the poet expresses his gratitude, would seem rather prosaic if the author had not earlier shown the intensity of his sorrow by saying, "then I understood why one cries,/ and then I understood why one kills."

The fourth and last group of poems in *The Rhymes*, those preoccupied with anguish and death, includes poems 52 through 76. In general, the poems of this group seem to be more detached from autobiographical experience, less charged with emotional intensity. Perhaps for this very reason, they are pervaded by a haunting lyricism.

One of the most famous poems ever written in Spanish is poem 53, the "Rime of the Swallows," which has been read and memorized by one generation after another. The poem expresses the brevity and the irreversibility of life and the unique value of every experience. The poet admits that the "dark swallows will return," but not "those that learned our names," "those . . . will not return!" He acknowledges that there will be flowers again on the honeysuckle tree, but not "those decorated with dew/ whose drops we used to see trembling," "those . . . will not return!" Finally, he concedes that "the fervent words of love/ will sound again in your ears," but "as I have loved you, . . . do not deceive yourself/ nobody will love you like that!

The last poems in the collection are dominated by the theme of death. When the poet asks himself about his origin and his end in poem 66, he ends his expression of radical loneliness by affirming that his grave will be "where forgetfulness lives." In poem 71, he hears a voice calling him in his sleep, and he concludes that "somebody/ whom I loved has died!" In another of his most famous poems, which is also the longest in the book, Bécquer describes the funeral of a girl, repeating at the end of each stanza, "my God, how lonely stay the dead!" The same experience may have inspired poem 74. In poem 74, it seems that he sees a dead woman, and at the spectacle of death his soul is filled with "a fervent desire": "as the abyss attracts, that mystery/ was dragging me towards itself." At the same time, the angels that are engraved on the door seem to speak to him: "the threshold of this door only God trespasses." In poem 74, which concludes the volume, Bécquer again describes the funeral of a woman and expresses his own wish to rest from the struggles of life: "oh what love so quiet that of death/ what sleep so calm that of the sepulchre."

OTHER MAJOR WORKS

SHORT FICTION: *Leyendas*, 1858-1864 (serial; partial translation in *Terrible Tales: Spanish*, 1891; also in *Romantic Legends of Spain*, 1909).

NONFICTION: *Historia de los templos de España*, 1857; *Cartas literarias a una mujer*, 1860-1861 (serial; *Letters to an Unknown Woman*, 1924); *Cartas desde mi celda*, 1864 (*From My Cell*, 1924).

MISCELLANEOUS: *Obras*, 1871; *Legends, Tales, and Poems*, 1907; *The Infinite Passion: Being the Celebrated "Rimas" and the "Letters to an Unknown Woman,"* 1924 (includes *Rimas, Letters to an Unknown Woman*, and *From My Cell*); *Legends and Letters*, 1995.

BIBLIOGRAPHY

Bécquer, Gustavo Adolfo. *Collected Poems (Rimas)*. Translated by Michael Smith. Exeter, England: Shearsman Books, 2007. This bilingual work is a modern translation of *The Rhymes*, with an informative introduction by the translator.

Bynum, B. Brant. *The Romantic Imagination in the Works of Gustavo Adolfo Bécquer*. Chapel Hill: University of North Carolina Press, 1993. Interpretation of Bécquer's work with an introduction to Romanticism and an extensive bibliography.

Havard, Robert. *From Romanticism to Surrealism: Seven Spanish Poets*. Totowa, N.J.: Barnes & Noble, 1988. Brief biography and critical analysis of Spanish poets of the nineteenth and twentieth centuries. Includes bibliographic references.

Mayhew, Jonathan. "Jorge Guillén and the Insufficiency of Poetic Language." *PMLA* 106 (October, 1991). Discusses the skepticism of Bécquer and other poets regarding the capacity of language to convey the poets' experiences.

Silver, Philip W. *Ruin and Restitution: Reinterpreting Romanticism in Spain*. Nashville, Tenn.: Vanderbilt University Press, 1997. Examines Bécquer and Luis Cernuda and their works in terms of Romanticism.

Rogelio A. de la Torre

PEDRO CALDERÓN DE LA BARCA

Born: Madrid, Spain; January 17, 1600
Died: Madrid, Spain; May 25, 1681

PRINCIPAL POETRY
Psalle et sile, 1741
Poesías, 1845
Obra lírica, 1943
Sus mejores poesías, 1954
Poesías líricas en las obras dramáticas de Calderón, 1964
Los sonetos de Calderón en sus obras dramáticas, 1974

OTHER LITERARY FORMS

Pedro Calderón de la Barca (kol-day-ROHN day lo-BOR-ko) is known primarily as a verse dramatist, an occupation to which he was dedicated during his entire life. He wrote more than one hundred plays, most of which were published during his life or soon after his death. Some of the better known include *Amor, honor, y poder* (1623; love, honor, and power); *El sitio de Breda* (pr. 1625; the siege of Breda); *El príncipe constante* (pr. 1629; *The Constant Prince*, 1853); *La dama duende* (pr., pb. 1936; *The Phantom Lady*, 1664); *Casa con dos puertas, mala es de guardar* (pr., pb. 1936; *A House with Two Doors Is Difficult to Guard*, 1737); *La devoción de la cruz* (pb. 1634; *Devotion to the Cross*, 1832); *Los cabellos de Absalón* (pb. 1684; *The Crown of Absalom*, 1993); *La vida es sueño* (pr. 1635; *Life Is a Dream*, 1830); *El mayor encanto, amor* (pr. 1635; *Love, the Greatest Enchantment*, 1870); *A secreto agravio, secreta venganza* (pb. 1637; *Secret Vengeance for Secret Insult*, 1961); *El mágico prodigioso* (pr. 1637; *The Wonder-Working Magician*, 1959); *El alcalde de Zalamea* (pr. 1643; *The Mayor of Zalamea*, 1885); *El médico de su honra* (pb. 1637; *The Surgeon of His Honor*, 1853); *El pintor de su deshonra* (pb. 1650; *The Painter of His Dishonor*, 1853); *La hija del aire, Parte I* (pr. 1653; *The Daughter of the Air, Part I* 1831); and *La hija del aire, Parte II* (pr. 1653; *The Daughter of the Air, Part II*, 1831).

ACHIEVEMENTS

Pedro Calderón de la Barca lived during Spain's Golden Age, his death marking the end of that most productive period of Spanish letters. He was known as a poet and dramatist in his teens, and in his early twenties, he took several poems to the poetic jousts held in 1620 and 1622 to commemorate the beatification and canonization of Saint Isidro. He was awarded a prize in the second contest, and Lope de Vega Carpio, who was the organizer of the two events, praised the young poet highly on both occasions.

Pedro Calderón de la Barca
(Library of Congress)

Indeed, throughout his life, Calderón continued to write lyric poetry, the great bulk of which, however, is incorporated into his plays. His first dated play, *Amor, honor, y poder* is from 1623, and subsequently he established himself so well in the theatrical scene that, when Lope de Vega died in 1635, Calderón became the official court dramatist, a position he held until his death. Calderón proved a worthy successor of Lope de Vega, for he wrote more than two hundred dramatic pieces, a total second only to that of Lope de Vega. Calderón produced several masterpieces, including *Life Is a Dream*, one of the great works of Spain's Golden Age. In addition, he was the supreme master of the *auto*, or Eucharist play, a dramatic form which he refined and improved progressively and to which he was dedicated almost exclusively during the last years of his life.

Biography

Pedro Calderón de la Barca was born in Madrid into a family of some nobility. His father, Diego Calderón de la Barca, came from the valley of Carriedo, in the mountains of Santander, and was a secretary to the treasury board under Philip II and Philip III. Calderón's mother, Ana María de Henao, was from a noble family of the Low Countries that had moved to Spain long before. Calderón was their third child.

Soon after Calderón was born, his family moved to Valladolid, following the transfer of the court, and there the boy learned his first letters. When the court returned permanently to Madrid, and with it his family, Calderón, then nine years old, was placed in the Colegio Imperial of the Jesuits, where he studied Latin and the humanities for five years.

Calderón's mother died in 1610, and his father married Juana Freyre four years later, only to die himself the following year. His death was followed by a bitter and costly lawsuit between Juana and the Calderón children, ending favorably for Juana. Calderón had entered the University of Alcalá de Henares in 1614, but, after his father's death, he transferred to the University of Salamanca to be under the supervision of his uncle. In Salamanca, he studied canon law and theology, planning to become a priest and take charge of a chaplaincy endowed by his maternal grandfather. Calderón abandoned his studies in 1620, however, and returned to Madrid, where for some time he led a turbulent life. He and his brothers, Diego and José, were engaged in a fight that resulted in the murder of Diego de Velasco. The father of Velasco demanded retribution, and the Calderón brothers settled the case by paying six hundred ducats (a substantial sum in those days).

While in Salamanca, Calderón had started writing poetry and drama; in Madrid, he entered the poetic competitions of 1620 and 1622, organized to celebrate the beatification and canonization of Saint Isidro. Calderón's entries won the praise of Lope de Vega, judge of the contests and editor of its proceedings. The works that Calderón presented to these jousts are of interest not only because they are his earliest extant poems but also because they are among his few surviving nondramatic poems.

The next few years took Calderón away from Spain. He enlisted in the Spanish army and went to Northern Italy and to Flanders, where he probably witnessed the defeat that the Spaniards inflicted on the Flemish, an event that he dramatized so well in *El sitio de Breda*. The poet returned to Madrid around 1625, and soon afterward he entered the service of Duke Frías. From that time on, Calderón fully committed himself to the theater, constantly writing new plays and staging them with all the available machinery and scenery. According to Pérez de Montalbán, Calderón had written many dramas by 1632—all of which had been performed successfully—as well as a substantial body of lyric verse. Consequently, he was enjoying an enviable reputation as a poet.

About that time, the dramatist was involved in another unhappy event. Pedro de Villegas wounded one of Calderón's brothers very seriously, and in pursuit of Villegas, Calderón, accompanied by some police officers, violated the sanctity of the Trinitarians' convent. The entire court reacted negatively to this event, including Lope de Vega, who protested violently because his daughter Marcela was in the convent. Calderón was reprimanded for his actions, but nothing more, and he even made fun of the affair in *The Constant Prince*. His popularity was already larger than the gravity of his actions, and, therefore, he came out of it unscathed.

In 1635, the Retiro Gardens and Palaces were opened with great festivities, and Calderón's play, *Love, the Greatest Enchantment*, was staged for the occasion. Lope de Vega died that same year, and Calderón became officially attached to the court, furnishing dramas for the exclusive entertainment of the Royal Palace. In recognition of his services, King Philip IV made Calderón a knight of the Order of Santiago in 1637. As such, he participated in the liberation of Fuenterrabía that same year, and with the army of Count Duke Olivares, he took part in the pacification of Catalonia, serving loyally and courageously until 1642, in recognition of which he was awarded a monthly pension of thirty gold crowns.

The war of Catalonia made an impact on Calderón, aggravated by the fact that his brother José lost his life in the conflict. Nevertheless, he went back to Madrid and continued his occupation as court dramatist, increasingly enjoying the favor of the king, who put in his hands the arrangement of the festivities for the arrival of the new Queen, Mariana de Austria, in 1649.

During these years, Calderón, about whose intimate life little is known, fathered a son out of wedlock. This son, born around 1647, died before reaching adulthood, while his mother died soon after his birth. Calderón, who had been contemplating the idea for some time, determined to become a priest. He was ordained in 1651, and two years later, Philip IV appointed him to the chaplaincy of the New Kings in the Cathedral of Toledo. Calderón moved to that city, but he kept in contact with Madrid, supplying the court with new plays and *autos* on a regular basis. While in Toledo, and inspired by the inscription of the cathedral's choir, he wrote the poem *Psalle et sile* (sing and be silent), an unusually self-revealing work.

Calderón returned to Madrid in 1663 as the chaplain of honor to Philip IV, who had created that position to ensure Calderón's presence in the court. Later that year, Calderón joined the Natural Priests of Madrid, and he became head of the congregation afterward, remaining in that position until his death. He led a quiet life during that time, dedicated to his priestly duties and restricting his literary activity to the writing of Eucharist plays and an occasional drama for the court. He still enjoyed an immense popularity, and his plays were staged frequently. Three volumes of his *Partes* (1636-1684; collected plays) appeared during this period (two had been published in 1636 and 1637), although he disowned four dramas of the last volume and one of the Eucharist plays. Preparation was under way to publish his entire dramatic production, a task that was undertaken by Juan de Vera Tassis after Calderón's death.

Calderón died on May 25, 1681; his death marked the end of the Golden Age of Spanish literature. Following his desires, the dramatist was buried during a simple ceremony, but a gorgeous one took place a few days later to satisfy the many admirers who wanted to pay homage to the playwright for the last time.

Analysis

There are extant only about thirty nondramatic poems by Pedro Calderón de la Barca. Most of them are short poems, composed for a particular occasion, usually in praise of someone in whose collection they would appear.

Use of sonnets

As he did in his plays, Calderón employed a variety of verse forms in his nondramatic poems, but the sonnet is the prevalent form. The sonnet had been an important part of Spanish poetry since Juan Boscán and Garcilaso de la Vega assimilated the Italian poetic form into Castilian verse, but it was losing popularity during Calderón's time, as he observes in one of his plays, *Antes que todo es mi dama* (pb. 1662; my lady comes before everything else). Fifteen of Calderón's nondramatic poems are sonnets; added to the sonnets that he included in his dramatic works and the one inserted in the longer poem *Psalle et sile*, they make a total of eighty-six sonnets, collected in a single volume by Rafael Osuna in 1974.

Calderón's sonnets reflect the main poetic currents of his times; Gongorism and *conceptismo* are both present, with a preference for the latter. In general, Calderón's sonnets reveal the poet's desire for a poetry of geometric perfection, evident in the parallel constructions, the *enumeratio* of concepts and *recopilación* or recapitulation of them in the final line, and other rhetorical techniques. They are also filled with the rich imagery that the poet uses in all his literary production. The nondramatic sonnets are, in general, less convincing than those found in the plays, given their occasional character, but some of them are well constructed and worthy of praise. Among these are the sonnet dedicated to Saint Isidro, beautiful in its simplicity; the one written in honor of Saint Teresa de Ávila, which shows a fervent respect for the reformer of the Carmelitans; the one inserted in *Psalle et sile*, which hails the Cathedral of Toledo as a symbol of faith; and the one praising King Philip IV's hunting skills, the best of all, according to Osuna.

Use of romance verse

Another poetic form that Calderón used with great skill is the romance. He gives a particular lightness to this traditional verse form, making the poem flow with ease, always adapting it appropriately to the theme he is poeticizing. In this meter, Calderón wrote his only two extant love poems, an ascetic composition, and a self-portrait in verse that reveals his comic genius. This last is, unfortunately, incomplete, yet the 173 lines of the fragment are rich in wit. Calderón first describes his physical appearance—not forgetting any part of his body—in a very unflattering manner. He proceeds to tell the reader about his studies in Salamanca, referring to his mother's desire that he become a priest, his dedication to the theater, and his days as a soldier, adding jokingly that none of these occupations enabled him to find a decent woman who would marry him. The poet, however, does not let this situation affect him, for he has learned that, "as a philosopher says, it makes good sense to adapt to the times." Based on this thinking, he involves himself with two women because he prefers two ugly maids to a beautiful lady. The poem ends abruptly in an argument against Plato's concept of love. The sarcastic tone of the opening lines informs the entire composition; for example, when referring to his lack of responsibility, the poet observes that his peccadilloes are excused by everyone because he is a Salamanca graduate. The tone of the poem is far from Calderón's characteristic sobriety, although it is possible that he wrote other poems of this nature that have not survived. Because of the reference to the time he spent in the army, the poem must have been written sometime between 1625 and 1637, for he became very disappointed with the reality of war during the Catalonian uprising.

"Decima"

It is in his serious compositions that Calderón shows his best abilities as a poet. In them, as in some of his philosophical plays, Calderón is preoccupied with the reality of death. The best poem of this type is "Décimas a la muerte" ("Decima"), the tone of which is reminiscent of Jorge Manrique's *Coplas por la muerte de su padre* (1492; *Ode*, 1823), although it is less impressive than that fifteenth century masterpiece. Its themes include the brevity of life; the justice of death, which ends every man's life equally; and the *ubi sunt* topos. Absent from it is the theme of fame, so strong in Manrique and present elsewhere in Calderón's works. Here, the poet is deeply pessimistic: "Everything resolves to nothingness,/ all comes from dirt, and dirt becomes,/ and thus it ends where it began." This sense of pessimism is heightened by the fact that there is only a vague reference to eternal life at the end of the poem. The emphasis is placed on the "end" of everything and the absurdity of life, on a pervasive lack of meaning.

A similar attitude is expressed in another poem, "Lágrimas que vierte un alma arrepentida" (1672; tears of a repentant soul). Written in Calderón's old age, "Lágrimas que vierte un alma arrepentida" reveals his strong religious sentiments. The poet presents himself with humility, declaring that he is a sinner, full of vices, and asks God to forgive him. The poem is an expression of love for Christ; it recalls Saint Teresa of Ávila and the anonymous "Soneto a Cristo crucificado" ("Sonnet to Christ Crucified").

Psalle et sile

Calderón's longest poem is *Psalle et sile*, written in Toledo while the poet was in charge of the chaplaincy of the New Kings (1653-1663). The 525-line poem was inspired by the words inscribed at the entrance of the cathedral's choir. Calderón tries to explain the meaning of the inscription, which, because of its location, implies a request or command to those who enter the choir. How is it possible to sing and be silent at the same time? The poet praises silence as the greatest moderation and as the language of God, with whom one can communicate only in the silence of one's soul. Calderón adds, however, that "he who speaks with propriety does not break silence." To speak with propriety, one has to concentrate on the subject of the conversation. In the same manner, one needs to concentrate when conversing with God, which can be done only by meditating. If one is immersed in meditation, then one is speaking the language of God—that is, one is truly silent. At the same time, one could sing songs without interrupting the mental conversation with God. Following this reasoning, it is possible to sing and to be silent simultaneously, utterly absorbed in spiritual communication with God.

OTHER MAJOR WORKS

PLAYS: *Amor, honor y poder*, pr. 1623; *El sitio de Breda*, pr. 1625; *El príncipe constante*, pr. 1629 (*The Constant Prince*, 1853); *La devoción de la cruz*, pb. 1634 (*The Devotion to the Cross*, 1832); *El mayor encanto, amor*, pr. 1635 (*Love, the Greatest Enchantment*, 1870); *La vida es sueño*, pr. 1635 (*Life Is a Dream*, 1830); *Casa con dos puertas, mala es de guardar*, pr., pb. 1636 (wr. 1629; *House with Two Doors Is Difficult to Guard*, 1737); *La dama duende*, pr., pb. 1636 (wr. 1629; *The Phantom Lady*, 1664); *A secreto agravio, secreta venganza*, pb. 1637 (*Secret Vengeance for Secret Insult*, 1961); *El mágico prodigioso*, pr. 1637 (*The Wonder-Working Magician*, 1959); *El médico de su honra*, pb. 1637 (*The Surgeon of His Honor*, 1853); *El alcalde de Zalamea*, pr. 1643 (*The Mayor of Zalamea*, 1853); *El gran teatro del mundo*, pr. 1649 (wr. 1635; *The Great Theater of the World*, 1856); *El pintor de su deshonra*, pb. 1650 (wr. 1640-1642; *The Painter of His Dishonor*, 1853); *La hija del aire, Parte I*, pr. 1653 (*The Daughter of the Air, Part I*, 1831); *La hija del aire, Parte II*, pr. 1653 (*The Daughter of the Air, Part II*, 1831); *El laurel de Apolo*, pr. 1659; *La púrpura de la rosa*, pr. 1660; *Antes que todo es mi dama*, pb. 1662; *Hado y divisa de Leonido y Marfisa*, pr. 1680; *La Estatua de Prometeo*, pb. 1683 (wr. 1669); *Los cabellos de Absalón*, pb. 1684 (wr. c. 1634; *The Crown of Absalom*, 1993); *Eco y Narciso*, pr. 1688 (wr. 1661).

BIBLIOGRAPHY

Acker, Thomas S. *The Baroque Vortex: Velázquez, Calderón, and Gracián Under Philip IV*. New York: Peter Lang, 2000. This comparative study places Calderón in both a literary and historical context. Contains bibliographical references.

Aycock, Wendell M., and Sydney P. Cravens, eds. *Calderón de la Barca at the Tercentenary: Comparative Views*. Lubbock: Interdepartmental Committee on Comparative Literature, Texas Tech University, 1982. An important collection of papers on the three-hundredth anniversary of Calderón's death. The essayists concentrate on comparing some of Calderón's contributions with other artistic impulses, such as German Idealist philosophy, Euripides, Mexican cleric characters, and William Shakespeare.

Cascardi, Anthony J. *The Limits of Illusion: A Critical Study of Calderón*. New York: Cambridge University Press, 2005. Valuable for the breadth and variety of its inquiry. Includes an index.

Hesse, Everett W. *Calderón de la Barca*. Boston: Twayne, 1967. Treats the Spanish theater of the Golden Age, the political and social arena, the structure of Calderón's work, the works in which he excelled, and Calderón's critical reception. Selected bibliography and index.

Maraniss, James E. *On Calderón*. Columbia: University of Missouri Press, 1978. Stresses Calderón's sense of "order triumphant" and moves through the canon examing the plays. Gives a sense of who the poet was.

Rupp, Stephen James. *Allegories of Kingship: Calderón and the Anti-Machiavellian Tradition*. University Park: Pennsylvania State University Press, 1996. An examination of Calderón's portrayal of the monarchy in literature and of his political and social views. Bibliography and index.

Suscavage, Charlene E. *Calderón: The Imagery of Tragedy*. New York: Peter Lang, 1991. Although concerned with the plays, focuses on Calderón's language and figures of speech. Bibliographical references.

Wardropper, Bruce W., ed. *Critical Essays on the Theatre of Calderón*. New York: New York University Press, 1965. Essays on Calderón's themes, characters, structure, political viewpoint, and theoretical perspectives. The opening article, by A. A. Parker, is a good summary of the justifications for ranking Calderón among the great writers of a great literary age.

Juan Fernández Jiménez

ROSALÍA DE CASTRO

Born: Santiago de Compostela, Spain; February 24, 1837
Died: Padrón, Spain; July 15, 1885

PRINCIPAL POETRY
La flor, 1857
A mi madre, 1863
Cantares gallegos, 1863
Follas novas, 1880
En las orillas del Sar, 1884 (*Beside the River Sar*, 1937)
Obras completas, 1909-1911 (4 volumes)
Poems, 1964
Poems, 1991

OTHER LITERARY FORMS

Rosalía de Castro (KOS-troh) was a novelist as well as a poet. Her five novels—*La hija del mar* (1859; *Daughter of the Sea*, 1995), *Flavio* (1861), *Ruinas* (1866; ruins), *El caballero de las botas azules* (1867; the knight with the blue boots), and *El primer loco* (1881; the first madman)—span the transition from Romanticism to realism. Although Castro herself put considerable stock in her novels, she is remembered only for her poetry.

ACHIEVEMENTS

Rosalía de Castro has been called Spain's foremost woman poet; Gerald Brenan has gone further, asserting that if she had written more in Spanish than in her native Galician dialect, she would be recognized as the greatest woman poet of modern times. Her unabashedly heart-throbbing lyrics are saved from mawkishness by her disciplined style. Castro's poetry, along with that of Gustavo Adolfo Bécquer, is the most representative of Spanish poetry at the time of its transition from Romanticism to the modern lyric. Some critics believe that she interacted with Bécquer—that in fact she lent him in 1857 a copy of Gérard de Nerval's translation of Heinrich Heine's *Tragödien, nebst einem lyrischen Intermezzo* (1823; *Tragedies, Together with Lyric Intermezzo*, 1905), a book said to have influenced Bécquer. It was not until the second decade of the twentieth century, when Azorín (José Martínez Ruiz) and Miguel de Unamuno y Jugo recommended her to the public, that her reputation as a poet became assured. Later, even poet Luis Cernuda, who found her work uneven and sentimental, recognized the rare timelessness of her observations. Antonio Machado borrowed images from her poetry, Juan Ramón Jiménez referred to her as "our Rosalía," and Gerardo Diego used her name as a metaphor in his own poetry. Her Galician poetry inspired Federico García Lorca to write his own "poemas gallegos," including a "Canzón de cuna pra Rosalía Castro, morta" ("Lullaby for the Late Rosalía de Castro").

With her contemporaries Manuel Curros Enríquez (who wrote an elegy for her) and Eduardo Pondal, Castro made up a triad of Galician poets who effected a renaissance of their provincial literature. Using the folk songs of Galicia as her models, she bonded modern Spanish poetry to oral forms that would have otherwise been lost. She led the way for subsequent poets to utilize folk tradition, and her work tolled the death knell for urban Romanticism. Modernist poets availed themselves of the revolutionary meters used by Castro (her ennea-syllabic verse in *La flor*—the flower—predates the so-called innovations of Rubén Darío), and her use of free verse heralded the boldness of contemporary poetry.

To a remarkable extent, Castro's Galician and Spanish poetry has been accepted into English-language anthologies of world verse, especially in those of women's poetry (such as *A Book of Women Poets: From Antiquity to Now*, rev. ed., 1992).

Biography

Rosalía de Castro was born in Santiago de Compostela in 1837, the child of María Teresa de la Cruz de Castro y Abadía. Her mother, who came from a once-wealthy family, was thirty-three when Rosalía was born; her father, Jose Martínez Viojo, was thirty-nine and a priest. Although her father could not acknowledge Rosalía as his daughter, he may have taken some interest in her welfare. Rosalía was brought up by Francisca Martínez, who, despite her surname, does not appear to have been the priest's sister. By 1853, Rosalía was living with her real mother, and there developed between them a deep bond. In Rosalía's eyes, her mother sanctified whatever sin she may have committed by reaffirming her obligation to her daughter in defiance of a hypocritical society.

A precocious child, Castro was writing verses by the age of eleven, and by the age of sixteen she could play the guitar and the piano, had developed a fine contralto voice, and could draw well and read French. She read the foreign classics in translation and was fond of Lord Byron, Heinrich Heine, Edgar Allan Poe, and E. T. A. Hoffmann. Judging from the spelling errors in hand-written manuscripts of her poetry, however, her formal education may not have been extensive.

As a teenager, Castro was taken from Padrón to Santiago, where she attended school and where she participated in the city's cultural life. At a young people's cultural society, she met Aurelio Aguirre, one of the most representative figures of the Romantic movement in Galicia, a man who was later to be the model of Flavio in her novel of the same name, and who dedicated to her a work called "Improvisation"—apparently an attempt to console her for the discrepancy between her enchanting poetry and her less than enchanting physical appearance. Perhaps it is too facile to attribute the characteristic wistfulness of her poetry to a failed love affair, but it has been suggested that the lost love recalled in her poems and her fiction was Aurelio Aguirre. Among the poems not included in her own collections but included in *Obras completas* is an elegy for Aguirre.

In 1856, Castro went to Madrid, where she stayed at the home of a relative. It is generally said that she went "on family business," but it is possible she left home with the idea of becoming an actress in Madrid. Exposed to the cultural life of the Spanish capital, she devoted herself to writing and was able to meet other contemporary writers. In 1857, her first book of poetry *La flor* appeared and was favorably reviewed by Manuel Murguía in *La Iberia*. According to Murguía, he was not acquainted with the young author, but this is rather unlikely, not only because some of his comments presuppose a direct knowledge of Castro's personality, but also because he, too, had recently come from Galicia and, in fact, was Aguirre's best friend. Castro and Murguía were married in Madrid on October 10, 1858. Murguía, like Aguirre a Galician of Basque descent, was a journalist and historian destined to be honored in Galicia for his role in promoting regionalist literature. The couple had seven children. Their first child, a daughter, was born in 1859; their second child, also a daughter, was not born until ten years later. One of the twins Castro bore in 1871, Ovidio, was an accomplished painter of Galician landscapes but died young. Her youngest son died in his second year as the result of a fall, and her youngest daughter was stillborn in 1877.

In 1862, Castro's beloved mother died, and Castro honored her with a privately printed collection of poems, *A mi madre* (to my mother) of limited literary value but elegiac and emotional.

It remains unclear what kind of a marriage Castro had with Murguía. Gerald Brenan believes that Murguía, envious of his wife's talents, mistreated her; it is certain that Murguía destroyed his wife's correspondence after her death. Castro scholar Marina Mayoral, on the other hand, prefers to see in Murguía—who survived his wife by thirty-eight years and wrote lovingly and abundantly about her—one of the few mainstays of Castro's sad life. Despite the fulfillment of children and the security of family life, she was frequently bored, and in both her poetry and her fiction, she mourned lost happiness.

It is important, however, not to exaggerate the pathetic nature of Castro's life. She loved the arts and took great pleasure from her endeavors in the fields of music, drawing, and acting. She was a great success when she acted in Antonio Gil y Zárate's play *Rosamunda* (1839), and for the greater part of her life she enjoyed exchanging ideas with her friends. Her daughter Gala, who lived until 1964, was especially concerned that her mother not be remembered as morose. As Victoriano García Martí points out, people who are authentically sorrowful often develop a profound love of humankind and achieve a different kind of contentment. This was especially true of Castro, and after her death a legend grew concerning her generosity to others, endowing her with a kind of saintliness.

Between 1859 and 1870, the couple lived in Madrid and Simancas, where Murguía had a position as a government historian, and they traveled extensively throughout

Spain. To Castro, any terrain that was not green, damp, and lush like her native Galicia was disappointing; thus, she disliked most of the rest of Spain. She became so consumed with nostalgia for her native land that she began her *Cantares gallegos* (Galician songs), written in Galician but given a Spanish title. In the 1870's, Murguía held positions in Galicia, and Castro spent much of her time at Padron, which she considered home. Having suffered from vague ill health all her life, she withdrew completely from society in her last decade; she died of uterine cancer in 1885. In the moments before her death, she received the Sacraments, recited her favorite prayers, and begged her children to destroy her unpublished manuscripts. With her last breath, she asked that the window be opened, for she wished to see the ocean—which in fact was not visible from her home.

Castro was buried near her mother in the peaceful cemetery of Adina in Padron, a place whose enchantment she had evoked in *Follas novas* (new leaves). On the very day of her death, accolades began to arrive, and as a result of the homage paid her in death, her remains were moved in 1891 to a marble tomb in the Convent of Santo Domingo de Bonaval in Santiago. In 1917, her compatriots, together with an organization of Galician emigrants in America, organized a campaign to raise a statue to their poet in the Paseo de la Herradura in Santiago, looking toward Padron. According to biographer Kathleen Kulp-Hill, this statue is faithful to portraits and descriptions of Castro. The figure is seated in a calm, pensive attitude, projecting an aura of strength and warmth.

Analysis

As Frédéric Mistral is to Provence and Joan Maragall to Catalonia, Rosalía de Castro is to Galicia, the northwest corner of the Iberian peninsula, linked politically with Spain but tied ethnically, linguistically, and temperamentally with Portugal. When Castro was nine years old, there was an unsuccessful insurrection in Galicia against the Spanish government. The unpleasant memory of the savage reprisals undertaken by the government may help explain her strong hostility toward Castile and Castilians, as in the lines, "May God grant, Castilians,/ Castilians whom I abhor,/ that rather the Galicians should die,/ than to go to you for bread."

Santiago de Compostela, Castro's birthplace, possesses the bones of Saint James the Apostle, for which reason Galicia became in the Middle Ages the third most holy shrine in Christendom (after Jerusalem and Rome). The steady stream of pilgrims traveling to Galicia from all parts of Europe made Santiago a medieval cultural center, and in the thirteenth century, Galician became the language of lyrical poetry throughout the Iberian peninsula. The Galician *jograles* (minstrels) sang characteristically of melancholy (designated in Spanish by its Galician and Portuguese name, *saudades*), as in, for example, their *cantigas de amigo*, the songs of women whose lovers were absent, either away at sea or fighting the Moors in Portugal. After the thirteenth century, however, there was an eclipse of Galician poetry, and it was not until the nineteenth century that an interest in the poetic potential of the Galician language was reawakened.

The poetry of Castro flows from line to line in a musical sequence and does not, as Gerald Brenan observes, condense well into a single epithet or phrase. She was not fond of metaphors but rather relied heavily on repetition—in such lines as ("Breezes breezes, little breezes/ breezes of the land I come from")—and contrast—as in "To them those frosts/ are the promise of early flowers;/ To me they are silent workers/ weaving my winding sheet." In her earlier poems, she sometimes used the *leixa-pren*, a special feature of the medieval *cantigas de amigo*, whereby each new stanza begins with an echo from the last line of the previous stanza. Her diction is almost colloquial, her syntax uninverted (except in her earliest poetry and in some of her later poetry), and her adjectives are always the least ornamental possible. There abound words for the lushness of Galicia, names of animals and birds, and especially of trees (such as the oaks sacred to the ancient Celts of Galicia; giant chestnuts; and the cedars of "our own" Lebanon). In her somber moods, she draws repeatedly on Spanish adjectives such as *torvo* (grim), *amargo* (bitter), and *triste* (sad), and uses verbs such as *anonadar* (to destroy), *agostar* (to wither up as in August), *hostigar* (to scourge), while she uses words such as *guarida* (lair), *nido* (nest), and *egida* (aegis) to express the security and coziness of home in Galicia. Galician, more than Spanish, is a nasal language (for example, Galician *min*, "my," as opposed to Spanish *mí*), and Castro uses its humming nasals as a tool to craft more sharply the gloom she suffers on Earth, as in the line "Pra min i-en min mesma moras" (for me and in myself you live), rom "Cando penso que to fuche" (when I think that you have gone), in *Follas novas*.

"I Used to Have a Nail"

One remarkable poem that reveals Castro's attitude toward sorrow is "Una-ha vez tiven un cravo" ("I Used to Have a Nail") in *Follas novas*. This painful nail, whether made of gold, iron, or love, leads the poet, weeping like Mary Magdalen, to entreat God to effect a miracle for its removal. When at last she gathers the courage to pluck it out, the void it leaves is something like a longing for the old pain. Some critics have speculated that without an abundant supply of sorrow for her to sublimate into poetry, Castro felt lost. This contradictory hunger for suffering cannot be reduced to the level of a personal neurosis, for it reflects the ideals of traditional Christianity. Castro believed that thistles, though harsh to the flesh, mark the road to heaven, and in "Yo en mi lecho de abrojos" ("I on My Bed of Thistles," from *Beside the River Sar*), avowedly preferred her destiny to a "bed of roses and feathers," which have been known to "envenom and corrupt."

Religion and superstition

Castro was conventionally religious; she needed God and sought him everywhere, and she fought herself for her faith, as Unamuno did. There are biblical references in her poetry, as well as her marginally Christian *sombras* ("shades"), the souls of persons no longer living whom Castro "invokes" from time to time and who respond by intervening in the lives of the living. She also draws on Galician lore concerning the supernatural world. Witches (*meigas, lurpias*), warlocks (*meigos*), and elves (*trasgos*) inhabit her forests, and the safety of the unwary nocturnal traveler may be jeopardized by the Host of Souls in Torment. In "Dios bendiga todo, nena" ("God Blesses Everything, Child," from *Cantares gallegos*), an old woman warns a young girl of the dangers of the world, whereupon the girl declares her intention never to leave her village without scapularies, holy medals, and amulets to protect her from witches. The fine line between religion and superstition is typified in "Soberba" ("Foolish Pride") in *Follas novas*, where a family frightened by a storm tries to placate God with candles, olive leaves, and prayers, and by scouring from their personal slates offenses that might have incurred his wrath. Nor is the imagery of the supernatural always to be taken literally. In an aubade, Castro has the heroine address her lover affectionately as "warlock" while he prepares to leave her bed, and elsewhere employs the same word to create a metaphor for sorrow: "N' hay peor meiga que un-ha gran pena" (there is no worse demon than a great sorrow).

CANTARES GALLEGOS

Castro's first important book of poems was *Cantares gallegos*. In the prologue to this volume, she acknowledges the inspiration of *El libro de los cantares* by Antonio de Trueba, published the previous year, and apologizes for her shortcomings as a poet, claiming that her only schooling was that of "our poor country folk." The poems are dedicated to Fernan Caballero (Cecilia Böhl de Faber), the pioneer of the realistic novel in Spain, who won Castro's appreciation with her unprejudiced portrayal of Galicians. Working without a grammar, Castro apologizes for her Galician; indeed, it is not a pure dialect unaffected by Castilian influence, and lexical and orthographic inconsistencies abound. She attempted to imitate modern Portuguese in her use of diacritical marks, contractions, and elisions, and included a short glossary of Galician words for the sake of her Castilian readers.

Castro's usual procedure was to begin her poems with a popular couplet and then to elaborate it into a ballad. Her masterpiece is perhaps "Airiños, airiños, aires" ("Breezes, Breezes, Little Breezes") in which she portrays the nostalgia of a Galician emigrant, playing upon the dual meaning of *airiños* as "little breezes" and "little songs." Everywhere this unfortunate emigrant turns in the strange country of her destination, people peer curiously at her, and she longs for the sweet breezes of home, those "quitadoiriños de penas" ("takers-away of sorrow") that enchant the woods and caress the land. Similarly as Galician poetry inspired the Castilian lyric of the fifteenth and sixteenth centuries, this poem influenced the revival of Spanish poetry that began thirty years after Castro's death. The *Romancero gitano, 1924-1927* (1928; *The Gypsy Ballads of García Lorca*, 1951, 1953) of Federico García Lorca, for example, with its themes and repetitions derived from folk tradition, owes much to this poem.

In "Pasa rio, pasa rio" ("Pass by, River, Pass By"), a disconsolate lover weeps tears into the ocean in hope that they may reach her beloved in Brazil, where he has had to emigrate. The plight of the Galician emigrant forced to leave his homeland because of economic necessity troubled Castro deeply. There are many poems of praise for Galicia, such as "Cómo chove mihudiño" ("How the Rain Is Falling Lightly"), in which she describes Padrón, lulled by the river where the trees are shady, and reminisces about the great house owned by her humanitarian grandfather. She dares to ask the Sun of Italy if it has seen "more green, more roses,/ bluer sky or softer colors/ where foam stripes your gulfs with whiteness"; and is reminded by a wandering cloud of the sad shade of her mother wandering lonely in the spheres before she goes to glory.

Follas novas

The poems of *Follas novas* are meant to be read and reflected upon, as opposed to the folk poems of *Cantares gallegos* with their marked oral quality. The 139 poems of *Follas novas* are more subjective and personal and bleaker than those of the earlier book, which radiate innocence and hope; they are also more innovative in form: Castro employed varying line lengths with metrical combinations then regarded as inappropriate for Spanish verse, such as combinations of eight with ten or eleven syllables or eight with fourteen. Dedicated to the Society for the Welfare of Galicians in Havana, the book was published simultaneously in Havana and Madrid in 1880. In her prologue, Castro expresses her concern for the suffering of Galicians in distant lands, and she also asserts her artistic independence as a woman. Certainly the successive deaths of her two youngest children within three months of each other in 1876-1877 did much to intensify her tragic sense of life, but many of the poems in this collection were written as long as ten years before the publication date.

Here, Castro's poetry is no longer concerned with aubades but rather with the departures of lovers and their separation. Love is no longer hopeful but rather furtive and anxious. In "¿Que lle digo?" ("What Should I Tell Her?") the emigrant may be plagued by *saudades* for his homeland but may wax cynical about love as well: "Antona is there, but I have Rosa here." The landscape of Galicia is always in the background, but is no longer decorative and is now interwoven with more complex emotions. Death is seen as a cure for the disease of life, and the poet asks God why suicide must be deemed a crime.

Although she occasionally dedicated her poems to worthy persons (such as her husband and Ventura Ruíz de Aguilera), Castro did not often exalt either historical figures or living persons in her poetry. One notable exception, written in classical form, is her elegy on the tomb of Sir John Moore, the affable British general who led a retreat to Corunna that ended in the British victory over the Napoleonic forces there in 1809, but which cost Moore his life. *Follas novas* also includes a translation into Galician of the poem "Armonias d'a tarde" (harmonies of the afternoon), by Ventura Ruíz de Aguilera, a contemporary poet who drew on the folk motifs of the Salamanca area.

BESIDE THE RIVER SAR

As a result of complaints made by her Galician readers that some of her material was scandalous, Castro vowed never again to write in Galician, and it is to this decision and the Spanish poems of her last collection, *Beside the River Sar*, that she owes her prominence in Spanish literature. Not all the critics, however, proclaim the superiority of these poems. Gerald Brenan, who prefers the softer, more tender tone of her Galician verse, finds the aloofness of her Castilian poems chilling. Many of the poems collected in *Beside the River Sar* were written between 1878 and 1884 and were published in periodicals, some as distant as *La nación española* of Buenos Aires. These late poems reflect a greater concern with ideas; they are characterized by unusual combinations of lines and broken rhythms, with lines of as many as sixteen or eighteen syllables, and by a syntactical complexity not previously seen in Castro's work.

In *Beside the River Sar*, Galicia is no longer a focal point, assuming instead the role of a backdrop, and the folk element is even less in evidence. Castro continues to excel in nature poetry, displaying in "Los robles" ("The Oaks") a distinctly modern concern for ecology when she protests the wasteful destruction of trees in Galicia with an almost druidic reverence for arboreal vitality. The River Sar of the title, the beloved river of her homeland, is a symbol for the flowing of life toward its unknown and unknowable destination.

In what is possibly her most frequently anthologized poem, "Dicen que no hablan las plantas" ("They Say That Plants Do Not Speak"), Castro asserts the importance that natural phenomena such as plants, brooks, and birds have for her. Although it seems that these natural phenomena view her as a "madwoman" because of her outlandish dreams, she exhorts them not to poke fun at her, because without those dreams, she would lack the wherewithal to admire the beauty that they themselves so generously display.

In her valorization of dreams (*sueños* or *ensueños*) and her refusal to accept the pathetic constraints by which humankind is necessarily bound, Castro prefigures the concerns of the Generation of '98, of poets such as Unamuno, Machado, and Azorín. Nevertheless, she must acknowledge that dreams can lead to folly, as they do in the poignant "La canción que oyó en sueños el viejo" ("The Song Which the Old Man Heard in His Dreams"), in which an old man, designated crazy in the poem, feels his blood pump and surge as his youthful passions return when in truth he should be reckoning with "infallible death" and "implacable old age."

In *Beside the River Sar*, the winter, symbolic of despair and the end of life in Castro's earlier work, is friendly, a herald, in fact, of spring, and is "a thousand times welcome." Even the desert of Castile, anathema in her earlier poetry and so drastically opposed to the lushness of Galicia, assumes a positive guise, coming to represent the realm beyond carnal suffering, lit by "another light more vivid than that of the golden sun."

One of the most interesting poems in the collection is the questioning and subsequently epiphanic "Santa Escolástica" ("Saint Scholastica"). In Santiago on a drizzly

April day, the poet allows herself to absorb the dismal atmosphere. "Cemetery of the living," she exclaims, as she contrasts the gloom she sees around her with the city's medieval glory. This leads to her own rephrasing of that tortured question, "Why, since there is God, does Hell prevail?" She enters the Convent of San Martín Pinario in search of comfort. Her female soul begins to feel the sacred majesty of the temple as vividly as it has felt the satisfactions of motherhood. Suddenly, the sun strikes the statue of Saint Scholastica and brings into sharper focus the saint's ecstasy, which in turn produces an ecstasy in Castro, who exclaims exultantly, "There is art! There is poetry! . . . There must be a heaven,/ for there is God."

Kulp-Hill contrasts this joyous poem from *Beside the River Sar* with a poem from *Follas novas* having the same setting, "N'a catedral" ("In the Cathedral"). In the latter, although the sun shines briefly into the dimly illuminated room, the shadows return, and the poet withdraws without consolation. As the contrast between the two poems suggests, Castro's last volume was a testament to hope.

In an age when poets declaimed, Castro had the courage to write honestly and realistically about issues that troubled her. She was unashamed to examine and interpret the feelings of the Galician peasantry, creating from their own forms and phrases a new poetry of rare beauty. As she explored her own hope and hopelessness and pondered the human condition in general, she translated her findings into poetry that speaks to all people.

OTHER MAJOR WORKS

LONG FICTION: *La hija del mar*, 1859 (*Daughter of the Sea*, 1995); *Flavio*, 1861; *Ruinas*, 1866; *El caballero de las botas azules*, 1867; *El primer loco*, 1881.

BIBLIOGRAPHY

Courteau, Joanna. *The Poetics of Rosalía de Castro's "Negra sombra."* New York: Edwin Mellen Press, 1995. A close critical examination of one of Castro's poems. Includes bibliographical references and index.

Dever, Aileen. *The Radical Insufficiency of Human Life: The Poetry of R. de Castro and J. A. Silva*. Jefferson, N.C.: McFarland, 2000. A comparison of Castro's and Silva's poetry. Their works have meaningful differences but share remarkable likenesses in theme, tone, and style, though it is unlikely that they knew of each other's work. Of interest to feminist critics is an interpretation of Castro's literary vocation within a patriarchal society.

Geoffrion-Vinci, Michelle C. *Between the Maternal Aegis and the Abyss: Woman as Symbol in the Poetry of Rosalía de Castro*. Madison, N.J.: Fairleigh Dickinson University Press, 2002. Examines the symbolism of Castro's poetry at length. Discusses her relationship with Manuel Murguía.

Kulp-Hill, Kathleen. *Manner and Mood in Rosalía de Castro: A Study of Themes and*

Style. Madrid: Ediciones José Porrua Turanzas, 1968. A thorough critical study of Castro's writing and a bibliography of her works.

_____. *Rosalía de Castro*. Boston: Twayne, 1977. Introductory biography and critical analysis of selected works. Includes an index and bibliography of Castro's writing.

Wilcox, John C. *Women Poets of Spain, 1860-1990: Toward a Gynocentric Vision*. Urbana: University of Illinois Press, 1997. This work on female poets in Spain in the second half of the nineteenth century contains a section on Castro.

Jack Shreve

LUIS CERNUDA

Born: Seville, Spain; September 21, 1902
Died: Mexico City, Mexico; November 5, 1963

PRINCIPAL POETRY
Egloga, elegía, oda, 1927
Perfil del aire, 1927
Un río, un amor, 1929
Los placeres prohibidos, 1931
Donde habite el olvido, 1934
Invocaciones, 1935
La realidad y el deseo, 1936, 1940, 1958, 1964
Las nubes, 1940
Ocnos, 1942, 1949, 1964 (prose poems; English translation, 2004)
Como quien espera el alba, 1947
Variaciones sobre tema mexicano, 1952 (prose poems; *Variations on a Mexican Theme*, 2004)
Poemas para un cuerpo, 1957
Desolación de la quimera, 1962 (*Desolation of the Chimera: Last Poems*, 2009)
The Poetry of Luis Cernuda, 1971
Poesía completa, 1973
Selected Poems of Luis Cernuda, 1977
34 Poemas, 1998
Written in Water: The Prose Poems of Luis Cernuda, 2004 (includes *Ocnos* and *Variations on a Mexican Theme*)

OTHER LITERARY FORMS

Although Luis Cernuda (sur-NEW-dah) is best known for his poetry, he was also a prolific essayist and critic. He published several works in prose, three of which, devoted to criticism, appeared during his lifetime. In his *Estudios sobre poesía española contemporánea* (1957; studies on contemporary Spanish poetry), Cernuda analyzes the most important trends in Spanish poetry since the nineteenth century. He bestows upon Gustavo Adolfo Bécquer the distinction of having reawakened poetry after more than one hundred years of lethargy, and he lauds Miguel de Unamuno y Jugo as the most important Spanish poet of the twentieth century. Cernuda's *Pensamiento poético en la lírica inglesa (siglo XIX)* (1958; poetic thought in English lyricism), a study of the theory of poetry as practiced by nineteenth century British poets, reveals Cernuda's deep appreciation of and attachment to English verse of the Romantic and Victorian periods.

Many of Cernuda's essays and magazine and newspaper articles—which appeared originally in such publications as *Caracola, Litoral, Octubre, Cruz y raya, Heraldo de Madrid,* and *Insula*—have been collected in the two-volume *Poesía y literatura* (1960, 1964; poetry and literature) and in *Crítica, ensayos y evocaciones* (1970; criticism, essays, and evocations). *Variations on a Mexican Theme*, often referred to as poetic prose, is an affectionate reflection by the poet on the people of Mexico, their music, their art, their churches, and their poverty and misery. Mexico was the poet's adopted homeland, after some years in what he perceived to be alien environments, and he felt warmed by the Mexicans, their culture, and their climate, so reminiscent of his native Andalusia. *Ocnos* is a meditation on time, a prose poem that becomes the lyrical confession of a poet writing about himself and his art. Because it contains Cernuda's analysis of his work, this volume is a useful companion to his poetry. Cernuda also undertook the translation into Spanish of the poetry of Friedrich Hölderlin, Paul Éluard, William Wordsworth, and William Blake, as well as plays by William Shakespeare. He did not devote much effort to fiction, leaving behind only three short pieces: "El indolente" ("The Indolent One"), "El viento en la colina" ("The Wind on the Hill"), and "El sarao" (the dancing party), all published in the collection *Tres narraciones* (1948; three narratives).

Achievements

While Luis Cernuda is recognized as an important member of the Generation of '27 (considered by some a second Spanish Golden Age), he did not receive during his lifetime the acclaim and recognition extended to some of his contemporaries, such as Federico García Lorca, Jorge Guillén, Rafael Alberti, and Vicente Aleixandre. Furthermore, Cernuda never enjoyed financial or professional security. His position as a self-exile—he never returned to Spain, even for brief periods, after 1938—might explain his lack of popularity during the 1930's and 1940's. In addition, his political sympathies (staunchly Republican), his open homosexuality, his reticence, and even the seemingly simple structure and language of his poetry were all factors that may have distanced him from an entire generation of readers. After his death, however, Cernuda's audience has been growing: A number of important critical studies have appeared, a complete edition of his poetry has been published, and a collection of many of his extant essays was issued in 1970—clear indications that Cernuda is being reappraised by a new generation of Spanish poets and critics.

However, as Carlos-Peregrín Otero has observed, it might still be premature to evaluate Cernuda's impact and his role as an innovator in Spanish letters. Cernuda displayed, first and foremost, a commitment to poetry and to the creative act. His work allowed him to express himself and served to sustain him. It was through his poetry that he came to understand himself and the world, and this understanding helped him endure the solitude and melancholy of his alienated and withdrawn existence. Through his writing, he was able to objectify his desire, his passion, and his love and to liberate himself in ways that his social persona never could. He also used his poetry to battle against his obsession with time and its relentless passage. These were the principal themes of Cernuda's works. He expressed them with increasing clarity and simplicity of language, yet, toward the end of his life, his work began to acquire the quiet, meditative tone of a man who is confident in the knowledge that his art, if nothing else, will escape decay.

Biography

Born to a comfortable middle-class family of Seville, Luis Cernuda y Bidón was the youngest of the three children of Bernardo Cernuda Bousa, a colonel of a regiment of engineers, and Amparo Bidón y Cuellar. In Cernuda's poem "La familia" ("The Family"), which appeared in *Como quien espera el alba* (like someone awaiting the dawn), the domestic environment of his youth is portrayed as grave, dark, and rigid like glass, "which everyone can break but no one bends." The poet does not reveal any warmth or affection for his parents or his two sisters. His parents, he adds, fed and clothed him, and even provided him with God and morality. They gave him all: life, which he had not asked for, and death, its inextricable companion. From an early age, Cernuda displayed a timidity and reticence which were to characterize his social interaction throughout his life.

Cernuda first began to appreciate poetry at the age of nine, when he came across some poems by Gustavo Adolfo Bécquer, the nineteenth century Romantic poet whose remains were transferred from Madrid to Seville for permanent interment in 1911, causing excitement among the residents of the city and renewed interest in the poet's work. After completing secondary school in a religious institution, Cernuda enrolled at the University of Seville to study law in 1919. He received his law degree in 1925 but never practiced. His most important experience during his university years was his contact with Pedro Salinas, the eminent poet whose first year as a professor at the university coincided with Cernuda's first year as a student. Their association—at first formal, impersonal, and restricted to the classroom—developed in the course of the next few years, as Salinas encouraged Cernuda and other students to pursue their poetic inclinations. Salinas recommended that Cernuda begin to read French authors, among them Charles Baudelaire, Stéphane Mallarmé, and André Gide. Gide's works helped Cernuda to confront and to reconcile himself to his homosexuality. Through the influence of Salinas, Cernuda was able to publish nine poems in the prestigious magazine *Revista de occidente* when he was only twenty-three. Two years later, in 1927, Cernuda published his first collection, *Perfil del aire* (air's profile). In spite of the coolness with which it was received, with one or two notable exceptions, Cernuda had determined to devote his life to writing, putting an end to any professional indecision he had felt earlier.

Upon the death of his mother in 1928—his father had died in 1920—Cernuda left Seville for good, traveling first to Málaga and then to Madrid, and meeting a number of the writers and poets who would be known as the Generation of '27, among them Manuel Altolaguirre and Emilio Prados (the editors of *Litoral*), Vicente Aleixandre, and Bernabé Fernández-Canivell (future director of the literary magazine *Caracola*, an outlet for Cernuda's poetry). He had met García Lorca in Seville in 1927. In the fall of 1928, through Pedro Salinas, Cernuda was offered an appointment as Spanish lecturer at the École Normale de Toulouse, a position that afforded the young poet the opportunity to spend some time in Paris. During his year in France, he immersed himself in the Surrealist movement and adopted a style and point of view to which he would adhere for the next four years.

The 1930's was a decade of steady productivity for Cernuda, marked by increasing recognition of his gifts among other writers of his generation. At the same time, it was a period of political instability that forced writers to take sides. Cernuda was a staunch supporter of the Spanish Republic and, for a brief period, around 1933, a member of the Communist Party, contributing several political articles to *Octubre*, a magazine edited by Rafael Alberti. In 1934, for a short time, he worked for Misiones Pedagógicas (pedagogic missions), an educational program sponsored by the Republican government to bring culture to remote areas of the country. Cernuda's job was to explain the great masterpieces of Spanish painting, presented to the audience in reproduction. Cernuda spent the first summer of the Spanish Civil War, in 1936, in Paris as a secretary to the Spanish ambassador to France, Alvaro de Albornoz, whose daughter Concha was a friend of Cernuda. Upon his return to Spain, Cernuda joined the Republican popular militia and fought in the Guadarrama. In the winter of 1938, he traveled to England to deliver a series of lectures arranged for him by the English writer Stanley Richardson. A few months later, while returning to Spain through France, Cernuda decided to go into exile permanently, first to Great Britain, where he taught in Surrey, Glasgow, Cambridge, and London, and then to the United States, where he arrived in the fall of 1947. His appointment as professor of Spanish literature at Mount Holyoke College, negotiated for Cernuda by Concha Albornoz, initiated the most stable and financially untroubled period of the poet's life. The New England climate and the isolation of the school, however, made Cernuda restless and caused him to explore the possibility of a teaching post at a university in Puerto Rico. In 1953, after several summers spent in the more hospitable Mexico, he resigned his tenure at Mount Holyoke and settled in Mexico, where he would remain—with only brief returns to the United States to teach at San Francisco State College and the University of California, Los Angeles—until his death from a heart attack in 1963. While in Mexico, he supported himself by his writing and by teaching several courses at the Universidad Autónoma in Mexico City.

Analysis

In the case of Luis Cernuda, it is impossible to separate the poet from the man—his personality from his literary production. As much as Cernuda himself protested that he loathed the intrusion of the person in the poem, he, much more than most of his contemporaries, can be said to have revealed himself through his writing. He offered readers a glimpse of his poetic world from one window only, as Jenaro Talens states, and that window is open to the main character, who is frequently—if not always—Cernuda himself. As a consequence, his poetic production reflects his development as a man and his awareness of himself. This, in turn, tends to focus most analyses of his work along closely chronological lines, as his poetry evolves from the vague and dreamy musings of youth to the bitter acceptance of the relentlessness of time and the inevitability of death.

PERFIL DEL AIRE

Beginning with the first book of poems, *Perfil del aire*—published as a supplement to the magazine *Litoral* and edited by Manuel Altolaguirre and Emilio Prados in 1927—Cernuda embarked upon a journey of self-discovery. In this first collection, the youthful poet presents an indifferent, indolent attitude toward the world; he is there, but he dreams and is surrounded by emptiness. Dreams and walls protect him, provide him with a haven for his loneliness; there, he can savor his secret pleasures and his unfulfilled yearnings. This first major effort, retitled "Primeras poesías" and revised before reappearing in the first edition of *La realidad y el deseo* (reality and desire), was not well received. Cernuda was criticized sharply for imitating Jorge Guillén, and his production was judged unoriginal. More recent criticism, while acknowledging Cernuda's debt to Guillén, dismisses these charges as exaggerated, praising this early work for its fine sensibility and for the musical quality of its language.

EGLOGA, ELEGÍA, ODA

The negative reception of his first book encouraged Cernuda to withdraw, at least personally, from what he considered the literary mainstream and, by his own admission, "to wish to cultivate that which is criticized by others." He began work on a second collection, *Egloga, elegía, oda* (eclogue, elegy, ode), a series of four poems patterned after classical and neoclassical models, particularly the works of Garcilaso de la Vega, whose meter and rhyme Cernuda imitated deliberately. Some years later, reflecting on his development as a writer, Cernuda said that, while this second work had permitted him to experiment with classical themes and strophes, its style did not satisfy him, for he was unable to find what he loved in what he wrote. Nevertheless, in *Egloga, elegía, oda*, the poet was able to express more forcefully some of the feelings first introduced in *Perfil del aire*. Vague yearnings have become a compelling attraction to beauty in all its forms; the poet's need to satisfy his desires is confronted by the opposition of desire to such satisfaction. In this set of poems, he begins to remove his cloak of ennui, revealing a strong, sensuous nature. The pursuit of pleasure replaces indifference as the antidote for solitude and sadness. Desiring to express himself in a more daring fashion and to rebel against the constraints of bourgeois society, which misunderstood him and his sexuality, Cernuda gravitated toward the Surrealists. He read the works of Louis Aragon, André Breton, and Paul Éluard, whose poetry he translated into Spanish.

UN RÍO, UN AMOR AND LOS PLACERES PROHIBIDOS

Cernuda's Surrealist stage began, not coincidentally, with his year in France (1928-1929) and resulted in two important works, *Un río, un amor* (a river, a love) and *Los placeres prohibidos* (forbidden pleasures). The most notable technical characteristic of *Un río, un amor* is Cernuda's use of free verse, which was also being adopted during this period by other Spanish poets, such as Aleixandre, García Lorca, and Alberti. Freed of external constraints, Cernuda's verse nevertheless retained a strong sense of meter, and the rhythm of his lines was preserved through accentuation and cadence. He also made use of reiteration, anaphora, and anastrophe. From this period onward, Cernuda began to experiment with longer lines, although they seldom exceeded eleven syllables. In *Los placeres prohibidos*, Cernuda continued to discard technical conventions, alternating between verse and prose poems. Thematically, Surrealism provided Cernuda with the opportunity to liberate himself from social restrictions. Asserting his linguistic and stylistic freedom, he wrote of "night petrified by fists," "towers of fear," "iron flowers resounding like the chest of man," "tongue of darkness," and "empty eyes."

Toward the end of *Un río, un amor*, Cernuda intimates what is expressed openly in *Los placeres prohibidos*; he accepts his homosexuality and admits to being possessed by love. This love takes the form of passionate physical desire, rendered no less glorious and pure because of its carnality; only the outside world tarnishes this love with its opprobrium. In *Un río, un amor*, love produces an emptiness and a vacuum. Man is like a phantom, without direction; he is indifferent to the world, as if he were dead. In *Los placeres prohibidos*, however, love ceases to be the object of dreams; it becomes something real, the primary goal of man's desire, the motive behind all he does and feels: To give in to this love, without reservation, is man's purpose. Its attainment is nevertheless elusive—except for some fleeting moments—and contains an element of pain; herein lies the source of the solitude and the impotence of man.

DONDE HABITE EL OLVIDO

A third work published during this period, *Donde habite el olvido* (where oblivion dwells), closes out Cernuda's Surrealist phase. It was written after a failed love affair, one that the author naïvely had believed would last forever. This accounts for the bitterness of its tone, the poet's desire for death, and the harsh indictment of love, which, once it disappears, leaves nothing behind but the "remembrance of an oblivion." In the fourth poem of this collection, Cernuda retraces his personal history, as if it were a life already lived, replete with regrets and unfulfilled expectations. The first part of the poem exudes optimism, expansiveness, and anticipation, conveyed by the spring moon, the golden sea, and adolescent desire. The light, however, turns into shadows; the poet falls into darkness and is ultimately a living corpse.

LAS NUBES

With his next major publication, *Las nubes* (the clouds), Cernuda introduced two important new themes into his poetry: historical time, with its specific focus on Spain as the abandoned and beleaguered homeland, and humanity's spirituality and religiosity. Love, the recurring topic of much of Cernuda's work, plays virtually no role in this collection. In "Un español habla de su tierra" ("A Spaniard Speaks of His Homeland"), the poet writes nostalgically of the happy days of the past, before his land succumbed to the conquering Cains. The bitter days of the present find sustenance in the fond memories of years gone by, an idealized past that might someday be re-created, yet to which the poet cannot return. When that day comes, and his homeland is free, it will come looking for him—only to discover that death has come to call first. Ironically, as one critic has pointed out, this poem was prescient in its chronology. In "Impresión de destierre" ("Impression of Exile"), the dislocated narrator—then in London—overhears a fatigued voice announce the death of Spain; "'Spain?' he said. 'A name./ Spain has died. . . .'"

Las nubes also contains the clearest expression of Cernuda's views on traditional religion. While his poetic use of belief in the supernatural has been described as a type of pantheistic hedonism based on Mediterranean mythology, his spiritual quest included attempts to find answers in more traditional Christian imagery by positing the existence of a God through whom humanity can achieve love. Cernuda devoted four poems in this collection to the broad question of the existence of God: "La visita de Dios" ("God's Visit"), "Atardecer en la catedral" ("Dusk in the Cathedral"), "Lázaro" ("Lazarus"), and "La adoración de los magos" ("The Adoration of the Magi"). In the long poem "God's Visit," the protagonist, in a voice filled with anguish, confronts God with the terrible wreckage of what is now the speaker's country, the poet's paradise of years gone by, perhaps destroyed by the casual wave of his hand. As the last hope for renewal, the protagonist begs God to restore to the world beauty, truth, and justice; without these, he warns, God could be forgotten.

"THE ADORATION OF THE MAGI"

More firmly rooted in Christianity is the five-part poem "The Adoration of the Magi," in which Cernuda's debt to T. S. Eliot is clear. The poem opens with a meditation by Melchior on the existence of God, reaching the conclusion that if he himself is alive, God, too, might well exist. This knowledge does not fully satisfy Melchior. To reason the existence of God is not enough; some more evocative proof is needed. The second part of the poem, "Los reyes" ("The Kings"), presents the Magi, each with a distinctive voice which expresses the conflicting visions of a single character: Melchior the idealist, Gaspar the hedonist, and Balthasar the skeptic. Through their intertwined monologues, the pilgrim searches for proof of the existence of God. The next section, "Palinodia de la esperanza divina" ("Palinode of Divine Hope"), is perhaps the most inventive; in it, the author expresses the disenchantment and disappointment felt by the Magi upon arriving in Bethlehem after a long journey and finding nothing but a poor child, a life "just like our human one," after expecting "a god, a presence/ radiant and imperious, whose sight is grace." In the fourth part, "Sobre el tiempo pasado" ("On Time Past"), the protagonist is the old shepherd (Father Time?) who remembers a period in his youth, long past, when three wise men came to look at a newborn child. The old man, however, has no recollection of a god; how can a humble shepherd, whose knowledge of man is so lacking, have seen the gods? The poem closes with a short fifth part, "Epitafio" ("Epitaph"), wherein man, as searcher, is told that he once found the truth but did not recognize it; now he can console himself by living his life in this world, as a body, even though he cannot be free from misery.

Passage of time as theme

The publication of *Las nubes* marked a new beginning for Cernuda, the man and the poet. He had departed from Spain; he was approaching the age of forty—an age which, for a man who associated beauty with youth and joy with youthfulness, must have created much anxiety. His prospects for recognition in Spain had been shattered by political events. Cernuda responded to this situation by creating a protagonist with a distinct identity; he created the poet, whose role it was to substitute as the main character for the author and who would, when called upon, assume all responsibility for failure. Thus, Cernuda created what Phillip Silver calls his "personal myth" and entered into the mature stage of his poetic production. Poetry became a means to understand and preserve the past. The need to fulfill a grand passion was discarded; man must resign himself to a world that belongs to the gods, a world in which he cannot partake of paradise. If man can be made into a myth, however, his life will be eternal and his beauty everlasting. In poems such as "Noche del hombre y su demonio" ("A Man's Night and His Demon") and "Río vespertino" ("Evening River") from *Como quien espera el alba*, Cernuda expresses an attitude of acceptance, as if recounting a life already lived. He anticipates, without fear, the inevitability of death. There is but one small consolation: There is no ash without flame, no death without life. In the long poem "Apología pro vita sua" from the same collection, the poet gathers up all the suffering of his existence: his obsessions as a poet, the war, his agnosticism, and his need and hope for a personal, intimate God. From his bedside, the protagonist summons first his lovers to help illuminate his world growing dim, for "Is passion not the measure of human greatness . . . ?" He then calls in his friends to help him renounce the light. As in a confessional, he admits to regrets, but only for those sins which he has not had the opportunity or the strength to commit. He asserts that he has lived without God because he has not manifested himself to him and has not satisfied his incredulity. The protagonist maintains that to die, people do not need God; rather, God needs people in order to live. In an apparent contradiction, a few lines later, he asks God to fill his soul with the light that comes with eternity.

The past, that which has been, and the inevitable passage of time become the dominating theme of the remainder of Cernuda's poetic output. In his mature verses, he recounts his life and his loves with the pessimistic tone of one who knows that they will never come again. Splendor, beauty, passion, and joy are juxtaposed to solitude, old age, and death.

OTHER MAJOR WORKS
SHORT FICTION: *Tres narraciones*, 1948.
NONFICTION: *Estudios sobre poesía española cont emporánea*, 1957; *Pensamiento poético en la lírica inglesa (siglo XIX)*, 1958; *Poesía y literatura*, 1960, 1964 (2 volumes); *Crítica, ensayos y evocaciones*, 1970; *Prosa completa*, 1975.

BIBLIOGRAPHY
Harris, Derek. *Luis Cernuda: A Study of His Poetry*. London: Tamesis, 1973. A critical study of Cernuda's poetry. Includes bibliographic references.
_____. *Metal Butterflies and Poisonous Lights: The Language of Surrealism in Lorca, Alberti, Cernuda, and Aleixandre*. Anstruther, Fife, Scotland: La Sirena, 1998. An analysis of the use of surrealism in the poetry of Cernuda and other poets. Includes bibliographical references.
Jiménez-Fajardo, Salvador. *Luis Cernuda*. Boston: Twayne, 1978. An introductory biographical and critical analysis of selected works by Cernuda. Includes bibliographic references.
_____, ed. *The Word and the Mirror: Critical Essays on the Poetry of Luis Cernuda*. Rutherford, N.J.: Fairleigh Dickinson University Press, 1989. A collection of critical essays dealing with Cernuda's works.
McKinlay, Neil C. *The Poetry of Luis Cernuda: Order in a World of Chaos*. Rochester, N.Y.: Tamesis, 1999. A brief biographical and critical study. Includes bibliographical references and index.
Martin-Clark, Philip. *Art, Gender, and Sexuality: New Readings of Cernuda's Later Poetry*. Leeds, England: Maney, 2000. A critical interpretation of selected works by Cernuda. Includes bibliographical references and index.
Soufas, C. Christopher. *The Subject in Question: Early Contemporary Spanish Literature and Modernism*. Washington, D.C.: Catholic University of America Press, 2007. This general work on Spanish literature in the early twentieth century has a chapter looking at the themes of absence and experience in the poems of Cernuda and Rafael Alberti.

Clara Estow

J. V. FOIX

Born: Sarría, Spain; January 28, 1893
Died: Barcelona, Spain; January 29, 1987

PRINCIPAL POETRY
Gertrudis, 1927
KRTU, 1932
Sol, i de dol, 1936
Les irreals omegues, 1948
On he deixat les claus . . . ?, 1953
Del "Diari 1918," 1956
Onze nadals i un cap d'any, 1960
L'estrella d'en Perris, 1963
Desa aquests llibres al calaix de baix, 1964
Obres poètiques, 1964
Quatre nus, 1964
Darrer comunicat, 1970
Tocant a mà, 1972
Antologia poètica, 1973
Quatre colors aparien el món . . . , 1975
Poemes de pedra, 2006

OTHER LITERARY FORMS

In addition to his poetry, J. V. Foix (fohsh) published a number of works that are impossible to define in terms of conventional genres. Typical of his idiosyncratic manner are his "letters" to Clara Sobirós and Na Madrona Puignau, both invented personages. The Sobirós missive, which appropriately heads both the *Obres poètiques* and the first volume of the *Obres completes* (1974-1990), is a veritable manifesto of Foix's aesthetics. In "Na Madrona," he combines commentaries on contemporary events with a peculiar expression of concern for the ills of his society. In a third epistle, written in 1962 and addressed to Joan Salvat-Papasseit, that most engagé of Catalan poets, Foix, while amicably vindicating the honesty of his own convictions, conveys to his former associate the warm sympathy of a kindred soul, rising, at long last, above all the differences in temperament and upbringing that poisoned their relationship. In *Allò que no diu La vanguardia* (1970; what *La vanguardia* does not say)—the reference is to the noted Barcelonese newspaper—Foix parodies the reporter's jargon, distorting the idiom of the short bulletin and the somewhat longer newspaper column until he attains a magnificent absurdity. In still another vein, he devised a tale of fantasy, *La pell de la pell* (1970; skin's skin), complete with outlandish apparitions and magical transformations of time and place; there are infernal links between this work and *Noranta set notes sobre ficcions poncianes* (1974; ninety-seven notes on fictions à la Ponç), a congeries of paragraph-length meditations and aphorisms, inspired by the paintings of his friend, Joan Ponç.

In *Catalans de 1918* (1965; Catalans of 1918), an ingenuous Foix becomes the James Boswell of a forgotten era. In an intriguing admixture of memoirs and character sketches, he evokes the zeitgeist of the decade between 1910 and 1920. Through autobiographical tidbits (reminiscences—deliciously recounted—of associations, confrontations, collaborations, casual acquaintances, and chance encounters), he introduces an entire gallery of famous and not-so-famous Catalans: revered masters, friends, and colleagues. Foix takes special care to recapture not only the speech of the personages in question but also the ambience that provides an appropriate foil for their cameo appearances. Worthy, too, of special attention is Foix's prolific and influential output as a journalist from 1917 to 1936, before the Spanish Civil War. The numerous articles he contributed to *La publicitat*, a biweekly newspaper he directed from 1931 to 1936, stand out as especially significant, for they attest sensibilities keenly attuned to the critical issues of the day. A select sample of these articles appears in a collection titled *Els lloms transparents* (1969; transparent loins), edited by Gabriel Ferrater.

Achievements

The domain of the Catalan language comprises most of the eastern sector of the Iberian Peninsula (Catalonia proper, that is, and the Valencian region), the Balearic Isles, the Republic of Andorra, and, to a lesser extent, the French territories of Cerdagne and Roussillon. The Catalan-speaking people boast their own distinctive Romance tongue, a time-honored cultural heritage, and a brilliant literary tradition that goes back to the dawning of the Middle Ages. Thanks to a dramatic resurgence (commonly called the Renaixença) that began in the early 1830's, Catalan literature and art flourished in the twentieth century, despite the cataclysmic convulsions brought about by the Spanish Civil War and the repressive measures imposed by the regime of Francisco Franco.

Together with a number of distinguished contemporary writers, painters, sculptors, and avant-garde artists of all types (Salvador Espriu, Joan Oliver, Mercé Rodoreda, Josep M. Subirachs, Joan Miró, Salvador Dalí, and Antoni Tàpies, to name but a representative few), J. V. Foix stands out as a worthy champion of the best that Catalan culture has to offer to Western civilization. Few Catalan writers can vie with Foix in devotion to motherland, erudition, breadth of vision, and sheer genius for bringing to fruition the highest potential of the Renaixença. Though worlds apart from Espriu in the ultimate resolution and implication of a truly personal and original poetic, Foix, like Espriu, strikes a happy balance between, on one hand, aesthetic sophistication and avant-garde exploration, and, on the other, a sound understanding of the solid, broad infrastructure of the living language of his society. What has earned Foix a rank of special distinction is, above all, his unique talent for articulating through poems, through essays, and, indeed, through his urbane lifestyle and cosmopolitan outlook, the canons of a staunch Catalanism, founded on the principles of moderation and tolerance, transcending chauvinism and partisan affiliation of any kind—canons formulated by Joan Maragall, Foix's illustrious turn-of-the-century predecessor, a thinker who oriented his ideals toward the prospect of a Catalan autonomy within the context of pan-Iberian federalism.

Cognizant of Foix's venturesome, indefatigable quest for ever-novel approaches to the creative process, and of his pursuit of what Northrop Frye and Carlos Bousoño have called, in reference to other writers, the "encyclopedic form" or the *pupila totalizadora*, and what Arthur Terry has termed, apropos of Foix himself, the *visió còsmica*, some of the more perceptive readers of Foix (Enrique Badosa, Patricia Boehne, Gabriel Ferrater, Pere Gimferrer, Albert Manent, David Rosenthal, and Terry, among others) have drawn parallels between him and such luminaries of twentieth century literature as Ezra Pound, T. S. Eliot, Federico García Lorca, and Fernando Pessoa. Indeed, Foix can mold into a collage of macrocosmic proportions strains issuing from both within and without the mainstream of the autochthonous tradition, techniques borrowed from the *stilnovisti* as well as from the Futurists and the Surrealists, echoes recaptured from the writers of ancient Greece as well as from homegrown classics (Ramon Llull, Ausiàs March, Jordi de Sant Jordi). Foix's overall production, then, projects the epiphany of an innovator endowed with a scrupulous social conscience. His stirring voice frequently has to cry out to bemoan the poet's personal anguish and that of many of his fellow citizens, who, though never having left their own country, have suffered from the malaise that Paul Ilie has perceptively diagnosed as "inner exile."

Because of the prejudicial policies of the centralist Spanish government, limited Catalan readership, and other inimical circumstances, Foix, like practically all his Catalan colleagues, does not enjoy the wide recognition he justly deserves. He does not lack, however, the enthusiastic acclaim of well-informed critics at home and abroad. His name occupies, as it should, a prominent place in the standard histories and anthologies of Catalan literature. He attracted the attention of numerous scholars, and a sizable body of his work has been translated into Castilian, English, French, and Italian. Foix is held in high esteem by the younger Catalan literati, and his influence is detectable among them, especially in the works of Ferrater and Gimferrer, outstanding poets in their own right.

In 1961, Foix was elected to the Catalan Academy (the Institut d'Estudios Catalans), and in 1973, on the occasion of his eightieth birthday, he was awarded the Premi d'Honor de les Lletres Catalanes. On that occasion, two prestigious magazines, *Destino* and *Serra d'Or*, dedicated special issues to him, and his friends published an homage anthology (*Antologia poètica*).

BIOGRAPHY

Josep Arseni Vicenç Foix i Mas, or J. V. Foix, was born of peasant stock. His father came from Torrents de Lladurs, a town in the province of Lérida (Western Catalonia).

The second of three children—he shared the household with two sisters—he received the usual schooling and exhibited an unusual, precocious interest in Catalan culture and literary studies. His formal education came to an abrupt end in 1911 after an unsuccessful bout with the study of law. Other occupations were to absorb the young Foix's attention. Following in his father's footsteps, Foix worked in earnest to build for himself a reputation as the premier *pâtissier* in his native town.

In retrospect, Foix presented the intriguing figure of a man with two private lives: One belongs to the bourgeois merchant, who plods a course marked by the work ethic leading to material rewards; the other pertains to the genuine artist fully devoted to a métier that thrives on the values of the spirit. Foix plied his trade by day and wrote at a feverish pace by night. The first fifteen years of his career (beginning, approximately, in the year 1915) were years of particularly intense activity. In *Catalans de 1918*, he provides a captivating account of his numerous sessions in libraries, his contacts with the many aspiring authors of his generation who later became his intimate friends and with established scholars and literati—Fabra, Mosén Jacinto Verdaguer, d'Ors, Carner, and Riba—who were all engaged in the epic task of shaping the future of Catalan culture. From 1917 on, various journals of the avant-garde mushroomed in Barcelona, and Foix contributed articles to all of them and directed some. Himself a central figure of the intelligentsia, he became acquainted with the prominent personalities who were creating a stir in the literary and artistic circles of the Catalan metropolis: Paul Éluard, García Lorca, Tristan Tzara, Dalí, Miró, and Luis Buñuel. Foix relished playing the part of a cultural middleman of sorts, an aesthetician at large. In this role, he introduced, in 1925, the first exhibitions of Dalí and Miró.

Foix's creative surge paralleled and in some cases even anticipated the artistic renewal experienced throughout Europe in the mid-1920's. While the revolutionary tendencies that were fermenting on the Continent were making their sensational impact in Catalonia, especially through the movements of Futurism and Surrealism, and García Lorca was publishing *Romancero gitano, 1924-1927* (1928; *The Gypsy Ballads of García Lorca*, 1951, 1953), Foix was reaping in *Gertrudis* the first fruit of a protracted labor. By 1930, he had completed the main components of those books that many years later would reach the printing press under the titles *KRTU, Del "Diari 1918," Sol, i de dol* (alone and in mourning), *Catalans de 1918*, and even some items of *Les irreals omegues* (the unreal omegas).

The advent of the Republic in 1931 and the subsequent five years of autonomy, which encouraged high hopes for the future of Catalan nationhood, enhanced Foix's consciousness of his civic responsibilities. Though he shunned direct involvement in politics, he acquitted himself brilliantly of his self-imposed duties as ideologue in *Revolució catalanista* (1934; the Catalan revolution), a book he coauthored with his friend Josep Carbonell. As a representative of the emerging Catalan state, he attended two international conventions of the PEN Club, held in Belgrade and in Dubrovnik in the early 1930's.

The civil war struck hard at the hopes of those who, like Foix, had set their hearts on tolerance and constructive dialogue. The abolition of the Catalan press, after Franco's victory, brought Foix's journalistic career to a standstill, but censorship could not dry up the fountainhead of his inspiration or stint the vitality of his poetic voice—which, fortunately, found an outlet in numerous books published after the Spanish Civil War. Following Franco's death, Foix had the satisfaction of witnessing a revitalized Catalonia, autonomous once again. He died in Barcelona, Spain, on January 29, 1987.

ANALYSIS

By 1930, J. V. Foix had developed the mainstays of his craft on which he would effect countless variations. In particular, he had perfected his favored techniques of antithesis: the old opposed to the new, the familiar articulated with the exotic, reason contravened by *follia*, fantastical narratives counterbalanced by references to the workaday world, Arcadia admixed with veristic depictions of the Catalan landscape. Other quintessential traits of Foix's resourcefulness readily come to mind: his lyric élan, his profuse language contained within exquisite conciseness of form elaborated to an adamantine luster, his play on perspectivism and the effects of trompe l'oeil, inviting analogies with the visual arts (especially with paintings of Giorgio de Chirico, Dalí, Yves Tanguy, René Magritte, and Miró). Foix's associations with the Buñuel of *Un Chien andalou* (1928) and *L'Âge d'or* (1930) fostered, no doubt, his strong penchant for transforming into devices of literature sudden shifts of focus, flashbacks and flash-forwards, telescopings and superimpositions of images, panoramic shots, foreshadowings, fade-outs, and other cinematic techniques.

Through his mimesis of the oneiric experience, Foix unfolds the wide horizons of a kaleidoscopic, constantly changing universe: He evokes a dreamlike world in a state of flux, brings about mutations upon a protean imagery, develops into full-fledged personal myths symbols rooted in the subconscious. In the final analysis, however, the universe he envisages remains, as Terry has perceptively pointed out, strikingly unified—paradoxical and mysterious though its unity may be. It is because of his convictions concerning an absolute order that governs all things and also because of his compelling drive toward explorations beyond well-trodden paths that Foix, despite his obvious indebtedness to the champions of Surrealism, is not merely another epigone of that movement.

Foix is a bold exponent of the avant-garde, "a poet, magician, speculator of the word," to use his own words, an "investigator of poetry." In his reflections on his own work, Foix employs distinctive terminology—*alliberament* (liberation), "el risc de la investigació estética" (the risk of aesthetic research), "un joc gairebé d'atzar" (a game of chance, just about), "l'exercici de la facultat de descobrir" (the exercise of the skill of making discoveries)—in order to describe his exploratory, "investigative" imagination. Though keenly aware of the pitfalls lurking in his risky ventures as an avant-garde artist,

Foix will not accept a road map or even, at times, general bearings from the Surrealists or from other revered masters. He insists on sallying forth, on his own, into uncharted realms of the imagination, so allured is he by prospects of serendipitous innovations and by the intuition of elusive *sobiranes certeses* (sovereign certainties).

"Without Symbolism"

Thus do Foix's, and the reader's, literary adventures begin. At the outset, the author dazzles the reader with an array of colors, odors, sounds, and other sensory perceptions. He frequently projects himself into the persona of the passionate lover, engulfed in one of his usual reveries about his femme fatale. Typical is the prose poem from *Gertrudis*, "Sense simbolisme" ("Without Symbolism"), in which a lover embarks upon a first-person account of a doomed amatory episode. "I abandoned the horse," says the lover, for a start, "that, by the most beauteous blinking of his eyelids, had converted the sun into an ornament for his forehead, and I made sure to take this ornament along with me that night—a very special lantern which guided me, faithfully, to Gertrude's garden." The lover finds his *amada* "tooting" his name "to the pretty cadence of a popular fox-trot." His attempt to embrace her is foiled by "the viscosity of a precise ray of moonlight." Ensuing scenes have the disjointedness of a dream. The sight of Gertrude's tresses stimulates a train of heady olfactory impressions: "The intense odor of the acacias anesthetized us so that we felt on the verge of a fainting spell. By sheer will power, I managed, though, to collect all the odors and enclose them in a case held shut by a ring studded with genuine jewels; and I felt at once revived by my audaciousness at this happy stroke of luck."

Lucky, however, the lover is not, as he soon discovers. In bold images of the type that Carlos Bousoña has labeled *visión*, Gertrude is shown as literally reaching for the stars: "She would unhook the stars one by one and would rinse them, with a shuddering of the infinite, in a pond half green, half silver, and would release them to the toads. . . ." This is clearly the high point of the episode. In contrast with a superwoman endowed with the might of a demiurge, the lover could not be cast in a more demeaning and ridiculous role. He is left to "harmonize" the "infamous croakings" of those denizens of stagnant waters "with the aid of a system of pedals that my beloved, with foresight, had providently arranged." He tries again, to no avail, to possess his beloved.

The distressed lover has little else to do but contemplate his fall from Earthly Paradise. Cognizant of the "heavy threat of the moon," he searches for his horse. The animal, now completely immersed in darkness, its eyes plastered over with "the stimulant of black tar," carries the lover and Gertrude to the rim of an abyss. Another odor—this time the unpleasant smell of the bramble bush—impels him to make a third try for the reward that, once again, proves unattainable. Overwhelmed by gloomy concerns—"torn asunder by fright" when assailed by various nightmarish flashes—the protagonist abandons the horse and tries to return home by taxi, but ends up, instead, in an unknown village. In his last fantasies, he feels a perverse pleasure in "purifying" himself "by gulping down as in a milk shake the smoke of all the chimneys in the neighborhood" and, finally, "in taking refuge beneath the crust of the large cities in order to capture the melody that the people's leaden footsteps create in homage to my littleness."

What order, one may ask, can ever transpire from the lover's stream of consciousness? At issue here is the recognition that "Without Symbolism" (the title proves to be obviously ironic) abounds in symbols that Foix cleverly disguises as principles of an overall design. Design, then, is the fountainhead of the order that an attentive reader will gradually intuit in Foix's composition. In effect, this intriguing piece evolves, organically, from a masterfully carried-out process that enhances the suggestiveness even as it fulfills the potential of a fundamental binary schema. This simple schema stems, in turn, from the atavistic opposition between male and female. To the exaltation of an apotheosized Gertrude, Foix counterposes the debasement of an antihero at the edge of annihilation. If the one shines in all her stellar splendor, the other lurks in the darkness of the netherworld.

"The Partisans of the Sun"

Foix, who in another prose poem, "The Partisans of the Sun," constructs a personal mythology on the antagonism between two primeval races—the partisans of the sun, who live in the open and gather at daybreak, and their adversaries, the cave dwellers, who come out only by moonlight—is well aware of the tension between two fields of symbols, the chthonian and the uranic, to borrow the terminology which Rupert C. Allen, Gustavo Correa, and others have employed in their illuminating studies of García Lorca: Definitely uranic is the portrayal of Gertrude in the accoutrements of a *donna angelicata*, and unmistakably chthonian the depiction of the lover's persona with the demeanor of a fallen angel. What may interest the reader is the affinity between Foix's and García Lorca's respective versions of stock symbols—the horse, the moon, and various elements of nature—versions that often involve an intermingling of the heavenly and earthly spheres, as when (to mention but a few illustrations from Foix) Gertrude from her lofty position casts the stars into the lowly pond, the menacing moon hangs "heavily" down on the fate of the lover, and the horse loses its association with the sun in order to become a demoniac figure, as lurid as such a common representation of human libido ought to be.

Affinities of this kind detract nothing from the fierce independence and the original genius of the two writers in question. A striking aspect of Foix's innovative spirit is the ambivalent treatment he accords to the Gertrude-lover dyad as a latter-day manifestation of the age-old courtly love tradition, one of the many aspects of medieval literature that has never ceased to fascinate Foix. Insofar as he expatiates on leitmotifs of the quasi-canonized damsel and the virtually doomed young gallant, Foix exhibits a faithful adherence to that tradition. A closer reading, though, brings to light telltale signs of distortions characteristic of parody and even of the burlesque. As he dwells on the veritable chasm that separates the distant, disdainful *belle dame sans merci* and her mournful admirer who stews in the juices of his own morbid passion, Foix appears less interested in revitalizing worn-out topics than in elaborating in his own rendition of the ridiculous Don Juan *manqué*, much in the grotesque vein which Ramón María del Valle-Inclán had developed into a new art form in his revolutionary *esperpentos* of the early 1920's. Foix is quite successful in reconciling the conventions of the past with the fashionable trends of his day. Tradition? Yes, but only up to a point. Not for anything does he declare in one of his more renowned sonnets: "I am excited by what is new and enamored by what is old."

Sol, i de dol

With *Sol, i de dol*, Foix's attention shifted directly to the refinement of the outer form of poetry. This sequence of seventy splendid sonnets evinces a control, balance, and precision that many would consider possible only in an author of the classical Renaissance—the Renaissance that the historical and political circumstances of the fifteenth and sixteenth centuries did not allow Catalan literature to experience.

Foix reached the zenith of his mastery, however, in the most complex of his literary modes, which, since it extends toward the farthest stretches of poetic signification, appropriately may be labeled "contextual." Most commonly found in *Les irreals omegues, On he deixat les claus...?* (where did I leave the keys...?), and *Desa aquests llibres al calaix de baix* (these books in the bottom drawer), the "contextual" composition exhibits, instead of a title, an epigraph or a rubric in prose, ranging from three to fifteen lines, followed by a section in verse of variable length, which constitutes the body of the poem proper. By the intertextual articulation of the epigraph (the "pretext," one may say) with the verse component (that is, the "text" proper), Foix creates a "con-text" rich in metaphysical, ethical, and aesthetic connotations. It is not unusual for Foix to challenge his readers to round out the context with their own insights into historical circumstances, merely hinted at either through clues interspersed within the composition itself or by the date included at the end of the piece. Thus, Foix tries to raise the consciousness of his readers about important social issues, even as he engages their full participation in the re-creation of the poem itself.

"I Was Riding at Full Gallop Around the City Walls, Pursued by a Throng of Superstitious Coalmongers"

Civic consciousness, social concern, and a sense of moral outrage are fully evident in Foix's poem "I Was Riding at Full Gallop Around the City Walls, Pursued by a Throng of Superstitious Coalmongers." The broad period the author specifies in the dating of the composition (July, 1929, to October, 1936) was one of the most turbulent in Spanish history. Brutalized victims of a religiosity of the worst kind, foisted on them by a reactionary Big Brother, Foix's *carboners* (coalmongers) have little to do with the *car-*

boneros whose naïve, innocent, blind faith Miguel de Unamuno y Jugo secretly admired. To Foix, they are the agents of blind passion, an unthinking multitude as loathsome to him as are their victimizers. The poem calls to mind the unctuousness and bigotry of some, the animosity and resentment of many, and the tensions that seethed within the masses until they exploded in the conflagration of 1936, and Foix's persona cannot but cry out in consternation: "Give me a lamp: —Where is my horse?/ Give me stone-hard coals and luminous pebbles/ Give me night walls in lunar cities." At the end of the poem, the persona attains the dubious distinction of speaking as a prophet of sorts, vexed by suspicions of an ominous handwriting on the wall; thus, Foix—with the prescience of García Lorca's *Poeta en Nueva York* (1940; *Poet in New York*, 1940, 1955), Pablo Neruda's *España en el corazón* (1937; *Spain in the Heart*, 1946), and Pablo Picasso's painting *Guernica* (1937)—cries out against man's inhumanity to man and warns of the danger that humankind will bring on itself the dreadful wrath of the gods.

OTHER MAJOR WORKS

SHORT FICTION: *Allò que no diu La vanguardia*, 1970; *La pell de la pell*, 1970.

NONFICTION: *Revolució catalanista*, 1934 (with Josep Carbonell); *Catalans de 1918*, 1965; *Els lloms transparents*, 1969; *Noranta set notes sobre ficcions poncianes*, 1974.

MISCELLANEOUS: *Obres completes*, 1974-1990 (4 volumes; includes his epistles).

BIBLIOGRAPHY

Boehne, Patricia J. *J. V. Foix*. Boston: Twayne, 1980. An introductory biographical study and critical analysis of selected works by Foix. Includes bibliographic references and an index.

Bohn, Willard. *Marvelous Encounters: Surrealist Responses to Film, Art, Poetry, and Architecture*. Lewisburg, Pa.: Bucknell University Press, 2005. Contains a chapter on the Catalan experience, with a discussion of Foix.

Cocozzella, Peter. Review of *Tocant a mà*. *World Literature Today* 68, no. 1 (Winter, 1994): 107. Cocozzella provides a summary in English of Joan R. Veny-Mesquida's introduction in Catalan to *Tocant a mà*. Complementing positivistic analysis with the insights provided by current literary theory, Veny-Mesquida, in a substantial introduction of some eighty pages, calls upon foreign and homegrown pundits—Norman Friedmann, Gerald Prince, Carles Miralles, Maurici Serrahima, Enric Sulla, Ferrater, and Gimferrer, among others—to help him shed light on Foix's engrossing masterpieces.

Rosenthal, David. *Postwar Catalan Poetry*. Cranbury, N.J.: Associated University Presses, 1991. Contains an introduction to Catalan poetry, and a chapter on Foix, followed by chapters on other Catalan poets.

Peter Cocozzella

FEDERICO GARCÍA LORCA

Born: Fuentevaqueros, Spain; June 5, 1898
Died: Víznar, Spain; August 19, 1936

PRINCIPAL POETRY
Libro de poemas, 1921
Canciones, 1921-1924, 1927
Romancero gitano, 1924-1927, 1928 (*The Gypsy Ballads of García Lorca*, 1951, 1953)
Poema del cante jondo, 1931 (*Poem of the Gypsy Seguidilla*, 1967)
Llanto por Ignacio Sánchez Mejías, 1935 (*Lament for the Death of a Bullfighter*, 1937, 1939)
Primeras canciones, 1936
Diván del Tamarit, 1940 (*The Divan at the Tamarit*, 1944)
Poeta en Nueva York, 1940 (*Poet in New York*, 1940, 1955)
Collected Poems, 2002 (revised edition)

OTHER LITERARY FORMS

The publisher Aguilar of Madrid issued a one-volume edition of the works of Federico García Lorca (gahr-SEE-uh LAWR-kuh), compiled and annotated by Arturo del Hoyo, with a prologue by Jorge Guillén and an epilogue by Vicente Aleixandre. In addition to the poetry, it includes García Lorca's plays, of which the tragic rural trilogy *Bodas de sangre* (pr. 1933; *Blood Wedding*, 1939), *Yerma* (pr. 1934; English translation, 1941), and *La casa de Bernarda Alba* (pr., pb. 1945; *The House of Bernarda Alba*, 1947) are world famous and represent García Lorca's best achievement as a poet become director-playwright. To portray all the facets of García Lorca's artistic personality, the Aguilar edition also includes his first play, *El maleficio de la mariposa* (pr. 1920; *The Butterfly's Evil Spell*, 1963); an example of his puppet plays, *Los títeres de Cachiporra: La tragicomedia de don Cristóbal y la señá Rosita* (pr. 1937; *The Tragicomedy of Don Cristóbal and Doña Rosita*, 1955); selections from *Impresiones y paisajes* (1918; impressions and landscapes), García Lorca's first published prose works, in which his genius is already evident in the melancholic, impressionistic style used to describe his feelings and reactions to the Spanish landscape and Spanish life; several short prose pieces and dialogues; a number of lectures and speeches; a variety of representative letters to friends; texts of newspaper interviews; poems from the poet's book of suites; fifteen of his songs; and twenty-five of his drawings.

Although the Aguilar edition reflects a consummate artist, still missing from its pages are a number of other works: a five-act play, *El público* (fragment, pb. 1976; *The*

Audience, 1958), and the first part of a dramatic biblical trilogy titled "La destrucción de Sódoma" (wr. 1936; the destruction of Sodom), on which García Lorca was working at the time of his death. Lost are "Los sueños de mi prima Aurelia" (the dreams of my cousin Aurelia) and "La niña que riega la albahaca y el príncipe pregunton" (the girl who waters the sweet basil flower and the inquisitive prince), a puppet play presented in Granada on January 5, 1923. "El sacrificio de Ifigenia" (Iphigenia's sacrifice) and "La hermosa" (the beauty) are titles of two plays whose existence cannot be substantiated.

Reportedly, García Lorca also collected a group of poems titled "Sonetos del amor oscuro" (sonnets of dark love), the title suggesting to certain critics the poet's preference for intimate masculine relationships. Until the 1960's, most of the works evaluating García Lorca centered on the events of his life and death and were only interspersed with snatches of literary criticism. Since his death, thematic and stylistic studies by such noted scholars as Rafael Martínez Nadal, Gustavo Correa, Arturo Barea, Rupert C. Allen, and Richard L. Predmore have served to illuminate García Lorca's symbolic and metaphorical world.

Achievements

The typically Spanish character of his plays and poetry, enhanced by rich and daring lyrical expression, have made Federico García Lorca one of the most universally recognized poets of the twentieth century. His tragic death in 1936 at the hands of the Falange, the Spanish Fascist Party, in the flower of his manhood and literary creativity, merely served to further his fame.

The first milestone of García Lorca's short but intense career was the publication of *The Gypsy Ballads of García Lorca*, which solidly established his reputation as a fine poet in the popular vein. His dark, brooding, foreboding ballads of Gypsy passion and death captured the imagination and hearts of Spaniards and foreigners, Andalusians and Galicians, illiterate farmers and college professors. Critics saw in García Lorca's poems the culmination of centuries of a rich and diverse Spanish lyric tradition. For example, Edwin Honig has noted that García Lorca's poetry took its inspiration from such diverse sources as the medieval Arabic-Andalusian art of amorous poetry; the early popular ballad; the Renaissance synthesis in Spain of classical traditions, as exemplified by the "conceptist" poetry of Luis de Góngora y Argote; and the *cante jondo*, or "deep song," of the Andalusian Gypsy.

Living in an era of vigorous cultural and literary activity, called by many Spain's second golden age, García Lorca clearly maintained his individuality. His innate charm and wit, his strong and passionate presence, his *duende*, or "soul," as a performer of Andalusian songs and ballads, and his captivating readings of his own poetry and plays drew the applause and friendship of equally talented writers and artists, such as Rafael Alberti, Pedro Salinas, Jorge Guillén, Vicente Aleixandre, Salvador Dalí, and Luis Buñuel.

The poet reached the peak of his popular success in the late 1920's. Both his *Songs* and *The Gypsy Ballads of García Lorca* were published to great critical acclaim. In the same period, he delivered two memorable lectures, the first at the *cante jondo* festival organized jointly with composer Manuel de Falla in Granada, and the second at the festival in honor of Góngora's tercentenary. His play *Mariana Pineda* (pr. 1927; English translation, 1950) was produced in Barcelona, and the following year he founded and published the literary journal *Gallo*. Despite these achievements, however, García Lorca suffered a grave spiritual crisis, to which he alludes in his correspondence but never really clarifies. This crisis led him to reevaluate his artistic output and turn to new experiences and modes of expression.

The result of García Lorca's soul-searching can be seen in his later works, especially *Poet in New York* and *Lament for the Death of a Bullfighter*. In the former, García Lorca fully unleashes his imagination in arabesques of metaphor that on first reading appear incomprehensible. *Poet in New York* is a difficult and frequently obscure work that has been viewed as a direct contrast to his earlier poetry. However, as Predmore has so painstakingly demonstrated, these poems extend rather than depart from García Lorca's established preference for ambiguous and antithetical symbolism.

The two threads that run throughout García Lorca's work are the themes of love and death: They lend a poetic logic and stability to what may otherwise appear chaotic and indecipherable. A study of these themes in García Lorca's poetry and plays reveals a gradual evolution from tragic premonition and foreboding, through vital passion repressed and frustrated by outside forces, to bitter resignation and death. Throughout his life, García Lorca's constant companion and friend was death. The poet Antonio Machado described this intimacy with death in his lament for García Lorca:

> He was seen walking with Her, alone,
> unafraid of her scythe.
> . . . .
> Today as yesterday, gypsy, my Death,
> how good to be with you, alone
> in these winds of Granada, of my Granada.

García Lorca's gift of imagination, his genius for metaphor and volatile imagery, and his innate sense of the tragic human condition make him one of the outstanding poets of the twentieth century. With his execution in Granada in 1936 at the outbreak of the Spanish Civil War, the frustrated personas of his poetry and plays, who so often ended their lives in senseless tragedy, materialized in his own person. In García Lorca, life became art and art became life. Combining the experience of two cultures, he addressed in both, the Andalusian and the American man's primal needs and fears within his own interior world.

Biography

Federico García Lorca was born on June 5, 1898, in Fuentevaqueros, in the province of Granada. His father, Don Federico García Rodríguez, was a well-to-do landowner, a solid rural citizen of good reputation. After his first wife died, Don Federico married Doña Vicenta Lorca Romero, an admired schoolteacher and a musician. García Lorca was very fond of his mother and believed that he inherited his intelligence and artistic bent from her and his passionate nature from his father. It was in the countryside of Granada that García Lorca's poetic sensibility took root, nourished by the meadows, the fields, the wild animals, the livestock, and the people of that land. His formative years were centered in the village, where he attended Mass with his mother and absorbed and committed to memory the colorful talk, the folktales, and the folk songs of the *vega* (fertile lowland) that would later find a rebirth in the metaphorical language of his poetry and plays.

In 1909, his family moved to Granada, and García Lorca enrolled in the College of the Sacred Heart to prepare for the university. This was the second crucial stage in his artistic development: Granada's historical and literary associations further enriched his cultural inheritance from the *vega* and modified it by adding an intellectual element. García Lorca wanted to be a musician and composer, but his father wanted him to study law. In 1915, he matriculated at the University of Granada, but he never was able to adapt completely to the regimentation of university studies, failing three courses, one of them in literature. During the same period, he continued his serious study of piano and composition with Don Antonio Segura. García Lorca frequented the cafés of Granada and became popular for his wit. In 1916 and 1917, García Lorca traveled throughout Castile, Léon, and Galicia with one of his professors from the university, who also encouraged him to write his first book, *Impresiones y paisajes*. He also came into contact with important people in the arts, among them Manuel de Falla, who shared García Lorca's interest in traditional folk themes, and Fernando de los Ríos, an important leader in educational and social reforms, who persuaded García Lorca's father to send his son to the University of Madrid.

In 1919, García Lorca arrived in Madrid, where he was to spend the next ten years at the famous Residencia de Estudiantes, in the company of Rafael Alberti, Jorge Guillén, Pedro Salinas, Gerardo Diego, Dámaso Alonso, Luis Cernuda, and Vicente Aleixandre. There García Lorca published his first collection of poems, *Libro de poemas*, and became involved with the philosophical and literary currents then in vogue. In 1922, García Lorca returned to Granada to conduct with Manuel de Falla a Festival of Cante Jondo.

The years from 1924 to 1928 were successful but troubled ones for García Lorca, marked by moments of elation followed by depression. During these years, García Lorca developed a close friendship with Salvador Dalí and spent several summers with the Dalí family at Cadaqués. He published his second book of poems, *Songs*, in 1927 and in that same year saw the premiere of *Mariana Pineda* in Barcelona and Madrid. In December of 1927, García Lorca participated in the famous Góngora tricentennial anniversary celebrations in Seville, where he delivered one of his most famous lectures, "The Poetic Image in Don Luis de Góngora." Gradually, García Lorca's fame spread, and his *The Gypsy Ballads of García Lorca* became the most widely read book of poems to appear in Spain since the publication of Gustavo Adolfo Bécquer's *Rimas* (*Poems*, 1891; better known as *The Rhymes*, 1898) in 1871. During the period from May to December of 1928, García Lorca suffered an emotional crisis that prompted him to leave Spain to accompany Fernando de los Ríos to New York. After spending nine months in the United States, a stay that included a visit to Vermont, García Lorca returned to Spain by way of Cuba with renewed interest and energy for his work. The clearest product of this visit was *Poet in New York*, one of his greatest books of poems, published four years after his death.

After his return to Madrid in 1930, García Lorca turned his focus increasingly to the dramatic. In 1932, under the auspices of the Republic's Ministry of Education, García Lorca founded La Barraca, a university theater whose aim was to bring the best classical plays to the provinces. In the same period, he saw the successful staging of *Blood Wedding* and *El amor de don Perlimplín con Belisa en su jardín* (pr. 1933; *The Love of Don Perlimplín for Belisa in His Garden*, 1941). His achievements in Spain were capped by another trip to the New World, this time to Argentina, where *Blood Wedding, Mariana Pineda*, and *La zapatera prodigiosa* (pr. 1930; *The Shoemaker's Prodigious Wife*, 1941) were staged and received with great enthusiasm. The years 1934 and 1935 saw the writing of the *Lament for the Death of a Bullfighter* and the premieres of at least four new plays. By 1936, García Lorca had decided to return to Granada for the celebration of his name day and also to bide his time until the political turmoil in Madrid abated. During his stay, the civil war broke out, and amid the fighting between the Nationalist and the Popular forces in Granada, García Lorca was detained and executed on August 19, 1936, in the outskirts of Víznar. His body was thrown into an unmarked grave.

Analysis

In imagery that suggests an "equestrian leap" between two opposing worlds, Federico García Lorca embodies a dialectical vision of life, on one hand filled with an all-consuming love for humanity and nature and, on the other, cognizant of the "black torso of the Pharaoh," the blackness symbolizing an omnipresent death unredeemed by the possibility of immortality. The tension between these two irreconcilable forces lends a tautness as well as a mystery to much of his poetry.

"Elegía a doña Juana la Loca"

A recurring theme throughout García Lorca's work that is expressive of this animating tension is that of thwarted love, repressed by society or simply by human destiny and ending inevitably in death. This obsession with unfulfilled dreams and with death is evident in the poet's first collection. In a moving elegy to the Castilian princess Juana la Loca titled "Elegía a doña Juana la Loca," García Lorca details in fifteen stanzas the lamentable fate of a woman driven to madness by her unrequited love for her husband, Felipe el Hermoso. Throughout the poem, García Lorca addresses her as a red carnation in a deep and desolate valley, to whom Death extended a bouquet of withered roses instead of flowers, verses, and pearl necklaces. Like other great tragic heroines of Spanish literature, such as Isabel de Segura and Melibea, and those of García Lorca's own creative imagination, she is a victim of fate.

The themes of violent passion and death, later more fully expressed in *The Gypsy Ballads of García Lorca*, are latent in the description of Juana as a princess of the red sunset, the color of blood and fire, whose passion is like the dagger, whose distaff is of iron, whose flax is of steel. Here, metallic substances are symbols of death; Juana lies in her coffin of lead, and within her skeleton, a heart broken into a thousand pieces speaks of her shattered dreams and frustrated life.

"Ballad of the Little Square"

In contrast to the bleak symbolism of these works, children and their world interested and delighted García Lorca, and he futilely sought in their charm and innocence a respite from the anguish of existence. In another poem from his first collection, "Balada de la placeta" ("Ballad of the Little Square"), the poet is listening to children singing. In a playful dialogue, the children ask the poet what he feels in his red, thirsty mouth; he answers, "the taste of the bones of my big skull." The poet's consciousness of death's presence mars his contemplation of youthful fun. Although he might wish to lose himself in the child's world, he clearly recognizes in a later poem, "Gacela de la huida" ("Gacela of the Flight"), that the seeds of death are already sown behind that childish exterior: "No one who touching a newborn child can forget the motionless horse skulls." Still, he tries to reject the physical destruction, the putrefaction of death that he so vividly describes in "Gacela de la muerte oscura" ("Gacela of the Dark Death") and in the *Lament for the Death of a Bullfighter*.

"The Song of the Horseman"

García Lorca was a master of the dramatic ballad, full of mystery, passion, and dark, sudden violence. His tools were simple words and objects culled from everyday living, which contrasted with and intensified the complex emotions underlying the verse. García Lorca's mastery of the ballad form is exemplified in "Canción de jinete" ("The Song of the Horseman"), from *Songs*. The horseman's destination is the distant city of Córdoba. Although he knows the roads well and his saddlebags are packed with olives, he fatalistically declares that he will never reach Córdoba. García Lorca never tells a story outright; he makes his audience do the work. Thus, Death is looking at the horseman from the towers of Córdoba, as he cries "Ay! How long the road! Ay! My valiant pony! Ay! That death should wait me before I reach Córdoba." How? Why? Who? Where? These questions are left to the imagination.

"Somnambule Ballad"

It is through the figure of the Andalusian gypsy that García Lorca best conveys his personal vision of life. With his characteristic techniques of metaphorical suggestion and dramatic tension, enriched by an artist's palette of colors, García Lorca in *The Gypsy Ballads of García Lorca* treats his usual subject matter of love and death, passion and destruction, with great lyrical fantasy. The refrain "Green, how much I want you green" establishes the enchanted atmosphere of the famous "Romance sonambulo" ("Somnambule Ballad"), where everything possesses the greenish cast of an interior world: "Green wind, green flesh, green hair." The best known of García Lorca's ballads, it only implies the story behind the death of a pair of lovers: his the result of a wound that runs from his chest to his throat, hers from drowning in the sorrow of having waited for him so long in vain.

The themes of passion and violence are underscored by the theme of liberty, denied to the lovers by fate and a false social order. The gypsy girl's death is already intimated in the first stanza, where she is described as having a shadow on her waist, with green flesh, hair of green, and eyes of cold silver that cannot see. On a first reading, the two lines "The ship upon the sea/ and the horse in the mountain," which precede the description, seem to be a discordant and senseless addition to the narrative. To understand their function, the reader must see them in relation to the theme of liberty. Humans are imprisoned by their passions, by destiny, death, a sense of honor, and social institutions. In contrast, the images of the ship upon the sea and the horse on the mountain suggest total freedom. The horse, which in García Lorca's work often represents male virility, prefigures the gypsy's attainment of the freedom that is his by nature. The image of the ship, on the other hand, has a long tradition of symbolizing liberty, especially in the Romantic period; its interpretation here, as such, is logical and expected. The description of the stars as white frost and the mountain as a filching cat foreshadows the violence of the characters' deaths.

Thus, "Somnambule Ballad" offers a profusion of surrealistic and seemingly disconnected images governed by a vigorous inner logic. In this, it is representative of García Lorca's finest works. The repetition of key images—of green, cold silver, the moon, water, and the night—unifies the poem. The gypsy girl and the gypsy are together in death and cannot hear the pounding of the drunken civil guard on the door. Death has granted them freedom, and all is as it should be: "The ship upon the sea, and the horse on the mountain." Using the local color and ambience of gypsy life, García Lorca gives voice to his own frustrations and those of humanity in general. Fettered by passion, destiny, and social norms, humanity's only escape is through death.

Poet in New York

The strange poems of *Poet in New York* are the work of a mature poet. In New York, García Lorca, who had loved life in all its spontaneity, who had grieved over the death of gypsies, their instinctive and elemental passions suffocated, was confronted with the heartless, mechanized world of the urban metropolis. In *Poet in New York*, the gypsy is replaced by the black person, whose instinctive impulses and strengths are perverted by white civilization and whose repression and anguish is embodied in the figure of the great King of Harlem in a janitor's suit. The blood of three hundred crimson roses that stained the gypsy's shirt in "Somnambule Ballad" now flows from four million butchered ducks, five million hogs, two thousand doves, one million cows, one million lambs, and two million roosters.

The disrespect for life in this landscape of vomiting and urinating multitudes is portrayed in the death of a cat, within whose little paw, crushed by the automobile, García Lorca sees a world of broken rivers and unattainable distances. Alone, alienated, and frustrated in his endeavors, humans cannot appeal to anyone for help, not even the Church, which in its hypocrisy and heathen materialism betrays the true spirit of Christianity. The poet sees death and destruction everywhere. His own loneliness and alienation, described in "Asesinato" ("Murder"), recall the haunting words and melody of the *cante jondo*: "A pinprick to dive till it touches the roots of a cry."

Lament for the Death of a Bullfighter

Considered by many to be García Lorca's supreme poetic achievement, *Lament for the Death of a Bullfighter* is the quintessence of the Spanish "tragic sense of life." In this lament, García Lorca incorporated aspects of a long poetic tradition and revitalized them through his own creativity. Based on a true incident, as were most of García Lorca's poems, the elegy was written on the death of his good friend Ignacio, an intellectual and a bullfighter, who was gored by a bull and died in August of 1934. The bullfight is elevated by García Lorca to a universal level, representing humanity's heroic struggle against death. Death, as always in García Lorca's poetry, emerges triumphant, yet the struggle is seen as courageous, graceful, meaningful.

The elegy is divided into four parts: "La cogida y la muerte" ("The Goring and the Death"), "La sangre derrameda" ("The Spilling of the Blood"), "Cuerpo presente" ("The Body Present"), and "Alma ansente" ("Absent Soul"). In general, the poem moves from the concrete to the abstract, from report to essay, from the specific to the general. Part 1 describes the events, the chaos, the confusion, the whole process of death in a series of images appealing to all the five senses. Phones jangle, the crowd is mad with grief, the bulls bellow, the wounds burn. What dominates is the incessant and doleful bell, reminding the poet, with each repetition of "at five o'clock in the afternoon," of the finality of death, worming its way into Ignacio's being, hammering its way into the public mind and into the poet's consciousness. The macabre sights and smells of death are detailed in all their colorful goriness: the white sheet, a pail of lime, snowy sweat, yellow iodine, green gangrene. Time ceases for Ignacio as all the clocks show five o'clock in the shadow of the afternoon. Refusing to look at Ignacio's blood in the sand, García Lorca vents his anger and frustration at seeing all that beauty, confidence, princeliness, strength of body and character, wit, and intelligence slowly seeping out as the moss and the grass open with sure fingers the flowers of Ignacio's skull.

The poet's initial reaction of shock and denial slowly softens into gradual acceptance. Using the slower Alexandrine meter in "The Body Present," García Lorca contemplates the form of Ignacio laid out on a sterile, gray, cold stone. The finality of death is seen in the sulphur yellow of Ignacio's face and in the rain entering his mouth in the stench-filled silence. García Lorca cannot offer immortality. He can only affirm that humankind must live bravely, and that death too will one day cease to exist. Hence, he tells Ignacio to sleep, fly, rest: Even the sea dies. Death, victorious, challenged only by the value of Ignacio's human experience, is dealt with in the last part. By autumn, the people will have forgotten Ignacio, robbed by death and time of the memory of his presence. Only those like the poet, who can look beyond, will immortalize him in song.

Lament for the Death of a Bullfighter expresses the fundamental attitude of the Spaniard toward death: One must gamble on life with great courage and heroism. Welcoming the dark angels of death, the "toques de bordón," or the black tones of the guitar, the poet is paradoxically affirming life. This is humanity's only consolation.

García Lorca's evolution as a poet was characterized throughout by this movement toward an all-encompassing death. Synthesizing a variety of themes and poetic styles and forms, García Lorca embodied, both in his life and in his verse, modern humans' struggle to find meaning in life despite the overwhelming reality of physical and spiritual death.

OTHER MAJOR WORKS

PLAYS: *El maleficio de la mariposa*, pr. 1920 (*The Butterfly's Evil Spell*, 1963); *Mariana Pineda*, pr. 1927 (English translation, 1950); *La doncella, el marinero y el estudiante*, pb. 1928 (*The Virgin, the Sailor, and the Student*, 1957); *El paseo de Buster Keaton*, pb. 1928 (*Buster Keaton's Promenade*, 1957); *La zapatera prodigiosa*, pr. 1930 (*The Shoemaker's Prodigious Wife*, 1941); *Bodas de sangre*, pr. 1933 (*Blood Wedding*, 1939); *El amor de don Perlimplín con Belisa en su jardín*, pr. 1933 (*The Love of Don Perlimplín for Belisa in His Garden*, 1941); *Yerma*, pr. 1934 (English translation, 1941); *Doña Rosita la soltera: O, El lenguaje de las flores*, pr. 1935 (*Doña Rosita the Spinster: Or, The Language of the Flowers*, 1941); *El retablillo de don Cristóbal*, pr. 1935 (*In the Frame of Don Cristóbal*, 1944); *Así que pasen cinco años*, pb. 1937, (wr. 1931; *When Five Years Pass*, 1941); *Los títeres de Cachiporra: La tragicomedia de don Cristóbal y la señá Rosita*, pr. 1937 (wr. 1928; *The Tragicomedy of Don Cristóbal and Doña Rosita*, 1955); *Quimera*, pb. 1938 (wr. 1928; *Chimera*, 1944); *La casa de*

Bernarda Alba, pr., pb. 1945 (wr. 1936; *The House of Bernarda Alba*, 1947); *El público*, pb. 1976 (wr. 1930, fragment; *The Audience*, 1958).

NONFICTION: *Impresiones y paisajes*, 1918; *Selected Letters*, 1983 (David Gershator, editor).

MISCELLANEOUS: *Obras completas*, 1938-1946 (8 volumes).

BIBLIOGRAPHY

Anderson, Reed. *Federico García Lorca*. London: Macmillan, 1984. Anderson's study focuses on García Lorca's dramatic art. The book has a fine overview of García Lorca's relationship to Spanish literature in general as well as insightful discussions of the early and mature dramas.

Binding, Paul. *Lorca: The Gay Imagination*. London: GMP, 1985. Binding's is a fine study focusing on García Lorca's work as it is an outgrowth of the poet's sexuality. Binding has a sympathetic sense of the modern temperament, and his readings, particularly of García Lorca's mature works, are excellent.

Bonaddio, Federico, ed. *A Companion to Federico García Lorca*. Woodbridge, Suffolk, England: Tamesis, 2008. Provides biographical information and critical analysis. Contains a chapter on poetry.

Delgado, Maria M. *Federico García Lorca*. New York: Routledge, 2007. A biography that looks at the life, politics, and mythology surrounding the poet and dramatist. Also looks at his legacy.

Gibson, Ian. *Federico García Lorca*. New York: Pantheon Books, 1989. A monumental biography that goes to the heart of García Lorca's genius with brilliant prose and telling anecdotes. Meticulously reconstructs the poet's periods in New York, Havana, and Buenos Aires. Vividly re-creates the café life of Spain in the 1930's and the artistic talents that were nurtured there. Evokes the landscapes of Granada, Almeria, Cuba, and Argentina celebrated in the poetry.

Johnston, David. *Federico García Lorca*. Bath, England: Absolute, 1998. Asserts that García Lorca, rather than celebrating, is deconstructing the essentials of Spain's culture of difference. Claims that the poet's most radical ultimate intention was the deconstruction of a civilization and the redefinition of the individual's right to be, not through the language of ethics or of the law but in terms of a natural imperative.

Mayhew, Jonathan, ed. *Apocryphal Lorca: Translation, Parody, Kitsch*. Chicago: University of Chicago Press, 2009. Literary criticism of García Lorca's works. Mayhew contrasts the perception of the poet in the English-speaking world to that in the Spanish-speaking world. He notes the poet's legacy among American poets.

Morris, C. Brian. *Son of Andalusia: The Lyrical Landscapes of Federico García Lorca*. Nashville, Tenn.: Vanderbilt University Press, 1997. In six chapters and an epilogue, Morris identifies the presence of Andalusian legends, traditions, songs, and beliefs in García Lorca's life and works.

Sahuquillo, Angel. *Federico García Lorca and the Culture of Male Homosexuality.* Jefferson, N.C.: McFarland, 2007. Examines García Lorca's life and works from the perspective of his sexuality.

Stainton, Leslie. *Lorca: A Dream of Life.* New York: Farrar, Straus and Giroux, 1999. Stainton, an American scholar who lived in Spain for several years, writes of García Lorca's sexuality, his left-wing political views, and his artistic convictions. Her detailed account is strictly chronological. García Lorca's work is described but not analyzed.

Katherine Gyékényesi Gatto

GARCILASO DE LA VEGA

Born: Toledo, Spain; 1501
Died: Nice, France; October 13, 1536

PRINCIPAL POETRY

Las obras de Boscán y algunas de Garcilasso de la Vega repartidas en quatro libros, 1543
Las obras del excelente poeta Garcilasso de la Vega, 1569
Obras del excelente poeta Garci Lasso de la Vega con anotaciones y enmiendas del Licenciado Francisco Sánchez..., 1574
Obras de Garci Lasso de la Vega con anotaciones de Fernando de Herrera, 1580
Garcilaso de la Vega: Natural de Toledo, Principe de los Poetas Castellanos, de Don Thomas Tamaio de Vargas, 1622 (*The Works of Garcilaso de la Vega surnamed the Prince of Castilian Poets*, 1823)
Obras de Garcilaso de la Vega, ilustradas con notas, 1765
Garcilaso: Works, A Critical Text with a Bibliography, 1925
Garcilaso de la Vega: Obras completas, Edición de Elías L. Rivers, 1964
Garcilaso de la Vega y sus comentaristas: Obras completas del poeta acompañadas de los textos íntegros de los comentarios de El Brocense, Fernando de Herrera, Tamayo y Vargas y Azara, 1966
The Complete Love Sonnets of Garcilaso de la Vega, 2005
Selected Poems of Garcilaso de la Vega, 2009 (bilingual edition)

OTHER LITERARY FORMS

Garcilaso de la Vega (gahr-see-LAH-soh day lo VAY-guh) is remembered only for his poetic works.

ACHIEVEMENTS

Garcilaso de la Vega revolutionized Castilian poetry, playing a unique role in Spanish literature and achieving a notable place in European literature as well. In accomplishing this poetic revolution, Garcilaso may rightly be called the first modern Spanish poet. Although the fifteenth century in Spain had seen efforts to introduce into Castilian poetry the Italian hendecasyllable, attempts such as those of the Marquis of Santillana, who composed a collection of "Sonetos fechos al itálico modo" (sonnets made in the Italian way), had not been successful. Equally unsuccessful had been the use of a non-Italianate hendecasyllabic line by the fifteenth century poets Juan de Mena and Francisco Imperial.

Garcilaso's perfection of the Castilian hendecasyllable, successful cultivation of both Italianate verse forms and metrical innovations, and his use of classical models, all contributed to a poetry of intimate sentiment, delicate metaphor, conceptual content, and musicality. Religious themes, so important in the poetry of even the late Middle Ages in Spain, are completely absent in his verse, which crystallized the introduction into Spain of the essentially secular values of the Renaissance. From fifteenth century Spanish poetry, Garcilaso retained a certain predilection for wordplay, along with the favorable influence of the Catalan poet Ausias March. While at times expressively manipulating syntax, Garcilaso created a poetic diction soon regarded as a model of lucid simplicity for the Spanish language.

In international terms, Garcilaso is also notable for having preceded by many years the introduction of Italianate forms and sentiment into both English and French poetry. His use of pastoral poetry to express interiorized sentiments, of interest to the student of comparative literature, also represents a notable contribution to the development of this international literary mode.

Garcilaso's poetry, all of which was published posthumously, was rapidly accorded classic status, and editions of his poems with copious annotation and commentary appeared within the sixteenth century. The first of these was the edition by the esteemed scholar Francisco Sánchez de las Brozas, initially published in 1574. The important poet Fernando de Herrera first published his annotated edition in 1580. Additional annotated editions were published by other editors in the seventeenth and eighteenth centuries. The 1543 edition included most of the sonnets currently known to be Garcilaso's or attributed to him, all the other poems in Italian meters, and one poem in a traditional Castilian verse form. Subsequent editions have gradually been enlarged by adding more sonnets, other compositions in Castilian verse forms, and several Latin poems, as well as some letters and the poet's will. Virtually all dating of his compositions is conjectural, and the numbers commonly assigned to specific poems do not correspond to their presumed order of composition.

Garcilaso's poetry in some sense became the model and inspiration for virtually all poetry written during the nearly two centuries of Spain's Golden Age and for much of Spanish poetry up to the present day. Although the traditional Castilian verse forms were championed by poets such as Cristóbal de Castillejo and his followers in the sixteenth century, the influence and acceptance of Garcilaso's innovations was so pervasive that it has been said that every Spanish poet "carries his Garcilaso inside himself." Garcilaso's own compositions in the traditional verse forms—and his Latin poetry—illuminate the development of his Spanish poetry in the new style but are not themselves of primary interest in defining or understanding his art. The poetical canon left by Garcilaso provided the inspiration and basis for both of the somewhat antithetical schools or styles of poetry that were to evolve later in the Golden Age. The statement of ideas without metaphorical adornment and Garcilaso's retention of wordplay and puns from medieval Spanish poetry evolved ultimately into the dense, conceptual style exemplified by Francisco Gómez de Quevedo y Villegas, while Garcilaso's manipulation of word order, sense of color, and use of metaphor were reflected in Luis de Góngora y Argote's hyperbatons, polychromatic palette, and extravagant imagery.

Garcilaso pioneered the use of six distinct verse forms in Spanish poetry. The Spanish sonnet, composed of fourteen hendecasyllabic lines divided into two quatrains and two tercets, possessed a fundamentally different structure from the sonnet subsequently developed in English by William Shakespeare. The *estancia* combined lines of eleven and seven syllables in a pattern established in the poem's first strophe and then repeated in the subsequent strophes. The *lira*, so called because of its use in an ode whose first line contained this word (meaning "lyre"), was a particular form of the *estancia*, which became standardized. The *tercetos* consisted of three-line stanzas of eleven-syllable lines, with the first and third lines rhyming, and the middle line rhyming with the first and third lines of the next stanza. The *octava real* was a stanza of eight hendecasyllabic lines, rhyming *abababcc*. Garcilaso also introduced into Spanish the use of blank verse.

Biography

Garcilaso de la Vega's brief but active life might serve as a model for that of the multitalented Renaissance man. Born in 1501 of a family with influence in the court of Ferdinand and Isabella and with several well-known authors in its antecedent generations, Garcilaso died in 1536 of wounds received in Provence while he was fighting for Emperor Charles V.

Garcilaso entered the emperor's service in 1519 or 1520, was first wounded in battle in 1521, and he participated in several important campaigns, for which he was awarded the prestigious Order of Saint James in 1523. During his accompaniment of the court in the subsequent years of the decade, his friendship with the poet Juan Boscán developed. This relationship was of profound significance for Garcilaso's literary career; when, for example, his friend Boscán was persuaded by the Venetian ambassador to employ the Italian hendecasyllable in Castilian verse, Garcilaso did likewise, changing Spanish poetry forever. It has been suggested that his sonnets 31 and 38 were written in this period.

In 1525, Garcilaso married Doña Elena de Zúñiga, a lady-in-waiting to Charles V's sister, Princess Leonore. The following year, he met and became infatuated with Isabel Freyre, who came to Spain from Portugal with Doña Isabel de Portugal when the latter married Charles V. Although his marital relationship apparently never saw expression in his poetry, Garcilaso's love for Isabel Freyre, seemingly unrequited, became a central poetic theme. The "Canción primera" ("First Ode") and sonnets 2, 15, and 27, probably from this period, express the poet's emotional state and his amorous devotion to an unnamed lady. The first numbered of his "Canciones en versos castellanos" ("Songs in Castilian Verse Forms"), on the occasion of "his lady's marriage," was presumably composed in response to Isabel Freyre's wedding. While with the retinue of Charles V in Italy, where the monarch had gone in 1529 or 1530 to receive the Imperial crown,

Garcilaso apparently composed his "Canción cuarta" ("Fourth Ode") and sonnet 6, perhaps reflecting his anguish over the affair with Isabel.

In 1531, however, Charles V withdrew his favor, banishing Garcilaso to a small island in the Danube River because he had persisted in supporting a marriage opposed by the royal family. Sonnets 4 and 9 and the "Canción tercera" ("Third Ode") reflect the poet's unhappiness during this period. Thanks to the intervention of the duke of Alba, however, the island confinement was altered to banishment to Naples, where the poet gained a position of confidence with the viceroy, earned the praise of Cardinal Bembo, and, as reflected in his sonnets 14, 19, and 33 and in the famous "Canción quinta, a la flor de Gnido" ("Fifth Ode, To the Flower of Gnido"), made the acquaintance of several other important Neapolitan literary figures. During this period, he also studied the classics and met the expatriate Spanish author Juan de Valdés, who mentioned Garcilaso in his *Diálogo de la lengua* (wr. c. 1535, pb. 1737; dialogue of the language). Garcilaso's "Egloga segunda" ("Second Eclogue"), probably composed shortly after his brief trip to Spain and return to Naples in 1533, praises the House of Alba, while the "Egloga primera" ("First Eclogue") and sonnet 10, both apparently composed during the period 1533-1534, reflect the death at that time of Isabel Freyre. It is reasonable to assume that during this time in Naples, the poet composed his several Latin poems and stopped composing in the old Castilian verse forms.

During 1535 and 1536, Garcilaso returned to the emperor's service. Sonnets 32 and 35 suggest that Garcilaso was wounded in an encounter with the Moors in an expedition to Tunis in 1535. With the emperor's entourage in Sicily after returning from Tunis, Garcilaso composed his "Elegía primera" ("First Elegy"), for the recent death of the brother of the duke of Alba, and the "Elegía segunda" ("Second Elegy"), addressed to his friend Boscán. The "Egloga tercera" ("Third Eclogue"), generally regarded as the poet's last work, was written when Garcilaso was again part of the emperor's court and in full favor, as Charles V decided to move against the French. It was while participating in this campaign that the poet was killed.

Boscán, Garcilaso's lifelong friend, gathered Garcilaso's poems, intending to publish them with his own. Upon Boscán's death in 1542, his widow carried out the project, realizing its publication in 1543.

Analysis

While Garcilaso de la Vega took much inspiration from Italian and classical models, he did not merely imitate them; rather, he assimilated and transformed these influences in the development of his own distinctive poetic voice.

"Second Eclogue"

This development is particularly evident in Garcilaso's eclogues. The "Second Eclogue," his longest composition, fully initiated the pastoral mode in his poetry. The poem possesses a balanced structure in which motifs and differing stanzaic forms—*tercetos, estancias, rima al mezzo* (interior rhyme)—are arranged in a symmetrical pattern centered on lines 766 through 933, which portray in dialogic form a chance encounter between the shepherd Albanio and Camila, his childhood playmate, who has earlier rejected his translation of their childhood friendship into love. On being rejected once more by Camila, after his hopes have been raised, Albanio goes mad. This central scene is preceded by a prologue in which Albanio laments his sad state; by several *estancias* inspired by Horace's *Beatus ille*; and by a section of dialogue between Albanio and Salicio in which Albanio recounts the story of his love for Camila, her negative response, and his present desire to kill himself. The dialogue, modeled on an episode in Jacopo Sannazzaro's *Arcadia* (1501-1504), is punctuated by an exchange in Petrarchan *rima al mezzo* in which Camila the hunter appears at the fountain where she first rejected Albanio and recalls the unpleasant incident.

Following the central scene between Camila and Albanio, a passage in *rima al mezzo* presents the struggle of Salicio and Nemoroso, another shepherd, to control the crazed Albanio. The following passage is in *tercetos*; with Albanio subdued, Nemoroso tells Salicio that Severo, a sage enchanter who had cured him, has come to Alba and can cure Albanio of his love woes. A brief dialogic *rima al mezzo* then leads to a lengthy panegyric by Nemoroso to the House of Alba. A short dialogue in *estancias* reaffirms the certainty of Albanio's eventual cure, and as dusk falls, the two shepherds discuss their leave-taking and the disposition of Albanio.

The "Second Eclogue" departs from the refinement of Vergilian bucolics and displays characteristics that separate it from the more perfected form that Garcilaso was to achieve in his "First Eclogue" (which, despite its designation, was composed after the "Second Eclogue"). The tranquility and idealization of nature and human feelings are disturbed by a number of familiar or rustic expressions and proverbs, concentrated in the dialogue between Albanio and Salicio that precedes Camila's appearance. These exchanges acquire an almost comic character that has caused some critics to regard them as constituting a dramatic farce in themselves. The poet engagingly steps outside the poetic conventions of the pastoral mode by having Albanio question Salicio's advice with the query, "Who made you an eloquent philosopher/ being a shepherd of sheep and goats?" There is a considerable amount of jocularity elsewhere in exchanges between Albanio and Salicio and in Nemoroso's initial resistance to helping Salicio subdue the crazed Albanio. Although it has been assumed that Albanio represents Garcilaso's friend and mentor the duke of Alba, a number of details suggest that Albanio is more plausibly Bernardino de Toledo, the duke's younger brother, whose death in 1535 occasioned Garcilaso's "First Elegy." Though somewhat distracting, these elements contribute to the originality of Garcilaso's poetic creation.

The "Second Eclogue" is also rich in conceits and various forms of wordplay. Some of these devices are reminiscent of Petrarch, while others have their antecedents in Castilian poetry of the fifteenth century. In its representation of Albanio's love as an anguished state, the poem recalls the Petrarchan influence evident in Garcilaso's earlier works.

"First Eclogue"

In "First Eclogue," Garcilaso attained perfect balance and equilibrium, a consistent and refined tone, idiom, and sentiment, and the definitive expression of the central amorous relationship in his life, the love for Isabel Freyre. A four-stanza prologue and dedication to the duke of Alba introduces two shepherds, again Salicio and Nemoroso, who lament respectively and in succession, each in twelve stanzas, their disappointments in love. The two successive speeches are separated by a one-stanza transition, and culminated by a single stanza conclusion, so that the poem as a whole comprises thirty fourteen-line stanzas.

In the two shepherds and their lamentations, the poet has represented himself ("Salicio" is an anagram of Garcilaso, while "Nemoroso" is a coinage based on the Latin root *nemus*, closely related in meaning to Spanish *vega*, a meadow) and expressed in a perfectly balanced duality the two essential elements of his relationship with Isabel Freyre: its failure, followed by her marriage to another, and her death. The lamentations begin at daybreak and end as the sun sets and the shepherds return with their flocks. Unity is achieved in the use of a single verse form throughout, the *estancia* (here a fourteen-line stanza of eleven- and seven-syllable lines); in the two shepherds' embodiment of the poet; and in the restriction of the action to a single day's time. Without calling attention to itself, an exquisite and seemingly effortless design governs the entire poem, which in its structure is similar to that of Vergil's "Eighth Eclogue."

The poem's opening six lines establish the delicacy and balance of the pastoral mode, exemplifying Garcilaso's expressive manipulation of word order to yield consonance of form and meaning. The first two lines, "The sweet lamentation of two shepherds/ Salicio jointly and Nemoroso," introduce the duality of the shepherds, separating and balancing them at the beginning and end of the poetical line. Here, the use of the first of many carefully positioned modifiers begins to create the idealized, gentle, tender ambience that defines the eclogue. The opening lines contain no active verbs, instead using infinitives, participles, and verbs of being. This construction suggests that the sheep are forgetful of their grazing, attentive rather to the shepherds' "savory song," a dreamlike oblivion and perfect harmony between nature and man. In an abrupt change, the next line addresses the duke of Alba, expressively heightening the contrast between the idyllic pastoral environment and the affairs of state or martial concerns that preoccupy the dynamic man of action.

The evocation of the duke's military activities in the succeeding stanzas touches a theme that was an important part of the poet's life and that finds expression in other of his poems, most notably the "Second Elegy." This poem, apparently written to Boscán from Sicily in 1535, expresses the poet's distaste for the petty politics of the emperor's retinue. Garcilaso depicts himself as a tender lover trapped in Mars's service, envying Boscán's tranquil, secure family life, and scorning the hypocrisy and ambition of those who surround the "African Caesar." The poem's opening lines, remarking on Vergil's presence in Sicily, through Aeneas, confirm Garcilaso's active awareness of Vergil during this period.

The stanza of the "First Eclogue," which connects the dedication to the duke with the beginning of Salicio's lament, returns to the idyllic natural setting. A characteristic hyperbaton represents the gradually rising sun, first rising above the waves, then above the mountains, and finally directly revealed at the beginning of the stanza's third line to introduce at daybreak the reclining Salicio. The pasture in which the shepherd is at his ease is crossed by a gurgling brook whose pleasant sound harmonizes with the music of the shepherd's sweet complaint. Assonant rhyme in addition to the usual consonantal rhyme, and internal rhyme in one verse, lend the passage a delicate musicality. As the clear brook flows unimpeded and burbling to accompany the shepherd's song, so too does the stanza, continuous, unimpeded, and without rigorous syntax.

The stanza that begins Salicio's complaint, addressed to the absent Galatea, who has not returned his love, is reminiscent of the plaints of several of Vergil's shepherds and provides a strident contrast to the sonorous passage preceding it. The shepherd first berates Galatea as harder than marble to his complaints and colder than ice to the fire that consumes him. The bitterness of these sentiments becomes death in the absence of the one who could give him life with her presence, then shame and embarrassment at his own pathetic state, then incredulity at the lady's refusal to command a soul that has always given itself to her, until it dissolves in the stanza's last line in the flowing tears bidden to emerge abundantly and without sorrow. This final line becomes a refrain at the end of the remainder of Salicio's stanzas, with the exception of the last one. Following stanzas contrast the permanence of the shepherd's sorry state with the daily changes of a delicately evoked nature, questioning the justice of his situation and reproachfully recalling his lady's falseness and deception.

While Salicio's unrequited love for Galatea recalls Garcilaso's disappointment in his love for Isabel Freyre, the shepherd Nemoroso's lament for his lost love, Elisa, recalls Garcilaso's mourning at Isabel's death. Nemoroso's lament confirms in a general way, though without many specific borrowings, Garcilaso's profound familiarity with Petrarch and his ability to equal or surpass the Italian model in his own poetry. Nemoroso's theme, the loved one's death, is also traditionally regarded as the subject of Garcilaso's famous sonnet 10, "Oh dulces prendas, por mi mal halladas" (O sweet favors, found to my woe), and sonnet 25. Sonnet 10, expressing the poet's grief on finding a token of his departed love, and contrasting the joy that love once brought him with the sadness it presently causes, is reminiscent of both Vergil and Petrarch. The sonnet is recalled in the "First Eclogue" when Nemoroso describes the consoling tears engendered by a lock of Elisa's hair, always kept at his bosom.

Nemoroso's song begins with an evocation of nature, distilled into select details each refined with adjectival description into exquisite perfection ("running, pure, crystalline waters," "green field," "fresh shade"). The natural setting is self-contained, turned in upon itself and vaguely anthropomorphic as green ivy winds its way among trees that see themselves reflected in the water. The harmony between man and his thoughts and an idealized natural surrounding is disturbed only by the suggestion of present sadness and by the last line's reference to joy-filled memories, implying that joy is past.

The following stanzas recall the happy times the lovers shared and mourn their brevity; in imagery that anticipates the Baroque violence of Góngora, the shepherd expresses his passion, his rage, and his desolation. In the final stanza of Nemoroso's lament, anger and despondency yield to a quiet prayer to the now-divine loved one to hasten the coming of the shepherd's death so that they may enjoy tranquilly together and without fear of loss the eternal fields, mountains, rivers, and shaded flowery valleys of the third sphere. Natural beauty is thus raised to a cosmic plane; in Salicio's plaint, the imagery that concludes the lament recalls its opening lines.

The dreamlike poetic moment of the two shepherds' lamentations is ended in the eclogue's final stanza. Looking at the pink clouds and sensing the creeping shadows that reverse the process of sunrise described at the poem's opening, the two shepherds awaken from their reverie and conduct their sheep home, step by step. So, too, does the reader leave an exquisite and incomparably evoked poetic world of true sentiment, delicate appreciation of nature, and harmony between man and his surroundings, representative of Garcilaso's enduring contribution to Spanish literature.

BIBLIOGRAPHY

Cammarata, Joan. *Mythological Themes in the Works of Garcilaso de la Vega*. Potomac, Md.: Studia Humanitatis, 1983. A critical analysis of Garcilaso's use of folklore and mythology. Includes bibliographical references and index.

Fernández-Morera, Dario. *The Lyre and the Oaten Flute: Garcilaso and the Pastoral*. London: Tamesis, 1982. A critical study of selected works by Garcilaso. Includes bibliographical references and index.

Garcilaso de la Vega. *Selected Poems of Garcilaso de la Vega: A Bilingual Edition*. Translated by John Dent-Young. Chicago: University of Chicago Press, 2009. This translation divides the poems into sonnets, songs, elegies, and eclogues, providing a short introduction to each.

Ghertman, Sharon. *Petrarch and Garcilaso*. London: Tamesis, 1975. Ghertman analyzes and compares the linguistic styles of Petrarch and Garcilaso.

Heiple, Daniel L. *Garcilaso de la Vega and the Italian Renaissance*. University Park: Pennsylvania State University Press, 1994. Heiple analyzes Garcilaso's work and its place in the history of Italian renaissance literature. Includes bibliographical references and index.

Helgerson, Richard. *A Sonnet from Carthage: Garcilaso de la Vega and the New Poetry of Sixteenth-Century Europe*. Philadelphia: University of Pennsylvania Press, 2007. Helgerson starts with a sonnet to Juan Boscán from Garcilaso and proceeds to examine Garcilaso's effect on the poetry of Europe.

Torres, Isabel. "Sites of Speculation: Water/Mirror Poetics in Garcilaso de la Vega, Eclogue II." *Bulletin of Hispanic Studies* 86, no. 6 (2009): 877-893. Examines Garcilaso's "Second Eclogue," noting water and mirror images in the poem.

Theodore L. Kassier

LUIS DE GÓNGORA Y ARGOTE

Born: Córdoba, Spain; July 11, 1561
Died: Córdoba, Spain; May 23, 1627

PRINCIPAL POETRY

Fábula de Polifemo y Galatea, 1627 (*Fable of Polyphemus and Galatea*, 1961)
Obras en verso del Homero español, 1627 (includes *Fábula de Polifemo y Galatea* and *Soledades*)
Soledades, 1627 (*The Solitudes of Don Luis de Góngora*, 1931; also as *The Solitudes*, 1964, Gilbert Cunningham, translator)
Obras poéticas de D. Luis de Góngora, 1921 (3 volumes; based on the Chacón manuscript of 1628)
Selected Poems of Luis de Gongora y Argote, 2007 (bilingual edition)

OTHER LITERARY FORMS

During the Golden Age of Spain, drama was the most prestigious literary form. Lope de Vega Carpio had developed Spain's national *comedia*, and Luis de Góngora y Argote (GAWNG-kuh-ro ee or-KOH-tay), like almost every other Spanish writer, tried his hand at theater. Góngora's plays met with little success. He completed two *comedias*: *Las firmezas de Isabela* (pr. 1610) and *El doctor Carlino* (pr. 1613). A third play, "Comedia venatoria," was left unfinished. Góngora's plays were unsuccessful because of their excessive difficulty; he was primarily a lyric poet, and therein lies his importance. Ironically, his greatest achievement in poetry constituted his main fault in drama: The dialogue was so complicated that the audience was unable to follow the plot, and the long lyrical sequences in the plays diverted attention from the main action.

ACHIEVEMENTS

The figure of Luis de Góngora y Argote has prompted critical polemics for the last three centuries. For a long time, critics divided his poetry into two categories: the easy-to-understand popular poems and the *culteranos*, complex works that are difficult to comprehend because of distorted syntax and a new poetic language. To quote a famous expression, Góngora became known as Prince of Light, Prince of Darkness. Research indicates, however, that his poetry developed in one constant line, culminating in the integration of opposing stylistic tendencies. The year 1613 marked the beginning of a literary controversy, yet unresolved, when the first manuscript copies of *Fable of Polyphemus and Galatea* were distributed at court. Literary circles in Spain were shocked, and opinion was drastically divided. On one hand, Góngora's ardent admirers proclaimed him to be the prince of poets. On the other hand, his enemies accused him of destroying both language and poetry. It is important to mention that among his severest critics were two of the leading Spanish poets of the Golden Age: Lope de Vega and Francisco Gómez de Quevedo y Villegas. With *Fable of Polyphemus and Galatea* and the first part of *The Solitudes*, distributed in 1613, Góngora nevertheless became the central figure of Spanish poetry. The impact of his complex style, *culteranismo*, was so powerful that even his worst enemies were ultimately influenced by his poetry.

Góngora's reputation fluctuated in succeeding centuries. His Baroque vision horrified the classicist souls of the eighteenth century, who held him responsible for the decadence of Spanish poetry. Nevertheless, they admired the "easy" Góngora, the Prince of Light. This attitude prevailed during the nineteenth century as well. The revaluation of Góngora's *culteranismo* did not begin until the end of the nineteenth century, when the French Symbolists, especially Paul Verlaine, praised Góngora's poetry as a brilliant attempt to create musicality and perfection. The most significant revaluation of his work, however, was initiated in 1927, when a group of young Spanish poets and critics joined to celebrate the third centennial of his death. The enthusiasm following the celebration led to the creation of the Generation of '27, the most brilliant group of Spanish poets since the time of Góngora. Critics today credit Góngora with perfecting the poetic language in Spanish. His work did not constitute a break with Renaissance models, but rather a culmination of its ideals. In the words of scholar Dámaso Alonso, Góngora was Europe's foremost seventeenth century lyrical poet. A young generation of international critics seems to agree with Alonso's judgment.

Biography

Luis de Góngora y Argote was born in Córdova, Spain, on July 11, 1561. He was the son of Francisco de Argote and Leonor de Góngora. His use of his mother's surname before his father's, not an unusual practice in Spain, was a result of economic considerations and a desire to carry a more euphonic name (Góngora was extremely fond of proparoxytonic words). It seems that, coming from an aristocratic family, his father originally intended to make his son a lawyer and to place him, through various political connections, in the court of the Habsburg rulers. Consequently, the young Góngora was sent to study at Salamanca, where he never completed his studies because he spent most of his time writing poems, flirting, and gambling. Góngora nevertheless was able to learn Latin, Greek, and classical literature and mythology. His maternal uncle, who held a hereditary position at the Cathedral of Córdova, convinced the young poet to enter the church. Góngora became a deacon and in 1585 inherited his uncle's position; he was not ordained as a priest until almost thirty years later.

The young poet was uncomfortable in his role as a churchman. There is a letter extant from the bishop of Córdova accusing Góngora of not fulfilling his ecclesiastical duties and of preferring bullfights to the chorus. Góngora was also accused of writing profane poetry. He replied sarcastically to these accusations, and a small fine was imposed on him. Thereafter, Góngora devoted himself to writing poetry, and his name became famous throughout Spain, especially because of his romances, which are included in many of the important collections of the time, such as the *Flores* of Pedro de Espinoza and the important *Romancero general* of 1600.

In 1613, with his *culteranos*, he became the central, if controversial, figure of Spanish poetry. The polemics and debates that his poems aroused, together with their success, moved him to abandon his native Córdova to settle in Madrid in 1617. His hopes of obtaining favors from the government proved futile, and this circumstance, combined with his passion for gambling and a luxurious lifestyle, soon consumed his limited capital. Sad, destitute, and frustrated, he returned to Córdova in 1627, where he died on May 23 of that year.

Analysis

Romances and *letrillas* constitute two important forms of popular Spanish poetry. The romance is customarily written in octosyllabic lines (although other metric forms are sometimes used). The rhyme is assonantic, or imperfect, meaning that after the tonic vowel, all other vowels are equal. This poetic mode has no stanzas, and only the even lines rhyme, usually with one assonance carried throughout the entire poem. The *letrillas* are generally written in octosyllabic lines and grouped in stanzas of either four, eight, or ten lines. The rhyme is consonantic, or perfect, meaning that all sounds after the tonic vowel are identical. The *letrilla* usually has a refrain. Both the romances and the *letrillas* were originally intended to be sung.

It would be a mistake to consider the romances and *letrillas* written by Luis de Góngora y Argote as "popular" or "easy" poems. His first dated poem (1580) is a romance; his last, dated 1626, is also a romance. This poetic form was basic to Góngora's work. Although the themes of the romances vary, they generally follow traditional Spanish subjects. Góngora wrote amatory, mythological, satirical, religious, and Moorish romances. Within the Moorish convention, some of his best romances correspond to the theme of the *cautivo*, the Christian prisoner of the Moors, who dreams of his homeland. It is important to remember that this theme is also present in many other authors. For example, having once been a *cautivo* in Africa, Miguel de Cervantes included this theme in a long fragment of *El ingenioso hidalgo don Quixote de la Mancha* (1605, 1615; *The History of the Valorous and Wittie Knight-Errant, Don Quixote of the Mancha*, 1612-1620; better known as *Don Quixote de la Mancha*). Hence, the situation described in the romances of captives is genuine. Góngora was able to re-create lyrically a popular feeling in a superior manner.

The *letrillas* are also numerous and cover a wide range of subjects. Many of them are satirical and were intended to evoke laughter. It is interesting to note, though, that some of Góngora's most accomplished creations in this genre are not sarcastic but deal with religious themes. Indeed, his *letrillas* devoted to the Yuletide are among his best poems.

"The Fable of Pyramus and Thisbe"

It is impossible to consider in detail the romances and *letrillas*. They total 215 compositions, with approximately forty-four additional ones attributed to the poet. One of the romances, however, deserves special attention: "Fábula de Píramo y Tisbe" ("The Fable of Pyramus and Thisbe"). The perfect conjunction of the two "styles" that critics noted in Góngora's poetry, it is a *culterano* poem in a popular form. Góngora took a mythological theme and inverted the topos into a cruel parody. This parody is also stylistic: Góngora took his own literary devices and converted them into a new form. "The Fable of Pyramus and Thisbe" is not "easy"; presupposing an extensive knowledge of mythology and Spanish Renaissance culture, the poem is a net of references, imagery, and ideas that captures in its lines the epitome of the Spanish Baroque. A work of 508 lines, it is a virtual encyclopedia of literary figures. The most prominent are metaphors of the first, second, and third degrees, metonymies, catachreses, and hyperboles. A typical example of the style of the poem is found in the description of Thisbe. Góngora follows all the Renaissance topoi of beauty: Her face, for example, is a crystal vase containing carnations and jasmines. The inversion of the topos follows immediately. Because her face is made of flowers, her nose should also be floral, but it is described as an *almendruco*, a small almond. The ending -*uco* in Spanish (the base word is *almendra*) carries a pejorative connotation. This example shows the vision that Góngora is trying to capture in the text: It is a contrasting world of light and shadows, of beauty and ugliness—a Baroque worldview.

Occasional sonnets

Góngora was the author of at least 166 sonnets; some fifty more are attributed to him. The sonnets, like the romances, span his entire literary life. It is important to remember that the sonnet form had not only a literary function in the Golden Age, but also a social one. Poets were expected to write for various special occasions, and most of the time, the sonnet was the chosen form; it was short and had a flavor of enlightenment and culture. Thus, Góngora often was compelled to write occasional sonnets. Many such poems were written for special festivities, such as births, weddings, and hunting parties, or were merely encomiastic compositions to celebrate sayings or actions of the nobility. Góngora managed to overcome the limitations imposed on him, composing masterpieces based on these stock themes. Not all his sonnets, however, were occasioned thus; many were born in the soul of the poet and offer lyrical expressions of his persona.

It is impossible to consider the sonnets individually, but the "Inscripción para la tumba de El Greco" ("Epitaph for the Tomb of El Greco") deserves mention. Critics have noted that there is a relation between Góngora's poetry and El Greco's art. Both responded to a distorted vision of the world that was typical of the Baroque period. Góngora's admiration for El Greco's painting is easy to understand in the light of his poetry. Both artists were successful in creating a new code and a new mode of expression.

Góngora frequently employed traditional Renaissance topoi. The carpe diem and *brevitas vitae* themes combine in a sonnet written in 1582 to create a typically Baroque worldview. The poet describes a beautiful woman in the spring of her life; the Baroque spirit emerges in the last stanza, when the poet asserts that the gold of her hair will become silver, that the freshness of her face will become a crushed violet, that beauty, youth, and the lady herself will become "earth, dust, smoke, shadow, nothingness."

FABLE OF POLYPHEMUS AND GALATEA

Fable of Polyphemus and Galatea is Góngora's masterpiece. The text is a re-creation of Ovid's fable of Acis and Galathea. Góngora transforms the 159 Latin hexameters into sixty octaves. The poem also contains an introduction of three octaves, for a total of sixty-three octaves (504 hendecasyllabic lines). The argument of the poem is basically the same as Ovid's: The horrible Polyphemus loves Galathea, a beautiful nymph, but she falls in love with the young and beautiful Acis. In a jealous rage, the Cyclops grabs a gigantic rock and crushes Acis under it. The young lover is changed into a river by Galathea's mother, Doris.

In *Fable of Polyphemus and Galatea*, Góngora created a completely new poetic language. The border between everyday and lyrical language had never before been so clearly delineated. Góngora found his tools in the rhetorical devices of the classical Roman and Greek writers, learning from them not only a new vocabulary but also a new syntax. His use of this new grammar offered the best means of giving the language a new "sound": He intended that only a highly educated and select few would be able to understand his work. The main syntactical innovation introduced by Góngora was the hyperbaton. This grammatical inversion had indeed been used before in Spanish but never taken to the extremes to which Góngora carried it. He consistently separated the noun from its adjective and the subject from its object; furthermore, as in Latin, he placed the verb at the end of the sentence. In addition to these grammatical anomalies, Góngora introduced hundreds of neologisms. A further complication was his use of words whose meaning had evolved through the centuries. Góngora used these words in their original metaphorical sense. He was able to develop a complete code of metaphors, based on mythology and private associations. Once the code was established, he constructed his images accordingly, creating such difficult texts that even the learned Spanish speaker needed a prose "translation" of the poem. Hence, the first critics and commentators did exactly that, and in the twentieth century, Alonso's work in reviving Góngora began with a prose version of the most complicated poems.

In spite of its difficulties, *Fable of Polyphemus and Galatea* is not unintelligible. Góngora's art is completely organized and follows a rigorous pattern. Even the most difficult passages respond to a logic that takes notice of the most minute details. The obvious conclusion is that even in his "darkest" moments, Góngora is still the Prince of Light. *Fable of Polyphemus and Galatea* shines with the magical light of inner order and beauty. It reveals a Renaissance attitude hidden behind a Baroque mask.

The Solitudes

Góngora originally conceived *The Solitudes* as four books, each being a long eclogue. Unfortunately, he completed only the first and a part of the second. Undoubtedly, the unfavorable reception of *Fable of Polyphemus and Galatea* and the *Soledad primera* (*First Solitude*) prompted his abandonment of the project. In the words of A. A. Parker, Góngora was too proud to cast any more pearls before swine. Although the poem is incomplete, Góngora left a substantial fragment. The *First Solitude* is composed of 1,091 lines, and the unfinished *Soledad segunda* (*Second Solitude*) of 979 lines. The external form of *The Solitudes* is the *silva*, a stanza combining seven- and eleven-syllable lines in a free pattern. After the rigid mode in which he composed *Fable of Polyphemus and Galatea*, Góngora probably thought that he could express himself more eloquently in a flexible stanza. Indeed, *The Solitudes* carry the difficulties of *Fable of Polyphemus and Galatea* to an even higher degree.

The argument of the poem is almost nonexistent. A young man survives a shipwreck and reaches the shore, where he is greeted by shepherds. The next morning, he sets out on a walk and meets a group of people celebrating a rural wedding. The rest of the poem describes the festivities that follow the ceremony. At sunset, the newly married couple goes off to enjoy their first night together. The *Second Solitude* begins the next morning, when the young pilgrim meets a group of fishermen on the banks of a river. He accompanies them to a nearby island, and again there is a description of the rest of the day. Throughout the following morning, the group observes a hunting scene. Góngora was probably near the completion of the *Second Solitude* when he stopped abruptly. It has been suggested that Góngora planned to write "solitudes" of the country, of the shore, of the woods, and of the desert. The first two books follow a similar pattern: the journey; the arrival, followed by a soliloquy, festivities, a chorus; and, finally, evening games in the *First Solitude* and hunting in the *Second Solitude*.

It is clear that the nature of the poem is not heroic but lyrical. What Góngora accomplished was to create a world that was both parallel to and removed from nature. In many ways, this new world was better than nature itself. At first, *The Solitudes* may appear to be superficial, without a "message" and preoccupied with only the technical aspects of poetry. However, after the difficulties of the text are overcome, one sees that the poem offers an optimistic view of the world: Things are intrinsically beautiful. The world is infused with light. Nature is perceived in an instant and is captured in its purest form. Góngora, the magician of sounds and colors, became a daemon with the power to create a new world.

Other major works

PLAYS: *Las firmezas de Isabela*, pr. 1610; *El doctor Carlino*, pr. 1613.

BIBLIOGRAPHY

Chemris, Crystal Anne. *Góngora's "Soledades" and the Problem of Modernity*. Woodbridge, Suffolk, England: Tamesis, 2008. Chemris argues that *The Solitudes* represent a reaction to the transition in worldviews from the Baroque era to the Renaissance.

Collins, Marsha S. *"The Soledades," Góngora's Masque of the Imagination*. Columbia: University of Missouri Press, 2002. Collins provides extensive analysis of *The Solitudes*, with the intent of making the poetry understandable to the modern reader by creating a conceptual map with which to navigate the poetry.

De Groot, Jack. *Intertextuality Through Obscurity: The Poetry of Federico García Lorca and Luis de Góngora*. New Orleans: University Press of the South, 2002. Compares and contrasts the poetry of Góngora and Federico García Lorca, looking at how Góngora influenced the later poet.

Foster, David William, and Virginia Ramos Foster. *Luis de Góngora*. New York: Twayne, 1973. A standard biography. Contains a good annotated bibliography, including entries for several studies in English.

Góngora y Argote, Luis de. *Selected Poems of Luis de Góngora*. Translated by John Dent-Young. Chicago: University of Chicago Press, 2007. This bilingual translation of Góngora's shorter poems, the *First Solitude*, *The Fable of Polyphemus and Galatea*, and "The Fable of Pyramus and Thisbe," contains commentaries on the poems that provide a wealth of information.

McCaw, R. John. *Transforming Text: A Study of Luis de Góngora's "Soledades."* Potomac, Md.: Scripta Humanistica, 2000. An extensive critical interpretation of *The Solitudes*. Includes bibliographical references.

Wagschal, Steven. *The Literature of Jealousy in the Age of Cervantes*. Columbia: University of Missouri Press, 2006. Examines the theme of jealousy in early modern Spanish literature. The two chapters on Góngora look at the beautiful and sublime as well as myth and the fractured "I."

Woods, Michael. *Gracián Meets Góngora: The Theory and Practice of Wit*. Warminster, England: Aris & Phillips, 1995. A critical study of the use of humor in the works of Góngora and Baltasar Gracián y Morales. Includes bibliographical references and indexes.

Francisco J. Cevallos

JORGE GUILLÉN

Born: Valladolid, Spain; January 18, 1893
Died: Málaga, Spain; February 6, 1984

PRINCIPAL POETRY

Cántico: Fe de vida, 1928 (revised 1936, 1945, 1950; *Canticle*, 1997)
Maremágnum, 1957 (translated in *Clamor*, 1997)
Clamor: Tiempo de historia, 1957-1963 (3 volumes; includes *Maremágnum*, *Que van a dar en el mar*, *A la altura de las circunstancias*; *Clamor*, 1997)
Que van a dar en el mar, 1960 (translated in *Clamor*, 1997)
A la altura de las circunstancias, 1963 (translated in *Clamor*, 1997)
Cántico: A Selection, 1965
Homenaje, 1967 (*Homage*, 1997)
Affirmation: A Bilingual Anthology, 1968
Aire nuestro, 1968 (includes *Cántico*, *Clamor*, and *Homenaje*; *Our Air*, 1997)
Y otros poemas, 1973
Final, 1981
Horses in the Air, and Other Poems, 1999

OTHER LITERARY FORMS

Jorge Guillén (gee-YAYN) is a literary theorist and translator as well as a poet. His critical work *Language and Poetry* (1961) was first published in English translation, appearing in Spanish as *Lengua y poesía* the following year. Guillén edited *El cantar de los cantares* (1561; *The Song of Songs*, 1936), a translation of the Song of Solomon by Luis de León, and the Aguilar edition of the works of Federico García Lorca; in addition, he published volumes of correspondence and essays on García Lorca and Gabriel Miró.

Guillén's translations of poetry into Spanish are included in *Homage* under the heading "Variaciones"; among them are three of William Shakespeare's sonnets; "Torment," by the Portuguese Antero Tarquínio de Quental; poems by Arthur Rimbaud; "The Lake Isle of Innisfree," by William Butler Yeats; several poems by Paul Valéry; and others by Jules Supervielle, Saint-John Perse, Archibald MacLeish, and Eugenio Montale.

Huerto de Melibea (pb. 1954; the orchard of Melibea) is a short poetic drama re-creating the Fernando de Rojas tragedy *Comedia de Calisto y Melibea* (1499; commonly known as *La Celestina*; *Celestina*, 1631); it was later incorporated into *Clamor* in *Our Air*.

Achievements

The most classical and intellectual member of the Generation of '27, Jorge Guillén is widely regarded as one of the greatest Spanish poets. The clean beauty of his lyrics has been recognized by contemporaries as diverse as García Lorca and Jorge Luis Borges. He has been called the Spanish equivalent of T. S. Eliot and Valéry. His greatness as a poet stems from the high quality of his verse rather than from the influence he has exerted.

Guillén's "Salvación de la primavera" ("Salvation of Spring") has been called one of the greatest love poems of the Spanish language. In the wake of a century of Spanish poetry that lacked interest in pantheism, Guillén and his friend Pedro Salinas are credited with creating a mode of poetry whereby hidden reality is disclosed by the contemplation of simple things.

Guillén was awarded the Etna-Taormina International Poetry Prize in 1961, and he received numerous other awards as well, including the Award of Merit Medal from the American Academy of Arts and Letters (1955), the Bennett Literary Prize (New York, 1976), the Miguel de Cervantes Prize (Alcaláde Henares, Spain, 1977), and several Italian literary prizes.

Biography

Jorge Guillén was the oldest of four children born to Julio Guillén Sáenz and Esperanza Alvarez Guerra, both of Valladolid. In "Patio de San Gregorio," Guillén recalls his childhood as both happy and difficult, filled with duties, studies, and games. He attended high school in Valladolid and at the Maison Perreyve of the French Fathers of the Oratory in Fribourg, Switzerland. He pursued his university studies at Madrid and Granada, and he graduated in 1913. Thereafter, he secured a teaching position at the Sorbonne, and he worked as a correspondent for the newspaper *La libertad* from 1917 to 1923. He received his doctorate from the University of Madrid in 1924, writing his dissertation on the "Fábula de Polifemo y Galatea" (1627; *Fable of Polyphemus and Galatea*, 1961) of Luis de Góngora y Argote.

In 1921, while in Paris, Guillén married Germaine Cohen, who bore him two children: Teresa in 1922 and Claudio in 1924. Germaine died in 1947, and in 1961, while in Bogotá, Colombia, Guillén married Irene Mochi Sismondi. Guillén reconciles his two marriages in the poem "Pasiones" ("Passions"), where he represents Germaine as France and Irene as Italy and proceeds to vow undying love for both countries, citing a vigorous confrontation with the future as the most effective way of keeping the past alive. The "In memoriam" section of *Clamor*, which became the central section of *Our Air*, is devoted to his love for Germaine, and the "El centro" ("The Center") section of *Homage* is devoted to his love for Irene.

Guillén assumed his first professorial chair at the University of Murcia in 1926. Three years later, he was offered a lectureship at Oxford, and from 1931 to 1938, he was a professor at the University of Seville. After being imprisoned in Pamplona for political reasons in 1938, he fled Spain, crossing the bridge between Irún and Hendaye on foot. He went to the United States, taught at Middlebury College in Vermont for one year, spent the following year at McGill University in Montreal, and then moved to Massachusetts, where he taught at Wellesley College until 1957. He taught one final year as Charles Norton Eliot Professor at Harvard, retiring in 1958.

In 1982, Guillén's native city of Valladolid staged a weeklong tribute to him; scholars and fellow poets from Spain and from abroad came to honor the venerable poet, who had published his most recent volume, *Final*, at the age of eighty-eight. On February 6, 1984, Guillén died of pneumonia in Málaga, Spain.

ANALYSIS

Jorge Guillén was stigmatized early in his career as a cold, intellectual poet, and although that is almost the opposite of the truth, it took a long time for his reputation to recover. He strove after the ideal of *poesía pura* (pure poetry) and sought to distill from experience its barest essence, weeding from his verse the incidental and the ornamental.

Guillén's concern for *poesía pura* was obviously influenced by Juan Ramón Jiménez and Valéry, while his pantheistic view of nature reveals the influence of José Ortega y Gasset. There was no such view of nature among the poets of nineteenth century Spain, and the radiance and intensity in Guillén's work are reminiscent of the Neoplatonic tradition of the sixteenth century poet Luis de León. In technique, Guillén was influenced by Francisco Gómez de Quevedo y Villegas (especially in the trenchant wit of his epigrams, which Guillén called *tréboles*) and Juan Meléndez Valdés, the great Spanish lyricist of the eighteenth century. In Guillén's classical Spanish rhythms and packed metaphors, he reveals the influence of Góngora, and there are also traces in his work of the creationism and Surrealism of the Chilean Vicente Huidobro.

Fond of assonance and short lines, Guillén uses a wide variety of meters. Often he uses the *décima* (with stanzas of ten octosyllabic lines) to express in simple form his ecstasy before the miraculous panorama of nature in a balance of rhythm, thought, and feeling. Contrary to the Spanish practice, he capitalizes the first word of each line of his poetry, and many of his poems have a circular structure, harking back in the last line to a keyword in the first.

Nouns that stress essence predominate in Guillén's poems, and his lexicon is basic and relatively spare. As fond as he is of onomatopoeia, he uses nearly as many nouns that are expressive of sound (such as *baraúnda, batahola, guirigay, algarabía*) as he does verbs. In "Alamos con río" ("Poplars with River"), for example, *arrullar* (to coo) appears as "Poplars that are almost music/ Coo to him who is lucky enough to hear." In addition, Guillén is fond of elliptical sentences and exclamations, colloquial expletives (such as *zas* and *uf*), and rhetorical questions. Although his poetry is not easy reading, his vocabulary is not difficult.

Guillén was well grounded in Spanish and world literature; quotations of and allusions to all periods abound in his work. His pieces are often headed by untranslated epigraphs in English, German, French, Italian, or Portuguese. He also makes moderate use of classical allusions, although often without encumbering the poetry with specific names.

CANTICLE

Many years of Guillén's poetic career were devoted to refining his *Canticle*, first published in 1928. The original collection included a mere 75 poems; in 1936, the poet added 50 more. The edition of 1945 contains 270 poems, and the 1950 volume contains 332.

First and foremost in *Canticle*, which, strictly speaking, is a "canticle" or "hymn of praise," Guillén wishes to communicate his ecstasy at the very existence of the created world. In the short poem "Beato sillón" ("Blessed Armchair"), for example, it is the armchair that gratefully puts him in touch with the physical universe and that allows him to transcend it ("The eyes do not see,/ They know"). He does not need magic to attain these heights, for he is fortunate enough to be able to savor the incidental properties of a world that, for him, is "well-made."

In *Canticle*, Guillén celebrates the perfection of the universe, ever grateful for its never-ending miracles. In a ten-line poem titled "Perfección" ("Perfection"), the poet submits to the beauty of one sunny day at noontime. He senses that the attributes of nature (the dense blue of the firmament "over-arching the day" and the sun at its zenith) reveal a superior order, which he perceives in architectural terms ("All is curving dome"). The sun reigns over the firmament, and its counterpart on Earth is the rose, humankind's perennial symbol of divine beauty. This moment so affects the poet that he feels time stop in a vision of the completeness of the planet. A corollary to this attitude is that death, as part of that natural order, is not to be feared, for without death, the perfect order of the universe would be impossible.

CLAMOR

After the overwhelming optimism of *Canticle*, it comes as somewhat of a relief, as G. G. Brown notes, to see that the poet is capable of recognizing some of the more negative features of life in his next volume, *Clamor* (in Spanish, the word *clamor* has more the connotation of "plaint" or "cry" than it does in English). Here, Guillén undertakes to describe the baseness of a Satanized world, even alluding to the horrors of the Spanish Civil War, a subject previously avoided in his work. As the poet grew older, he found it more difficult to savor nature in self-absorbed tranquillity. Guillén himself, however, insisted that *Clamor* is not a negation of *Cántico*, but rather a further perceptual step.

In *Clamor*, there are such titles as "Dolor tras dolor" ("Pain After Pain"), "Zozobra" ("Anguish"), and "El asesino del planeta" ("The Murderer of the Planet"); the vehement political statement of "Potencia de Pérez" ("Power of Pérez"); and references to Avernus, pollution, the vulgarity of television and pornography, nuclear holocaust, and the biblical Cain, the first murderer. (In a much later poem, Guillén uses the neologism *cainita* to describe the agony of his struggle in Spain before he chose to become an exile). A unique feature of *Clamor* is Guillén's insertion among the poems of his *tréboles* (literally "shamrocks" or "clover"), three-line or four-line statements that variously resemble epigrams, haiku, and other brief forms (for example, "Yours is the dawn, Jesus/ Watch how the sun shines/ In an orange-juice sky").

HOMAGE

In *Homage*, there is somewhat of a reconciliation between the rapture of *Cántico* and the bitterness of *Clamor*, as the poet seeks consolation from art, which allows some of his earlier optimism to resurface. In the section "Al Margen" ("Marginal Notes"), Guillén documents his reactions to many of the world's great thinkers and writers, from Sappho to César Vallejo. Guillén expresses his appreciation of Aristophanes for making him laugh ("While I laugh, I do not die"), of the converted Spanish Rabbi Sem Tob for his wisdom, of the erudition of Alfonso Reyes, and of the Italian Communist Antonio Gramsci ("From the prison there flashes before the astounded/ Like a revelation, that incredible/ capacity for injustice that is man's"). There are also some less charitable observations (concerning Arthur Schopenhauer, for example). At the end of this section, under the heading "Al margen de un Cántico" ("Marginal Notes on a Cántico"), Guillén includes five poems of commentary glossing his own earlier poems, thereby reserving a place for himself in his own literary history.

This section is followed by the love poems of "The Center," written to Guillén's second wife, followed in turn by the section "Atenciones" ("Attentions"), which consists of verse portraits of writers ranging from Juan Ruíz to Rubén Darío. "Attentions" includes a five-poem cycle that honors the memory of José Moreno Villa, Salinas, García Lorca, Emilio Prados, and Manuel Altolaguirre. The final section of *Homage* includes Guillén's translations of an impressive number of poems from world literature, as well as sundry poems of his own.

LOVE AND LOVERS

It comes as no surprise that a poet who is keenly aware of the miraculous should frequently concentrate on the nature of love. For Guillén, the love between man and woman suggests the larger relationship between humans and the cosmos and allows one to become greater than one is, to transcend the confines of time and space, of history and geography. In addition, love can give the assurance that death itself has been transcended, synchronizing the lovers with the natural cycle of the world. Moreover, the lover can be the salvation of the beloved by protecting that person from "phantoms" that might keep the beloved from communicating with his or her own inner vitality.

For Guillén, the body of a woman is the epitome of perfect creation. In "Desnudo" ("Nude"), for example, the poet observes that the female body needs no embellishment, no backdrop to improve its perfection, for that perfection consists not in its "promise" but in its "absolute presence." Another example of a sensuous achievement is the epithalamium "Amor dormido" ("Love Asleep"). The poet and his beloved are together in bed, bathed by moonlight. He contemplates her as she sleeps. Without waking up, she embraces him, and the poet feels himself transfigured, drawn into the realm of her dream.

WOMEN

Guillén has a special tenderness for the company of women, and his students at Wellesley became the subjects of a number of affectionate poems such as "Muchachas" ("Girls"), "Poesía eres tú" ("You Are Poetry"), "Nadadoras" ("Swimmers"), and "Melenas" ("Hair"). He is emphatic about the need for a man to become a man in the total sense, through the welcome intercession of a woman, and in a short poem, "El caballero" ("The Gentleman"), Guillén writes contemptuously of the typical Spanish café scene ("All men, terrible world of men/ Life that way could not be uglier"). Here, he employs a humorous neologism, *machedumbre* (composed of *macho*, meaning "male," and *muchedumbre*, meaning "crowd") to convey precisely how ridiculous and unthinkable such a world without women would be for him. The strong convictions that Guillén holds on this subject lead him to pontificate, in a later poem, "Sucesos de jardín" ("Garden Happenings"), that "He who never embraces [the other sex] is ignorant of everything."

Despite the foregoing quotation, Guillén is generally successful in avoiding clichés and seldom indulges in arrant nostalgia. In "Su persona" ("Her Person"), for example, the poet chides himself for attempting to feast on the memory of an old love, a figment of mist not anchored concretely in his current physical reality. He refuses to allow "phantoms" to convert him into a phantom, and love as a memory is condemned as a "fictitious delight." According to Guillén, one can relive and enjoy the past most profitably by continuing to savor new experiences rather than by wallowing in memories.

HUMOR AND RELIGION

Humor and self-deprecation are not alien to Guillén. In "Perfección de la tarde" ("Afternoon Perfection"), for example, the poet depicts a garden setting in lofty imagery, complete with alliteration and ecstatic utterances. In the midst of this garden idyll, however, a robin's dropping lands smack on the poet's bald pate, and the poet stands humbled in his pomposity.

Guillén himself has characterized *Canticle* as a "dialogue between man and the world," wherein "man affirms himself in affirming creation," and there is a noticeable absence of traditionally religious subject matter in this volume. In *Clamor*, there is clearly a greater emphasis on the message of Christianity, as in "Epifanía" ("Epiphany")—in whose manger scene the helpless infant "says in silence: I am not a king,/ I am the way, the truth and life"—and in "Viernes santo" ("Good Friday"): "A centurion already understands./ The three Marys weep. Sacred Man./ The Cross." A poem in *Homage*, "La gran aventura" ("The Sublime Adventure"), may provide a more balanced view of Guillén's religious stance. In this poem, he speculates whether the creation of humans by God or the creation of God by humans is the worthier marvel, concluding that in either case, there is no escape from the miracle of creation—that "the earth is a sublime adventure."

Guillén's achievement as a poet stems from his rare ability to seize a fragment of time and transform it into a single, simple jewel of articulation. When his lapidarian stance became obsessive and threatened to dehumanize his poetry, he dared to change and strove for means to make his work more human. Nor was he oblivious to evil and suffering; rather, he sought to be attentive to the "well-made world" while in the shadow of the other, "badly made world." The words that Guillén once wrote in a dedicatory passage to his readers were true of himself as well: He was eager to share life like a fountain and to realize that life more fully through the power of words.

OTHER MAJOR WORKS
PLAY: *Huerto de Melibea*, pb. 1954.
NONFICTION: *En torno a Gabriel Miró*, c. 1959; *Federico en persona: Semblanza y epistolario*, 1959; *Language and Poetry*, 1961 (*Lengua y poesía*, 1962).

BIBLIOGRAPHY
Havard, Robert. *Jorge Guillén, Cántico*. London: Tamesis, 1986. A critical study of Guillén's *Canticle*. Includes bibliographic references.
MacCurdy, G. Grant. *Jorge Guillén*. Boston: Twayne, 1982. An introductory biography and critical study of selected works by Guillén. Includes bibliographic references.
Machado, Antonio, Pablo Neruda, Federico García Lorca, and Jorge Guillén. *Cuatro Poetas: Poems of Antonio Machado, Pablo Neruda, Federico García Lorca and Jorge Guillén*. Translated and edited by Albert Rowe. Ilfracombe, Devon, England: Original Plus, 2004. This bilingual edition gathers some of the best-known poems by Guillén and three other poets. Contains a brief but detailed biography of each poet with some analysis.
McMullan, Terence. *The Crystal and the Snake: Aspects of French Influence on Guillén, Lorca and Cernuda*. Anstruther, Fife, Scotland: La Sirena, 2002. Contains two essays on Guillén, examining, in particular, the influence of Paul Valéry on his work.
Matthews, Elizabeth. *The Structured World of Jorge Guillén: A Study of Cántico and Clamor*. Liverpool, England: F. Cairns, 1985. Matthews analyzes Guillén's *Canticle* and *Clamor*. Includes bibliographic references.

Miller, Martha La Follette. "Self-Commentary in Jorge Guillén's *Aire Nuestro.*" *Hispania* 65, no. 1 (March, 1982): 20-27. A critical study of Guillén's works.

Sibbald, K. M., ed. *Guillén at McGill: Essays for a Centenary Celebration.* Ottawa, Ont.: Dovehouse, 1996. A collection of critical essays on Guillén's works. Text in English and Spanish. Includes bibliographical references.

Soufas, C. Christopher. *The Subject in Question: Early Contemporary Spanish Literature and Modernism.* Washington, D.C.: Catholic University of America Press, 2007. Contains a chapter analyzing the poetry of Guillén and Vicente Aleixandre and provides context for understanding Guillén's poetry.

Jack Shreve

JUAN RAMÓN JIMÉNEZ

Born: Moguer, Spain; December 23, 1881
Died: San Juan, Puerto Rico; May 29, 1958

PRINCIPAL POETRY
Almas de violeta, 1900
Ninfeas, 1900
Rimas, 1902
Arias tristes, 1903
Jardines lejanos, 1904
Pastorales, 1905
Elegías puras, 1908
La soledad sonora, 1908
Elegías intermedias, 1909
Elegías lamentables, 1910
Baladas de primavera, 1911
Pastorales, 1911
Laberinto, 1913
Estío, 1916
Diario de un poeta recién casado, 1917 (*Diary of a Newlywed Poet*, 2004)
Poesías escojidas, 1917
Sonetos espirituales, 1917 (*Spiritual Sonnets*, 1996)
Eternidades, 1918
Piedra y cielo, 1919 (*Sky and Rock*, 1989)
Segunda antolojía poética, 1922
Belleza, 1923
Poesía, 1923
Canción, 1936
La estación total, 1946
Romances de Coral Gables, 1948
Animal de fondo, 1949
Libros de Poesía, 1957
Tercera antolojía poética, 1957
Three Hundred Poems, 1905-1953, 1962
Dios deseado y deseante, 1964 (*God Desired and Desiring*, 1986)
Selected Poems, 1974
Le realidad invisible, 1983 (*Invisible Reality (1917-1920, 1924)*, 1986)
Naked Woman = La mujer desnuda, 2000
The Poet and the Sea, 2009

Juan Ramón Jiménez
(©The Nobel Foundation)

Other literary forms

Somewhat ironically perhaps, Juan Ramón Jiménez (hee-MAY-nuhs) is probably best known for his *Platero y yo* (1914, enlarged 1917; *Platero and I*, 1956), a collection of sketches in prose largely about his native Moguer. As always in Jiménez's noncritical work, however, his poetic vision and lyric expression are most apparent.

Achievements

In 1903, Juan Ramón Jiménez revealed himself as a prolific poet, and by 1916, no one could surpass Jiménez's position and influence as a poet in the Hispanic world. His twenty-two years spent in the United States, Puerto Rico, Cuba, and South America from 1936 to his death indicated no overall diminution of his creativity as a writer or of his authority as a critic. Appropriately, both for the excellence of his work and the half century devoted to it, he received the Nobel Prize in Literature in 1956, the first Spaniard to win it since 1920.

Biography

Juan Ramón Jiménez was born in Moguer, a typical town in Andalusia, Spain, steeped in tradition, colorful but slow-moving. His father, Victor, had come from north-central Spain to make his fortune in viniculture, acquiring extensive vineyards and numerous wineries in Moguer. Purificación, Jiménez's mother, was a native Andalusian and a very good mother, although perhaps too indulgent toward her youngest child, Juan Ramón. The future poet had a comfortable and happy early childhood in the family's new home on the Calle Nueva. Later, he learned to ride and, on horse or donkey, developed his love of nature in the beautiful countryside, which offered some compensation for the scant cultural stimulation of the town. After four or five years of elementary education in Moguer, Jiménez, then eleven years old, was sent with his brother to a Jesuit school near Cádiz, where he completed his secondary studies at age fifteen.

The *colegio* offered the best education available in the region, and Jiménez was a good, well-behaved student. Although somewhat homesick and averse to the school's regimentation, he was alert, imaginative, and intellectually curious, enjoying a variety of subjects, especially drawing and literature. His meditative mind and love of nature inclined him to religion and, despite later aversion to the Roman Catholic Church, among the six schoolbooks that he kept permanently were the Bible and Thomas à Kempis's *Imitatio Christi* (c. 1427; *The Imitation of Christ*, c. 1460-1530). Upon graduation, Jiménez went to Seville to study painting and to develop his passion for poetry. His father had wanted him to study law at the university, but he had no interest in prelaw studies and neglected them for the arts. The family's prosperity made it possible for Jiménez to indulge himself and choose between two financially unpromising careers. Some early paintings show that he might have become a fine painter, but the publication of his first poems evoked favorable criticism and turned him to poetry.

Fatigue and emotional strain in Seville put Jiménez under the care of doctors in Moguer, yet he continued to write feverishly, sending poems to magazines in Madrid and establishing contacts with poets there. Somewhat capricious and unreasonable, he shunned social events in Moguer and, despite two or more youthful love affairs, preferred to be alone. The poems sent by Jiménez to *Vida nueva* met with such favor that the magazine's editor, Francisco Villaespesa, and Rubén Darío, the Nicaraguan poet and leader of *Modernismo* who had been in Spain since 1899, invited the young poet to visit Madrid to help them reform Spanish poetry. Life in Madrid was exciting. Jiménez became close friends with Darío and other contemporary poets, and despite some excesses criticized by the academicians, his first collections were hailed as the work of a promising newcomer. His father's sudden fatal heart attack in 1900 caused Jiménez's nervous illness, which had recurred during the stimulating sojourn in Madrid, to worsen to the point that he required care in a sanatorium in Bordeaux.

In France, Jiménez read Charles Baudelaire and the Symbolist poets and continued to write, expressing his grief, sometimes in the excessively sentimental manner of the nineteenth century, sometimes in a more dignified, authentic style. Returning to Madrid rather than Moguer in 1901, the young poet continued his sheltered, privileged life in the Sanatorio del Rosario. Surrounded by tranquillity and beauty, Jiménez entertained friends and relatives more than ever before, and his retreat became a literary salon and social center. His work soon became known in the New World, and his popularity and influence grew with each volume. In 1903, Jiménez and a number of other young poets began to publish the literary journal *Helios*, the eleven issues of which exercised great influence—so much so that Miguel de Unamuno y Jugo, certainly not identified with *Modernismo*, was willing to be a contributor. While Darío gave Spanish poetry new subtlety, beauty, and music, Unamuno's influence deepened and intensified it. Later in 1903, Jiménez went to live with his physician and friend, Luís Simarra, with whom he remained for two years. With Simarra's encouragement and that of other scholars, Jiménez expanded his knowledge in several fields by reading and attending lectures at the Institución Libre de Enseñanza. The liberal views at this institution further eroded Jiménez's already weakened traditional religious convictions.

Unlike most of his colleagues, Jiménez felt less comfortable in Madrid than in a more rural setting. In 1905, ill again and homesick, he returned to Moguer, where he remained for six years, not with his family but in a house at Fuentepiña owned by them. There he rested and wrote, avoiding society for the most part. In 1910, at the age of twenty-eight, Jiménez was elected to the Royal Spanish Academy, but he declined membership, not only then but also on two subsequent occasions under different political regimes. With his sisters' marriages and other changes, including financial ones, the family's situation declined. Although Jiménez preferred solitude and nature, there were periods of tedium and depression for him, especially as he continued to suffer sporadically from ill health. Occasional amorous interludes were followed by disenchantment, bitterness, and remorse. In 1912, it seemed time to return to Madrid, where, except for brief visits to Moguer, the poet remained until 1936.

In four years at the Residencia de Estudiantes, the heart of intellectual and literary activity in Madrid, in the company of celebrated thinkers and writers, Jiménez completed two volumes of poetry and his prose masterpiece, *Platero and I*. His experimentation in content and form continued, and he gave evidence of increasing maturity in every way. In 1912, too, Jiménez had met Zenobia Camprubí Aymar; they soon became engaged and were married in 1916. Zenobia, who was part American, was lovely—as had been other women in the poet's life—and intelligent, interested in the same things that interested Jiménez. Above all, Zenobia was lively, a quality that proved very helpful for the sober, moody Jiménez. After a trip to New York and his wedding, Jiménez published his *Diary of a Newlywed Poet*, a work marking his entrance to full maturity and long considered his best by the critics and author alike. He continued to grow in all respects, producing more significant poetry in the years from 1916 to 1923 than during any other period in his life, and might have become the "grand old man" of poetry had his temperament permitted.

Like so many other Spanish refugees from the Civil War, Jiménez headed for the United States in 1936, first visiting Washington, D.C., briefly as a cultural emissary of the Spanish Republic, then visiting Puerto Rico and Cuba for three years, finally settling for six years in Coral Gables, Florida, and later in Washington, D.C. His fame as a poet and critic was great, especially in Hispanic circles, and he lectured, read his poetry, and wrote numerous critical essays but produced no new poetic works for a time. Between 1942 and 1951, however, he published four major works and began a fifth that he was not to complete. Despite numerous invitations, Jiménez and his wife rarely left the United States. In 1956, Jiménez won the Nobel Prize in Literature, two days before Zenobia's death from cancer. He died in 1958 and is buried in Moguer with his wife.

Analysis

The Spanish intellectuals and writers of the Generation of '98 saw the need to arouse the national conscience and envisioned a vigorous, creative Spain in every aspect of life. The presence of Darío in Madrid had drawn many to the city and to *Modernismo*, the literary movement of which he was the chief exponent. Both the French Symbolists, who had largely inspired *Modernismo*, and Darío himself strongly influenced Juan Ramón Jiménez's poetry for more than a decade. In 1903, Jiménez published a collection of lyric poems, *Arias tristes*, which revealed that he had abandoned the excessive sentimentality and random experimentation and imitation of his earlier collections for a more mature position based on firmer understanding of his talents.

Arias tristes

Arias tristes is divided into three "movements," each prefaced by the score of a *Lied* by Franz Schubert and dedicated to a friend. In addition, the second part has an epigraph taken from Paul Verlaine, and the third, one from Alfred de Musset. The second part is further prefaced by Jiménez's commentary on his own work, which is "monotonous, full of moonlight and sadness," and concludes with an evocation of Heinrich Heine and Gustavo Adolfo Bécquer as well as of Verlaine and Musset and an entreaty to all kindred spirits to weep for those who never weep. A vague, subdued sadness prevails here as in much Symbolist poetry. Avoiding novelty for the sake of novelty, Jiménez employs the verse of the romance exclusively and with a versatility that remains unmatched. Seemingly artless in its simplicity, the verse reveals great mastery in the use of enjambment to give it fluency and grace and in its diction, chosen for maximum musicality as well as meaning. Among the best poems in the collection are those that capture Jiménez's love of his native Andalusian landscape in delicate and original imagery.

Jardines lejanos and Pastorales

In part under the influence of Unamuno, who wrote for Jiménez's journal, *Helios*, but favored exploiting traditional Spanish inspiration, but more so under the influence of his doctor and close friend Simarro, who introduced him to the principles of liberal education of the Institución Libre de Enseñanza, the poet began to explore sources other than Symbolism and *Modernismo*, and in 1904 and 1905, respectively, produced two collections of verse, *Jardines lejanos* (distant gardens) and *Pastorales*. The former is full of musical allusions that convey Jiménez's emotional, often sad responses to music, and it has a new, conventional, and superficial eroticism that separates it from his earlier work. The second volume, like *Arias tristes* and *Jardines lejanos*, is prefaced with musical notations (from Christoph Gluck, Felix Mendelssohn-Bartholdy, and Robert Schumann), and its verse is chiefly that of the romance (usually four-line stanzas, odd lines unrhymed, even lines assonanced), but it is less introverted, less morbid, and less sorrowful than its predecessor. Jiménez's prolonged stay in the Guadarrama Mountains had completed his cure and brought him back to an appreciation of nature, albeit in solitude and mystery.

BALADAS DE PRIMAVERA

For Jiménez, the years from 1906 to 1912, spent in his native Moguer, represented both a physical and a spiritual renewal, as well as a return to *Modernismo*. In no less than nine books of poetry, he again emulated Darío in his experimentation with forms, fascination with the music of words, and joyous eroticism in nature. *Baladas de primavera* (ballads of spring) exemplifies this phase of Jiménez's development. In *Baladas de primavera*, he eschews the exotic figures and decor so typical of the Parnassians, Symbolists, and modernists; here, his sensuality is simpler, more tender, and closer to that of Musset, Verlaine, and Francis Jammes, experienced more personally than vicariously. Again, there is the inspiration from the heritage of popular Spanish poetry, evident both in form—as in the use of a rhythmic line as a musical refrain, conveying no particular meaning but with an appealing lilt—and in content, where ingenuous and simple expression belies profound thought or poignant emotion.

LA SOLEDAD SONORA

Jiménez's trilogy of elegies—*Elegías puras*, *Elegías intermedias*, and *Elegías lamentables*—marked a return to the Baudelairean Decadence of some earlier volumes. These poems have little of the spontaneity and musicality of the pastorals and ballads, largely because of the poet's efforts to adapt his material to the fourteen-syllable Alexandrine, usually in four-line stanzas with assonance in the even lines, not Jiménez's best poetic medium. The poet continued to modify and perfect the Alexandrine as well as other forms in four more volumes, *La soledad sonora* (the sonorous solitude) being the most representative. This collection articulates with particular clarity the poet's personal view of the world.

The epigraph of *La soledad sonora* is taken from Saint John of the Cross, reinforcing the link with the sixteenth century mystical poet suggested by the title of the collection.

The apparent paradox in the antithetical "sonorous solitude" disappears when the reader becomes aware that solitude here does not mean withdrawal from the world but rather intimate communion with it. Moreover, this work contains much more auditory imagery, along with the characteristic range of visual and other sensuous images, than found in earlier works, a change made possible for Jiménez by his solitude. The poet's normal tendency to Impressionism extends here to synesthesia, a common feature of *Modernismo* and one to which Jiménez's keen sensory perception easily adapted. The poet's skill in prolonging the perfect instant to render it infinite, occasionally disturbed by thoughts of the passage of time and death, is epitomized in his contemplation of the pine tree by his house at Fuentepiña. Jiménez's perceptions of the odor and sounds of the tree that best characterizes the Andalusian scene are transformed from sensations of the moment into a mystical experience in which he finds himself attuned to the eternal.

Spiritual Sonnets

Back in Madrid until his exile from Spain, Jiménez associated with many prominent artists and intellectuals, but by this time in his career, he was less open to stylistic influences. His *Spiritual Sonnets* are unique in his oeuvre in that they are composed almost exclusively of classic eleven-syllable sonnets with the traditional *abba* rhyme scheme. The discipline of these poems, which are characterized by a high degree of technical perfection, is matched by great emotional restraint. Here, Jiménez achieves a balance between thought and feeling. Despite the great mastery of form and the structural and verbal precision of these poems, genuine emotion prevents exclusive concern with intellectual subtlety, formal perfection, and verbal agility for its own sake. The introductory "Al soneto con mi alma" ("To the Sonnet with My Soul"), with its physical images translated in each case into ideal images and arranged in pairs, contains the essence of the volume.

Estío

Estío (summer) marks further Jiménez's maturation in terms of emotional and poetic authenticity; most notable in *Estío* are the variety, flexibility, and verbal economy of the verse. Jiménez's treatment of love in this volume, inspired by his love for his fiancé, is in marked contrast to the immature eroticism of earlier works.

Diary of a Newlywed Poet

Less than a year after his wedding, Jiménez published *Diary of a Newlywed Poet*, a combination of free verse and brief prose pieces generally recognized as a key work, his best, in the poet's own opinion. This collection is composed of six groups of poems, each with a title that identifies its theme. The principal themes of the volume are married love and the poet's metaphysical reflections on his ocean voyage to the United States and return voyage to Spain. This was not only his first contact with America but also his first experience of the sea. The expanse, monotony, and solitude of the gray ocean and gray sky immediately gripped him; he was most impressed by the endless, restless motion of the sea, like the beating of a huge, cosmic heart, giving the ocean a kind of immortality that he had never perceived before. Jiménez's awareness of the sea as an image of the entire physical world, changing constantly yet remaining fundamentally the same, gave *Diary of a Newlywed Poet* a metaphysical dimension previously lacking in his verse. The collection marked the mature poet's search for more universal values in poetry and life at a time when the vogue of *Modernismo* had passed. *Diary of a Newlywed Poet*, followed by *Eternidades* (eternities), *Sky and Rock*, *Poesía*, and *Belleza* (beauty), set a new direction for Spanish poetry and established decisively Jiménez's position and influence.

Exploiting Spanish heritage

Like Unamuno and Antonio Machado, Jiménez continued to keep abreast of the latest movements in literature and the arts yet sought inspiration primarily in Spanish traditions. Although it cannot be said that, either by age or temperament, Jiménez had become the "grand old man" of Spanish poetry, he did not recommend novelty for novelty's sake to his fellows, and he began to find fault not only with imitations of foreign works but also with the innovations of the Spanish vanguard poets. (Indeed, he had grown somewhat crotchety and, except for his wife, more solitary than ever.) His own originality was no longer achieved in defiance of tradition, but rather in a harmonious blend of change with the traditional. The *romancero*, Saint John of the Cross, Luis de Góngora y Argote, and Bécquer exemplify the vital heritage that Jiménez and the greatest of his contemporaries would continue to exploit. In fact, the Generation of '27 indirectly took its name from Góngora, whose tricentenary was celebrated in that year and to the admiration of whose virtuosity Jiménez had contributed. The Mexican essayist Alfonso Reyes, Jiménez's longtime friend, compared him physically and spiritually to Góngora as well as to the tortured figures in many of El Greco's paintings.

Poetry from the New World

During the first part of Jiménez's life in the New World, spent in Puerto Rico and Cuba, the poet wrote many articles for newspapers and magazines published in every country of Latin America. For several years, however, he wrote no new poetry, publishing several volumes that were no more than anthologies or rearrangements of old materials, perhaps because he thought that his American readers would find them new. Finally, in Florida, his inspiration returned and, before a trip to Argentina and Uruguay in 1948, he produced *La estación total* (total season) and *Romances de Coral Gables*. Although the former also contains some of his earlier work, Jiménez added much that was a distillation of all his poetic experience and a reaffirmation of the values of *Diary of a Newlywed Poet*. *La estación total* not only acts as a summation, but also points the way to the joyous sense of fulfillment of *Animal de fondo* (animal of depth).

In the collections immediately preceding *La estación total*, Jiménez had expressed the fundamental tension in his being—both a source of inspiration and a soul-wearying affliction. Torn between light and shadow, truth and falsehood, hope and doubt, he would be whole only when these opposites were united, perhaps only in death. In contrast, "Desde dentro" ("From Inside"), the first poem of *La estación total*, is positive and confident; in this collection, Jiménez finally attains the transcendent reality that he had grasped imperfectly and fleetingly in earlier work. "Plenitude" might well be the title of the volume, which reveals the poet's awareness of plenitude in three dimensions: the "eternal," seen in nature; the "external," experienced through the senses; and the "inner reality," discovered intuitively. Communicating a sincere, intensely personal religious experience through language alone, these poems are inevitably marked by a certain obscurity and ambiguity, desirable if readers are to be permitted their own interpretations.

ANIMAL DE FONDO

Animal de fondo was to be the first part of *God Desired and Desiring*, a much larger work that Jiménez never completed. The twenty-nine poems of the collection were not intended to be read as individual pieces but rather as links in a continuous chain. A dynamic rhythm, strongly suggestive of the motion of the ship on which Jiménez sailed to South America, prevails throughout the sequence. Soothed by the gentle movement of the sea, the poet is as satisfied as a child rocked and comforted in his mother's arms, attaining at last the complete sense of fulfillment that he has sought since childhood and to which he has aspired throughout his long, arduous efforts as a poet. Contrary to the tradition of Spanish mysticism, which expresses the divine through the language of human love, Jiménez uses religious metaphors to deify his sensitivity to the beautiful, for poetic creation is also a religious experience, an intimate union, although not, as in the customary mystical sense, a union with God. The theme of "La transparencia Dios, la transparencia" ("Transparency, God, Transparency") is that of the whole collection, expressing the struggle between the poet and his personal god to achieve successful union in art and love, "as a fire with its air" in its ardor. There is some ambiguity in the poems that follow, as Jiménez attempts to distinguish his god from God, often in paradoxical and contradictory terms. Among the several attributes of his god, Jiménez discovers love, found in all the elements but not solely spiritual or divine. "En mi tercero mar" ("On My Third Sea") reveals his god to be one of human love also, that of the poet for his wife, as much physical as spiritual. The poet's "great knowledge" is his awareness of being complete when, as perceiver, he merges with that which is perceived. On the sea, his god is the "mirror" of himself, but in "La fruta de mi flor" ("The Fruit of My Flower"), the imagery becomes more abstract, and Jiménez's vision turns inward. The sensibility that has been like a halo about him through life now enters his being, and the flower of promise bears the fruit of fulfillment. Whether Jiménez's mysticism is orthodox or not, the joyous yet humble religious attitude, the flexible meter and other aspects of prosody, and the novel imagery of *Animal de fondo* often remind one of the *canciones del alma* (songs of the soul) of Saint John of the Cross.

It is neither as theologian nor as philosopher but as a great lyric poet that the author of *Animal de fondo* is remembered. Unfortunately, recurring depression prevented Jiménez from maintaining in his last poems the optimism of *Animal de fondo*. In more than fifty years of poetic production, however, Jiménez's aesthetic and spiritual vision remained clear and his creative ability vigorous. Constant renewal kept his work from becoming dated, although his roots were always deep in the Spanish traditions that sustained his entire poetic creation.

OTHER MAJOR WORKS

SHORT FICTION: *Historias y cuentos*, 1979 (*Stories of Life and Death*, 1985).

NONFICTION: *Platero y yo*, 1914, enlarged 1917 (*Platero and I*, 1956); *Españoles de tres mundos*, 1944; *Monumento de amor*, 1959; *El trabajo gustoso*, 1961; *La corriente infinita*, 1961.

MISCELLANEOUS: *Tiempo y espacio*, 1986 (*Time and Space: A Poetic Autobiography*, 1988).

BIBLIOGRAPHY

Fogelquist, Donald F. *Juan Ramón Jiménez*. Boston: Twayne, 1976. An introductory biography and critical analysis of Jiménez's major works. Includes a bibliography of the poet's works.

Jiménez, Juan Ramón. *The Complete Perfectionist: A Poetics of Work*. Edited and translated by Christopher Maurer. New York: Doubleday, 1997. Maurer, who has written widely on Spanish literature, has collected and categorized the thoughts and aphorisms recorded by Jiménez in his quest for perfection in life and his work. Maurer provides context for the maxims set down by Jiménez, allowing the reader to begin to know Jiménez as a person and a poet as well as a philosopher.

_____. *Time and Space: A Poetic Autobiography*. Translated by Antonio T. de Nicolás. New York: Paragon House, 1988. Nicolás provides some excellent translations and a detailed introduction to the prose work *Tiempo* and the prose and poetry of *Espacio*. His well-documented presentation is supported by analysis in a historical context.

Predmore, Michael P. Introduction to *Diary of a Newlywed Poet: A Bilingual Edition of "Diario de un poeta reciencasado,"* by Juan Ramón Jiménez. Translated by Hugh A. Harter. Selinsgrove, Pa.: Susquehanna University Press, 2004. The extensive, multipart introduction contains information about the life of the author as well as critical analysis that examines the nature of the work, its use of the prose poem and free verse, the European influence on the author, and its autobiographical nature.

Wilcox, John C. *Self and Image in Juan Ramón Jiménez*. Chicago: University of Illinois Press, 1987. Examines the evolution of the poetry from premodern origins through modernism and its endurance through the postmodern era. Focuses on the work as process and reader interpretations from various perspectives, including formalist, structuralist, and poststructuralist readings as well as other critical readings of the enigmatic poet's prolific corpus.

_____. "T. S. Eliot and Juan Ramón Jiménez: Some Ideological Affinities." In *T. S. Eliot and Hispanic Modernity, 1924-1993*, edited by K. M. Sibbald and Howard Young. Boulder, Colo.: Society of Spanish and Spanish-American Studies, 1994. A discussion of Jiménez's connections with literary movements in England and the United States.

Young, Howard T. *The Line in the Margin: Juan Ramón Jiménez and His Readings in Blake, Shelley, and Yeats*. Madison: University of Wisconsin Press, 1980. This analysis demonstrates the influences upon the poet's work by English poets William Blake, Percy Bysshe Shelley, and William Butler Yeats. Jiménez had translated their poetry, and the Spanish poet's admiration is evident in his own poetry as he departed from his Spanish and French models. This investigation yields interesting biographical data as well as critical readings and literary analyses. The poet's affinity for British literature was evident in his life and work.

Richard A. Mazzara

SAINT JOHN OF THE CROSS
Juan de Yepes y Álvarez

Born: Fontiveros, Spain; June 24, 1542
Died: Úbeda, Spain; December 14, 1591

PRINCIPAL POETRY
"Vivo sin vivir en mí," wr. 1573 ("I Live Yet Do Not Live in Me")
"Adónde te escondiste," wr. 1577 ("The Spiritual Canticle")
"En el principio moraba," wr. 1577 ("Ballad on the Gospel 'In the Beginning Was the Word'")
"En una noche oscura," wr. 1577 ("The Dark Night")
"Llama de amor viva," wr. 1577 ("The Living Flame of Love")
"Que bien sé yo la fonte," wr. 1577 ("Although by Night")
"Encima de las corrientes," wr. 1578 ("Ballad on the Psalm 'By the Waters of Babylon'")
"Entréme donde no supe," wr. c. 1584 ("Verses Written on an Ecstasy")
"Tras de un amoroso lance," wr. c. 1584 ("A Quarry of Love")
The Complete Works of St. John of the Cross, 1864, 1934, 1953
Poems, 1951

OTHER LITERARY FORMS

Saint John of the Cross wrote several prose works that use methodologies of Scholastic criticism to explicate themes in his poetry: *Cántico espiritual* (c. 1577-1586; *A Spiritual Canticle of the Soul*, 1864, 1909), *La subida del Monte Carmelo* (1578-1579; *The Ascent of Mount Carmel*, 1864, 1922), and *Llama de amor viva* (c. 1582; *Living Flame of Love*, 1864, 1912). Discussion of them in the text is parallel with that of the poems.

ACHIEVEMENTS

With Saint Teresa of Ávila, Saint John of the Cross carried out the reform of the Carmelite Order and defended the Descalced Carmelites' rights to self-determination within obedience. In addition to becoming rector of the Carmelite College at Alcaláde Henares and founder of the Descalced Carmelite College in Baeza, John was vicar of the El Calvario Convent in Andalusia and prior of Los Mártires in Granada and of the Descalced Carmelite Monastery in Segovia. Moreover, he participated in the foundation of at least eight Descalced Carmelite houses throughout Spain. John was beatified in 1675 by Pope Clement X, canonized in 1726 by Pope Benedict XIII, and declared Doctor of the Church in 1926 by Pope Pius XI.

In Spain, John is considered to be the most successful lyric poet of the sixteenth century because of his harmonious resolution of popular and medieval traditions with the new learning and literary forms of the Renaissance. Beyond Spain, perhaps because of his singular dedication to one ideal and the strength of his vision, his poetry continues to rank among the finest love poetry written in any language.

Biography

Saint John of the Cross was born Juan de Yepes y Álvarez in 1542 in the town of Fontiveros in the kingdom of Old Castile. His father, Gonzalo de Yepes, and his mother, Catalina Álvarez, had worked in that small village for thirteen years as silk weavers and merchants, aided by John's older brother, Francisco. Gonzalo de Yepes's great-grandfather had been a favorite of King Juan II; one uncle was an Inquisitor in Toledo; three others were canons; and one was the chaplain of the Mozarabic Chapel in Toledo.

Because of her lower social status, Catalina Álvarez was hated by her husband's family, so much so that on Gonzalo's death they refused to help her support his three children, forcing them to live in poverty. In 1548, they moved to Arévalo, where Francisco was apprenticed as a weaver and John, without success, attempted a variety of trades.

From Arévalo, the Yepes family moved to the town of Medina del Campo, famous since the Middle Ages for its annual three-month-long international trade fair. There, John learned his letters and learned to beg for his Jesuit school. His brother married, and his mother, Catalina, in spite of their difficulties, took in a foundling. In 1556, when Emperor Charles V stopped at Medina on his way to his retirement at the monastery at Yuste, John saw the hero of European spiritual unity. The great moment did not, however, contribute to John's learning a trade. In 1563, he was taken to the Hospital de la Concepción by Don Alonso Álvarez de Toledo, where he became a nurse, working in that profession until he was twenty-one years old.

In 1563, having rejected the offer to become the hospital's chief warder, John left it to profess in the Order of Mount Carmel. The young Spaniard followed the rule of the Order in perfect obedience, according to contemporary accounts, but he spent hours searching for the spirit of the primitive rule in *A Book of the Institutions of the First Monks* (reprinted in 1507). In this fourteenth century work, John discovered the tradition of the eremitical way, which leads through austerity and isolation to the experience of the Divine Presence. John received permission to follow the old rule when he made his final profession before Ángel de Salazar, who had recently allowed Teresa to found the Order of Descalced Carmelites in Ávila.

After professing in 1564, the young friar traveled to the University of Salamanca, to which the Spanish then referred as *Roma la chica* because of its large international student body and its superb reputation in theology. He spent the first three years at Salamanca as an *artista* and the fourth as a theologian studying, not with the famous

Francisco Vitoria, founder of international law, nor with Luis de León, who taught there between 1565 and 1573, but with the more traditional Father Guevara and Father Gallo, who taught Thomas Aquinas's *Summa theologiae* (c. 1265-1273; *Summa Theologica*, 1911-1921) and Aristotle's *Ethica Nicomachea* (n.d.; *Nicomachean Ethics*, 1797). The effect of this study appears in John's later writing. Rather than posing a threat to his mystic contemplation, Scholasticism served to keep his mystic effusions within the confines of reality, fostering a clarity of language and logical development, a lyricism of thought, and a psychology of common sense that made his work accessible to all readers.

The faculty during those years at Salamanca longed for intellectual emancipation, and many, such as Luis de León, were cautioned and often jailed for years by the Inquisition. The debate was between the Scholastics, who authorized only the Latin Vulgate, and the Renaissance-inspired Scripturalists, who wished to translate the Hebrew and Koine Greek into modern languages. Typically, John did not involve himself in this intellectual turmoil but continued to seek the solitary spirit of Mount Carmel. His zeal was so great that in 1566, those Carmelite students who were entrusted to his tutelage by the vicar general of the Order, Juan Bautista Rubeo, complained of John's rigor, self-discipline, and near-constant state of contemplation. John's course was not the outward one. Instead of finishing his university career, he left Salamanca in 1567 for Medina del Campo, where he said his first Mass at the Church of Saint Anne in the presence of his brother, the latter's family, and his mother, Catalina Álvarez.

Because it was permissible to do so among the Carmelites, John immediately decided to enter the Carthusian Order for a life of total silence, solitude, and contemplation. His decision was delayed, however, by his meeting Teresa, who had come to Medina del Campo, with Vicar General Rubeo's blessing, to establish a convent for Descalced Carmelite nuns. Teresa convinced John to follow the contemplative way within his own Order so that her nuns would have a confessor. Moreover, at the time of Teresa's visit, King Philip II wrote to Father Antonio Heredia, the prior of Saint Anne's, giving him permission to reform the Carmelite Order of Monks as well, telling him that a wealthy gentleman had donated a house in the hamlet of Duruelo for that very purpose.

In August, 1568, Teresa, three nuns, one Julián de Ávila, and John left Medina del Campo for the city of Valladolid and for Duruelo. Teresa taught John the old rule through example as she commanded his aid in establishing the Convent of El Río de los Olmos outside Valladolid. She then changed his name from Juan de San Matías to John of the Cross. She also persuaded him that recreation in the form of music, song, and dance were necessary (as well as taking long walks, which prevented the Carmelites from becoming surly) and sent him with one workman to prepare the house at Duruelo for the eventual arrival of Father Heredia from Saint Anne's.

During their five weeks of rigorous labor, John revived the mode of desert life of the original Carmelites, going barefoot, wearing serge vestments, fasting, praying, and doing penance. When Father Heredia arrived to take charge, John was careful to observe Vicar General Rubeo's dictates not to depart in principle from the Unmitigated Carmelite Order as already defined, so as to avoid antagonizing them. While Teresa's letters to Heredia reveal her concern regarding the severity of the brothers' penances and flagellations, John's mother, Catalina Álvarez, came to be their cook, his brother Francisco came to sweep their cells, and Ana Isquierda came to wash and mend their clothes.

From Duruelo, John went to establish religious houses in the towns of Mancera and Pastrana, and in 1570, he went to the University of Alcaláde Henares to found a college for the Order. At Alcalá, John tutored his charges in Thomist philosophy, heard their confessions and those of the nuns at the Imagen Convent, and directed the friars in their contemplative life.

In 1571, Teresa called John to be the confessor at the Convent of the Incarnation in Ávila. She relates that, during the months of December and January, she began to have access to the ineffable experience of *matrimonio* and that John was of immense help to her: "One cannot speak of God to Father John of the Cross because he at once goes into ecstasy and causes others to do the same," she writes. The practical-minded Teresa complained that John's desire to bring everyone to spiritual perfection was a source of constant annoyance. Moreover, testimony from his living companions, Father Germaine and Brother Franciso, claimed that John was tormented with frightful night apparitions and on one occasion was severely beaten by an enraged countryman—all of which he welcomed.

Suddenly, the reformed Order began to encounter difficulty on every level. In 1570, Philip II appointed visitors to examine the houses, an action that angered Vicar General Rubeo. He retaliated by appointing various defenders, who were sent to each of the provinces. Teresa left the Convent of the Incarnation and met Father Gracián, who persuaded her to disregard Vicar General Rubeo's orders not to establish houses in Andalusia simply because the vicar general felt that the vitality of southern Spain was incongruent with the contemplative way. With Gracián's assurance that Philip II would support her, Teresa, then sixty-three years old, went ahead and established houses in Seville, Peñuela, and Granada. Rubeo accordingly declared the Descalced Order disobedient and ordered the immediate evacuation of the Andalusian convents in 1575. Gracián and Teresa refused; he was excommunicated, and she was ordered by the Council of Trent to pick a convent where she would spend the remainder of her days. She refused and decided to spend another year in Seville.

Meanwhile, John was still serving as confessor at La Incarnación in Ávila, until Gracián called him and other Descalced Carmelites to Almodóvar in 1576. Father Gracián proposed that the reformed Order name its own definitors and provincials, in effect making themselves independent of the Unmitigated Carmelites under Father Rubeo. At this meeting, John wished, as usual, to avoid conflict. In fact, he opposed the election of officers from among the reformed Order, since the Calced brothers already fulfilled these duties, leaving the followers of the reformed Order to their meditations. John's voice went unheard, and Gracián succeeded.

Rubeo reacted by sending Father Jerónimo Tostado to visit the Spanish Descalced houses to discourage their expansion. Supposedly, had Teresa and Gracián taken their case to Rome, the pope could have settled their differences with Rubeo. Philip II, however, was eager to maintain the traditional Spanish monarchical sovereignty over the Church Militant and impeded Gracián and Teresa's move in that direction.

In 1577, Teresa attempted to return to La Incarnación in Ávila, but Tostado excommunicated all the nuns who voted for her reinstatement as prioress. He evicted them from the convent and denied them access to their confessors. He then tried to persuade John to abandon Teresa and reenter the unreformed Order, promising him a priorship. John refused.

While visiting Teresa, who was living in secrecy in Toledo, John was arrested by the secular arm of the Roman Catholic Church, beaten, and locked in isolation. When he was led out for interrogation, he succeeded in escaping back to his cell to destroy letters, only to be recaptured and imprisoned within the Carmelite monastery in a closet at water level on the River Tajo. There he remained from December, 1576, until his escape in August, 1577. Teresa repeatedly wrote Philip II regarding the situation, but her letters went unanswered. Rubeo and Tostado considered Teresa's work finished and John to be a rebel who had disobeyed by serving as confessor to the Convent of the Incarnation in Ávila without Rubeo's express permission.

While he was imprisoned, John composed, among others, his poems "The Spiritual Canticle" and "The Living Flame of Love," which, according to nineteenth century Spanish critic Menéndez y Pelayo in his *Historia de los heterodoxos españoles* (1887), "surpass all that has ever been written in Spanish." John was fed bread and water only three times a week on the floor of the refectory, after which he was beaten by each of the friars, who verbally insulted his kneeling form. Occasionally, so that he would not collapse from hunger, he was given rancid sardines.

After loosening the bolts of his cell door during his jailer's absences, John lowered himself down a rope made of bedclothes to the monastery garden. There, a stray dog showed him a route of escape. Believing that the Virgin Mary was lifting him, he succeeded in scaling two walls to reach the street. By hiding in doorways of various houses, he made his way in full daylight to the Carmelite Convent of San José, where he found refuge for several days until the nobleman Don Pedro González de Mendoza arranged for his recuperation at the Hospital of Santa Cruz. During John's stay with the nuns of San José, he spoke of his captors in glowing terms as his benefactors who had brought him to an understanding of grace, to which he referred as "the dark light." He recited to the nuns the poems he had composed while in captivity, and one of the nuns wrote them down.

Because Tostado's persecution of the Order had abated, John was soon appointed vicar of the El Calvario monastery in Andalusia. John customarily led the thirty monks into the mountains for evening meditations. According to tradition, they ate only salads made from wild herbs that were carefully chosen by an expert, the cook's mule. On feast days, they dined upon *migajas*, bread fried in oil. At El Calvario, John wrote *The Ascent of Mount Carmel*.

One year later, in 1579, John was ordered by Father Ángel de Salazar to take three friars to the university town of Baeza and set up a monastery in an old house; this was to become the College of Our Lady of Mount Carmel. The college quickly became an object of intense curiosity among the faculty at the university, who, believing that John enjoyed infused wisdom, respected his insight into the mysteries of the faith and attended his lectures on morals and religious questions. John, however, prudently sent his charges to the university to study theology.

In 1581, John and his companion, Brother Jerome, established a convent of four nuns in Granada. The following year, John was elected prior of the Carmelite monastery there, Los Mártires. The revolt of the Alpujarras, in which Moorish converts to Christianity had elected a king and rejected their new religion, had been suppressed by Philip II ten years prior to John's arrival. Consequently, many of the children born to apostate families now served as slaves or protected servants in the homes of wealthy Old Christian families. Moreover, during those years there lived in Granada a ninety-year-old woman remembered as La Mora de Ubeda, who had gained a reputation among contemporary Muslim theologians for mystic wisdom acquired through the *faqir* tradition. The young *moriscos* drawn to their fathers' faith were threatened with years of rowing in the king's galleys should they wear Moorish clothes; carry Moorish weapons; speak, read, or write Arabic; bathe too frequently; dance the zambra; or play Moorish instruments. John served as confessor to *moriscos* and Old Christians alike, and to those seduced by the splendors of the city crowned by the Alhambra and the Generalife, he taught that "we travel not in order to see but in order not to see."

In Granada, John wrote the books *A Spiritual Canticle of the Soul* and *Living Flame of Love* to distinguish the contemplative way to unity according to the Divine Will from both natural and Muslim mysticism, which often took the form of possession and madness. According to John, these states were outwardly nearly indistinguishable from the transports of the dark light of grace; they occurred, he said, not only among Christians drawn to the Illuminist movement but also among the young *moriscos*, on whom he was often called to perform exorcisms.

While John was still at Baeza, a wealthy young Genoese, Jesús María Doria, professed within the Descalced Order and quickly found favor with Teresa through Philip II's recommendation. Doria was to be John's nemesis. Teresa, well aware of the Italian's keen mind, sent him to her friend Gracián, who in turn sent him as their representative to Rome. In 1582, Doria returned to Spain with special papal privileges, determined to reorganize the Order of Descalced Carmelites according to the *machina* of the Italian houses. In order to do so, he succeeded in having himself elected vicar general of the Order and unsuccessfully tried to send his former superior and continual rival, Gracián, to Mexico. In 1588, through a general conference, he revamped the Order's governing structure. Meanwhile, John, while founding monasteries and convents in Córdoba, Segovia, and Málaga, sought to mediate between Doria's missionary zeal to send Carmelites throughout all Christendom and beyond and Gracián's equal determination to keep the Order small and confined to Spanish soil. At a general meeting in Almodóvar, John actually spoke out against the hunger for power he saw invading the Order in the guise of worthy projects—but to no avail.

In 1588, John was appointed prior to the convent in Segovia, which became the seat of government of the Order during Doria's frequent trips abroad. Philip II learned of John's able administration and commended him for it. John's companions, however, attested that he scourged himself regularly, was sickly, wore sparto-grass undergarments and chains that drew blood, fasted almost continuously, and refused to wear anything but the heaviest clothing the year round. He slept only three hours each night and still heard confessions and ministered to the sick while trying to reconcile Gracián and Doria. His inner life was such that on occasion he was incapable of carrying out the simplest task, so frequent and overwhelming were his raptures. The last time he saw his brother Francisco, whom he claimed to have loved more than anyone else, John told him of a vision in which Christ asked him his desire. To Christ, John replied, "Suffering to be borne for Your sake and to be despised and regarded as worthless." His prayer was to be answered.

In 1589, the nuns of the Order, convinced that Doria was determined to abolish the reforms initiated by Teresa, petitioned Gracián and John to be separated from the Brothers over whom Doria ruled. Doria learned of the conspiracy from Luis de León and, suspecting that both Gracián and John were supporting the feminine rebellion against him, denounced the two to Philip II, who intervened directly with an order that the nuns remain.

At the next chapter meeting, John was denied any post whatsoever. First the council accepted and then rejected his offer to lead twelve Carmelites to Mexico. He and Gracián were to learn the extent of Doria's anger. In Seville during the chapter meetings, there was such fear of Doria that no one dared to oppose him. John bravely spoke out, accusing Doria of destroying charity, free discussion, and the right to self-determination within the rule. Doria reacted by sending John into exile, to the solitude of the desert monastery of Peñuela in Extremadura. Gracián suffered a worse fate, being stripped of his habit, expelled from the Order, and sent begging justice to Rome. The accusation against him was disobedience.

In Peñuela, John became seriously ill with an infection and went to Úbeda seeking aid. There, the prior treated him badly because, years earlier, John had scolded him for his manner of preaching. John's ecstatic prayer in Segovia, as reported by his brother Francisco, was answered in Úbeda: "not to die a superior, to die where he was unknown and to die after great suffering."

Analysis

The work of Saint John of the Cross, although not copious, presents a synthesis of medieval learning and Renaissance form, couched in the tradition of Spanish realism. He sought through his poems and books to explain to his Order the nature of the three steps through contemplation to union with the Divine Presence: the *via purgativa*, the *via iluminativa*, and the *via unitativa*. The poem "The Dark Night" and the poet's book-length explication *The Ascent of Mount Carmel* address the beginner or novice, revealing the two spiritual revolutions he will experience; the poem "The Spiritual Canticle" and its book-length explication *A Spiritual Canticle of the Soul* address the *aprovechantes*, who intermittently see their aspirations fulfilled; the poem "The Living Flame of Love" and its explication *Living Flame of Love* address those perfect religious aspirants who seldom cease to experience the dark light of grace. The three poems were written during the imprisonment of John in Toledo in 1577, the first book during his priorship at El Calvario in 1578, and the remaining two while he was prior of Los Mártires in Granada in 1581. Although the works become clearer when read in the context of sixteenth century Spain, John's method of combining medieval, Renaissance, and popular traditions to explain the mysteries of the faith in terms of universal human experience frees his writing from its historical limitations.

John's prose explicates his poetry: *The Ascent of Mount Carmel*, *A Spiritual Canticle of the Soul*, and *Living Flame of Love* use the methodology of Scholastic criticism to explain the doctrine contained in his three major poems. The author readily admits that the intellect hinders rather than aids one's progress toward meditation, but he maintains that reason, in theology as well as in physics and psychology, is the only reliable guide. Reason and the concomitant qualities of simplicity and clarity are extolled as those values most to be esteemed in the religious life of prayer and discipline, so that the contemplative may avoid the danger of becoming attached to the intricate beauty of the ritual rather than to its spirit. The contemplative must present a tabula rasa—freeing his will from the self so that he may be charitable, his understanding from knowledge so that he may have faith, and his memory from continuity so that he may have hope—before he may receive grace.

Reason enables John to distinguish the contemplative's two passages through the "dark night," first from initiate to *aprovechante*, then to perfect, from the states of melancholy, *aboulia*, and possession that they closely resemble. The initiate's enthusiasm soon becomes anger in the form of the frustration experienced by a child denied the rewards he seeks, and he is then subject to pride, restlessness, boredom, envy, impatience, fetishism, and dishonesty until, when he least expects it, he "stand[s] alone in the bitter and terrible dark night of the senses" in which the world appears inverted. The initiate entering the first dark night manifests total distraction and fear that he is lost. All his attempts to regain the source of his former well-being are foiled. Some initiates attempt to begin their discipline again, to no avail. Most, on entering the first dark night, manifest madness in the form of extreme sexual desire, blasphemy, and vertigo.

Once they have overcome these trials, however, the *aprovechantes* may lose their humility and attack with too much confidence, to the point that their experience of grace is self-deceiving and they become blinded by hallucinations, voices, and transports. Since the *aprovechantes* have not completely overcome their former affections, they are in danger of becoming physically and psychologically ill.

According to John, the second passage through the dark night to perfection is even more difficult and may last many years. For the physically weak, it is unbearable. The *aprovechantes* experience spiritual poverty, helplessness, detachment, incomprehension, an absence of will, and anguish over losing mind and memory. They may by chance finally acquire wisdom in the form of the dark light of the fire described in *Living Flame of Love*. The perfect is then enjoined to make of his soul a hiding place where the beloved may live with gracious company in pleasure and ease.

Although John's psychology is limited to three faculties (the will, reason, and memory) and four interrelated emotions (pleasure, pain, fear, and hope), he provides a clear view of the spiritual adventure of a sixteenth century Spaniard who is not called to the territorial adventure of imperial expansion. In an interesting image, John compares the reluctant adventurer to a canvas that refuses to be still for the artist's brush.

"THE DARK NIGHT"

In "The Dark Night," John presents the momentary union of the novice's soul with God in terms of the fulfillment of the desires of two lovers who have been separated. Most directly, the poem re-creates the escape of the beloved at night from her house to a meeting with her lover outside the walls of the city, where they surrender themselves to the rapture of their passion. The beloved recalls her fear, her desire, the necessary deceptions and precaution, the shock of being found by her lover, and the joy of the encounter, with its consequential loss of self in a union with all and nothingness.

The simplicity of the poem gives it its strength and almost hypnotic power. The Spanish is rustic, although not uncultured, and it characterizes the beloved with a pastoral simplicity and innocence as she ventures forth to meet her lover. Morphologically and syntactically, the poet gives the beloved's words some features of that dialect between Gallego-Portuguese and Castilian that characterizes the standard literary form of rustic speech known as *sayagués*. Moreover, the poet employs a stanza that discourages elaboration in favor of simplicity, clarity, and precision. From the soldier-courtier Garcilaso de la Vega (1501-1536), who two decades earlier had revolutionized Spanish poetry by successfully adapting the softer Italian hendecasyllable to the more regularly accented and rigid medieval Spanish verse, John borrowed the *lira*. By alternating three heptasyllables and two hendecasyllables within a rhyme scheme that seals the lines by pairing them without regard to length, the poet using the *lira* directs his thought inward and inhibits elaboration. The inward direction of the poem, reflecting the recollection necessary for the beloved's escape, is reinforced by the poet's skillful use of repetition within and between the strophes. Through onomatopoeia, he re-creates with sibilants and voiceless fricatives the darkness, silence, secrecy, and softness of the adventure.

To overcome the temporal limitation of the language of the poem, the poet uses a series of apostrophes to the night. The poem is a re-creation of the encounter in which the beloved attributes to the night the same immediacy ascribed to the lover. Again, in response to the inward direction of the poem, the apostrophe culminates in the center of the poem, in which the metamorphosis of lover-beloved occurs on the morphological level: "amado con amada/ amada en el amado transformada." The fusion of the lovers becomes confusion, and the sounds of the poem overwhelm the sense, so that the original gender distinction between the allomorphs "amado" and "amada" disappears into "transformada."

"THE SPIRITUAL CANTICLE"

"The Spiritual Canticle" enlarges the theme of "The Dark Night" to include mortification and illumination. The poem, comprising forty *liras*, is an eclogue, modeled on those of Garcilaso, in which John presents the lovers in a dialogue as shepherds who are now espoused. (In "The Dark Night," they had to escape in order to be united.)

The first stanzas present the beloved initiate moving through the *via purgativa* as a young shepherdess seeking her lover, who has abandoned her soon after revealing his love. Her sense of loss turns her life into an attenuated death and a desperate search for reunion. First, she tries to reach him through other shepherds. Then she abandons both her fears and her pleasures to look for him on her own. As she wanders, the beauty she discovers reminds her of his grace, until she is overwhelmed by longing. The shepherds who speak to her of him merely increase her pain, because she cannot understand the meaning of their words. As she has already surrendered her will to him, she believes her punishment is unjustified, yet she hopes that by his possession of her, she will regain the self she has lost and the reason for being that she lacks. When she least expects it, her lover's eyes appear to her, reflected in a fountain where she quenches her thirst. The *via purgativa* ends with the medieval motif of the maid at the fountain overtaken by a stag.

The next step toward union, the *via iluminativa*, begins with fear. The beloved flees in panic until the lover's words assure her that her flight merely attracts him more, and therefore her attempt to escape is futile. Since the beloved has not acquired perfection, the *via iluminativa* of the *aprovechante* and the *via unitativa* of the perfect become confused. The beloved may ascend to union and also descend to mortification on the secret ladder introduced by the poet in "The Dark Night." In the fourteenth and fifteenth stanzas, the beloved finds union with her lover, expressed as an ecstatic vision of mountains, valleys, strange islands, sweet melodies unheard, and sonorous silence. The vision is enriched by imagery reminiscent of the Old Testament Song of Songs and, because of the absence of verbs, is made to appear simultaneous.

The beloved must descend from union, presented as a garden in Zion, first to mortification in which she defends their vines from foxes; then to illumination in which she weaves their roses into garlands; then back to mortification in order to defend their solitude, to conjure the rain-laden western wind, to restrain the envious, and to hide her lover away in silence while distracting him with the delights of her raptures. To aid his beloved, the lover proudly commands his creation, through song, to abandon them to their rapture. He then proceeds to raise her again to union, regaling her with the fulfillment of her desire, healing her sorrow, defending her tranquillity with the controlled power of lions, the wealth of gold shields or coins, the luxury of purple hangings, and the peace derived from a social structure based on others' admiration and awe before the brilliance of their passion and the fragrance of their wine that, because of its age, gives delight without sorrow.

In stanzas 26 through 29, the beloved addresses those same admirers of her rapture in order to explain her distraction. She reveals that it derives from the wine that she shares with her lover and that consequently her only concern has become to learn to love well. She explains to them that she will no longer be among them on the commons, because she has become entranced with loving, losing herself only to be found by her lover. In the last ten stanzas, unconcerned that their admirers overhear, she addresses her lover and reveals to them the source of their love. His passion derives from one insignificant grace, presented as a single hair blown across her throat. Because of her humility and unworthiness, the continuation of that passion arises from the beauty that flows from his eyes, and is reflected in her, as her passion arises from discovering her reflection in him. The verbal tenses of these last eight stanzas refer not to chronology but to the fulfillment of the lover and beloved's purpose. The distinctions among past, present, and future disappear as the lovers explore profound and lofty mysteries. Accordingly, the eclogue ends not in the classical manner of the shepherd's departure with the setting sun, but with the image of horses descending a hill to drink water once the siege they had resisted is lifted.

"THE LIVING FLAME OF LOVE"

The third of the poems written by John while in the monastery prison of Toledo, "The Living Flame of Love," continues the allegory of "The Dark Night" and "The Spiritual Canticle." This work presents in four *liras* the song of the beloved to her lover's passion during their ecstatic union. The beloved is now perfect inasmuch as her grace is actual rather than potential. These *liras*, having six rather than five lines and deriving from Garcilaso's friend and immediate literary predecessor, Juan Boscán, are freer, less vacillating and inwardly directed than the first two poems.

The poem is one of the most intense moments in a powerful literary tradition. In it, the beloved sings of the lover's passion as a life-giving and living fire that consumes with fulfillment rather than destruction. The beloved rejoices in her total surrender and pleads to have the rapture made complete by his destruction of the barriers that still divide them. His passion captures, wounds, and subdues her with a gentleness that reveals to her the nature of eternity. The taste of this knowledge turns her heart from the sorrow of living an attenuated death apart from her lover to the joy that his presence infuses as she comes into being through his love. The dark light emanating from her lover's fire illuminates the entirety of her beauty when the poem ends abruptly with her lover's breath rousing her passion again as he awakens on her breast.

Three other poems written in Toledo at the same time do not achieve as perfect a synthesis of the eclogue, Song of Songs, and folk motifs derived from the tradition of the romances and courtly lyrics of the *villancicos* as do the three poems presented here. The *coplas de pie quebrado*, known as "Although by Night ," present the medieval motif of the *fonte frida* in such a way that the night acquires at least thirteen different meanings through an equal number of contexts. In the nine *romances* that constitute the "Ballad on the Gospel 'In the Beginning Was the Word,'" the poet employs the same method as in his major poems, explaining the mysteries of the faith in terms of the varieties of human love. In "Ballad on the Psalm 'By the Waters of Babylon,'" the ascetic's sense of alienation and his consequent rejection of the world are presented in terms of the Babylonian captivity of Israel's people, who refuse to sing the jubilant songs of Zion.

OTHER MAJOR WORKS

NONFICTION: *Cántico espiritual*, c. 1577-1586 (*A Spiritual Canticle of the Soul*, 1864, 1909); *La subida del Monte Carmelo*, 1578-1579 (*The Ascent of Mount Carmel*, 1864, 1922); *Llama de amor viva*, c. 1582 (*Living Flame of Love*, 1864, 1912).

MISCELLANEOUS: *The Complete Works of St. John of the Cross*, 1864, 1934, 1953.

BIBLIOGRAPHY

Brenan, Gerald. *St. John of the Cross: His Life and Poetry*. 1973. Reprint. New York: Cambridge University Press, 1989. This biography includes a translation of John's poetry by Lynda Nicholson. Bibliography.

Gaylord, Mary Malcolm, and Francisco Marquez Villanueva, eds. *San Juan de la Cruz and Fray Luis de León: A Commemorative International Symposium*. Newark, Del.: Juan de la Cuesta, 1996. This collection of works from a symposium examines mysticism in literature, focusing on John and Luis de León. Includes index.

Hardy, Richard P. *John of the Cross: Man and Mystic*. Boston: Pauline Books and Media, 2004. This biography covers John's life from its start to end. Contains an appendix on how to read his works and one with selected texts.

_____. *Search for Nothing: The Life of John of the Cross*. New York, Crossroad,

1982. Hardy wrote this biography to explore John's humanity and make his personality accessible to the modern reader. Hardy provides a necessary corrective to more traditional accounts of John's life.

Herrera, Robert A. *Silent Music: The Life, Work, and Thought of Saint John of the Cross*. Grand Rapids, Mich.: W. B. Erdmans, 2004. This biography of John sees him as a man "whose life was a heroic attempt to assimilate and to be assimilated by the Divine." Places John in his contemporary world and examines his writings in context.

Kavanaugh, Kieran. *John of the Cross: Doctor of Light and Love*. New York: Crossroad, 1999. A study of John that reprints the poems and includes useful features such as a select bibliography. Illustrated.

Payne, Steven. *Saint John of the Cross*. New York: Continuum, 2005. This biography in the Outstanding Christian Thinkers series looks at the saint's life and works, in particular examining his mysticism.

———, ed. *John of the Cross: Conferences and Essays by Members of the Institute of Carmelite Studies and Others*. Washington, D.C.: ICS, 1992. This collection of essays deals with John's thinking on a variety of theological topics, useful to the scholar as well as the general reader. Each essay includes bibliographical notes.

Perrin, David Brian. *For Love of the World: The Old and New Self of John of the Cross*. San Francisco: Catholic Scholars Press, 1997. This work examines the beliefs of John and places him within the history of the Roman Catholic Church. Includes index.

Ruiz, Federico, et al. *God Speaks in the Night: The Life, Times, and Teaching of John of the Cross*. Translated by Kieran Kavanaugh. Washington, D.C.: ICS, 1991. This book commemorates the fourth centenary of John's death with almost one hundred short essays authored by Spanish Carmelite scholars and is lavishly illustrated with beautiful color photographs and illustrations. Organized around the central events of John's life, this volume provides a wealth of information of use to the scholar as well as the general reader. Includes an index of names and places.

Kenneth A. Stackhouse

JUDAH HA-LEVI

Born: Tudela, Kingdom of Pamplona (now in Spain); c. 1075
Died: Egypt; July, 1141
Also known as: Abū al-Ḥasan; Yehuda ben Shemuel ha-Levi; Yehuda Halevi

PRINCIPAL POETRY
Dīwān, twelfth century
Selected Poems of Jehudah Halevi, 1924, 1925, 1928, 1942, 1973
Die schönen Vermasse, 1930
Kol Shirei Rabbi Yehudah Halevi, 1955
Shirei ha-qodesh, 1978
Ninety-two Poems and Hymns of Yehuda Halevi, 2000

OTHER LITERARY FORMS

Primarily famous as a poet, Judah ha-Levi (JEW-duh haw LEE-vi) also wrote an apologetic religious treatise, the *Kuzari* (twelfth century; English translation, 1947), and several letters, in the rhymed prose characteristic of formal Hebrew and Arabic letters of the Middle Ages, which have been preserved and are of interest for their literary style. One of these is translated in Benzion Halper's *Post-Biblical Hebrew Literature* (1921) and reprinted in Franz Kobler's *Letters of Jews Through the Ages*. Some important Judeo-Arabic letters were translated into English by S. D. Goitein, "Judeo-Arabic Letters from Spain," in J. M. Barral, editor, *Orientalia Hispanica*, 1974.

ACHIEVEMENTS

To understand Judah ha-Levi's position as one of the foremost Hebrew poets not only of the medieval period but also of all time, it is necessary to survey briefly the "firmament" in which he is said to be one of the shining stars—that is, medieval Hebrew poetry. Hebrew poetry began with the Bible, and it would even be possible to argue that secular poetry began there as well, if such books as the Song of Songs may be understood to be secular rather than allegorical. In the Hellenistic period, Jewish poets wrote some Greek verse, and apparently some verse in Persian during the period of the post-Talmudic era in Babylonia. It was the influence of Arabic poetry, however, throughout the Muslim world—where the majority of Jews in the medieval period lived—that aroused Jewish intellectuals to attempt a renaissance of the Hebrew language. Hebrew had long been relegated to religious poetry (*piyyut*) for recitation in the synagogue and some few compositions on purely religious subjects. Simply by composing Hebrew poetry on secular themes, and using adaptations of Arabic meter, ha-Levi's predecessors were effecting a linguistic revolution. These first efforts began in Muslim Spain in the tenth century, and quickly reached a level of excellence in the eleventh century with the generation preceding ha-Levi.

Samuel ibn Nagrillah, born in Córdoba at the height of the cultural flourishing of Muslim civilization in Spain, rose to a position of power almost unheard of for a Jew at that time and in that area; he became prime minister and commander in chief of the armies of the Muslim kingdom of Granada (there were other Jewish ministers and even prime ministers in Muslim Spain and elsewhere, but he was the first known Jewish general since the one who served Cleopatra). As an active soldier, fighting battles against the enemies of his kingdom every year for eighteen years, he wrote virtually the only Hebrew war poetry extant. In addition, he found time to compose no less than three volumes of Hebrew poetry on a variety of themes, as well as a work on grammar and a book on Jewish law.

Solomon ibn Gabirol was the other outstanding Hebrew poet of that period. Although his life was marked by frustration and suffering, his poetry can only be described as brilliant, often rising above whatever his misfortunes may have been to sing the lyric themes of love, nature, wine, and other topics. He began writing while still a teenager and expressed the audacity and hubris of youth in some of his early poems, praising his own poetry and fame. He was a philosopher and a mystic—more famous in the Christian world for his *Fons vitae* (the Latin translation of his original work) than among his fellow Jews. Both of these elements are present in many of his poems, some of which reveal profound philosophical insights or are tinged with mystical longings. Most famous of these is the lengthy religious-mystical-philosophical poem *Keter malkhut*, translated frequently into numerous languages (perhaps the best version in English is *The Kingly Crown*, translated by Bernard Lewis).

Contemporary with ha-Levi, although his senior and for many years his mentor and friend, was the great Moses ibn Ezra of Granada. Perhaps the finest of the Hebrew poets of medieval Spain and certainly the most complex, he has been the least understood and appreciated. His poetry is far from simple; it consists of an intricate filigree of biblical language, with allusions to the Talmud, the Midrash, and Arabic poetry and letters. This texture is characteristic of the other medieval Hebrew poets as well, but Ibn Ezra's style is particularly complex. A philosopher as well as a poet (his work in this field still has not been completely edited), he also wrote the only important medieval work on Hebrew poetics. This work details the history of Hebrew poetry and poets to his time, analyzing at length the various rhetorical devices and poetic embellishments employed over the years.

Ha-Levi thus came at the end of what could be termed the "classical period" of medieval Hebrew poetry, and the period in which he lived and wrote was by no means as conducive to creative production as that of the previous generations of poets. Following a civil war that led to the destruction in 1013 of the central caliphate of Córdoba, the Muslim part of Spain was divided into a series of *taifa* (city-state) kingdoms, such as that of

Granada, of which the poet Ibn Nagrillah was prime minister. These were generally weak and divided among themselves, with constant fighting and quarreling, thus providing the opportunity for which the Christians had long been waiting. Ferdinand I was able to unite Leon and Castile and begin the "reconquest" of Muslim Spain. Alfonso VI succeeded in conquering Toledo in 1085; in response to this loss of territory, the Muslims invited the fanatic Almoravids of North Africa to invade Spain and help rid them of the Christian threat. In 1090, the Almoravid troops entered Granada, an event that came just after the massacre of many Jews there. The Christian reconquest itself had serious repercussions for the entire Jewish community, both in Christian and in Muslim Spain. Caught between invading Christian troops and Almoravid Muslim forces, Jews fought and suffered on both sides. The poet Moses ibn Ezra was forced to flee from Granada, as were most of the Jews there, and he spent many years wandering in exile in Christian Spain, primarily in Navarre. During the same period, ha-Levi wandered from city to city in Muslim Spain, and it appears almost fruitless to try to trace these wanderings. In spite of this less-than-ideal situation, he managed to produce a very respectable body of poetry, both secular and religious in theme.

Even in his own time, or soon thereafter, ha-Levi was recognized as one of the greatest of the Spanish Hebrew poets. His contemporary and friend Ibn Ezra may not have shared this opinion, since in his work on poetics, he mentions ha-Levi only as a composer of some riddles, but this judgment may have been written before the poet had done most of his best work. Judah al-Harizi (who lived in the early thirteenth century) said of ha-Levi's poems that they are "sweeter than honey," adding that "he took all the treasures from the treasury of poetry and locked its gate after him." Abraham Bedersi of Provence (who also lived in the thirteenth century) said of ha-Levi, "He prevailed over his fellow-poets; to ha-Levy say: My perfection and my light." Nearly all the nineteenth century scholars who pioneered in the study of Hebrew poetry concurred. Heinrich Heine, who acquired his limited knowledge of Hebrew poetry from reading the German works of some of these scholars, joined in praise of ha-Levi. Heine, in his "Princezzin Sabbath" ("Princess Sabbath"), erroneously attributes to ha-Levi the famous *piyyut* "Lekha dodi", (actually written by Solomon Alkabes) recited at Friday evening services.

Heine dedicated four lengthy poems to ha-Levi. The first of these is a highly romantic and inaccurate picture of the poet's youth. The second, "Beiden Wassern Babels," one of Heine's finest poems, has a reference to "Ghaselen" as one of the various kinds of poems that ha-Levi wrote. This may puzzle some readers: The term is a transliteration of Arabic *ghazal* (erotic poetry), a form in which ha-Levi excelled. In the final poem, "Meine Frau ist nicht zufrieden," Heine explains to his wife that the three stars of Hebrew poetry were ha-Levi, Ibn Gabirol, and Ibn Ezra; he advises her to abandon her theaters and concerts long enough to devote some years to studying Hebrew so that she can read their poems in their original language.

Biography

Judah ha-Levi, in Arabic surnamed Abū al-Ḥasan, was born in Tudela, Spain. His father is referred to in a letter as a rabbi and great scholar, but this may have been merely a courtesy. Otherwise, nothing is known of him. There is absolutely no evidence to support the oft-repeated claim that ha-Levi studied either with the great Isaac Alfasi in Lucena or with his successor Joseph ibn Megash. It is true that ha-Levi composed a eulogy on the death of the former, but this was not unusual considering that Alfasi was the greatest rabbi in Spain, and many poets composed eulogies in his honor. At some time during his youth, certainly not later than 1089, ha-Levi left Christian Spain for Andalusia in Muslim Spain and sent a letter to Ibn Ezra in Granada, together with an imitation of one of Ibn Ezra's poems. Thus began a long friendship with Ibn Ezra and his brothers that lasted until their death.

Like many Jews in medieval Spain, ha-Levi was trained in medicine, and he practiced as a doctor at a later period in his life. Although he was probably wealthy and even engaged in commerce in his later years, in his younger life, he received financial support by writing poetry in praise of patrons.

Ha-Levi had one daughter, who is supposed to have written at least two poems and who was married to Isaac ibn Ezra (the son of the great biblical commentator Abraham ibn Ezra, himself a poet but not related to Moses ibn Ezra). Isaac ibn Ezra, also a poet of note in later years, accompanied his father-in-law on his famous journey, when, at about the age of fifty, ha-Levi decided to leave his beloved Spain and go to the Holy Land. He and his companions arrived in Egypt in 1140. He remained in Egypt for a year, and died there in July, 1141.

Analysis

Judah ha-Levi may not entirely deserve his reputation as the greatest of medieval Hebrew poets, a reputation that is based largely on nineteenth century scholarship, when little was known of the work of other Hebrew poets of the period; certainly, however, he is one of the four greatest. He mastered most of the themes typical of Hebrew poetry: wine, love (both of women and of boys), nature, friendship, panegyric, complaint, and humor. Ha-Levi wrote a number of religious or "liturgical" poems as well. Like most of the religious poems that come from the Spanish school, they are far simpler in style and vocabulary than the secular verse. His secular poetry, which constitutes the largest part of his work, is often difficult and at times stiff, but he can move the modern reader with his emotions; he can arouse a smile and even a laugh. Some of his love poetry, dealing with both sexes, ranks among the finest in Hebrew verse. There is no doubt, however, that the poetry for which he is most famous and was best remembered is his "Zion" poetry. The poet came to the conclusion that, like the rabbi in his religious treatise, the *Kuzari*, he had to abandon his "temporary home" in the Exile and go to the land scared to his people: "My heart is in the East [Zion] and I am in the ends of the West

[Spain]; How can I taste what I eat, and how can it be sweet?"

Leaving his home was not easy, however, and one of ha-Levi's most poignant poems describes his emotions about leaving his daughter and his grandson and namesake, Judah:

> I do not worry about property or possessions
> nor wealth nor all my losses—
> Except that I foresake my offspring,
> sister of my soul, my only daughter.
> I shall forget her son, a segment of my heart,
> and I have, except for him, nothing to discuss—
> Fruit of my womb and child of my delights;
> how can Judah forget Judah?

"ODE TO ZION"

Of all the poems that ha-Levi wrote while contemplating his trip and during the perilous sea voyage that he so well describes (the meter of one poem makes the reader "feel" the motion of the sea during a storm), none is more famous than the "Zionide" ("Ode to Zion"), which has been translated into numerous languages in many versions. Of all the poems ever written by Jew or Gentile in praise of Zion, this is surely the best known and the most stirring.

The poem opens with the poet's plaintive query to Zion concerning the scattered Jewish people who daily seek the welfare of Zion: "Do you inquire of the welfare of your captives?" There follows the famous line in which the poet says that in his dreams of the return of the people to Zion, he is "a lute for [their] songs." He mentions his desire to wander in the now-desolate land, and all the places that he names are places where God appeared to Jacob; thus, they are symbolic of the holiness of the land and also reflect ha-Levi's interest in revelation, an interest that is central also in the *Kuzari*. "There," in Jerusalem, "your Creator opened facing the gates of heaven your [Zion's] gates," he says, reflecting the rabbinic allegory, borrowed in turn by Christian writers, indicating that there is a heavenly city of Jerusalem corresponding to the earthly one, the gates of which are the gates of Heaven. In Jerusalem, the poet says, he shall prostrate himself "and delight in [the city's] stones exceedingly and favor [its] dust," a reference to Psalm 102:15.

From his ecstatic vision of himself walking barefoot in the land, verging on allegory ("the life of souls is the air of your land, and of flowing myrrh the dust of your earth, and flowing honey your rivers"), the poet turns to polemics against the Muslims, who had conquered and inhabited the land, profaning, in his eyes, the sacredness of the place. The reader must remember that this poem was written while the poet was still in Muslim Spain, and—almost as if he were afraid to express anti-Muslim sentiment openly, even in Hebrew—he hides behind allusions; for example, "How can the light of day be sweet to my eyes while I see in the mouths of crows the corpses of your eagles?" becomes fully intelligible only when the reader realizes that the Hebrew word for ravens (or crows), *orvim*, is almost identical in sound to the Hebrew word for "Arabs," *Aravim*.

From the pit of captivity, he says, the exiled people are longing for return: "the flocks of your multitude which have been exiled and scattered/ from mountain to hill and have not forgotten your folds." These lines echo Jeremiah 50:6: "My people hath been lost sheep, their shepherds have caused them to go astray . . . they have gone from mountain to hill, they have forgotten their resting place." Because the Jews of medieval Spain knew the Old Testament books almost by heart, such allusions would not have been lost on them.

Another significant allusion is found in the line "Shinar and Pathros—can they compare to you in greatness , or their vanity be likened to your perfection and enlightenment?" Shinar and Pathros are biblical terms for Babylonia and Egypt, but the reader cannot help feeling that there is yet another meaning: the medieval Muslim lands that represented the culture with which the Jews of Spain, at least, were trying to compete.

From praise of Jerusalem, the poet turns, prophetlike, to consolation, declaring that God longs once again to make the city a habitation for his glory. The poem concludes in a mood that is both a challenge and a litany of praise: "Happy he who waits, and arrives, and sees the ascendancy of your light, and upon whom breaks your dawns—/ To see the goodness of your chosen and to rejoice in your happiness in your return to your former youth!"

Legacy

"Ode to Zion" became almost an anthem of the Jewish people in the Middle Ages and for centuries afterward, although astonishingly few know it in the twenty-first century. It entered into the liturgy and was recited in synagogue services throughout the world. No other Hebrew poem was so frequently imitated by so many poets in different lands.

In the late twentieth century, the revival of Hebrew as a living language prompted renewed interest in the entire corpus of Hebrew poetry, and several excellent anthologies were published, ranging from biblical verse to modern Hebrew poetry written in Israel. In this renaissance of Hebrew poetry, the works of ha-Levi were discovered by a new generation of readers.

Other major work

NONFICTION: *Kuzari*, twelfth century (English translation, 1947).

Bibliography

Brener, Ann. *Judah Halevi and His Circle of Hebrew Poets in Granada*. Boston: Brill/ Styx, 2005. Part of the Hebrew Language and Literature series, this volume looks at the lives of Judah ha-Levi and the other Hebrew poets in Spain. Includes translations of selected poems.

Halkin, Hillel. *Yehuda Halevi*. New York: Schocken, 2010. This biography notes the importance of poetry to Andalusian Jews and provides in-depth analysis of it in telling the story of Judah ha-Levi's life.

Judah ha-Levi. *Ninety-two Poems and Hymns of Yehuda Halevi*. Translated by Thomas Kovach, Eva Jospe, and Gilya Gerda Schmidt. Edited by Richard A. Cohen. Albany: State University of New York Press, 2000. Provides translations of Judah ha-Levi's hymns and poems, including "Ode to Zion." Also includes an introductory essay.

Menocal, Maria Rosa, Raymond P. Scheindlin, and Michael Sells, eds. *The Literature of Al-Andalus*. New York: Cambridge University Press, 2000. Part of the Cambridge History of Arabic Literature series, provides a biographical look at the literature of Judah ha-Levi in Arabic Andalusia.

Scheindlin, Raymond P. *The Song of the Distant Dove: Judah Halevi's Pilgrimage*. New York: Oxford University Press, 2008. Examines Judah ha-Levi's pilgrimage, using the poems as one of the sources of information.

Silman, Yochanan. *Philosopher and Prophet: Judah Halevi, the Kuzari, and the Evolution of His Thought*. Translated by Lenn J. Schramm. Albany: State University of New York Press, 1995. Explores the whole range of Judah ha-Levi's philosophical and religious thought, from Aristotelianism, to form and matter, divinity, theology, anthropology, god and world, and more.

Yahalom, Joseph. *Yehuda Haveli: Poetry and Pilgrimage*. Jerusalelm: Hebrew University Magnes Press, 2009. Follows the poet from Muslim Spain to Zion. To describe the journey, uses his *Dīwān* as well as autobiographical letters and correspondence from the Cairo Geniza collections.

Norman Roth (including original translations)

LUIS DE LEÓN

Born: Belmonte, Spain; 1527
Died: Madrigal de las Altas, Spain; August 23, 1591
Also known as: Fray Luis

PRINCIPAL POETRY
Poesías originales, 1637
Poesías traducidas de autores clásicos y renacentistas, 1637
Poesías traducidas de autores sagrados, 1637
Poems from the Spanish of Fra. Luis Ponce de León, 1883
Lyrics of Luis de León, 1928
The Unknown Light: The Poems of Fray Luis de León, 1979

OTHER LITERARY FORMS

Luis de León (LEW-ees duh lay-OHN) is considered the greatest Spanish prose writer of the sixteenth century as well as one of Spain's greatest poets. His prose masterpiece, *Los nombres de Cristo* (1583; *The Names of Christ*, 1926), is a treatise on the various names given to Christ in Scripture. *La perfecta casada* (1583; *The Perfect Wife*, 1943) is a commentary on Proverbs 31, with observations on marriage customs pertaining to medieval and sixteenth century women. His translations include the Song of Solomon, *El cantar de los cantares* (1561; *The Song of Songs*, 1936), and the Book of Job, *El libro de Job* (wr. c. 1585, pb. 1779).

ACHIEVEMENTS

Luis de León's life and work have come to symbolize for generations of Spaniards and Latin Americans the struggle for truth within the intellectual tradition of the Spanish Golden Age (1492-1680), a tradition that valued faith above knowledge. During his career of forty-seven years at the University of Salamanca, in all his writings in Latin and Castilian, this Augustinian friar (frequently referred to as Fray Luis) fought valiantly to reconcile the Humanist tradition of the Renaissance with faith in the medieval Scholastic tradition based upon the authority of Aristotle and the church fathers.

In theology and exegesis, the two principal disciplines of the medieval university, the new learning implied for Fray Luis an uncompromising literalist position regarding sacred and classical texts. His insistence on an untranslatable spirit made concrete in language, his virulent criticism of his peers' imperfect understanding of texts, and the occasional unorthodox position that was a consequence of his understanding of Hebrew and Greek resulted in five years of prison while the Inquisition investigated his work for signs of heresy. Legend, unfounded in fact, has it that after his exoneration, he resumed his university lectures in the usual manner with the words, "As we were saying yesterday . . ." Fray Luis has grown to represent the quality of forgiveness of those who misunderstood his passionate dedication to the pursuit of knowledge.

Fray Luis's translations from Greek, Latin, and Italian into Spanish, which constitute two-thirds of his poetic production, attest eloquently his knowledge of the nature of language and the art of translation. His work within the Augustinian Order and his prose writings reveal his belief in the perfectibility of humans and human institutions as well as the strength of his faith. Most important, however, Fray Luis's original verse established the Salamancan school of Spanish poetry, which rejected the full aesthetic force of the language in favor of a simplicity of style and profundity of thought that would lay bare the poet's struggle to reconcile modern concerns with awesome traditions.

BIOGRAPHY

One of six children, Luis de León was born Luis de León y Varela, the son of Lope de León and Inés Varela, in 1527 in the town of Belmonte. His family on both sides was extremely successful and included a professor of theology, a royal treasurer, a lawyer at the royal court, the secretary to the duke of Maqueda, and the general Cristóbal de Alarcón, who had won fame and wealth in the Italian campaigns of Charles V. Lope de León himself was a successful lawyer in Madrid and Valladolid and was able to give his sons an outstanding classical education. When Luis was fourteen years old, he began to follow his father's and uncles' footsteps in the Faculty of Law at the University of Salamanca.

Perhaps because of the international reputation of the Salamancan theologians, perhaps because of a strong religious vocation, at age seventeen Luis de León professed in the Order of Saint Augustine and, instead of studying law, began to study in the Faculty of Sacred Letters. His first public speech before the order reveals his determination that no kind of intimidation would force him to swerve from the truth as he perceived it. In that speech, Fray Luis claimed that, having given his life to Christ rather than to personal ambition, neither hypocrisy nor deception could constrain him to obedience. Within six years, he had begun the career that he would continue until his death, that of professor of theology at Salamanca.

Fray Luis was faced with winning and then every four years defending his position in public debates until he won a *cátedra*, or lifetime appointment to a chair with a fixed salary. These appointments became the source of fierce rivalry and heated debates between Augustinian and Dominican friars, and Fray Luis used every legal means available to guarantee his post until he had won a chair. Even then, to improve his position, he continued to challenge other professors for better-paying chairs as death provided opportunities. In one such opposition, he brought to trial Fray Bartolomé de Medina, a Dominican, for irregularities in Medina's appointment. The Salamanca conference decided in Medina's favor because of the latter's popularity among his students and colleagues. Fray Luis took the case to the royal council of Philip II, which decided in Fray Luis's favor by virtue of his seniority. This process and similar cases soon incurred his colleagues' disfavor and mistrust.

Fray Luis remained undefeated at Salamanca until he opposed León de Castro. Fray Luis denounced the latter's *Comentarios sobre Isaias* (1570) to the Inquisition and succeeded in having it suppressed. The *Comentarios sobre Isaias* contained a thinly veiled assault on the dangers of the Humanists' approach to Scripture because of their reliance upon Greek and Hebrew. León de Castro preferred the traditional Scholastic method of syllogistic deduction to the literalist method of translation, claiming that the literalist approach, particularly in the work of Martínez de Cantalpiedra and Gaspar de Grajal, represented a threat to the authority of the Vulgate (vulgar Latin) Bible. On a personal level, León de Castro attacked Martínez and Grajal and, by association, Fray Luis, as heretics.

In March of 1572, the seeds of dissension bore fruit. An accusation against Fathers Grajal and Martínez implicating Fray Luis was filed with the Inquisition in Valladolid, calling for an investigation into their orthodoxy. Fray Diego González initiated the process, declaring that he had learned from León de Castro that, like Grajal and Martínez, Fray Luis taught that the rabbinical interpretation of Scripture was as valid as that of the saints, that the prophets' words are meaningful to Christian and Jews alike, that there was no promise of eternal life in the Old Testament, and that the Vatablo and Pagninus Bibles were superior to the Vulgate. All three men, Diego González claimed, were *conversos* (converted Jews) who desired to observe the faith and law of their Jewish ancestors.

It is well known that Fray Luis, like Teresa de Jesús and much of the Spanish nobility, had Jewish forebears , that Fray Luis's maternal grandmother and great aunt had renounced Christianity and had been put to death in an *auto-da-fé*. During the Counter-Reformation in Spain, as during the plague-ridden fourteenth century, Spanish popular concern with *limpieza de la sangre* (purity of blood) reached fanatical proportions. On March 30, 1572, Fray Luis was arrested in Valladolid, where he would remain until 1577.

While in prison, Fray Luis finished *The Names of Christ*. The record of the trial reveals that Fray Luis valiantly refused to confess or to acknowledge his accusers' interpretations of the texts in question. While his judges declared that they felt Fray Luis was a dissembler and a deceiver, they refused to submit him to torture because of his delicate health. He was declared innocent of the charges only after the principal Augustinian professor of theology at Salamanca, Fray Domingo Báñez, turned the trial around by giving a Catholic meaning to Fray Luis's more ambiguous theological proposals. Báñez afterward advised Fray Luis that regarding scriptural studies, one might think with the minority but must speak with the majority. He was released with the threat of excommunication should he discuss the trial with anyone or try to seek out his accusers.

Fray Luis returned to Salamanca in triumph, but not to his original chair; he was given a lectureship in theology instead. On another occasion, he was denounced again to the Inquisition for opposing the teachings of Saint Thomas Aquinas and Saint Augustine regarding the nature of grace and predestination. Fray Luis held that grace was not a free gift of God but determined in part by people's actions or merit. This time the Inquisition refused to try the case.

Fray Luis left Salamanca in 1585 to represent the interests of the University in Madrid, specifically to defend the Colegio del Arzobispo against charges of irregularities in the granting of degrees. He was never to return, in spite of the efforts of Salamanca to have him back. Instead, he remained in Madrid, finished his commentary on the Book of Job, and became a close friend of Madre Ana de Jesús, a follower of Saint Teresa of Ávila in the establishment of Reformed Carmelite convents.

Fray Luis's friendship with Madre Ana de Jesús and his sympathy with the Carmelite reforms were to become the strongest concerns of the last years of his life. When an opportunity arose in Salamanca to act upon the very issue for which he had been imprisoned by the Inquisition—the opportunity to correct the Vulgate in the light of Hebrew and Greek texts—he turned it down. He stated that such an undertaking was interminable and impossible since what was requested was not a literal translation but a re-creation of the spirit of the original texts, with the inevitable result that each revision would be worse than the last. Instead, in 1588, he visited Philip II at El Escorial Palace to speak with the king's confessor about the establishment of cloistered monasteries for Augustinian friars. The request was granted.

Later, Fray Luis aided Madre Ana de Jesús's efforts, as did Saint John of the Cross, to establish autonomy for the Reformed Carmelite nuns from the ambitious rule of Jesús María Doria. Fray Luis and Teresa de Jesús's favorite, Father Gracián, wrote Pope Sixtus V and received permission to provide a separate council for the nuns. Doria reacted by appealing to Philip II, and the king, in turn, ordered Fray Luis to desist in his support for the nuns. Fray Luis reacted by calling a general council to act immediately upon the directive of Pope Sixtus V. Doria appealed to the king, who sent an order to the meeting forbidding any innovations until the opinion of the new pope, Gregory XIV, could be assessed.

Reportedly, Fray Luis left the meeting saying that none of his Holiness's orders could be carried out in Spain. This comment was overheard and reported to Philip II, who retaliated by temporarily blocking Fray Luis's appointment to provincial of his order. Pope Gregory XIV eventually revoked the brief of Sixtus V, and Fray Luis died soon after in Madrigal de las Altas, having finally been appointed provincial.

Analysis

The poetry of Luis de León presents the pursuit of knowledge as a form of spiritual exultation. For him, the intellectual's contemplation of creation constitutes a joy approaching mystic rapture. In almost all his original poems, he holds Neoplatonic philosophy and medieval Christianity in a tenuously balanced, unstable harmony that creates tremendous aesthetic tension. During his early years, his poems circulated in random manuscript form until he collected them at the request of his friend Don Pedro Portoarrero as a defense against misinterpretation. He divided his work into three books: original poems; translations from Horace, Vergil, Pindar, and Pietro Bembo; and translations of Holy Scripture.

In 1631, a similarly spirited poet, Francisco Gómez de Quevedo y Villegas, published all of Fray Luis's poetry. Quevedo recognized Fray Luis's depth and clarity, qualities that contrasted strongly with the elaborate Baroque preciosity of the style that was to become known as *Gongorismo*. Quevedo likewise recognized that Fray Luis's translations were in keeping with the classical orientation that informed his theory of language in *The Names of Christ* and that had led him to conclusions often dangerously at variance with those of his colleagues. In *The Names of Christ*, Fray Luis asserts that language when used by true and sound minds will reflect reality accurately without distortion; the triple complexity of words—in thought, speech, and writing—can obtain absolute truth. This absolute, shared by many minds, leads to a harmonious world. Within this essentially Neoplatonic framework, Fray Luis includes the tradition of the Kabbala and attributes to words an unconscious depth of meaning, realized through secret references and arbitrary associations.

RELIGIOUS POETRY

In Fray Luis's religious poetry, there is an intimacy of feeling and an occasional self-doubt that appear nowhere else in his work. The poem "En la fiesta de todos los santos" ("On the Holiday of All Saints' Day") illustrates the characteristic antithetical organization of his verse. The greatness of the remote past contrasts so strongly with the inadequacies of the present that the devotion to the early Christian saints continues to increase with each generation. A sense of being abandoned imbues his poem "En la ascensión" ("On the Ascension"), in which the poet asks Christ where his sheep will turn now that he has left them.

In one of his songs dedicated to the Virgin, "A Nuestra Señora" ("To Our Lady"), Fray Luis, in the depths of his despair at the persecution he has suffered, calls upon the Virgin Mary and, protesting his innocence and declaring his unworthiness, beseeches her to intercede for him against the hatred of his enemies and against their deceptions. He asks her to free him from the prison in which their misunderstanding has cast him. In this poem, Fray Luis expresses self-doubt, saying that if indeed he has succumbed to evil unknowingly, the Virgin's virtue will shine more brightly in forgiving a darker sin.

"TO CHRIST CRUCIFIED"

The song "A Cristo crucificado" ("To Christ Crucified"), by virtue of the brutal realism of the imagery and the poet's legalist perspective, reveals Fray Luis's faith in the law. While (for Fray Luis) the Virgin is the summa of the Divine Essence, Christ's humanity and suffering make him humble in Fray Luis's eyes and, therefore, accessible. The poem elaborates the theme of Christ the advocate fulfilling the law by granting pardon to all who call on him. He cannot flee because his feet are nailed. His heart is revealed through his gaping wounds, and two words from a thief are sufficient to steal it. He dictates his will and New Testament before dying and, from the Cross, can deny no one's wish. His head drops upon his chest, and Fray Luis calls upon witnesses to affirm the gesture as a sign that the poet's request for pardon has been granted. Finally, since no testament is legally valid until the testator is dead, Christ fulfills the law to the letter and dies. While concluding the poem with the lines that Heaven, Earth, and Sun mourn Christ's death, the poet, because of his intellectual and legalistic perspective on the Crucifixion, demands—rather than seeks—justice.

"To Santiago"

The same intensity found in "To Christ Crucified" characterizes Fray Luis's *liras* dedicated to Saint James the Apostle and Moor Slayer, "A Santiago" ("To Santiago"). The poet portrays Saint James as the disciple who, after bringing Spain to Christ and returning to the East to suffer martyrdom, reappears during the Wars of Reconquest (780-1492) to avenge Spanish blood spilled by the Infidels. The poem exalts the theocratic dynamics of Spain's imperial expansion: the Spaniard's thirst for vengeance against the Moor, the Isabeline politics of African expansion, and the taste for awesome power, wealth, and fame acquired by the valiant conqueror who wages war for Christ. In this poem, Fray Luis proves that his range includes the grandiloquence associated with his contemporary Fernando de Herrera, founder of the Sevillian school.

The Perfect Wife

Fray Luis's book *The Perfect Wife* still enjoys popularity in the Spanish-speaking world. Through a commentary on the last chapter of Proverbs, Fray Luis acknowledges that love between husband and wife is the strongest of all human bonds. It is forged by nature and enhanced by grace, being the only institution in existence before the Fall of Adam and Eve. It is reinforced by social custom and tied by intricate mutual obligations. Fray Luis writes that the role of wife is more difficult than that of the average husband because, aside from the chastity that is universally assumed, she is duty bound to profit her husband by managing his household economically, rearing his children wisely, and bringing him comfort and joy. Fray Luis contrasts the ideal wife with vain women who are incapable of physical work because they spend their days with cosmetics and jewelry, who scold servants to prove their authority, or who destroy their neighbors' reputations with frivolous gossip. Because of her role as wife and mother, Fray Luis insists, a virtuous woman is the most powerful agent in society, providing she speak wisely and gently. He writes that, since reason cannot deceive and love does not wish to deceive, a loving and reasonable woman can bring her husband to perfection.

PEACE THROUGH SERVICE

For Fray Luis, in *The Names of Christ* and *The Perfect Wife*, perfection consists simply of fulfilling well one's station in life. In his own life, as a friar and scholar, service to the Church was of paramount importance. The poem "A la vida religiosa" (on the religious life) reveals through a dream the nature of Fray Luis's vocation. In the pastoral setting he so often prefers, he is called to exchange the glory of Earth for the glory of Heaven by renouncing present contentment, comfort, and wealth. Rather than follow the career of his father and uncles, the rewards of which he believes are feigned, he chooses the monk's bare cell, plain frock, hair shirt, and flagellation in order to free himself of vice, the world, the Devil, and the flesh. Thus freed, Fray Luis believes he will have everything the secular person strives for simply by serving God.

For Fray Luis, the ascetic life does not lead, as it did for Saint John of the Cross, to mystic union with God. Rather, it frees him to engage in intellectual pursuits unencumbered by personal concerns. Through acquired rather than infused knowledge, he hopes to envision, enjoy, and realize in a social context his ideal of peace. His most famous and successful poems present this theme of peace through knowledge. This peace is obtained by achieving the Neoplatonic ideal of harmony, first within the soul, next between the individual and nature, and, finally, between the individual and a well-ordered society. Thus, in his poem "Morada del cielo" ("Dwelling Place in Heaven"), Fray Luis harmonizes the Renaissance idea of utopia with the Christian concept of Heaven through the conventions of the pastoral tradition. The Good Shepherd leads his flock to fields where knowledge becomes aesthetic delight, obliterating the sorrow, pain, and injustice of an imperfect temporal world.

This vision of peace stands in marked contrast to Fray Luis's combative life, yet in spite of his fierce competitiveness, in spite of his tendency to win through litigation what he could not win through friendship and approval, there are in his poems moments of that wholeness he so desperately desired. In "Dwelling Place in Heaven," Fray Luis reveals the height of his spiritual ambition, to hear the divine, silent music of the spheres played by God himself, the music that will transport him from his prison of imperfection to the eternal companionship of those who live free from error.

Fray Luis reveals his empirical certainty that such a paradise exists in his three most famous poems, "Vida retirada" ("The Secluded Life"), "A Salinas" ("To Francisco Salinas"), and "Noche serena" ("Serene Night"). Whenever he perceives the concert of number and harmony of disparities as he does in these poems—whether it be in the pastoral vision of nature, in the aesthetic pleasure of polyphonic music, in observing the heavens within a mythic Copernican perspective, or in the language of Humanistic dialogue and Renaissance verse forms—Fray Luis reaffirms his ideal of perfection and his belief in the perfectibility of humanity and its institutions. Because of the intensity of his struggle to harmonize the new learning of the Renaissance with the medieval traditions of Post-Tridentine Spain (after the Council of Trent, 1545-1563) and because of the valor of his struggle for intellectual integrity against his contemporaries' lack of understanding and his own self-doubts, Fray Luis has a permanent place in the history of Spanish culture.

OTHER MAJOR WORKS

NONFICTION: *La perfecta casada*, 1583 (*The Perfect Wife*, 1943); *Los nombres de Cristo*, 1583 (*The Names of Christ*, 1926).

TRANSLATIONS: *El cantar de los cantares*, 1561 (*The Song of Songs*, 1936); *El libro de Job*, 1779 (wr. c. 1585).

BIBLIOGRAPHY

Bell, Aubrey. *Luis de León*. Oxford, England: Clarendon Press, 1925. A biographical study in the context of the Spanish Renaissance.

Durán, Manuel. *Luis de Léon*. New York: Twayne, 1971. An introductory biography and critical study of selected works by Fray Luis. Includes bibliographic references.

Fitzmaurice-Kelly, James. *Fray Luis de León: A Biographical Fragment*. Oxford, England: Oxford University Press, 1921. A brief biography issued by the Hispanic Society of America.

Gaylord, Mary Malcolm, and Francisco Márquez Villanueva, eds. *San Juan de la Cruz and Fray Luis de León: A Commemorative International Symposium*. Newark, Del.: Juan de la Cuesta, 1996. This collection of works from a symposium examines mysticism in literature, focusing on John of the Cross and Fray Luis. Includes index.

Hildner, David Jonathan. *Poetry and Truth in the Spanish Works of Fray Luis de León*. Rochester, N.Y.: Boydell & Brewer, 1992. A critical analysis of selected works by Fray Luis. Includes bibliographical references.

Nowak, William J. "Virgin Rhetoric: Fray Luis de León and Marian Piety in 'Virgen, que el sol más pura.'" *Hispanic Review* 72, no. 4 (Autumn, 2005): 491-510. Nowak examines Fray Luis's poem "Virgen, que el sol más pura" and argues that it is not simply an expression of the poet's Marian piety.

Thompson, Colin P. *The Strife of Tongues: Fray Luis de León and the Golden Age of Spain*. 1988. Reprint. New York: Cambridge University Press, 2009. A critical study of Fray Luis's works with an introduction to the history of Spain in the sixteenth century.

Vossler, Karl. *Fray Luis de León*. Buenos Aires: Espasa-Calpa Argentina, 1946. A short biography of Fray Luis.

Kenneth A. Stackhouse

LUCAN

Born: Corduba, Roman Province of Spain (now Córdoba, Spain); November 3, 39 C.E.
Died: Rome (now in Italy); April 15, 65 C.E.
Also known as: Marcus Annaeus Lucanus

PRINCIPAL POETRY
Bellum civile, 60-65 C.E. (*Pharsalia*, 1614)

OTHER LITERARY FORMS

Thirteen of the lost works of Lucan (LEW-kuhn) were known to Vacca, one of his major biographers, living in the sixth century. Vacca implied that these works were still extant; and several of them were confirmed by Suetonius, another biographer. Vacca is clear that the thirteen are minor works compared with the epic on the civil war, *Pharsalia*, but feels that some, at least, are valuable. The items on Vacca's list include the *Iliacon* from the Trojan cycle; the *Laudes Neronis*; the *Orpheus; De incendio urbis*, a description of the great fire that nearly destroyed Rome; *Saturnalia*, on the gaieties of December; ten books of miscellaneous *Silvae*; the unfinished tragedy of *Medea*; a series of letters called *Epistulae ex Campania* (which, if they had survived, would surely have proved to be a fascinating addition to our specimens of ancient letter writing); as well as speeches for and against Octavius Sagitta. The latter suggest that (in 58 C.E.) Lucan, perhaps acting on the detective instinct, seized upon one of the most exciting murder trials of the day as material for two clever rhetorical showpieces.

ACHIEVEMENTS

Lucan's poetry covered a great variety of genres, although only his incomplete epic, the *Pharsalia*, is extant. Based on the titles, the subjects of a number of lost works range from tragedy to satire to occasional verse. The bulk of Lucan's poetry, including the ten books of the *Pharsalia*, was probably produced in about five years, beginning in 60 C.E. In the light of this information, his production can only be described as prodigious. The output is all the more remarkable when one considers that Lucan composed much of his poetry while he was involved in a political career. Most poets of antiquity who were also politicians postponed their poetic endeavors until they had withdrawn or retired from state business.

Lucan, then, enjoyed neither the leisure time of the retired senator nor the professional poet's singleness of purpose. Vergil was able to spend eleven years of his mature creative life working almost exclusively on the *Aeneid* (c. 29-19 B.C.E.; English translation, 1553), and the *Thebais* (c. 90 C.E.; *Thebiad*, 1767) occupied Statius for twelve years, but Lucan, still in his early twenties, worked on the *Pharsalia* for no more than five years and possibly less than three. While he worked, he held an augurate and a quaestorship and joined a conspiracy to kill the emperor Nero.

Biography

Marcus Annaeus Lucanus was born in Corduba on November 3, 39 C.E. The determining factors in his career were his descent from two prominent Spanish families and his rhetorical education. His father, Marcus Annaeus Mela, was the brother of Seneca the Younger (the philosopher, poet, and statesman) and the son of Seneca the Elder. Lucan's mother was the daughter of Acilius Lucanus, a Corduban speaker of note. Thus, by birthright Lucan belonged to one of Spain's most distinguished families, whose talents had been widely recognized and who had obtained considerable wealth. Lucan was brought to Rome at an early age, where he enjoyed all the wealth and prestige that the Annaei could provide, particularly after 49 C.E., when Seneca was recalled from exile to become the tutor to Nero, the heir apparent to the throne. After formal training at the school of a grammarian, Lucan became the pupil of the Stoic philosopher Annaeus Cornutus, whose name suggests that he may have been a freedman of Lucan's own family.

Considering Seneca's position in Roman public affairs, which grew even stronger between 49 C.E. and 60 C.E., it is not surprising that Lucan was quickly drawn into the very heart of Roman social and political life. While this introduction to court life proved to be an incentive to Lucan, it ultimately caused his ruin. Lucan probably spent considerable time with Nero himself. After all, Lucan and Nero were only two years apart in age and both had a keen interest in literature. When Lucan left Rome for Athens to pursue his education, Nero recalled him to join his entourage, the *cohors amicorum*. Soon, honors were being conferred upon Lucan, such as the quaestorship before the regular age of twenty-five and an augural priesthood. In 60 C.E., then twenty-one years old, he achieved his first public literary triumph with his *Laudes Neronis* at the festival of the Neronia, a newly established celebration in honor of the emperor.

At that time, Nero and his young admirer were on the best of terms; Lucan's position, however, became less secure as Nero's dislike for his tutor Seneca increased. Lucan, perhaps foolishly, entered a competition against Nero and so incurred the enmity of the emperor, who was clever, conceited, and egotistical. Suetonius, a biographer of Lucan, implies that the break between Lucan and Nero arose partly from Lucan's imagining that Nero's attitude toward his works was deliberately insulting and partly from Lucan's unbecoming mockery of the emperor's verses. Vacca attributes the quarrel to Nero's jealousy of Lucan's genius. In any case, Lucan was forbidden to engage in further poetic production or the pleading of law cases. The only avenue left open to the poet was covert satire, and he was prompted by Nero's persecution to join the Pisonian conspiracy. When the intrigue was discovered, Lucan was condemned to death. To avoid execution, after a sumptuous feast, he had his veins opened. His last moments were spent reciting a piece of his own about a soldier similarly bleeding to death. When the emperor cut short Lucan's career, his epic was incomplete and published only in part.

Analysis

Lucan was an audacious author. In touch with an imperial court, he dared to write his long poem *Pharsalia* glorifying the opposition to the founder of imperial power in Rome. Lucan must have been sufficiently aware of the arbitrary tyranny of Nero to recognize that in writing such an epic he played a game involving the highest of stakes. Conscious of his genius, independent in spirit, and impetuous in his youth, he was perhaps fascinated by a hazard with double danger. It was dangerous enough to challenge Nero in literary competition, but it was even more perilous to celebrate the defenders of the ancient Republican system. Theirs had been a lost cause, yet Lucan makes idols of Pompey and Cato and so implicitly challenges Caesarism. There were several justifications for this anti-Caesarism. Corduba, the Spanish seat of his family, acknowledged a traditional allegiance to Pompey, and Lucan's own youthful imagination dreamed up rosy visions of a Republican past. His readings of Livy, the great propagandist for the Republic, confirmed his attitude. Nero's unfairness in trying to silence him drove him to detest the Caesarean dynasty.

Lucan's independent spirit affected not only the subject of his epic but also its composition. He broke away from epic tradition by resolutely rejecting mythology. Lucan's originality lay not so much in the choice of a Roman historical theme—there had been many epics, renowned and unrenowned, on national history—but in the treatment of his theme without the conventional introduction of the gods. The way in which Lucan introduced mythology as an appendix to geography served only to measure his contempt for it. When he described a region that had a legend, he told the legend with the proviso that it was not true. For Lucan, the strongest motive for relating a legend was that it was an incredible explanation of facts for which no credible explanation was forthcoming. Aware of the intrinsic greatness of the figures in a colossal struggle, Lucan relied for his effects more on history than on romance. In his theme, therefore, he broke away from Vergilian precedent and for legendary glamour substituted interest in a human conflict of a comparatively recent time.

Pharsalia

Pharsalia is the only work by Lucan extant, and only ten books survive. This epic treats the war between Caesar and Pompey that erupted in 49 B.C.E. The title *Pharsalia* is borrowed from book 9, verse 985 of the poem. It consists of more than eight thousand hexameters but still does not complete the poet's design; the tenth book, about 150 lines shorter than the next shortest, ends abruptly, leaving Caesar at war in Egypt.

Modern critics have tended to condemn Lucan as tasteless and uninspired, and his *Pharsalia* is frequently (as has been said about John Milton's *Paradise Lost* of 1667,

1674) more talked about than read. In the Middle Ages, however, few classical authors were more widely read or praised than Lucan. In eighteenth century England, the *Pharsalia* not only was popular but also was considered to be the work of a poet even greater than Vergil. Lucan must be given credit for picturesque and striking language, but above all for his attempt to reinfuse a somewhat wilted Roman literature with the spirit of life. As Vergil had correctly seen, historical themes were not well suited to epic treatment. Nevertheless, Lucan was right in perceiving that Roman literature could not go on forever dealing with mythological fantasy, with ancient never-never lands and legendary history. If literature was to have any real meaning, it had to bring itself back to reality.

Lucan's attempt to make philosophy and science serve as the divine and mythological machinery had once served, however, is less than successful. The philosophical portions of the poem seem pompous, forced, and insincere, and require entirely too much argument. The scientific and pseudoscientific episodes are too long and detailed and clog the narrative. Lucan also failed to notice that if he was to write about real people and real history, he must write about them in "real" language and not in the high-flown, artificial style of the rhetorical schools.

The conflict between character and circumstance, each always victorious on its own ground, is the subject that gives interest and dignity to the *Pharsalia*. The poem opens with a delay of the action as Lucan describes the emperor Nero as a god and addresses him as sufficient inspiration for a poet. Lucan anticipates Nero's apotheosis and acknowledges that civil war was not a heavy price to pay for the blessings of Nero's reign. This opening probably owes something to Seneca, and certainly the poet is not at first so violently opposed to Caesar as he later becomes. Lucan is able to recognize that the war was a result of Pompey's inability to endure an equal and Caesar's inability to endure a master. It is a solitary gleam of insight. Referring to Pompey's lack of recent battle experience, Lucan unduly stresses his advanced age. In his fifty-seventh year, he was only four years older than his opponent, and, as Lucan more than once reminds his readers, had become Caesar's son-in-law by marrying Julia, whose death made the breach between them more probable. The poet, although sincerely embracing Pompey's cause, perceives him as a man overconfident because of previous battles and too trusting in the power of his name. The contrasting figure of Caesar is drawn forcefully although not sympathetically. He is a character who relies much on the sword and who enjoys creating havoc.

The strict narrative begins with Caesar's passage across the Alps, bringing his big plans to the small river Rubicon. (The adjectival antithesis is Lucan's.) Caesar is confronted with the majestic image of his native country protesting against further advance. The Rubicon is crossed; Arminium is taken; Caesar is met by his supporters. A summons for troops from Gaul presents an opportunity for digressions on Gallic tribes, tides, and Druids; then, a description of panic in Rome at Caesar's approach leads to the introduction of omens and expiatory rites. The book ends gloomily amid presages of disaster. Lucan, while he removes from his historical epic the conventional gods of epic poetry, puts in their place the supernatural, represented here by the symbolic figure of Roma, by portents, and by the prophecy of both an astrologer and a clairvoyant matron who has a vision of Pompey already lying dead.

Philosophy hesitantly opens book 2. The philosophical foundation of the *Pharsalia* is popular Stoicism, and the Stoics were perpetually confronted with the problem of reconciling belief in fate with divination. Why, asks Lucan, is humanity allowed to know future unhappiness through omens? He ends his philosophical discussion with a prayer that there might be hope amid fear and that the human mind be unaware of the coming doom. Mourning falls on Rome, and men pray for a foreign attack in preference to civil war. The passage is rhetorical in its earlier portion and argumentative at its close. The chief incidents of the book are: first, the remarriage of Cato to his former wife Marcia; second, the resistance to Caesar offered by Domitius, pointedly introduced because he was an ancestor of Nero; and, finally, the retreat of Pompey to Brundisium and overseas. Padding consists of digressions on the civil wars between Marius and Sulla and on the rivers of Italy. The introduction of Cato here is significant for book 9, where he plays a commanding part. For Lucan, Cato is the incarnation of virtue, never before guilty of shedding his country's blood, but now drawn by force into the struggle. Full of admiration for Cato's ascetic ordering of his life, the poet proudly describes his Stoic ability to combine self-sufficing virtue with altruistic claims.

Book 3, mainly concerned with Caesar's activities on his return to Rome and his siege of Massilia, is ruined by a wearisome list of Pompey's eastern allies and the account of an interminable series of ingeniously horrible deaths that befall the soldiers. Among the compensating passages, however, are descriptions of Pompey's farewell to Italy and the eerie forest near Massilia. The former opens the book with a note of poetry and pathos, and the latter, describing the grave of the Druids, is a somber study touched with the spirit of Celtic romance. The reader is placed in a haunted wood at twilight, a place polluted by inhuman rites, shunned by birds, beasts, and forest deities. The leaves of the trees quiver, although there is no wind, and the whole forest is awesome with decay and nameless terrors.

Three episodes constitute most of the action of book 4: Caesar's Spanish operations, the failure of one of three Caesarean rafts to escape the Pompeian blockade in Illyria, and the arrival of a Caesarean general, Curio, in Africa, where he is defeated by Iuba and meets his death. The thirst suffered by the Pompeians in Spain prompts one of Lucan's denunciations of luxury, while the advice of the Caesarean commander to his men trapped on the raft to commit "mutual" suicide rather than surrender is argued in the strained style of a course in rhetoric. When the crew carries out their mutual slaughter, characteristic realism is employed to describe the crawling, bleeding, writhing agony of the lacerated men. This mass suicide closes with a reflection that consoled many of Nero's subjects as well as Lucan: Death is a ready way to elude tyranny. It is the Stoic speaking, recognizing the theoretical obligation of suicide and admitting that it was in certain circumstances defensible.

Book 5 opens with the assembly of the Senate friendly to Pompey and closes with his decision to send his wife, Cornelia, to Lesbos for safety. Nevertheless, Caesar is the dominant figure, especially when he cows the mutineers and crosses the Adriatic in a small boat on a stormy night to bring Antony. Caesar's willpower is dramatized in his defiant braving of the storm despite a fisherman's warning. He is content to have Fortune as his sole attendant in crossing the sea, but the storm is irresistibly tempting for Lucan. He exhausts his use of contending winds and then turns to hyperbole; mountains, having struggled in vain, crumble into the sea, as the waves roll portentously. Still full of hyperbole, but much more human, is the concluding episode, in which Pompey, deeply affected, can scarcely bring himself to tell his wife that for her safety they must part.

Overloaded with digressions, details of Caesar's scheme to enclose his enemy at Dyrrachum, and hyperbolical praise of the repulse of Pompey, book 6 is not on the whole successful. The action concentrates on one outstanding Caesarean who offers the resistance of an African elephant, tearing out and stamping on his own eyeball along with the arrow that pierced it. This and much more is neither poetry nor common sense. The rest mainly concerns the temporary setback of Caesar, who retreats to Thessaly and is followed there by Pompey. The mention of Thessaly offers the opportunity for digressions on geography and magic. There is a catalog of Thessalian spells for love, weather, rivers, mountains, and laws of the universe. The witches of Thessaly are more convincing in the work of Apuleius; yet Lucan does achieve a gruesome effect through Sextus Pompey's morbid longing to learn the future, not from oracles but from necromancy. He makes his way to the sorceress Erichtho and holds a midnight séance with her. Agreeing to his request, she selects a dead warrior, who is brought back to life by loathsome ingredients in order to foretell the future. The revelation is that the shades of the dead await both Sextus's father and his house. With that ominous response, Sextus returns to his father's camp before daybreak.

Although book 7 is not free from extravagance, it is the greatest book of the poem. It describes the feelings of both rivals before Pharsalus, as well as their fortunes in the battle. Pompey's men shout for battle and criticize their leader's caution. In a historically inaccurate scene, Cicero, who was not actually present, is introduced as urging Pompey to give battle. Pompey consents under protest. His men have their way, but many presage death in their pale coloring. The harangues to each side by the respective commanders are vigorous, full of bravado, and very readable. Despite Pompey's claim that his is the better cause, tyranny—in Lucan's view—is triumphant at Pharsalus. Lucan contrasts the fugitive Pompey, looking back upon lost greatness, with Caesar, whose adversary from this point on is not Pompey but freedom and who, to discerning eyes, might be an object of pity: It was worse to win. The picture of the conqueror is not flattering. According to Lucan, Caesar encouraged his men to plunder, was the leader of the guilty side, callously surveyed the dead, withheld rotting corpses from cremation, and was hunted, Orestes-like, by avenging Furies.

The main interest of book 8 lies in Pompey's flight to Egypt and his murder as he is about to land. It is broken by reflections and apostrophes on both Egypt and Pompey. A prey to nervous fears, the defeated warrior escapes in a small boat to Lesbos, where he tries to console his grief-stricken wife. He sets sail with her in anxiety great enough to make unnatural his conversation with the pilot about astronomy. He holds a council of his supporters on his destination, suggesting they land in Parthia. His advisers consider this action dishonorable and persuade him to try Egypt, whose king, Ptolemy, owes his throne indirectly to Pompey. Thus does Pompey sail to meet death. Overmastering fate arranges that Pompey is enticed into a small boat where, in view of his wife and son, he is stabbed by a traitor. Pompey's head is cut off and carried to the boy-king Ptolemy. Having noted the majesty of Pompey's looks as preserved in death, Lucan yields to his obstructive passion for realism and spoils the pathos of the scene. Instead of Vergil's dignity in the face of sorrow, or beauty of simile, there are repulsive details of the still-gasping mouth and the drooping neck laid crosswise to be hacked through; there are sinews and veins to be cut; there are bones to break. Such realism is rendered unnecessary by the moving description of Pompey that follows. The headless body is retrieved from the sea by one of Pompey's Roman attendants and, after an incomplete cremation, is hastily buried. The book ends with imprecations and wild rhetoric on Egypt.

Pompey's apotheosis begins book 9. The lamentations of Cornelia, the threats of vengeance by Pompey's son, and Cato's dignified praise of the dead leader are preliminaries to the central theme of the book: the heroism of Cato. He marches with his men to Africa and gives many demonstrations of his endurance and courage. Cato's inspiring bravery is, however, almost smothered by a mass of irrelevant details about the origin of serpents in Africa and by catalogs of various species of serpents and various sorts of deaths from snakebite.

Book 10, on Caesar in Egypt, would fit better into an epic on mighty Julius than into the *Pharsalia*, yet it has energy in spite of a digression on Alexander the Great. The principal events are Caesar's visit to Alexander's tomb, his affair with Cleopatra, her magnificent banquet after a reconciliation with Ptolemy, and the plot to kill Caesar. The tenth book is incomplete, and there are many indications of an unfinished scheme. There is, for example, a reference to the postponement of a fated penalty, which implies that the poem was designed to continue up to Caesar's assassination in 44 B.C.E.

LEGACY

When it is remembered that the aim in academic rhetoric was to appear clever and striking at all costs, the central characteristic of Lucan's epic is at once grasped. The dominant note is one of display. The object is not to be natural but above all to be piquant and impressive. The parade of erudition that leads to catalogs and digressions employs

Lucan's rhetorical training. The realistic detail is calculated to cause a shudder, the subtlety of argument makes a debating speech cogent, the hyperbole arrests attention, and points, epigrams, and antitheses produce memorable phrases.

Realism in Lucan is morbid and grotesque. Too often it is paired with the desire to terrify the audience by dwelling on the horrible. Hence he enjoys describing tortures, the agonies of the wounded, the repulsive ghoulishness of a witch, and the revolting aspects of cremation. When realism is strained to the breaking point, it becomes unreal.

Despite such overemphasis on gory realism and hyperbole, Lucan's rhetoric is often brilliant, expressing his thought in brief, pointed form, often assisted by antithesis. These economical lines and phrases epigrammatically summarize a character, a situation, or—in the older meaning of *sententia*—a general truth.

Lucan's mannerisms and willful faults can blind his audience to his merits. It is true that he is rhetorical and sensational, yet when all his inaccuracies, distortions, and digressions have been held against him, his great passages prove that in spite of artificiality he can be fiery and irresistible.

BIBLIOGRAPHY

Bartsch, Shadi. *Ideology in Cold Blood: A Reading of Lucan's "Civil War."* Cambridge, Mass.: Harvard University Press, 1997. Bartsch approaches Lucan's *Pharsalia* as a paradoxical work, a combination of poetry and history in which the historical "facts" are less important than the underlying "meanings" that Lucan imposes on them.

Braund, S. H. Introduction to *Civil War*, by Lucan. 1992. Reprint. New York: Oxford University Press, 2008. Braud's solid, meticulous translation of *Bellum civile* is put into literary and historical context through his introduction, which reviews both the subject matter and style of the work and its altering reputation over the centuries.

D'Alessandro Behr, Francesca. *Feeling History: Lucan, Stoicism, and the Poetics of Passion*. Columbus: Ohio State University Press, 2007. This study examines Lucan's poem, especially his use of apostrophes (figures of speech in which an absent or dead person is addressed as if present or alive).

Henderson, John. *Fighting for Rome: Poets and Caesars, History and Civil War*. New York: Cambridge University Press, 1998. Henderson looks at Lucan's *Pharsalia* as an attempt to rewrite history in terms of explaining its meaning if not changing its course. An interesting approach to what Lucan was attempting to do with his poetry and how successful he was in the task.

Johnson, W. R. *Momentary Monsters: Lucan and His Heroes*. Ithaca, N.Y.: Cornell University Press, 1987. Studies the flaws in Lucan's "heroes"—Caesar, Cato, and Pompey—which cause them to become "momentary monsters" at crucial periods during the action of the poem. The question, which Lucan never resolves, is whether these flaws are prompted by events or are themselves the cause of those events.

Joyce, Jane Wilson. Introduction to *Pharsalia*, by Lucan. Ithaca, N.Y.: Cornell University Press, 1993. Wilson prefaces her lively and intelligent translation of Lucan with an introduction that places the poem in historical and literary context. While accepting much of the traditional scholarship that addresses the "poetry vs. history" puzzle the poem raises, she goes further to point out the underlying qualities that link the poem to other epics of the ancient world.

Masters, Jamie. *Poetry and Civil War in Lucan's "Bellum Civile."* New York: Cambridge University Press, 1992. Lucan's *Bellum civile* not only is about civil war, Masters explains, but also manages to mimic the conflict in its structure, style, and characters. The tensions of the poem thus help re-create the struggle of the civil war itself, making form and contents merge.

Matthews, Monica. *Caesar and the Storm: A Commentary on Lucan "De bello civili," Book 5, Lines 476-721*. New York: Peter Lang, 2008. This work closely examines a section of the fifth book of *Pharsalia*.

Sklenar, R. *The Taste for Nothingness: A Study of Virtus and Related Themes in Lucan's "Bellum Civile."* Ann Arbor: University of Michigan Press, 2003. This work looks at the concept of *virtus*, Latin for heroism on the battlefield and rectitude in the conduct of life, and how Lucan did or did not use it in his writing.

Shelley P. Haley

ANTONIO MACHADO

Born: Seville, Spain; July 26, 1875
Died: Collioure, France; February 22, 1939

PRINCIPAL POETRY
Soledades, 1902 (dated 1903)
Soledades, galerías, y otros poemas, 1907 (*Solitudes, Galleries, and Other Poems*, 1987)
Campos de Castilla, 1912 (*The Castilian Camp*, 1982)
Poesías completas, 1917
Nuevas canciones, 1924
De un cancionero apócrifo, 1926
Obras, 1940
Eighty Poems of Antonio Machado, 1959
Antonio Machado, 1973
Selected Poems of Antonio Machado, 1978
Selected Poems, 1982
Times Alone: Selected Poems of Antonio Machado, 1983
Roads Dreamed Clear Afternoons: An Anthology of the Poetry of Antonio Machado, 1994
Lands of Castile / Campos de Castilla, and Other Poems, 2002 (bilingual)
Border of a Dream: Selected Poems of Antonio Machado, 2004

OTHER LITERARY FORMS

Although the majority of the published work of Antonio Machado (mah-CHAH-doh) is poetry, he collaborated with his brother, Manuel, on a number of plays for the Madrid stage. These began in 1926 with adaptations of Spanish dramas of the Golden Age and culminated in 1929 with the very successful *La Lola se va a los puertos* (the Lola goes off to sea). The last of their plays to be staged in Madrid was *El hombre que murió en la guerra* (the man who died in the war), in 1941. Several series of prose commentaries on a variety of subjects, principally literary and philosophical, originally appeared in periodicals and were eventually collected and published in 1936 in the somewhat amorphous yet interesting *Juan de Mairena* (English translation, 1963).

ACHIEVEMENTS

Antonio Machado was one of the two great lyric poets of Spain's Generation of '98, the other being Juan Ramón Jiménez. In 1927, Machado was elected to the Royal Spanish Academy.

BIOGRAPHY

Antonio Cipriano José María y Francisco de Santa Ana Machado was born into an interesting family of relatively successful professionals. His paternal grandfather had been to the New World, studied medicine in Paris, and practiced for a time in Seville, where he published a philosophical and scientific journal and became governor of the province. Machado's father studied but never practiced law, devoting himself to the study of Spanish folklore, especially flamenco song and poetry, and publishing four important collections. His mother was a vivacious woman who dedicated herself to her family and four sons, most particularly to Antonio, who was attached to her throughout life and whose death preceded hers by only a few days. Machado's memory of the home where he was born and for eight years led a peaceful existence in charming surroundings never left him.

When Machado's grandfather received a professorship in Madrid, the family accompanied him there. Life in the capital was turbulent and somewhat more hazardous than in Seville. Machado and two of his brothers were enrolled in the Free Institute, a private school founded by Francisco Giner de los Ríos, a friend of the Machado family, and dominated by the principles of *Krausismo*, named after an obscure German philosopher Karl Christian Friedrich Krause (1781-1832), whose system of philosophy, which attempted to combine pantheism and theism, was promoted in Spain by Julián Sanz del Río in an effort to establish a new, liberal educational system. Although Machado completed his secondary education in Catholic institutions, he was to remain faithful to the tenets of *Krausismo* and anticlerical to the end. When Machado concluded this first phase of his education, his family was undergoing a reversal of fortune, and in 1892 and 1895, respectively, his father and grandfather died.

Although Machado became "the man of the family," he did not assume any responsibilities. Rather, he led a somewhat Bohemian life, as before, and began a literary career by writing satirical sketches for *La caricatura* under the pseudonym of "Cabellera" ("Long Hair")—his brother Manuel wrote as "Polilla" ("Moth")—meanwhile thinking of entering the theater. In 1899, Antonio and Manuel at last obtained paid positions as translators and editors for Garnier Brothers in Paris. What they accomplished at Garnier Brothers is not clear, but they did frequent the literary circles of Paris and became acquainted with many of the celebrities of the day, such as Jean Moréas and Rubén Darío. At the same time that the Machados were exploring new interests, they were reading, discussing, and beginning to write poetry.

Little is known of Antonio's first efforts in France and Spain, but the small volume *Soledades* appeared in 1902 (although it was dated 1903) and soon began to enjoy some success in Madrid. Dissatisfied with the *Modernista* aestheticism of these early poems, however, Machado immediately started work on an expanded *Soledades*, in which the spiritual and the ethical would dominate and from which a number of the earlier poems would be excluded. During this period of rapid growth and maturation, the great influence on the poet was that of Miguel de Unamuno y Jugo, who, in an open letter of 1904 in *Helios*, had urged Machado to abandon the principle of art for art's sake. In an article of 1905 on Unamuno's *La vida de Don Quijote y Sancho* (1905; *Life of Don Quijote and Sancho*, 1927), Machado admires his mentor's re-creation of Miguel de Cervantes' hero, in which spirit and feeling transform ideas into poetry.

As a result of his contact with Unamuno, Machado abandoned his semi-Bohemian life and, during 1906 and 1907, prepared for a serious profession. Considering himself too old to attend a university, he studied French and Spanish language and literature at home and passed the arduous examinations to become a professor. He was appointed to a post at the Institute in Soria, in the heart of Old Castile, where he spent five years. Soria was not what it had been in ancient and medieval times, and the Institute ran pedagogically and politically in ways far removed from the principles of *Krausismo*. Patient and unassuming, Machado adjusted to the school's dull atmosphere, accepting old-fashioned patterns of unenthusiastic teaching and rote learning and ignoring local politics. His salvation lay in a few friendships with men of strong cultural interests and in the setting, steeped in the history and traditions of Spain.

Although an attractive man, Machado was timid and unaggressive with women, as was characteristic of the generally unromantic Generation of '98, who placed the blame on old Spanish customs regarding courtship. In late 1907, however, when he was past thirty, Machado met Leonor Izquierdo, the daughter of the family in whose boardinghouse he lived. The girl was only thirteen at the time, and Machado had to wait until she was fourteen to court her; they were married in 1909. A simple, provincial girl of limited education, augmented only by short stays in Madrid and Paris, Leonor nevertheless pleased her husband, and his love for her endured well beyond the grave. While they were in Paris in 1911, where Machado had been awarded a fellowship, she fell seriously ill with tuberculosis. She died in 1912, some time after their return to Soria.

After his wife's death, Machado secured a transfer to Baeza in Jaén. His native Andalusia did not comfort him, however, and he sank into a depression that brought him close to suicide. His mother joined him for a time, which must have helped, and the success of *The Castilian Camp* made Machado aware that he possessed a useful talent that he did not have the right to destroy. His faith in life was restored above all by a serious study of philosophy, including not only the work of modern philosophers, especially Henri Bergson, but also that of the ancients and the languages to read them in the original. Unable to emulate Unamuno in his mastery of Greek, Machado nevertheless managed during several summers in Madrid to pass the necessary examinations to acquire his doctorate in 1918, at the age of forty-three.

In Baeza, Machado, older, heavier, and careless of his appearance, resumed his old way of life. He was a seemingly aimless, somewhat lame, but indefatigable walker, usually alone. He sought the company of a few friends in a *tertulia*, at the Institute, or in the local pharmacy. Sometimes there would be an organized excursion to visit a point of interest; other times he would participate in the literary homages that are a part of Spanish culture, as when he read his "Desde mi rincón" (from my corner) in Aranjuez to honor José Martínez Ruiz (Azorín) and Castile. In 1915, Federico García Lorca, also an Andalusian, came to meet Machado at a cultural gathering in Baeza. Machado continued his work as a critic of Spanish society, concentrating on that of Baeza as most typical of the nation, except for Madrid. In his correspondence with Unamuno, he decried the state of religion in Baeza, dominated as it was by women. Both Machado and Unamuno were evolving from the Cain-Abel theme applied to Spain to a reaffirmation of Jesus's principle of Christian charity, yet Machado was not yet prepared to be an open activist.

Resigned but not satisfied in Baeza, and his inspiration grown thin, Machado obtained a post in Segovia in 1919. Segovia possessed everything that Soria had offered the poet and more, and Madrid was near. He would toil during the week in Segovia, pursuing other interests, especially in the theater, on his weekends in Madrid. Machado's scant poetic production during this time is varied in nature and high in quality. Outwardly he revealed little of his thoughts and feelings, but his mind was teeming with ideas and projects. One project that Machado eagerly worked to realize was the Segovian activists' Popular University. To it he contributed, with all its political overtones, his philosophy of an active Christian brotherhood outside the hierarchy of the Church. Further, he delivered a lecture on Russian literature in which he declared the Revolution a failure because of a lack of philosophical tradition, but praised Russian literature for its universality, founded on Christian brotherhood.

In the mid-1920's, Machado began to feel discontented with his image as a somewhat eccentric widower and schoolteacher and as an isolated poet exploiting a few memories. Furthermore, the poets of the Generation of '98 were being displaced by those of the Generation of '27. It was time to do something new. During this period, Machado began to collaborate with his brother on a series of plays. His desire for rejuvenation also led him henceforth to use pseudonyms and to seek and find a new love. As Machado's passion was at first for an imaginary lady, it was long thought that his "Guiomar" did not exist, but he met Pilar Valderrama in 1926 and soon was in the grip of a schoolboy's infatuation for the mediocre poetess, who was also a married woman and a mother of three. It was an infatuation that, despite her coolness, he maintained for many years, deriving from it a metaphysical system for all consolation.

Except for the theater, Machado's significant production after 1925 consisted of two open-ended, interrelated works. In 1926, he published a brief, intensely concentrated book in prose and verse, *De un cancionero apócrifo* (apocryphal songbook), in which his first important persona, Abel Martín, expresses Machado's persistent belief that the poet is constantly torn between philosophy and poetry. All great poets must be backed by an implied metaphysics, so that, like Plato and perhaps Machado, poet and philosopher are one. The prose parts explain Machado's ideas, each of which is illustrated by a poem. The idea of love is expressed, for example, in "Canciones a Guiomar" ("Songs to

Guiomar"). *Juan de Mairena*, published as a series in the *Diario de Madrid* and as a book in 1936, was entirely in prose, with increased emphasis by Mairena-Machado on political themes, for the Spanish Civil War was then in progress.

In 1927, Machado was elected to the Royal Spanish Academy, normally the greatest of honors for a man of letters in Spain, but his increasingly revolutionary political ideas made him less sympathetic toward the conservative academy, and he never completed his acceptance speech. In 1931, under the Republic created after the abdication of Alfonso XIII, Machado was appointed professor of Spanish literature at the Instituto Calderón de la Barca in Madrid, but his hope for the future of Spain could not keep him from putting all his creative energy into *Juan de Mairena*, and he continued to be a dry, dull professor.

In the tradition of civil wars, the Spanish Civil War set the Machado brothers against each other, Manuel producing propaganda for the Nationalists in Burgos, Antonio performing the same service for the Republicans, first in Madrid, then in Valencia, and finally in Barcelona. In January, 1939, as that city was about to fall to the Nationalists, Antonio, his mother, and others of the family fled to France. Both mother and son were gravely ill, and Antonio died in Collioure of pneumonia on February 22; his mother died three days later. After the war, Machado's work continued to be honored, and today the poet is widely recognized as one of the greatest of the Hispanic world.

Analysis

The two great lyric poets of the Generation of '98, Jiménez and Antonio Machado, were both Andalusians. The latter is equally representative of Castile, however, in his preference for intellectual, philosophical, and classical solutions to existential problems. At first influenced by the *Modernismo* of Darío, who characterized him as profound, Machado soon abandoned that style as superficial in its constant striving for effect. For him, true lyricism consisted of deep spirituality, of an animated exchange between the soul and the world.

Machado's output was not large, and his themes were few in number. His *Soledades* (solitudes) stressed recollections of his youth and the dreams of a young man in an Andalusian setting. In *The Castilian Camp*, the landscape with which Machado communes is that of the province that historically and culturally came to epitomize Spain, and that after many years of residence, he adopted as a second native region. In this collection as in *Nuevas canciones* (new songs), there are also memories of Leonor Izquierdo, the young woman whom Machado met, married, and soon lost to death in Soria; wishes for the renaissance of Spain, shared with the other intellectuals of the Generation of '98; and meditations on the passage of time, life, death, and the search for God. Discarding early in his career the influences of Impressionism, French Symbolism, and Hispano-American *Modernismo*, Machado forged a personal yet traditional style. His restrained, highly concentrated verse provided a valuable alternative to the aestheticism of his great contemporary, Jiménez.

SOLEDADES

The editions of Machado's *Soledades* dating from 1917 remained substantially unchanged and represent the mature poet. Despite successive modifications and excisions, the collection continues to reflect important influences of earlier poets. Gustavo Adolfo Bécquer, a Sevillian post-Romantic who wrote intimate lyrics in opposition to the realistic or bombastic poetry of his day, persisted in Machado's literary affections. Bécquer's idea of poetry as high perfection, impossible to attain, is symbolized by a disdainful virgin or a fleeing doe (poem 42 in *Soledades*), or, as life became sadder and more disappointing, illusion turned to chimera (poems 36 and 43). Like Bécquer, Machado became the poet of reverie par excellence, creating brief, intimate lyrics of traditional octosyllabic lines and subtle assonance.

Inevitably, he was somewhat influenced also by Darío's work, especially the brilliant and erotic *Prosas profanas* (1896; *Prosas Profanas, and Other Poems*, 1922). Although Machado, like the others of his grave generation, eschewed the sensual, he fell under the spell of Darío's "Era un aire suave" ("The Air Was Soft") when he composed "Fantasía de una noche de abril" (fantasy of an April night) in elegant *arte mayor*, musical twelve-syllable lines of balanced hemistichs. Although Machado relegated the poem to a minor section of *Soledades*, he did not reject it. In the poem, the poet ardently seeks love one night in Moorish Seville, but lacking confidence and considering himself an "anachronism," his hopes disintegrate with the elaborate form of the poem.

Another strong though brief influence on Machado's work was that of Paul Verlaine, particularly the Symbolist's use of nature, as in the garden with a fountain, to express the poet's feelings at a given moment, as well as the Edgar Allan Poe-like theme of fatality discovered through the French poet. Although by 1907 he had rejected most of his poems in the manner of Verlaine, Machado became a poet who, like Marcel Proust in his poetic novels, developed memory as a powerful instrument to reveal his inner self.

The poetic renovation accomplished by Machado's *Soledades*, a traditional title well suited to his purpose, progressively and rigorously excluded frank confession and the anecdotal as well as the stylistic excesses of Luis de Góngora y Argote. Here, Machado is preoccupied with time, and as he reworks a few symbols, such as the gallery, the road, the fountain, and the river, he seeks constantly to re-create the past and meditates on a possibly better future. Many lines in these simple poems strike deep and lasting chords in the reader responsive to the same existential problems.

THE CASTILIAN CAMP AND NUEVAS CANCIONES

Although somewhat late in joining Unamuno, Azorín, and Pío Baroja in their celebration of Castile, with *The Castilian Camp*, Machado earned membership in the Generation of '98, the only poet to do so, for Jiménez chose not to write on the Spanish theme. Influenced above all by Unamuno and Azorín, considerable portions of *Nuevas canciones* exploited the theme further. Machado dealt with the problems and destiny of Castile and Spain, centered on Soria as typical of the region and nation. Along the same lines, another group of poems praised those who advanced the culture of Spain. A third group gave the history of Machado's love for his wife, the shock of her death, and the continuing sense of loss, all in the same setting of Soria.

In the long run, however, the outer view was not the one with which Machado felt most comfortable. Toward the end of *The Castilian Camp*, in a poem unique in tone, "Poema de un día" or "Meditaciones rurales" ("Poem for a Day" or "Rural Meditations"), he offhandedly details his extreme loneliness and expresses his intention to withdraw once more into philosophy. The form is a rather complex variation of Jorge Manrique's medieval elegy; in his solitude, the poet is intensely conscious of his surroundings—the changing winter weather outside, the constant ticking of the clock inside. The latter causes him to think about the meaning of time, and the former leads him mentally to follow the raindrops to the fountain, then to the river, and finally to the sea, which symbolically evokes the anguish of the agnostic. Machado's only consolation lies in his books, particularly those of Unamuno, whose latest work, probably *Del sentimento trágico de la vida en los hombres y en los pueblos* (1913; *The Tragic Sense of Life*, 1921), he possesses. As for his old master, Bergson, Machado ironically accepts the author's conclusion in *Essai sur les données immédiates de la conscience* (1888; *Time and Free Will*, 1910) that time and being according to his definitions made free will inescapable. After a walk amid the banalities of Baeza and its provincials to clear his head, the poet returns to his study, again ready to face solitude and his own efforts to cope with the human condition.

Despite the inclusion of many different kinds of poems, *The Castilian Camp* presents a relatively unified picture of Machado in his effort to reach out to the reality of Spain—its landscape, its problems, its important cultural figures—and to create a meaningful personal life. Moreover, there is a strong continuity from *Soledades* to *The Castilian Camp*, for many of the symbols of the former became realities in Soria, and the poet's obsession with time found a firm basis in the strong sense of history in the typical Castilian town. When his wife's death forced him back into himself, Soria became more vivid as he sought to re-create time and life in memory. It is interesting to note in passing that what the Andalusian Machado did for Castile, his contemporary, Robert Frost, did for his adopted New England.

PROVERBIOS Y CANCIONES

The third and most complex body of poems by Machado is that in which he strove hardest to reconcile his metaphysical and aesthetic concerns. First in *The Castilian Camp*, then in *Nuevas canciones*, one finds long series of "Proverbios y canciones" (proverbs and songs), poems of one stanza presenting a bit of philosophy in highly concentrated form. They culminated in the major poems with prose commentaries, somewhat in the tradition of Saint John of the Cross, of the two parts of the *De un cancionero apócrifo* in *Obras completas de Manuel y Antonio Machado* (1946). This collection clearly reflects the poet's need to renew his inspiration and his desire to find love again.

DE UN CANCIONERO APÓCRIFO

As his protagonists represent Machado in his dramas, so do a series of related personas in the *De un cancionero apócrifo*. Lacking systematic training in philosophy, the poet hesitated to express himself directly. Moreover, the use of spokesmen permitted him a degree of objectivity in dealing philosophically with the great themes of love, God, and death, which were either disturbing personally or shocking to a Catholic readership. Noteworthy, too, is the mask of ironic humor that the poet wears throughout to conceal his anguish.

It is clear that Machado thought of poetry as the expression of intimate, personal experience. When, in the second part of the prose discussions in the *De un cancionero apócrifo*, he attacks Spanish Baroque poetry of the seventeenth century as too conceptual and artificial and insufficiently intuitive, he is attacking also the poetry of his day and of all the vanguard to the present. More important, Machado, through another of his spokesmen, Jorge Meneses, satirizes the mechanistic, materialistic society of the contemporary world, which has rendered individual sentiment unnecessary and ineffectual for poetry. Meneses has invented a kind of protocomputer into which are fed the terms significant in the kind of poetry desired; the machine thus produces a poem for the masses. When, with the words "man" and "woman," the computer is programmed to create a love poem, however, the result merely proves that love and the heightened existence that it is supposed to provide are illusory. As before, then, Machado acknowledges defeat for lyric poetry and for himself as a poet, a defeat brought about by excessive intellectualization. However accurate his predictions for the future of lyric poetry, Machado's poetic work nevertheless lives on, as fresh and human as when he conceived it.

OTHER MAJOR WORKS

PLAYS (with Manuel Machado): *Desdichas de la fortuna, o Julianillo Valcárcel*, pr., pb. 1926; *Juan de Mañara*, pr., pb. 1927; *Las adelfas*, pr., pb. 1928; *El hombre que murió en la guerra*, pr. 1941 (wr. 1928); *La Lola se va a los puertos*, pr., pb. 1929; *La prima Fernanda*, pr., pb. 1931; *La duquesa de Benamejí*, pr., pb. 1932.

NONFICTION: *Juan de Mairena*, 1936 (English translation , 1963).

MISCELLANEOUS: *Obras completas de Manuel y Antonio Machado*, 1946 (includes *De un cancionero apócrifo*).

BIBLIOGRAPHY

Cobb, Carl W. *Antonio Machado*. New York: Twayne, 1971. An introductory biography and critical study of Machado by an expert in Spanish poets and the translation of Spanish poetry into English. Includes a bibliography of Machado's work.

Hutman, Norma Louise. *Machado: A Dialogue with Time—Nature as an Expression of Temporality in the Poetry of Antonio Machado*. Albuquerque: University of New Mexico Press, 1969. A critical analysis of selected poems by Machado. Includes a bibliography of Machado's poetry.

Johnston, Philip G. *The Power of Paradox in the Work of Spanish Poet Antonio Machado (1875-1939)*. Lewiston, N.Y.: Edwin Mellen Press, 2002. In this study of paradox in Machado's writing, chapters 2 and 4 examine the poetry.

Krogh, Kevin. *The Landscape Poetry of Antonio Machado: A Dialogical Study of "Campos de Castilla."* Lewiston, N.Y.: Edwin Mellen Press, 2001. Krogh analyzes Machado's description of the countryside of Castile. Includes bibliographical references and indexes.

Ribbans, Geoffrey. *Antonio Machado, 1875-1939: Poetry and Integrity*. London: Hispanic and Luso Brazilian Council, 1975. A transcription of a lecture dealing with Machado's life and poetry. Ribbans has written extensively on various figures in Spanish literature and has edited collections of Machado's poetry.

Round, Nicholas Grenville. *Poetry and Otherness in Hardy and Machado*. London: Queen Mary and Westfield College, 1993. A critical study comparing the poetic works of Thomas Hardy and Machado. Includes bibliographical references.

Walters, D. Gareth. *Estelas en el mar: Essays on the Poetry of Antonio Machado*. London: Grant and Cutler, 1992. This collection of essays from the Glasgow Colloquium focuses on technical aspects of specific poems. Studies such as "Questioning the Rules: Concepts of Deviance and Conformism in *Campos de Castilla*," by Robin Warner, reevaluate the works' meanings in their historical contexts. Other studies analyzing neomysticism, the nostalgic vision of Canciones a Guiomar, and the poetry of cultural memory offer fresh approaches to contemporary classics.

Whiston, James. *Antonio Machado's Writings and the Spanish Civil War*. Liverpool, England: Liverpool University Press, 1996. A study of the influence on Machado's writing of Spanish Civil War propaganda and the resulting schism between the poet and his brother.

Richard A. Mazzara

JORGE MANRIQUE

Born: Paredes de Nava, Palencia, Castile (now in Spain); c. 1440
Died: Castle of Garci-Muñoz, Cuenca, Spain; 1479

PRINCIPAL POETRY
Coplas por la muerte de su padre, 1492 (wr. 1476; *Coplas on the Death of His Father*, 1833)

OTHER LITERARY FORMS
Jorge Manrique (mon-REE-kay) is known only for his poetry.

ACHIEVEMENTS
Jorge Manrique was a major Spanish poet. His *Coplas on the Death of His Father* is celebrated as a philosophical and theological reflection on the brevity and fragility of life. It is perhaps the most famous elegy written in Spanish and is still read in the twenty-first century.

BIOGRAPHY
It is generally believed that Jorge Manrique de Lara y Figueroa was born in the town of Paredes de Nava in about 1440; however, some scholars conjecture that Manrique's birthplace was Segura de la Sierra. Manrique's father, Rodrigo Manrique, was the count (*conde*) of Paredes de Nava, constable (*condestable*) of Castile, grand master (*maestre*) of the Order of Santiago, and one of the principal figures of the Kingdom of Castile in the fifteenth century. Manrique followed a great line of forebears who had distinguished themselves in their literary virtuosity. He was the great-nephew of Iñigo López de Mendoza (the marqués of Santillana); nephew of Gómez Manrique, the famous soldier and poet; and a descendent of Pero López de Ayala, the famed author of the *Libro Rimado de Palacio* (c. 1378-1403). Manrique's mother died while he was still a child, and the boy was raised largely by his father in the courtly tradition of humanism and the arts of war. Like his forebears, the young Manrique became a soldier, a courtier, and a literary figure.

Politically, the Manrique family allied itself with the Infante Alfonso, brother to King Henry IV and a pretender to the throne of Castile. In 1470, Manrique married Guiomar, one of his stepmother's younger sisters. Upon Alfonso's death, the Manriques took up the cause of Isabella, Henry's half-sister, and denied their support to Henry's daughter, Juana ("La Beltraneja"). Manrique fought at his father's side in support of Isabella in numerous clashes with Henry's supporters, such as those at Montizón, where in 1474, he distinguished himself for his bravery; Calatrava; Uclés; and at the castle of Garci-Muñoz, where, according to the historian Hernando del Pulgar, he was killed in battle in 1479. Some scholars, such as Jerónimo Zurita, believe that Manrique survived the battle only to die several days later in Santa María del Campo de Rus. It is believed that both Manrique and his father, Rodrigo, are buried in the cathedral of Uclés, in the province of Cuenca, although this has not been scientifically verified.

Analysis

Jorge Manrique's secular verse, which mostly treats of love, is typical of fourteenth and fifteenth century courtly poetry. Modeled in large measure after Ovid's *Ars amatoria* (c. 2 B.C.E.; *Art of Love*, 1612) and following the great tradition of Spanish adaptations of this work, most notably Juan Ruiz's *Libro de buen amor* (c. 1330; *The Book of Good Love*, 1933), Manrique's work was published in *cancioneros*—collections of poetry—with verse by other poets. Most of his poems are located in Hernando del Castillo's celebrated *Cancionero general* (1511). No autograph manuscript of Manrique's work is known to exist. Manrique's love poetry was not published separately until the latter half of the sixteenth century and not in its entirety. Even in the sixteenth century, critics recognized that Manrique's greatest contribution to Spanish literary history lay in his *Coplas on the Death of His Father*. Manrique's love poetry is typical of late-medieval and early-Renaissance works in its return to classical allusions and its pagan outlook on life, especially in questions of love. It was strongly influenced by the Provençal poets of southern France, whose work had become popular among nobles and in courtly circles in northern Spain during the late twelfth and thirteenth centuries. Manrique was a man of his day and, as such, embodied the great tradition of the courtier—the man of arms and letters, of war and of liberal arts.

Love poetry

Manrique's love poetry was published in *cancioneros*, or collections of poems by various writers. His composition, "De Don Jorge Manrique quexándose del dios del amor, y cómo razona el uno con el otro" (of Jorge Manrique complaining to the god of love, and how the one reasons with the other") is reminiscent of Ruiz's rendition of the dispute between the Arcipreste and don Amor in the *Libro de buen amor*. Manrique's composition shows no particular innovation, in that he follows the late-medieval and Renaissance convention of a return to a classical vision of love that depends on the actions of don Amor (Sir Love). In Manrique's case, the "debate" shows a curious mixture of the pagan and the Christian, which is also typical of fifteenth century Spanish love poetry. The poetic voice, who seeks love but does not find it, complains to don Amor that he has promised much and given nothing. In each instance, don Amor responds to the accusations leveled against him, urging that the "plaintiff" appeal his case to a "higher God" who can judge them both. The "plaintiff" doubts that God will help him:

> That high God without equal
> well do I know that he is the mightiest
> but, with my erring,
> I have made Him very upset

Other poems are directed to Fortune ("A la Fortuna"; this may also be understood as fate), a blind force that annihilates the hopes and dreams of lovers and soldiers alike, bringing all to a bitter end.

COPLAS ON THE DEATH OF HIS FATHER

Manrique's father, Rodrigo, died in Ocaña in 1476 after a protracted struggle with facial cancer, sending the young poet into a state of psychological and spiritual distress. Manrique's creative response to this disaster is the celebrated *Coplas on the Death of His Father*, his greatest work, and one of the most famous works of the entire Hispanic literary canon. The coplas are composed of forty strophes of *pie quebrado* verse (two eight-syllable lines followed by a four-syllable line, repeated four times per strophe) that follow *rima perfecta* (full rhyme) of *abc-abc-def-def*. The forty strophes can be divided into four thematic sections. The theme of the first section, strophes 1-15, is a general consideration of the shortness and purpose of life on Earth (in Latin, the *topos*, or literary commonplace, is called *tempus fugit*). The second, strophes 16-24, deals with the question of where all the great and powerful people of the past have gone (in Latin, this *topos* is called *ubi sunt*). The third section, strophes 25-37, is a panegyric to Rodrigo Manrique. The fourth section, strophes 38-40, deals with Rodrigo's acceptance of death and his prayer to Jesus, as well as a description of Rodrigo as an example to others. The first strophe of *Coplas on the Death of His Father* is one of the most famous in all of Spanish literature:

> Recuerde el alma dormida,
> abiue el seso e despierte
> contemplando
> cómo se passa la vida
> cómo se viene la muerte
> tan callando,
> quánd presto se va el plazer,
> cómo, después de acordado,
> da dolor;
> como, a nuestro parescer,
> qualquiere tiempo passado
> fue mejor.
>
> Let the sleepy soul remember,
> let the mind come to life and awaken
> contemplating
> how life passes by,

> how death comes
> creeping up so silently,
> how quickly pleasure fades,
> how, after being remembered,
> it brings us pain
> how, in our eyes,
> any time in the past
> was better.

This strophe sets the theme for the entire poem, namely, that time and life slip away before one knows it, and thus, every minute is to be savored and used wisely. While Manrique adduces two great topoi of classical and medieval Western literature, *tempus fugit* and *ubi sunt*, he locates them squarely in the realm of Roman Catholic theology. Manrique uses the Spanish of his day, which differs significantly from contemporary Spanish. Note the use of "u" for "v" in "abiue," the double consonant in "passa," the "z" for "c" in "placer ," the "sc" for "c" in "parescer," and the use of "q" with "uá" in "quánd"; unusual also is the phrase "cómo se viene la muerte/ tan callando" and the use of the medieval form "seso" for "mind."

Manrique employs a simple, yet beautiful, metaphor to speak of the endless movement of time and of people's lives toward death: "Nuestras vidas son los ríos/ que van a dar en la mar" ("Our lives are rivers/ that will empty into the sea"). This evocation of nature is at once filled with the beauty of creation, the inexorableness of the "flow" of time, and a recognition that human beings are merely a small part of a much bigger world. It is interesting to note that Manrique uses the feminine form, *la mar* (the sea), rather than the more common masculine form, *el mar*, a convention often employed by native speakers to show tenderness and affection for the ocean. The metaphor is particularly moving in that Manrique applies this form of endearment to the sea that is "el morir" (death) in the following line. Indeed, as the poet explains, this sea (death) is the great leveler that erases all differences between the great and the small, the rich and the poor.

In the fifth copla, Manrique presents the metaphor of life as a road that leads to everlasting life, the kingdom of heaven, where there are no worries and where people will find rest. The poet urges people to hurry along the road of their present lives, so as to reach the goal of their eternal reward without delay:

> Este mundo es el camino
> para el otro, qu'es morada
> sin pesar;
> mas cumple tener buen tino
> para andar esta jornada
> sin errar;
> partimos quand nascemos,
> andamos mientra viuimos,

> y llegamos
> al tiempo que fenecemos:
> assí que quando morimos
> descansamos.
>
> This world is a road
> to the other, that is a dwelling place
> without worry;
> it is well to move quickly
> in making this journey
> without erring;
> we leave when we are born,
> we travel while we live,
> and we arrive
> at the time when we die:
> such that when we die
> we rest.

The *Coplas on the Death of His Father* are celebrated for their lyrical beauty, their vivid images and examples from history, their directly stated message, and their clear affirmation of the Roman Catholic understanding of the present life as a time of preparation for the eternal life to come. Manrique's praise of his father as a model Catholic courtier is heartfelt, endearing, and a singularly powerful confession of faith in an age of great religious and intellectual confusion in Spain.

BIBLIOGRAPHY

Darst, David. "Poetry and Poetics in Jorge Manrique's *Coplas por la muerte de su padre*." *Medievalia et Humanistica* 13 (1985): 197-206. A brief but valuable study of the medieval attitudes and poetic theories at work in Manrique's work.

Domínguez, Frank. "Body and Soul: Jorge Manrique's *Coplas por la muerte de su padre*." *Hispania* 84, no. 1 (2001): 1-10. A brief review of the theological question of the relationship between the body and the soul, as this is presented in the Manrique's work.

———. "Jorge Manrique (circa 1440-21 April 1479)." In *Castilian Writers, 1400-1500*, edited by Frank Domínguez and George Greenia. Detroit: Gale, 2004. A general study of the life and works of Manrique, written by one of the best authorities to publish in English on the subject.

———. *Love and Remembrance: The Poetry of Jorge Manrique*. Lexington: University of Kentucky Press, 1988. This study of Manrique's works is thorough and carefully researched and is among the most important studies of the subject in English.

Grossman, Edith, trans. *The Golden Age: Poems of the Spanish Renaissance*. New York: W. W. Norton, 2006. This anthology contains a translation of Manrique's most famous work, along with information about the poet. An introduction by Grossman and one by poet Billy Collins provide context for understanding Monrique.

Kennedy, Kristin. "Fame, Memory, and Literary Legacy: Jorge Manrique and the *Coplas por la muerte de su padre*." In *Negotiating Heritage: Memories of the Middle Ages*, edited by Mette B. Bruun and Stephanie Glaser. Turnhout, Belgium: Brépols, 2008. This article is helpful in understanding the complex relationship between the medieval topoi (commonplaces) of fame and memory as these are expressed through the cultural patrimony of Christian literature.

Krause, Anna. *Jorge Manrique and the Cult of Death in the Cuatrocientos*. Berkeley: University of California Press, 1937. One of the earliest full-length studies in English of Manrique's major work, situating the coplas in the literary and theological context of fifteenth century Spain.

Montgomery, Thomas. "Jorge Manrique and the Dynamics of Grieving." *Hispania* 18, no. 3 (1995): 483-490. This brief study seeks to go beyond the study of theological aspects of Manrique's work so as to understand it as an expression of Manrique's grief at the loss of his father.

Mark DeStephano
(including original translations)

MARTIAL

Born: Bilbilis, Hispania (now near Calatayud, Spain); March 1, c. 38-41 C.E.
Died: Hispania (now in Spain); c. 103 C.E.

Principal poetry
Liber spectaculorum, c. 81 C.E. (also known as *Epigrammaton liber*; *On the Spectacles*, 1980)
Xenia, c. 84 C.E.
Apophoreta, c. 85 C.E.
Epigrammata, 86-98 C.E. (*Epigrams*, 1860)

Other literary forms

Martial (MAHR-shuhl) is unknown to have written anything beyond the fifteen thousand short poems and epigrams that appeared in his published work.

Achievements

Martial brought the centuries-old art of the epigram to new heights, perfecting the witty, barbed, quotable "zinger" while providing intimate glimpses of everyday life in Rome. Part vulgar gossip columnist, part ancient blogger, and always a keenly observant and skilled versifier, Martial was one of the most popular social commentators of his day during a volatile time—the first century C.E.—in which the Roman Empire greatly expanded, Christianity was introduced, and emperors rose and fell, sometimes violently.

Martial was active for more than thirty years in the midst of the world's most powerful military, political, and cultural force. A financially strapped survivor capable of a vast range of styles (fawning appeals to the wealthy, clever topical lists, straightforward reports of historical events, crude pornography), Martial moved across all social strata, rubbing elbows with the famous and infamous, and achieved nobility. His short poems record snapshot-like impressions in well-composed verse featuring every variation of human behavior witnessed first-hand in all settings imaginable, from the lowest dives to the court of the imperial palace. In the course of his life and work, Martial reinvented the style of the epigram, giving it a surprise ending, a "sting in its tail." Nearly two thousand years after his death, modern wits, public speakers, politicians, and poets still follow Martial's example of driving home a point in the last line to lend extra emphasis to what they say or write.

Biography

Marcus Valerius Martialis was the son of ordinary Roman citizens living in Spain, a colony of the Roman Empire. His parents were Fronto and Flaccilla, one of whom was of Celtic-Iberian heritage. His given name, Marcus, celebrates his birth on March first, probably late in the reign of the insane, ill-fated emperor, Caligula. Martial received a liberal education at home, and in 64 C.E., he journeyed to Rome with the intention of making his living as a poet.

Upon his arrival in the capital, Martial was welcomed into the literary circle of two fellow Spaniards, as well as into the patronage system that permitted starving artists of all disciplines to work under the financial sponsorship of the wealthy and powerful. Seneca the Younger, an elderly and noted dramatist, philosopher, and statesman, and Lucan (Seneca's nephew), a rising young epic poet about Martial's age, introduced the newcomer to Gaius Calpurnius Piso, a wealthy, influential senator. With such support, Martial's future seemed secure. However, in 65 C.E., Seneca, Lucan, and Piso were implicated in a conspiracy against reigning Emperor Nero and were forced to commit suicide. For the next fifteen years, Martial eked out a living, probably soliciting the rich to write occasional, ephemeral verse in the hope of landing a permanent, well-heeled patron.

Martial's earliest surviving work is *On the Spectacles*, a collection of epigrammatic poems written to celebrate the completion of the Colosseum in 80 C.E. Several years later, he published a pair of companion epigram collections, *Xenia* and *Apophoreta*. The first volume of his best-known work, *Epigrams*, appeared in 86 C.E. Due to the apparent popularity and notoriety of his work, he brought out a fresh collection of new poems every year or two.

Although Martial never gained a fortune from his writing, he did eventually achieve a measure of fame. He could count among his acquaintances the emperors Titus and Domitian, aristocrat-soldiers such as Frontinus, and many of the leading literary lights of the day, including poet-satirist Juvenal, letter-writer extraordinaire Pliny the Younger, rhetorician Quintilian, historian Tacitus, and epic poet Silius Italicus. Martial, relying on patronage for his subsistence for most of his working life, inherited a small farm near Nomentum, and in his mid-fifties acquired a modest house in Rome. He was granted a nominal imperial annual stipend and was made an honorary tribune of the equestrian order.

Late in life, with the financial assistance of Pliny the Younger, Martial returned to the town of his birth in Spain and spent his last years on a farm that a female patron, Marcella, had given him, and probably died there. He apparently never married and left no legitimate heirs.

ANALYSIS

Like many writers across the ages, before Martial made his mark on literature, he learned to compose by following the examples of earlier authors. Martial was an outspoken admirer of Catullus, a Roman poet of the previous century, and used his mentor's techniques to carve his own literary niche.

Throughout an effective—if not especially lucrative—working career spanning several decades in the heart of bustling, scandalous, fascinating first century Rome, Martial built a loyal following for well-crafted, sharp-pointed, often eyebrow-raising verse. Borrowing freely from the stylistic toolbox employed by Catullus and other epigrammatists, Martial made deft use of elegiac couplets (dactylic hexameter/dactylic pentameter, expressing a complete thought in as few as two lines), with occasional hendecasyllables (eleven-syllable lines) and choliambics (also known as scazons, which reverse the iambic meter in the last foot of a line) for rhythmic variety. Like Catullus, Martial achieved broad readership dealing with small, everyday, easily understood subjects and real contemporary figures, rather than mammoth epics of gods and heroes past. His direct, epigrammatic poetry drilled through the tumult of events, hammered home truths, and skewered individual behavior. His craftsmanship in constructing memorable two-liners (a set-up followed by a meaningful punch line) is still evident and still inspires to this day.

Although he may have attempted other types of writing, every extant work of Martial is in verse. Virtually all are of epigrammatic nature, most commonly of two to twelve lines, and seldom more than twenty lines long.

From the beginning of his career, Martial demonstrated both an eye for telling detail and a talent for marketing. His first known work, *On the Spectacles*—an eyewitness account of the first games held in the newly completed Colosseum—colorfully describes gladiatorial contests and battles among various species of animals. *On the Spectacles* opened with a poem boasting of the new facility's splendor, comparing it favorably to the pyramids of Egypt, the hanging gardens of Babylon, and other world wonders. This was followed by a dedication to the emperor before Martial launched into a series of brief, exciting glimpses of the action from the games.

Xenia and *Apophoreta* were likewise produced in timely fashion to capitalize on the celebration of Saturnalia (in 84 or 85 C.E.), a major weeklong celebration in December when masters and slaves reversed roles, gifts were given, and there was considerable merrymaking. Martial's elegiac couplets in *Xenia*—also prefaced with a sycophantic dedication to the emperor—were intended as clever tags to accompany gifts of food and wine, as though following course after course of a fabulous banquet. *Apophoreta*, containing couplets that occasionally use hendecasyllables, provides mottoes for more general Saturnalia gifts—artwork, books, animals, and other items.

EPIGRAMS

Martial's tour de force, and the work for which he is best remembered, is *Epigrams*, the collections of short poems he released between 86 and 98 C.E. A dozen of these books were produced during Martial's lifetime, and his earlier works, *Xenia* and *Apophoreta*, similar in structure and content, were later incorporated into the collection, as books 13 and 14, respectively. During his age and afterward, Martial earned a reputation for providing quality and quantity: Each book offered at least a hundred well-crafted epigrams. There was something for every taste: formal dedications, clever observations, gentle reminders, epitaphs and eulogies, friendly advice, birthday greetings, love poems, couplets in praise of the living and the dead, blatant appeals for patronage, scurrilous attacks, and crude scatological material—all in polished verse best appreciated in the original Latin. (Translations of Martial vary widely: Some preserve the meter and flavor of the poems, others gloss over the more sexually explicit of Martial's couplets.)

Book 1 of the *Epigrams* established the pattern that later entries would follow. In the opening poem, Martial addresses the reader, claiming, tongue-in-cheek, that he has exercised self-control and downplaying the significance of his poems, calling them merely jests. He summons the memory of previous epigram writers—Catullus, Marsus, Pedo, Getulicus—to justify the nature of the collection, apologizes in advance for sometimes blunt language, and cautions against reading too much meaning into his words. Other introductory material includes an obligatory dedication to the current emperor, Domitian, and the emperor's supposed reply—also in terse epigram form. Martial demonstrates a very modern sense of promotion, claiming in successive poems that he is known worldwide for his humorous work and informing interested readers exactly where his books (published on parchment in small, handheld editions, the precursor of nineteenth century "penny dreadfuls" and twentieth century paperbacks) can be purchased.

Though there are occasional poems concerning places ("On Regulus") and nonhuman subjects ("To a Hare"), the bulk of book 1, like each subsequent entry in the *Epigrams* series, consists of short pieces aimed at specific individuals (for example, "To Maximus," "To Decianus," "On Gemellus and Maronilla," "On Accerra"). These are intended to illuminate and poke fun at a particular human characteristic, behavior, or activity. Though it may be presumed that Martial had an actual acquaintance in mind for every pointed barb, the living objects of his scorn are disguised behind a generic precognomen (otherwise, he would have provided full names, as in Marcus Valerius Martialis). This was undoubtedly done to avoid potential legal action for libel or defamation of character, which, for a man of modest means, could have been ruinous.

The use of such pseudonyms allowed Martial the freedom to write with impunity about whatever caught his fancy, without worrying about the consequences. Thus he could lampoon a certain Sextilianus's excessive drinking, mock a miser called Tucca who put cheap wine in casks labeled for an expensive vintage, insult a Fidentius who is accused of plagiarizing from Martial, or ridicule Laevina, who left her husband for a younger man.

Martial's work, in the twelve books of *Epigrams* and in the two posthumous inclusions of his earlier writings, ranges far and wide, and its content has a timeless quality that still resonates. The outstanding epigrammatist of his time covers, like no one before him and few afterward, the full panoply of foibles—pride, envy, greed, lust, gluttony, sadism, selfishness, and the other flaws all humans exhibit—demonstrating once again the aphorism first noted more than two millennia ago in Ecclesiastes, that there is nothing new under the sun.

BIBLIOGRAPHY

Califf, David J. *A Guide to Latin Meter and Verse Composition*. London: Anthem Press, 2002. Focuses on the different types of classical meter employed to achieve specific purposes, using examples from Latin literature to demonstrate how ancient writers used rhythm and nuance to achieve subtle effects.

Conley, Thomas M. *Toward a Rhetoric of Insult*. Chicago: University of Chicago Press, 2010. Examines Martial's epigrams, along with the work of many other writers, for their insulting qualities.

Fain, Gordon L. *Writing Epigrams: The Art of Composition in Catullus, Callimachus, and Martial*. Brussels: Editions Latomus, 2008. Examines how Martial and two other writers wrote epigrams.

Fitzgerald, William. *Martial: The World of the Epigram*. Chicago: University of Chicago Press, 2007. Focuses on Martial's body of work, demonstrating how the poet's epigrams, addressed to an ancient audience, also speak to modern readers.

Garthwaite, John. "*Ludimus Innocui*: Interpreting Martial's Imperial Epigrams." In *Writing Politics in Imperial Rome*, edited by William J. Dominik, J. Garthwaite, and P. A. Roche. Boston: Brill, 2009. Examines the political aspects of Martial's epigrams.

Howell, Peter. *Martial*. London: Bristol Classical Press, 2009. Contains biographical information on Martial and analysis of the epigrams.

Nauta, Ruurd R., Harm-Jan van Dam, and Johannes J. L. Smolenaars, eds. *Flavian Poetry*. Boston: Brill Academic, 2005. This collection of scholarly papers deals specifically with the literature produced during the late first century reign of the Flavian emperors, under whom Martial lived and worked.

Rimell, Victoria. *Empire and the Ideology of Epigram*. New York: Cambridge University Press, 2009. This study examines Martial's poetic style and themes in the context of ancient Roman literature, culture, and history.

Wills, Garry. *Martial's "Epigrams": A Selection*. New York: Viking Adult, 2008. Presents Martial's most memorable short poems, newly translated, including about 150 examples from across the full range of his work.

Jack Ewing

BLAS DE OTERO

Born: Bilbao, Spain; March 15, 1916
Died: Majadahonda, Spain; June 29, 1979

PRINCIPAL POETRY
Cántico espiritual, 1942
Ángel fieramente humano, 1950
Redoble de consciencia, 1951
Pido la paz y la palabra, 1955
Ancia, 1958
Parler clair, 1959 (*En Castellano*, published in a French/Spanish edition)
Esto no es un libro, 1963
Blas de Otero: Twenty Poems, 1964
Que trata de España, 1964
Expresión y reunión: A modo de antología, 1969, 1981 (as *Blas de Otero: Expresión y reunión*)
Mientras, 1970
Selected Poems: Miguel Hernández and Blas de Otero, 1972
Todos mis sonetos, 1977 (*All My Sonnets*, 1997)
Poemas de amor, 1987

OTHER LITERARY FORMS

Blas de Otero (oh-TAYR-oh) experimented with progressively freer verse forms. An evolution began with the collection *Pido la paz y la palabra* (I ask for peace and the right to speak) and continued until his poetry approached prose. In their brevity, their imagery, and their dependence on sound effects, the pieces collected in his only full-length book of prose, *Historias fingidas y verdaderas* (1970; false and true history), resemble poetry more than prose, as in "Andar" (walking): "And I saw the world as a sea churning with people, hanging on to one another as they went down; and the world just risen among broken tombs and inscriptions that lied."

As Geoffrey Barrow has noted, Otero's prose represents a further slackening of poetic convention rather than an abjuration of poetry. The first section of *Historias fingidas y verdaderas* includes fifty-six pieces in which Otero meditates on his own personality. The next section comprises his thoughts on Spain, its long and tangled history and how it could profit from the Socialist revolution. The third section is devoted to speculation on the human condition in general. In contrast to the confidence that typified his writing of the previous decade, he raises doubts about the effectiveness of his role as a poet; it is now self-scrutiny rather than faith in the revolutionary potential of the majority that occupies him. Although no political theory of art emerges from his desultory observations, he attributes the social marginality he experiences as a poet to the written nature of the transference of his poetry. The secular millenarianism to which he subscribes, his belief in the imminent redemption of Spain and the world heralded by the Cuban revolution, betokens the incontrovertible romanticism of his revolutionary stance.

Achievements

During his lifetime, Blas de Otero certainly did not lack recognition and praise. He was hailed as one of the most virile poets Spain had produced since its civil war; Dámaso Alonso placed his sonnet "Hombre" (man) in the company of the sonnets of Francisco Gómez de Quevedo y Villegas; and the social and metaphysical concerns of his poetry have prompted comparisons to the work of Miguel de Unamuno y Jugo, William Blake, Arthur Rimbaud, Gerard Manley Hopkins, and Robert Lowell. Otero was awarded the Premio Boscan in 1950 and later the Premio de la Critica and the Premio Fastenrath from the Real Academia Española de la Lengua. His works have been translated into many languages, and criticism of his work has appeared in all the major European languages.

Biography

Blas de Otero Muñoz was born in 1916 in the industrial city of Bilbao, Spain, that "dark lap" of his youth, a city "damp with rain and smoky with priests." His ancestry was Basque, and though he boasted of being a "universal Basque" and occasionally wrote poems to fellow Basques such as the poet Gabriel Aresti, his powerful love for Spain as a single entity precluded regional or ethnic partialities.

Otero was a laconic man who did not leave behind an abundance of biographical detail. "I write and am silent," he wrote in one of the most valuable autobiographical documents available, the poem "Biotz-Begietan"; when Otero was questioned on whether the poem were indeed autobiographical, he replied with one word: "Almost."

His early schooling in Bilbao was typically Basque: traditional, Catholic, and Jesuit in an environment of fear, severity, and intellectual repression that contributed to the distrust he felt toward priests and the Catholic Church. He began writing poetry at an early age; he tells the story of being struck at school by a priest who disliked some of his youthful verses. Although many of Otero's poetic anecdotes from childhood are painful, he speaks warmly of such things as the light of August streaming down upon the cherry trees of his grandmother's orchard, the happy days of his confused adolescence in Madrid, and the laughter of a youthful girlfriend nicknamed Little Porcelain Jar. He graduated from high school in Madrid, earned a law degree at the University of Valladolid (although he never practiced law), and then began the study of literature at the University of Madrid. By the time he was nineteen, he had published several poems, including "Baladitas humildes" (humble little ballads) and "Cuerpo de Cristo, por mi amor llagado" ("body of Christ, by my love wounded"), in the *Revista de la Congregación (Kostkas) de Bilbao*. Then, the Spanish Civil War erupted, and Otero, apparently caught between shifting lines of battle, found himself fighting on one side and then the other. The postwar period was for Otero as painful as the war itself, and his desperate search for God, as it became more and more emotional, turned eventually into a desperate struggle with God. The poet who, in 1942, wrote, "oh beautiful God, oh flesh of my flesh and of my soul/ that, without You, would disappear like the fog," would write sarcastically in 1963, "What a shame there is not/ a god as excellent as they say."

Luis Romero describes Otero in 1946 as thin, ascetic-looking (although then not so much as he would later appear), ironic, a convincing polemicist, preoccupied, and looking more like a mystic or a philosopher than a poet. At this time, he lived on the Alameda Recalde in Bilbao with his widowed mother and an unmarried sister, of whom he rarely spoke. He earned his living as a tutor of private students, but this did not occupy much of his time.

Otero made his first trip outside Spain to Paris in 1951, where, according to his poem "Biotz-Begietan," he suffered "pangs of the spirit." Soon he became interested in Communism and for the rest of the 1950's was continuously preoccupied with leveling criticism at the Francisco Franco regime. If Otero lost interest in his search for God, he did not lose his sense of messianic purpose (his own life he called Calvary, and he titled a poem about himself "Ecce Homo"), which he transferred to his search for brotherhood among men. Even after his commitment to Marxism, his literary work expresses a longing for revolution in primarily moral and religious terms.

From 1955 to 1958, Otero lived in Barcelona; in 1959, he participated in the homage for Antonio Machado at the Sorbonne in Paris, where he read his poem "Palabras reunidas para Antonio Machado" (words put together for Antonio Machado). In 1963, he traveled to the Soviet Union and to China and had insuperable difficulties with the Spanish censors. *En Castellano* (in plain words), which was published in Paris in 1959 (*Parler clair*), was still not available in Spain, so Otero decided to permit its bowdlerized publication; when it came out, more than a hundred poems were missing.

Otero spent three years in Cuba, from 1965 to 1968, and returned to Spain with the word *guajiro* (Cuban peasant) in his vocabulary and with images of *los yanquis* (yankees) taking unfair advantage of everyone in the Americas. Soon after his return to Spain, he had a malignant tumor removed, a fact to which he refers in his chilling "Cantar de amigo" ("friend's song"): "Where is Blas de Otero? He's in the operating room, with his/ eyes open . . ./ Where is Blas de Otero? He is dead, with his eyes/ open." Throughout the 1970's, he continued assembling anthologies of his past work and writing new poetry which appeared primarily in magazines. In 1976, in ill health, he participated in commemorative services for Federico García Lorca at Fuentevaqueros. Apparently late in life, he was married to Sabina de la Cruz, who wrote the introduction to the posthumous edition of his anthology *Blas de Otero: Expresión y reunión*. Otero died in 1979 at his home in Majadahonda, outside Madrid.

ANALYSIS

Blas de Otero was fond of embedding his own name in his poems, and he did not shrink from acknowledging by name other poets whom he admired in his own work. The title *Ángel fieramente humano* (angel fiercely human) is admittedly taken from Luis de Góngora y Argote; *Esto no es un libro* (this is not a book) is from Walt Whitman; and *Historias fingidas y verdaderas* is from Miguel de Cervantes; Otero also makes ample use of epigraphs for his poems, taken from the Bible, popular Spanish songs, Saint John of the Cross, Machado ("A solitary heart is not a heart at all"), Francis Thompson, Augusto Ferrán, Rubén Darío ("Shall we be silent now in order to cry tomorrow"), and Luis de León.

Otero addresses poems to Machado, Quevedo, the Basque poet Aresti, Nobel Prize winner Vicente Aleixandre, the Turkish Communist poet Nazim Hikmet ("Considering how you have moved me/ at this time when tenderness is so difficult"), Paul Éluard, and Miguel Hernández, and recognizes by name as kindred spirits Pablo Neruda, the Bulgarian poet Nicolai Vaptzarov, Rafael Alberti, César Vallejo, Gabriel Celaya, and León Felipe.

Similarly, he made no secret of his scorn for the idea that poetry, not accessible to everyone, is for the "immense minority," as advanced by Juan Ramón Jiménez; thus was inspired his own commitment to the "immense majority." Otero was also vocal in denying Unamuno's influence on his thinking, an idea put forth by the critic Emilio Alarcos Llorach, and his attitude toward Cervantes and his knight errant is complicated by his resentment that both of them helped to perpetuate the myth of idealism.

LANGUAGE AND STYLE

As regards Otero's style, he is partial to words that convey violence and passion (such as *rasgar*, "to tear"; *arrancar*, "to wrench") and derivative verbs and participles using the prefix *des-* (such as *desterrar*, "to drive away"; *desarraigar*, "to uproot"; *desgajar*, "to wrench off"), the violence of which presents a striking contrast to the more positive condition of the word without the prefix (*terra*, "land"; *arraigo*, "stability"; *gajo*, "branch"). He commonly adds the suffix *-azo* to nouns, thereby incorporating the strong Castilian *th* pronunciation (as in *trallazo*, "whiplash"; *zarpazo*, "thud"). Among colors, yellow (*amarillo*) appears the most frequently, redolent of aging and decay.

In contrast, when moments of violence and anger give way to resigned melancholy and "when roses spring forth from the wall of grief," some of Otero's favorite words are *paz* (peace), *luz* (light), the neologism *frondor* (the lushness of fronds), and the names of various birds and flowers. Generally, Otero adheres to a basic Spanish vocabulary, almost colloquial, and for the most part, he avoids literary or unusual words. An exception is his delight in some of the more unusual designations for rugged terrain (such as *llambria, galayo, cantil*), whose very "difficulty" seems to mimic that which they denote.

Otero's conception of humanity as adrift in a vast abysmal ocean, straining to grasp some support, or as an island, floating with its flora of anxieties and its fauna of appetites, leads the poet to employ a full panoply of nautical terms, some of which are technical enough to sound awkward in English translation. The same is true of the poet's reliance on the imagery of directional winds, such as *cierzo* (cold northerly wind) and *galerna* (stormy northwest wind). The word *zafarrancho*, metaphorically "struggle," which Otero uses to sum up his life in a later poem, is another nautical term, originally referring to the drudgery of cleaning the deck of a ship.

Otero also creates new words, which he does by agglutination (as in the title "Españahogándose" / "Choking on Spain"), by blending (as in *Ancia*, composed of the first syllable of *Ángel fieramente humano* and the last syllable of *Redoble de consciencia* ("drumroll of conscience"), which also suggests *ansia*, "anguish," one of the key words in Existential philosophy), and by analogy ("alángeles y arcángeles," where the former is created on the model of the latter to denote another type of angel). Another feature of Otero's style is his tendency to freshen clichés and lines from other poets by making slight changes. Thus, the idiom "cogido de la mano" (hand in hand) is converted to "cogidos de la muerte": "You and I, linked by death" instead of "You and I, hand in hand." Otero takes a line from León, "espaciosa y triste España" (sad and spacious Spain), and recasts it as "esta espaciosa y triste cárcel" (this sad and spacious prison). A famous line from Gustavo Adolfo Bécquer, "While there exists one beautiful woman,/ there will always be poetry," becomes for Otero "Where there is in the world/ one single word,/ there will be poetry."

"Déjame"

To inculcate an idea, Otero does not avoid repeating the same or near-synonymous words (for example, "doors, doors, and doors. And more doors"). He is also fond of enjambment, which serves to speed up the rhythm of some of his poems or, conversely, to slow down their progress, as it does in the following lines from "Déjame" (leave me), where it suggests the uneven, ill-defined quality of the poet's relationship with God:

> You do me harm, Lord. Take your hand
> from upon my head. Leave me with my vacancy,
> Leave me. For an abyss, with my own
> I have enough. Oh God, if you are human,
> take pity, remove your hand
> from my head. It does me no good. It makes me cold
> and scared.

Other noteworthy techniques operative in Otero's poetry are the hyphenation of words in such a way as to permit an ambivalence of meaning: frequent use of the rhetorical question and experimentation with unconventional punctuation.

WOMEN AND LOVE POETRY

Although Otero did not customarily write love poetry unmarred by the dark thoughts connected with one or another of his compulsive searches, he was not reluctant to name names, and he identifies in his poems a significant number of women important to him. In his earliest poems, he treats the desired woman as a virginal symbol and his potential union with her as a union of body and soul: "Mademoiselle Isabel," apparently his teacher of French as an adolescent, with her carnation-colored breasts and rose-colored body; "Little Porcelain Jar," who smelled of hyacinth; and "La Monse" reclining in a field of yellow flowers. A special case is Tachia, nickname of Conchita Quintana, who, little more than a teenager when she befriended Otero, then in his thirties, gave the poet some of the happiest moments of his life. In fact, it was Tachia who helped the poet to realize the futility of his marathon bout with God, and it was she who invited him to concern himself instead with the brotherhood of humankind: "You said: Entwine your grief with mine,/ like a long and jubilant tress;/ immerse your dreams in my kind; push aside/ your thirst for God. My kingdom is of this world."

In later poems, this ethereal love becomes tainted by the tantalizing pain caused by the body of a woman, and Otero's imagery becomes less dainty: The poet lifts the warm skirts of one woman to find a shadow, fear, and a "silent hole," and he writes cheerlessly of the impoverished Laura, who has a "little accordion/ between her legs." In the relatively late "La palmatoria de cobre" ("the copper ferule"), Otero avails himself of the appellation "sister," borrowed from the biblical Song of Solomon to address the consoling female subject of his poem. The consolation of love with women, however, is not enough to provide the poet with a permanent distraction from his *Weltschmerz*. In fact, one of the only times he speaks of women generically is in the form of a savage diatribe, where women are characterized as "Cunning, calculating, liars/ lily-white in public, notorious with their masks."

CÁNTICO ESPIRITUAL

Otero destroyed hundreds of early poems, or so he claims in "Es a la inmensa mayoría" (to the immense majority). His attempts to maintain his faith in God after the horrors of the Spanish Civil War are the theme of his first published work, *Cántico espiritual* (spiritual canticle), written in homage to Saint John of the Cross on the occasion of the fourth centenary of his birth (1942). These homage poems, which establish the relationship of God and humanity as the product of a violent meditation ("I moan and clamor for You like a sin"), Otero never allowed to be reprinted, and in comparison to his later poems, they seem rather less spontaneous.

ÁNGEL FIERAMENTE HUMANO

For the next eight years, Otero published in the Basque literary magazine *Egan* and began to acquire a following. In 1950, *Ángel fieramente humano* appeared, dedicated to the "immense majority" and bringing into sharper focus Otero's personal quarrel with God and his conception of the vacancy and loneliness to which humankind is subjected in this life. The Existentialism of these poems recalls Søren Kierkegaard; Otero's views during this period were influenced by discussions among the young Basque intellectuals connected with *Egan*. Otero speaks of the terrible silence of God, a silence made to seem even more terrible in the wake of the unnecessary killing (twenty-three million, by Otero's count) in World War II. When the poet raises his hand, God, clearly the angry God of the Old Testament rather than the loving Jesus of the New, lops it off; when he raises his eyes toward God, God gouges them out. If man is an angel in the image of God, then his wings are like chains. Nevertheless, there are still to be found in this work vestiges of Otero's deep religious feeling, as in "Salmo por el hombre de hoy" ("Psalm for the Man of Today"), written as a prayer: "Raise us, O Lord, above death./ Extend and sustain our gaze/ so that it can learn henceforth to see You."

REDOBLE DE CONSCIENCIA

Otero's next collection, *Redoble de consciencia*, was devoted to the same theme and written mainly in free verse. The lament of Job that he was ever born serves as the epigraph of the sonnet "Tierra" (land), and Saint John's observation that the soft hand of God can weigh heavily on the soul of humans, serves to introduce "Déjame" (leave me). In the latter poem, Otero, equal in pride to God who made him, reaches the point of wishing he could kill God as God kills humans; a godless abyss without hope is thus preferable to an abyss reigned over by an oppressive God who tantalizes with a hope that is unattainable.

PIDO LA PAZ Y LA PALABRA

In *Pido la paz y la palabra*, Otero, heeding the advice of Tachia, devoted himself to the working class in poems which J. M. Cohen has called monotonous in their anger. Such apparently self-indulgent lines as "I have seen few Calvaries like the one I have" and "I am a man literally beloved by all sorts of ruin" are relieved somewhat by subsequent pledges to offer his life "to the gods/ who live in the country of hope" and "to leap up to the beautiful towers of peace," "sway other breezes," and "call at the doors of the world." One remarkable poem from this collection is "Hija de Yago" (daughter of Saint James), which depicts Spain on the map of Europe as its bloody heel which trod upon the face of a torpid America.

ANCIA

In 1958, Otero published *Ancia*, comprising a selection from *Ángel fieramente humano* and *Redoble de consciencia* as well as thirty-eight new poems, some of which were from the earlier periods of his life and among which is Otero's version of Matthew Arnold's "Dover Beach," a poem addressed to Tachia and titled "Paso a paso" (step by step). As the drum rolls from one side of Europe to the other, he begs his beloved to put death behind her; "The night is long, Tachia/ ... Listen to the sound/ of daybreak/ opening its way step-by-step—between the dead."

EN CASTELLANO

En Castellano, which did not pass the Spanish censors and had to be published in France in a bilingual edition as *Parler clair* in 1959, contained Otero's most unconventional poetry to date. Here, Otero broke up his customary hendecasyllables by distributing the words of a single line over several lines or by introducing short lines of another measure. He was increasingly concerned with eliminating decorative rhetoric and achieving the most direct style possible. The collection includes this now-famous dictum: "Formerly I was—they say—an existentialist./ I say that I am a co- existentialist." Much of its content, however, was aimed at the Franco dictatorship and is of limited interest to the contemporary reader.

ESTO NO ES UN LIBRO

Esto no es un libro, so called because its poems deal with real people and places, was published in Puerto Rico in 1963. It is a thematic anthology containing poems from different periods of the poet's life as well as several poems he was forced to omit from *Que trata de España* (all about Spain), which was published in Barcelona the following year and is confined to expressing the beauty and the misery of Otero's native land. Although in this book he evokes memories by the mention of place-names (130 of them) or words for regional phenomena (such as *orvallo* and *sirimiri* for "rain"), and although many of the images are beautiful in their own right ("the mountains of Leon glitter/ like a blue sword/ waved in the mist"), Otero manages to insert social criticism into every poem, touching on everything from consumerism and agrarian reform to Vietnam and the United Nations. If he rhapsodizes about "bright Catalonia," "pure Leon," and "Segovia of ancient gold ," he ends the poem with a tweak of conscience about "fertile Extremadura,/ where people and bread/ are parted unjustly."

QUE TRATA DE ESPAÑA

The original, uncut edition of *Que trata de España*, published by Ruedo Ibérico in Paris in 1964, contains 155 poems, subdivided thematically into five parts: "El forzado" (he who is forced), "La palabra" (the word), "Cantares" (songs), "Geografía e historia" (geography and history), and "Verdad comun" (common truth). The first section depicts the poet as the child of a miserable and beautiful mother and stepmother who is Spain, a proud country soaked by centuries of fratricidal bloodletting and disdainful of science and progress. It is to the people that Otero speaks, a people broken and burned beneath the sun, hungry and illiterate in their millenarian wisdom and "hospitable and good,/ as the bread they do not have."

The second section reflects the poet's admiration for simple words, especially for the simple, vivid (albeit sometimes ungrammatical) speech and eloquent gestures of the Spanish peasants. By this time, Otero had begun to realize that his poetry was not reaching the working person for whom it was written, and in defense of his original premise he added to one of his poems an epigraph (author unidentified): "In the condition of *our hemisphere* poetry is for the majority not because of the number of its readers, but because of its theme."

Spain has a richer inheritance of epic poetry and folk ballads than does any other European country, with the possible exception of England, and it was in appreciation of this inheritance that Otero named his third section "Cantares." All the poems included here have some link with the folk poetry of Spain or with folk-inspired modern poetry, such as that of García Lorca, and Otero's use of certain archaic variants of poetic words underscores this folk element. It is in this section that Otero launches a violent diatribe against the lie of literature and proffers the advice, "if you want to live peacefully,/ don't be corrupted by books."

In the fourth section, Otero paints more loving vignettes of Spain and probes deeply into the sad history of the country, invoking the aid of the painter Diego Rodriguez de Velázquez to forge an iron tongue on the anvil of truth; there is also a memorial poem to Machado and a collage poem on the death of Don Quixote. The final section attempts to join Spain with other countries of the world in a common hope for a better future: "we/ open our arms to life,/ we know/ another fall will come, heavy with gold,/ beautiful as a tractor in the wheat."

MIENTRAS

The collection *Mientras* (in the meantime), which the poet later wished to have incorporated into a larger work to be called "Hojas de Madrid con la galerna" (pages from Madrid with the northwest wind), contains poems written in Madrid after his return there from his three-year residence in Cuba and often shares metaphors, allusions, and symbols with the prose pieces of *Historias fingidas y verdaderas*, published the same year. The poems are characterized by the subjectivity and reflectiveness of a dying man who reviews and evaluates the facts of his life. In "Morir en Bilbao" (to die in Bilbao), he observes that although he loves Moscow as he does his right arm, he is Bilbao with his entire body in a way he can never be Moscow. The burden of being so peculiarly Spanish, however, is no longer as oppressive as it was in the earlier poems; the poet concedes that in part, his wishes for peace have been granted, and the subject of death no longer inspires defiance in him.

Whether Otero was struggling against the dreadful aloneness of humanity, as in his earlier work, or against the evils of war and political dictatorship, as he did in his later work, he plied his trade with subtlety and power. The justice he sought for Spain, "disheveled in its grief" under fascism, he grew to demand for citizens of the entire world, even if within a political framework as extreme in the other direction as the fascism that he loathed. His voice is sometimes sarcastic and often bitter, but it never quavers, and it is never without hope for a tomorrow better than today.

OTHER MAJOR WORK

NONFICTION: *Historias fingidas y verdaderas*, 1970.

BIBLIOGRAPHY

Barrow, Geoffrey R. *The Satiric Vision of Blas de Otero*. Columbia: University of Missouri Press, 1988. A critical examination of Otero's work. Includes bibliographic references and an index.

Cannon, Calvin, ed. *Modern Spanish Poems: Selections from the Poetry of Juan Ramón Jiménez, Antonio Machado, Federico García Lorca, and Blas de Otero*. New York: Macmillan, 1965. A collection of twentieth century Spanish poetry with commentary by the editor. Contains a discussion of Otero.

Debicki, Andrew Peter. *Spanish Poetry of the Twentieth Century: Modernity and Beyond*. Lexington: University Press of Kentucky, 1994. Debicki examines the sweep of modern Spanish verse, which he situates in the context of European modernity, tracing its trajectory from the Symbolists to the postmodernists. Touches on Otero.

Mellizo, Carlos, and Louise Salstad, eds. *Blas de Otero : Study of a Poet*. Laramie: Department of Modern and Classical Languages, University of Wyoming, 1980. A collection of critical essays in English and Spanish. Includes bibliographic references and an index.

Winfield, Jerry Phillips, ed. *Twentieth-Century Spanish Poets: Second Series*. Vol. 134 in *Dictionary of Literary Biography*. Detroit: Gale Research, 1994. Contains an entry on Otero that provides background and criticism.

Jack Shreve

PEDRO SALINAS

Born: Madrid, Spain; November 27, 1891
Died: Boston, Massachusetts; December 4, 1951

PRINCIPAL POETRY
Presagios, 1923
Seguro azar, 1929 (*Certain Chance*, 2000)
Fábula y signo, 1931
La voz a tí debida, 1933 (*My Voice Because of You*, 1976)
Razón de amor, 1936
Largo lamento, 1936-1938
Lost Angel, and Other Poems, 1938
Truth of Two, and Other Poems, 1940
El contemplado, 1946 (*The Sea of San Juan: A Contemplation*, 1950)
Todo más claro, y otra poemas, 1949
Confianza, 1955
Poesías completas, 1971
To Love in Pronouns, 1974

OTHER LITERARY FORMS

Although the reputation of Pedro Salinas (sah-LEE-nahz) is based primarily on his poetry, which forms the bulk of his work, he also wrote literary criticism, essays, translations, short stories, a novel, and plays. Through his literary criticism and essays, he contributed significantly to an understanding of the process of literary creation and to the appreciation of particular Spanish authors. His critical masterpiece, *Reality and the Poet in Spanish Poetry* (1940), contains six essays which focus on six different Spanish poets from medieval times to the nineteenth century. Salinas attempts to capture and comprehend the main theme of each author's work by assessing his attitudes toward reality. The variety and scope of Salinas's interpretations are also evident in his celebrated studies of the *Modernista* poet Rubén Darío and the medieval poet Jorge Manrique, and in the two published collections of his articles: *Literatura española: Siglo XX* (1941, 1949; twentieth century Spanish literature) and *Ensayos de literatura hispánica: Del "Cantar de mío Cid" a García Lorca* (1958; essays in Hispanic literature: from "Poem of the Cid" to García Lorca).

In contrast to his poetry and literary criticism, which he wrote and published throughout his creative years, Salinas's narrative prose represents the work of two distinct periods: his early beginnings as a writer and his final years. The early works are ex-

Pedro Salinas

tremely lyric and impressionistic, almost like poems in prose, and they contain the same themes ever prominent in his poetry: love, illusion, fate, and the poet. The later short stories represent a marked development in Salinas's narrative art. Each possesses a complex plot in which he combines lyricism, mystery, irony, humor, and criticism of the modern world. Salinas's only novel, *La bomba increíble* (1950; the incredible bomb), develops his concern about the ominous contemporary possibility: the destruction of the world by the atomic bomb. This allegorical satire of modern life ends, however, with the triumph of love.

Salinas's plays (two three-act plays and twelve one-act plays) are the fruit of his mature years. With respect to their content, they, like the narratives, are for the most part an extension of his poetic work. Of particular significance are the themes of communication, love, brotherhood, illusion versus reality, human happiness, the poetic imagination, and the dehumanization of modern humankind.

Achievements

Pedro Salinas, the eldest member of the celebrated Generation of '27, was a leader in its vigorous revival of Spain's poetic past. He and his contemporaries successfully renewed appreciation of Spain's lyric tradition and fused this wealthy heritage with contemporary literary trends: The result was a second golden age of poetry in Spain. Although the Spanish Civil War (1936-1939) led to the disruption and displacement of the Generation of '27, Salinas flourished in exile and continued to stimulate interest in Spanish literature—not only as a poet but also as a teacher and critic.

BIOGRAPHY

Jorge Guillén, poet, critic, and intimate friend of Pedro Salinas y Serrano, divided Salinas's sixty years into thirty years of preparation and thirty years of production. The early years Salinas spent in Madrid, obtaining his primary education from the Colegio Hispano-Francés, his secondary education at the Instituto San Isidro, and his licentiate degree in romance philology from the University of Madrid (1913). He then left for Paris and the Sorbonne, where from 1914 to 1917, he taught Spanish literature and completed his doctoral dissertation on the illustrators of Miguel de Cervantes's *El ingenioso hidalgo don Quixote de la Mancha* (1605, 1615; *The History of the Valorous and Wittie Knight-Errant, Don Quixote of the Mancha*, 1612-1620; better known as *Don Quixote de la Mancha*). While in Paris, he married Margarita Bonmatí; they later had two children. During the years in Paris, Salinas came into contact with many of the prominent writers and literary trends of the time. These modern influences, in combination with an attachment to the Spanish literary tradition, are evident in his poetry and in that of the other members of the Generation of '27.

Salinas was the oldest of this group of poets, whose prominent members include Rafael Alberti, Vicente Aleixandre, Dámaso Alonso, Manuel Altolaguirre, Luis Cernuda, Jorge Guillén, Federico García Lorca, and Emilio Prados. The Generation of '27 (1927 was the three-hundredth anniversary of the death of Golden Age poet Luis de Góngora y Argote) was responsible for rehabilitating the reputation of Góngora, for many years considered a writer of mostly obscure and frivolously ornate poetry. The revival of Góngora was indicative of the renewed appreciation of Spain's literary past, which, fused with a variety of vanguardist currents—Symbolism, *Modernismo*, Creationism, pure poetry, and Surrealism—characterized the works of Salinas and his contemporaries.

After his return from Paris, Salinas accepted a post as professor of Spanish literature at the University of Seville, where he taught for eight years. During that time, he published his first volume of verse, *Presagios*, translated Marcel Proust's *Á la recherche du temps perdu* (1913-1927; *Remembrance of Things Past*, 1922- 1931), contributed to numerous magazines, and published two critical editions and his early prose sketches. Also, he spent one year as a lecturer on Spanish literature at Cambridge University.

Salinas then moved to Madrid and worked as a researcher in Spain's Center for Historical Studies. There, in the country's literary center, he thrived on closer associations with his contemporaries. He taught at the University of Madrid and in 1933 founded the

International Summer University of Santander. All the while, his reputation as a poet was growing. By 1936, he had published his famous love poetry along with numerous scholarly studies.

In 1936, after the outbreak of the Spanish Civil War, Salinas taught at Wellesley College as a visiting professor. Thus began his permanent exile from his native land and the period of his most prolific creative output. During the last fifteen years of his life, Salinas produced two more volumes of poetry, his finest literary criticism, his plays, a novel, and short stories. In 1940, he was appointed Turnbull Professor of Hispanic Literature at The Johns Hopkins University in Baltimore, Maryland, a position he held until his death. He spent summers at Middlebury College in Vermont and lectured at universities throughout the United States and South America.

Salinas was a very cosmopolitan man, stimulated by all sorts of intellectual currents. At the same time, he felt an attachment to classical tradition and culture and, in his later years, a strong nostalgia for his native Spain. He was an extremely cordial man, who was devoted to his family, loved by his students, and involved in close friendships, yet he was also a profoundly private person, who attempted to penetrate the varied experiences of life through literary creation. A deeply spiritual orientation is evident in all his works, but particularly in his poetry, the most profound expression of his concern with the nature of reality, the creative process, love, and existence in the modern world.

ANALYSIS

Pedro Salinas's nine volumes of poetry can be divided into three groups, with each group representing a stage in his poetic development. In *Presagios* (presages), *Certain Chance*, and *Fábula y signo* (fable and sign), the poet reflects seriously on his inner and outer world, preoccupied with the creative process and with the deceptive nature of reality. The second period is his love cycle, for which he is best known: *My Voice Because of You*, *Razón de amor* (love's reason), and *Largo lamento*. The final three volumes make up the poetic production of Salinas in exile. *The Sea of San Juan*, composed during the two especially happy years he spent in Puerto Rico, is a love-filled portrayal of the Caribbean Sea. *Todo más claro, y otros poemas* (all more clear and other poems) combines the poet's positive reflections on the art of poetry with his anguish over the ravages of war, uncontrolled technology, and other aspects of modern life. *Confianza* (confidences) continues these themes, but here Salinas also communicates his hope and confidence in the future. Although differences of style and focus can be seen in the three phases, they overlap considerably, and there is no doubt that the poetry of Salinas forms an integral whole, in a voice that intensifies from *Presagios* to *Confianza*.

The poems of the first stage show Salinas's early attempts to come to terms with the act of creating poetry. The poet must face material reality, internalize it, and somehow transform it into a purer, more external reality. In the poem "Suelo" ("Soil"), for example, the soil or ground represents external reality. In a simple chain of connections, Salinas links it with artistic creation and with a newer, more permanent vision: "on the soil the feet are planted," "on the feet the body erect," "on the body the head firm," "in the lee of the forehead, pure idea," "in the pure idea, the tomorrow, the key—tomorrow—eternal." However, the process is far from simple. Faced with the blank page, the poet finds it difficult to incorporate into a lyric experience his interior harmony and that which he perceives around him. The poem "Cuartilla" ("Sheet of Paper") illustrates this difficulty and also provides a representative example of Salinas's early style.

"Sheet of Paper"

In "Sheet of Paper," Salinas likens the writing down of one's first word to a battle. The pen is the "point of steel," "against the white." In addition to this most obvious metaphor, the poem contains a wealth of other metaphors and images that suggest whiteness and conflict and reveal the mixture of traditional and modern influences that inspired Salinas and his generation. The vocabulary is very much that of *Modernismo*, with its many indications of coldness, whiteness, flight, and opulence: "winter," "marble," "snows," "feathers," "tall columns," "flights of doves," "wings," "snowflakes," "ermines." The intertwining of metaphors and images, of paradoxical and opposing elements is reminiscent of Baroque poetry: "Light as feathers, illusive tall columns uphold roofs of white clouds"; "The snowflakes begin sudden attacks, noiseless skirmishes, snows, ermines, opposed." The "doves" are the thoughts of the poet, who stands on a border between his inner and outer worlds: "Flights of doves uncertain between white above and below, hesitant, withhold the whiteness of their wings." Finally, the pen conquers, and the word emerges, likened to "sun and dawn." The poet is engaged in a constant pursuit of clarity; the goal of poetry is to penetrate, harmonize, and illuminate internal and external reality.

"Here"

In the course of his pursuit, the poet sometimes rejoices in his discoveries. The poem "Aquí" ("Here") communicates his acceptance, exaltation, and idealization of external reality and manifests themes that will dominate his later poetry: love and the sea. The poet is completely content: "I would remain in all/ as I am, where I am;/ calm in the calm water,/ silent, deeply submerged/ in love without light." Here, he claims to require no illumination, and never to need to retreat inward: "Never shall I go from you/ in a ship with wind singing/ at the sail." Nevertheless, the poet does withdraw, because so often he beholds the illusive and deceptive nature of reality. In the poem "Pregunta más allá" ("Further Question"), the love theme is again present, and the poet questions both his loved one and himself: "Why do I ask where you are,/ if I am not blind,/ if you are not absent?" He is afraid to trust appearances, and his comparison of her body, which terminates in a voice, with a flame that rises in smoke, "in the air, impalpable," is ultimately a metaphor for what he fears will be the fate of their relationship. The skepticism, the dialogue form, the simple, almost conversational language, the images of smoke and fire, and similar opposing elements—light/shadow, clear sky/mist—reappear with intensified force in the final two stages of Salinas's poetic production.

THE LOVE CYCLE

Salinas's love trilogy is generally considered to be his best poetry. *My Voice Because of You* traces the history of a love relationship from its first stages to fulfillment, to separation, to a recovery of the experience by means of the poet's internalization of his past happiness. In *Razón de amor*, the poet continues to reflect on past love. In his emotional meditations, he resolves the conflicts concerning love's illusive nature and proclaims love a permanent, redemptive reality for human existence. In *Largo lamento*, as the title suggests, some of the poet's bitterness returns. The poems of this volume foreshadow the disenchantment and preoccupation with the fragility of life that Salinas expresses in *Todo más claro, y otros poemas*. Each poem of the love cycle forms an independent unit and at the same time is a part of the trilogy in its entirety.

Critics disagree on whether the poems are addressed to a real or an imaginary woman. She is never named, and all information about her is conveyed through the poet's internal consciousness. She remains quite vague, but the experiences of the poet in the love relationship are extremely vivid and deeply moving.

MY VOICE BECAUSE OF YOU

One of the most beautiful poems in *My Voice Because of You* is "¡Sí, todo con exceso!" ("Yes, Too Much of Everything"), in which the poet communicates his ecstasy in the plenitude of love. A central metaphor and its numerous variations give the poem its structure: love compared with numbers. Salinas's predilection for paradox is evident in his juxtaposition of the "oneness" of love with love's infinity and freedom from all limits. There are images of ascension—"to mount up," "our slender joys . . . aloft to their height"—yet the lovers surrender "to a great uncertain depth" from which the culminating expression of love's infinity emerges: "This is nothing yet./ Look deeply at yourselves. There's more." The language is simple, often prosaic, antipoetic: "from dozens to hundreds," "from hundreds to thousands," "writing tablets, pens, machines," "ciphers," "calculations." Nevertheless, the result is poetry: "everything to multiply/ caress by caress/ embrace by wild passion." "Light" and "sea" are again present in this immeasurable experience—"too much light, life and sea/ Everything in plural,/ plural lights, lives and seas"—but gone are the more complicated metaphors and imagery of his earlier works. Salinas employs more wordplay, internal rhythm, and short phrases, but his work still possesses elegance and still makes use of traditional Spanish meters in varied combinations, in unrhymed verses, that echo Spanish Golden Age poets.

In "No quiero que te vayas" ("Sorrow, I Do Not Wish You"), the poet engages in a dialogue with his pain and desires to hold onto it as the "last form of loving." A profoundly emotional piece, the poem describes how the poet tries to cope with separation from his beloved. There are no metaphors in this poem; its tension and profundity are bound in clear, conceptual speech containing opposing elements. The poet's sorrow is the proof that his beloved once loved him: "Your truth assures me/ that nothing was untrue." He can thus live in "that crumbled reality which/ hides itself and insists/ that it never existed." In later poems, he no longer feels such anguish, but he clings to the sorrow. For example, in "¿Serás, amor?" ("Will You Be, Love?"), Salinas writes, "From the beginning, to live is to separate." He asks that love be "a long good-bye which never ends," because, for him, love is the most authentic reality: "And that the most certain, the sure is good-bye."

Eventually, the poet-protagonist reestablishes harmony in his soul. In "Pensar en ti esta noche" ("To Think of You Tonight"), he feels love rooted not only within him but also in all nature. The poem begins with his characteristic use of paradox: "To think of you tonight/ was not to think of you." Love in this poem relates to his earlier themes: It serves as a link between inner and outer reality ("An agreement of world and being"), and as a lyric inspiration ("the canticle singing for you in my heart"). The poet beholds love everywhere and believes that its omnipresence transcends even death (". . . in a love changed to stars, to quest, to the world,/ saved now from the fear/ of the corpse which remains if we forget"). This optimism prevails in the final stage of Salinas's poetic and spiritual development.

The Sea of San Juan

Salinas's last three volumes of poetry are quite different from one another in tone and content, but all reveal the poet's continued probing of the relationships between his inner and outer worlds. In *The Sea of San Juan*, Salinas speaks to the sea in what amounts to one long dialogue. The initial poem is labeled "El contempledo: Tema" ("Theme"), and it is followed by fourteen "Variaciones" ("Variations"). The poet rejoices in his beloved sea. Just as he finds spiritual harmony and permanence in love, so, too, he discovers the sea to be a symbol of everlasting beauty, life, and inspiration. The language and style are much like that found in his love poetry.

One of the central metaphors of this volume is that of the sea as the poet's light. In the fifth variation, "Pareja muy desigual" ("Pair So Unequal"), he completely surrenders to the sea's radiance "as a blindman to the hand" of his guide. The sea gives more to the poet than the poet can ever return with his glance. If the poet can hold its clarity in his eyes, "the past will never vanish." Through the sea, however, the poet recognizes his own temporality. In the fourteenth variation, "Salvación por la luz" ("Salvation Through the Light"), the poet writes, "Now, here, facing you, . . ./ I learn what I am: I am but a moment/ of that long gaze which eyes you." This does not disturb the poet, because he feels a bond with his "former brothers . . . blinded by death," who once contemplated the sea as he does now. He believes himself to be renewing their sight. Contemplation brings salvation: "perhaps your eternity,/ turned to light, will enter us through our eyes."

TODO MÁS CLARO, Y OTROS POEMAS

In many of the poems of *Todo más claro, y otros poemas*, Salinas denounces the destructive and dehumanizing aspects of modern life. One of the strongest expressions of Salinas's horror is his 1944 "Cero" ("Zero"), in which he prophetically envisioned nuclear holocaust (which occurred just months later in Hiroshima). This, his longest poem, depicts the annihilation of a city by a bomb dropped from a plane. The eyes of the poet overflow with tears: "Invitation to weeping. This is a plaintive cry,/ eyes, crying endlessly." With bitter irony, he narrates how the insensitive pilot, upon seeing the white clouds of destruction, is reminded of tufts of wool, of his playful childhood romps with little lambs in fields of clover. Salinas goes on to contrast what might have flowered had it not been for the tragic effects of misguided technology. His images are haunting, and they display the poet's high level of culture and continued immersion in literary tradition. After the nothingness, or "zero," falls upon everything, the poet gropes in the rubble for his dead. He finds "total shipwreck" in the sea of destruction. The desolation is overwhelming, but the poet keeps on searching. Even in this darkest of visions, the poet, in the closing stanza, finds a glimmer of hope: "I am the shadow searching the rubbish dump."

CONFIANZA

Salinas's final volume of verse, *Confianza*, is a reaffirmation of his faith in life. His serenity returns; in "La nube que trae un viento" ("The Cloud That Bears Wind"), for example, he sings to a harmony he believes must exist: "The cloud that bears wind, the words that bring pain,/ other words cleanse those, another wind carries away." He finds this harmony in nature as seen in poems "Pájaro y radio" ("Bird and Radio"), "Nube en la mano" ("Cloud in Hand"), "¿Qué pájaros?" ("What Birds?"), and "En un trino" ("In the Trill of a Bird"). He also finds harmony in love with "Presente simple" ("Simple Present"), in art with "La estatua" ("The Statue"), and in his creation of poetry with "Ver lo que veo" ("Seeing What I See") and "Confianza" ("Confidence").

REALITY AND THE POET

Critics have followed Salinas's own guidance in *Reality and the Poet in Spanish Poetry* and have tried to determine the author's vision of the world by establishing his basic attitude toward reality. Their opinions differ greatly. He has been viewed as one who wavers between acceptance of reality and nothingness, as an escapist, a romantic idealist in search of the absolute, a kind of Neoplatonist, and a mystic. Those critics who point to Salinas's varying perspectives on reality are probably more correct. His works represent a synthesis of several possible attitudes toward reality: exaltation, idealization, escape, revolt, and acceptance. However, if one attitude can be said to prevail, it is Salinas's basic acceptance of reality. Although certain volumes convey the desire of the poet to look beyond his circumstances from a variety of perspectives, a fundamental acceptance of life is the ground note of Salinas's oeuvre .

OTHER MAJOR WORKS

LONG FICTION: *La bomba increíble*, 1950.

NONFICTION: *Reality and the Poet in Spanish Poetry*, 1940; *Literatura española: Siglo XX*, 1941, 1949; *Jorge Manrique: O Tradición y originalidad*, 1947; *La poesía de Rubén Darío*, 1948; *Ensayos de literatura hispánica: Del "Cantar de mío Cid" a García Lorca*, 1958.

BIBLIOGRAPHY

Allen, Rupert C. *Symbolic Experience: A Study of Poems by Pedro Salinas*. Tuscaloosa: University of Alabama Press, 1982. A critical interpretation of selected poems by Salinas. Includes an index and bibliography.

Crispin, John. *Pedro Salinas*. New York: Twayne, 1974. An introductory biography and critical study of selected works by Salinas. Includes bibliographic references.

Hartfield-Méndex, Vialla. *Woman and the Infinite: Epiphanic Moments in Pedro Salinas's Art*. Cranbury, N.J.: Associated University Presses, 1996. Examines the role of women in Salinas's works.

Newman, Jean Cross. *Pedro Salinas and His Circumstance*. San Juan, P.R.: Inter American University Press, 1983. A biography of Salinas offering a historical and cultural background of his life and works.

Shaughnessy, Lorna. *The Developing Poetic Philosophy of Pedro Salinas: A Study in Twentieth Century Spanish Poetry*. Lewiston, N.Y.: Edwin Mellen Press, 1995. A critical analysis of the philosophy evident in Salinas's poetry. Includes bibliographical references and an index.

Stixrude, David. *The Early Poetry of Pedro Salinas*. 1967. Reprint. Princeton, N.J.: Princeton University Press, 1975. A critical study of Salinas's early works. Includes bibliographic references.

Susan G. Polansky

MIGUEL DE UNAMUNO Y JUGO

Born: Bilbao, Spain; September 29, 1864
Died: Salamanca, Spain; December 31, 1936

PRINCIPAL POETRY
Poesías, 1907
Rosario de sonetos líricos, 1911
El Cristo de Velázquez, 1920 (*The Christ of Velázquez*, 1951)
Rimas de dentro, 1923
Teresa, 1924
Romancero del destierro, 1928
Poems, 1952
Cancionero: Diario poético, 1953 (partial translation as *The Last Poems of Miguel de Unamuno*, 1974)

OTHER LITERARY FORMS

Miguel de Unamuno y Jugo (ew-nah-MEW-noh ee HEW-goh) wrote prolifically throughout his life and produced numerous novels, short stories, dramas, and essays, as well as volumes of poetry. A mediocre dramatist who, under the influence of Henrik Ibsen, created talky stage works with uninspired characters, Unamuno achieved his greatest success with fiction, poetry, and the essay. His outstanding works of fiction include *Niebla* (1914; *Mist: A Tragicomic Novel*, 1928); *Abel Sánchez: Una historia de pasión* (1917; *Abel Sánchez*, 1947); and *San Manuel Bueno, mártir* (1931; *Saint Manuel Bueno, Martyr*, 1954). A philosophical author, Unamuno explored rich and complex ideas in all his works, regardless of genre. Particularly noteworthy are two long collections of essays, *Del sentimiento trágico de la vida en los hombres y en los pueblos* (1913; *The Tragic Sense of Life in Men and in Peoples*, 1921) and *La agonía del Cristianismo*, 1925 (in French as *L'Agonie du Christianisme*; in Spanish 1931; *The Agony of Christianity*, 1928, 1960), regarded by many critics as his central works.

ACHIEVEMENTS

Miguel de Unamuno y Jugo embodied the Spanish spirit and temperament in profound ways not seen in any Spanish writer since the Golden Age of Miguel de Cervantes, Lope de Vega Carpio, and Pedro Calderón de la Barca. In an oddly ironic twist, Unamuno began his career by attempting to "Europeanize" what he believed to be a backward Spain. Believing—as did many young Spanish artists—that Spain had lagged far behind the other European countries in its literature, art, music, and philosophy, Unamuno hoped to be able to take what was best in recent European advances and, by

Miguel de Unamuno y Jugo
(Library of Congress)

planting those seeds, allow new cultural life to grow in Spain. However, by the end of his prolific and distinguished career, Unamuno had not opened the windows of Spain so that new European light might shine on his land; instead, through his writing, he had given his country its own unique literary character. As artist and philosopher, Unamuno was a distinctly Spanish figure—a figure whose works the rest of Europe was forced to contemplate, explore, and assimilate. Throughout his career, Unamuno thrust Spain and the Spanish character at the rest of Europe, from his glorification of the Spanish landscape in such great poems as "Salamanca" and "On Gredos" to his assertion of the Spanish temper and the Spanish soul as it was mirrored in his own poetry and personality.

Unamuno was passionate in his convictions and claimed to understand philosophy only as poetry and poetry only as philosophy. In seeking to blur the distinction between poetry and philosophy, he was deliberately attempting to change the nature of poetry in his time. He had no interest in the elegance, decorum, and refinement of the poetry of his day. Poetry was held captive, in Unamuno's vision, by a precious "literatism," and he sought to free it from its literary bonds by proclaiming poetry the proper sphere of philosophy. Poetry could once again become a field of turbulent emotions and passionate thought if its smooth sheen of polished craft and beautiful art were fired by suffering, fear, doubt, and death. Even his seemingly most traditional poetic work, *Teresa*, a collection of love poems by a supposedly "unknown poet" to his beloved in the manner of Dante, Petrarch, or Torquato Tasso, is given a typical and characteristic twist by Unamuno. The poems are written to the beloved after her death. The whole series is not an ordinary cycle of love poems, but rather a study of the "metaphysics of love" and the spiritual link between love and death.

Unamuno believed that the basis for all art must be religious, and he believed that much of the art of his time had become the mere eruption of petty egos. He had little regard for Charles Baudelaire, Paul Verlaine, or Stéphane Mallarmé, preferring the more ambitious, if less refined, work of Algernon Charles Swinburne, Robert Browning, and Walt Whitman. In creating poetry more concerned with substance than with form and in forcing large philosophical ideas back into the closed and refined poetry of his day, Unamuno not only made his poetry the living testament of a struggling soul, but also brought Spanish poetry into the forefront of the play of ideas in Europe.

Biography

Miguel de Unamuno y Jugo was born in Bilbao, Spain, an industrial center of the Basque province, on September 29, 1864. He remained in Bilbao until he was sixteen and then attended the University of Madrid, where he received a doctorate in 1884. Returning then to the Basque region of northern Spain, he began to work as a tutor and to write articles for the local newspapers, all the while preparing himself for a teaching career. During this time, he also began work on his first novel, *Paz en la guerra* (1897; *Peace in War*, 1983) and devoted himself to the study of foreign languages. In 1891, he was appointed to the chair of Greek at the University of Salamanca. In that same year, he married Concepción Lizárraga (Concha), a woman who remained in the background when her husband became a public figure, but who gave him a refuge from the limelight, a happy home, and nine children. His devotion to her was absolute throughout his life.

In 1897, one of Unamuno's sons contracted meningitis, resulting in terminal hydrocephalus. As a result, Unamuno suffered a grave religious crisis and, after years of Roman Catholic upbringing and devoted observance of the faith, lost his trust in Catholicism. His spiritual struggle lasted for the rest of his life and came to be the major subject of many of his works—the torment of a soul that feels itself a Christian and yet is besieged by doubt.

Named rector of the University of Salamanca in 1900, Unamuno wrote extensively during the next fourteen years in many different forms—producing fiction, poetry, essays, and travel books—and completed his seminal philosophical work, *The Tragic Sense of Life in Men and in Peoples*. Dismissed from the rectorship in 1914, he continued to teach, to write prolifically, and to be an outspoken public figure. His forthright criticism of the dictatorship of Miguel Primo de Rivera resulted in the loss of his position at the university and his exile to Fuerteventura in the Canary Islands in 1924. Although he escaped to Paris, he was unhappy and longed to return to his native land. He moved to Hendaye, a border town that offered him a view of the Basque mountains and thus some contact with his land, his home, and his family.

Unamuno's exile came to an end in 1930 when Primo de Rivera was overthrown. Unamuno returned to Spain in triumph, and, after the establishment of the republic in 1931, the University of Salamanca reappointed him as rector; he was also elected deputy for the city of Salamanca to the Constituent Assembly. The same year his second great philosophical work, *The Agony of Christianity*, was published. Within two months in the spring and summer of 1934, Unamuno lost his wife and a daughter, Salomé, and that fall he retired as a professor and was named lifetime rector of the university. At the outbreak of the Civil War in July, 1936, Unamuno lent his support to General Francisco Franco but soon became disillusioned with the intolerance of the military leaders and openly denounced them in a speech delivered at the University of Salamanca on October 12, 1936. He was promptly dismissed from his post and was confined to his home, where he died of a heart attack on December 31, 1936.

ANALYSIS

In an essay titled "Mi religión" ("My Religion"), Miguel de Unamuno y Jugo states that he has expressed his religion in his "song," in the poetry to which he devoted so much of his literary career. His poems do not offer logical explanations or reasoned analyses of his faith; rather, they are the cries of his soul. Unamuno's poetry represents a great accomplishment in the field of religious verse, but perhaps more important, it records the spiritual journey of a tormented soul through all the avenues of hellish doubt and divine exultation, a brutally honest record of a human soul through all the vicissitudes of faith, doubt, love, despair, and hope. Only a handful of modern writers—among them August Strindberg, Fyodor Dostoevski, and John Berryman—have confronted religious questions and their effects on heart and mind with such honesty, energy, and passion.

Poetry became the natural place for Unamuno to set down his philosophical ideas. After his spiritual crisis of 1897, he broke with the faith of his childhood because he could no longer tolerate the certainties of a dogmatic faith, the notion that the existence of God and the principal mysteries of the Christian religion could be proven through human reason and then codified by a worldly institution. For Unamuno, doubt was the fuel of faith. He became the enemy of rational attempts to systematize religious faith and championed the antirational believer, one who strives toward knowledge and ultimately faith, but does so through the pain of doubt, suffering, and despair.

MEDIUM FOR PHILOSOPHY

In Unamuno's view, humans are defined by their yearning for immortality, but each person in his or her lifetime seeks that immortality and hence finds faith by a unique path. Poetry, Unamuno believed, could offer a place for the individual voice to express its unique pain, its unique insights. In poetry, the sacred flame that had been extinguished by dogma could be rekindled. That process could only begin, however, through suffering. In Unamuno's philosophical work, *The Agony of Christianity*, "agony" is used in the Greek sense of *agon* or struggle, not in the narrower modern sense of the product of pain. The struggle of each questioning soul is unique, and can only be expressed in a form such as poetry or fiction, which makes no pretensions to scientific objectivity.

As these emphases suggest, Unamuno was an important figure in the development of existentialism, standing between Søren Kierkegaard, a writer he admired deeply, and later thinkers such as Martin Heidegger, Jean-Paul Sartre, and Albert Camus. William Barrett observes that Unamuno's vision helped bring questions of life and death back into the philosophical arena and thus spurred the development of modern existential thought.

Indeed, poetry offered Unamuno an ideal medium for his philosophy. Fiction and drama required the transformation of his voice into other voices, the transformation of his life into other lives. In poetry, his voice could speak directly of its suffering, its pain, its ecstasy. Poetry opened itself to the display of pure emotion and could be a vehicle of antirationalism. In Unamuno's verse, structure and form are often deliberately subordinated to idea and content; the criticism—that his poetry lacked discipline—he wore as a badge of honor.

If he often neglected structure, however, Unamuno was obsessed with the precision and the perfection of the word. Poetry and the poet, in depending on the importance of the word, in caring for the precise truth of the word and in creating new life and new thoughts through the word, might reach toward the ultimate Word, the Word that was made flesh. Unamuno constantly asserts the parallel between the word in poetry and the Divine Word, even in his earliest poems, published in 1907. For example, in "¡Id con Dios!" ("Farewell, Go with God!"), he speaks directly to his own verse:

> Go with God, since with Him you came to take
> in me the form of words: like living flesh.

The role of the poet becomes the role of the priest, the function of art a sacred function, for in the creation of poetry the poet makes the Word flesh.

THE CHRIST OF VELÁZQUEZ

Unamuno's greatest poetic achievement, *The Christ of Velázquez*, is a long sequence of poems that meditate on Diego Velázquez's famous painting of the figure of Christ on the Cross. The poet never moves his eyes from the vision of the Savior; instead, he explores each element of the painting, each detail of the crucified body and each response of his own mind and heart. The canvas unveils to Unamuno the pain, the mystery, and the hope of all Christian thought, and he creates songs of complex beauty that explore his own love and fear, despair and hope. The titles of the individual poems in this "liturgical epic"—"Luna" ("Moon"), "Ecce Homo," "Dios-obscuridad" ("God-Darkness"), "Sangre" ("Blood"), "La vida es sueño" ("Life Is a Dream"), "Paz en la guerra" ("Peace in War"), "Alba" ("Dawn"), "Rosa" ("Rose"), and so on—offer hints as to the individual sparks of inspiration for each poem.

At first, all thought and the universe itself are embodied in the figure of the crucified man-God, as in the poem "Moon," where the whiteness of Christ's body against the enveloping darkness of the background offers the poet assurance of God's presence and light, just as the moon in the black night radiates the light of the invisible sun. As the poems proceed, however, Unamuno comes to focus solely on the body of Christ itself, examining each detail of his human form in poems titled, "Corona" ("Crown"), "Cabeza" ("Head"), "Pelo" ("Hair"), "Frente" (" Forehead "), "Ojos" ("Eyes") , "Orejas" ("Ears"), and so on. The body becomes the poems. Throughout all the poems, images hurtle wildly by, for the suffering figure contains the whole universe and becomes the link for wide-ranging thoughts.

Unamuno's ideas are presented antirationally and nonlogically, for thought resides in his response to Christ's Passion and all it suggests of life and death, humans and God, time and eternity, and not in reason or analysis. The poems are sprinkled with references to and paraphrases from both Old and New Testaments, the sources of the quotations being duly noted in the margin. The sacred texts become natural elements of the individual poems as the poet deliberately blends his own voice with the Divine Word of the Almighty. Above all, Unamuno reproduces for the reader the promise of freedom from time and death that he feels as he views Velázquez's painting. The painter's art is re-created for the reader: Art becomes a source of hope.

Cancionero

Unamuno's last major work of verse, his *Cancionero* (book of songs), consists of more than fifteen hundred brief meditations and hymns. Published in 1953, many years after Unamuno's death, these compositions record the poet's thoughts from 1928 to 1936, constituting a kind of spiritual diary. Each of the poems was composed by Unamuno in the morning after he had read a chapter of the Bible. These meditations on biblical passages provided a measure of his spiritual state as he began to "resume . . . strife" for another day.

The poems of *Cancionero* reach the ideal form that Unamuno had long been seeking for his poetry; they do not pretend to be anything other than direct meditations and do not need any other subject than the Word of God and the mind and heart of the poet himself. They possess an intimacy and immediacy that go to the heart of Unamuno's philosophy. Moment by moment, the soul searches for the sacred, recording its quest with precision and reverence.

This immersion in and love for the details of life's reality follows from Unamuno's

Christian beliefs. When God became man and descended to assume flesh, he invested earthly life with eternal importance. Thus, there is nothing odd in Unamuno's addressing poems to a dead dog, a wild reed, or the "Forefinger of the Right Hand" of the crucified Christ. All life, all matter provokes meditation. For Unamuno, poetry is meditation, a means to stretch the soul: "the deeper into yourself you go,/ the larger your boundaries, my soul."

Legacy

Unamuno once wrote of Blaise Pascal that his *Pensées* (1670; *Monsieur Pascal's Thoughts, Meditations, and Prayers*, 1688; best known as *Pensées*) do not invite the reader to study a philosophy, but rather to become acquainted with a man, to penetrate the sanctuary of a soul bared to the quick. Unamuno's poetry makes the same invitation, for though it is philosophical poetry, the soul of the poet in all his complexity animates the poems. A poetry of philosophy, contemplation, meditation, religious hope, and the agony of doubt, Unamuno's verse is most memorable for the unique, unswervingly honest voice of the poet himself. Indeed, Unamuno's poetry is more dramatic than his dramas, for in his poetry, he brings his own character to startling life. Unamuno's intensity of personal vision combines with the ambition and universality of his themes and the precise energy of his language to create a poetry of richness, range, and lasting importance.

Other major works

LONG FICTION: *Paz en la guerra*, 1897 (*Peace in War*, 1983); *Amor y pedagogía*, 1902; *Niebla*, 1914 (*Mist: A Tragicomic Novel*, 1928); *Abel Sánchez: Una historia de pasión*, 1917 (*Abel Sánchez*, 1947); *Tres novelas ejemplares y un prólogo*, 1920 (*Three Exemplary Novels and a Prologue*, 1930); *La tía Tula*, 1921 (*Tía Tula*, 1976); *San Manuel Bueno, mártir*, 1931 (*Saint Manuel Bueno, Martyr*, 1954); *Dos novelas cortas*, 1961 (James Russell Stamm and Herbert Eugene Isar, editors).

SHORT FICTION: *El espejo de la muerte*, 1913; *Soledad y otros cuentos*, 1937; *Abel Sánchez, and Other Stories*, 1956.

PLAYS: *La esfinge*, pr. 1909 (wr. 1898); *La difunta*, pr. 1910; *La princesa doña Lambra*, pb. 1913; *La venda*, pb. 1913 (wr. 1899); *Fedra*, pr. 1918 (wr. 1910; *Phaedra*, 1959); *El pasado que vuelve*, pr. 1923 (wr. 1910); *Raquel encadenada*, pr. 1926 (wr. 1921); *Sombras de sueño*, pr., pb. 1930; *El otro*, pr., pb. 1932 (wr. 1926; *The Other*, 1947); *El hermano Juan: O, El mundo es teatro*, pb. 1934 (wr. 1927); *Soledad*, pr. 1953 (wr. 1921); *Teatro completo*, 1959.

NONFICTION: *De la enseñanza superior en España*, 1899; *Nicodemo el fariseo*, 1899; *Tres ensayos*, 1900; *En torno al casticismo*, 1902; *De mi país*, 1903; *Vida de Don Quijote y Sancho según Miguel de Cervantes Saavedra, explicada y comentada por Miguel de Unamuno*, 1905 (*The Life of Don Quixote and Sancho According to Miguel de Cervantes Saavedra Expounded with Comment by Miguel de Unamuno, 1927); Recuerdos de niñez y de mocedad, 1908; Mi religión, y otros ensayos breves, 1910; Soliloquios y conversaciones, 1911 (Essays and Soliloquies, 1925); Contra esto y aquello, 1912; Del sentimiento trágico de la vida en los hombres y en los pueblos, 1913 (The Tragic Sense of Life in Men and in Peoples, 1921); La agonía del Cristianismo, 1925 (in French as L'Agonie du Christianisme; in Spanish 1931; The Agony of Christianity, 1928, 1960); Cómo se hace una novela, 1927 (How to Make a Novel, 1976); La ciudad de Henoc, 1941; Cuenca ibérica, 1943; Paisajes del alma, 1944; La enormidad de España, 1945; Visiones y commentarios, 1949; Tratado del amor de Dios, 2005 (wr. 1905-1908; Treatise on Love of God, 2007).

MISCELLANEOUS: *De Fuerteventura a París*, 1925; *Obras completas*, 1959-1964 (16 volumes).

BIBLIOGRAPHY

Ch'oe, Chae-Sok. *Greene and Unamuno: Two Pilgrims to La Mancha*. New York: Peter Lang, 1990. A comparison of the Christian fiction of Unamuno and Graham Greene. Includes bibliography and index.

Ellis, Robert Richmond. *The Tragic Pursuit of Being: Unamuno and Sartre*. Tuscaloosa: University of Alabama Press, 1988. Compares and contrasts the existentialism revealed in the works of Unamuno and Jean-Paul Sartre. Includes bibliography and index.

Gonzalez, Pedro Blas. *Unamuno: A Lyrical Essay*. Mountain View, Calif.: Floricanto Press, 2007. Provides literary criticism of his poetry as well as of two novels.

Hansen, Keith W. *Tragic Lucidity: Discourse of Recuperation in Unamuno and Camus*. New York: Peter Lang, 1993. A comparison of the political and social views of Unamuno and Albert Camus, as evidenced in their literary works. Includes bibliography.

Little, William Thomas. Introduction to *The Velázquez Christ*, by Miguel de Unamuno y Jugo. Translated by William Thomas Little. Lanham, Md.: University Press of America, 2002. Little provides a scholarly introduction and commentary on each of the poems in his translation of Unamuno's poem sequence.

Luby, Barry. *The Uncertainties in Twentieth- and Twenty-first Century Analytic Thought: Miguel de Unamuno the Precursor*. Newark, Del.: Juan de la Cuesta, 2008. Examines the philosophy of Unamuno as revealed in his writing, looking at truth, reality, religion, and language.

Nozick, Martin. *Miguel de Unamuno*. New York: Twayne, 1971. A basic biography of Unamuno that covers his life and works. Includes a bibliography.

Round, Nicholas G., ed. *Re-reading Unamuno*. Glasgow: Department of Hispanic Studies, University of Glasgow, 1989. This collection of papers from a conference on Unamuno provides literary criticism of his works. Includes bibliographies.

Sinclair, Alison. *Uncovering the Mind: Unamuno, the Unknown, and the Vicissitudes of Self.* New York: Manchester University Press, 2002. An examination of the fictional works of Unamuno in respect to his portrayal of the self. Includes bibliography and index.

David Allen White

CÉSAR VALLEJO

Born: Santiago de Chuco, Peru; March 16, 1892
Died: Paris, France; April 15, 1938

PRINCIPAL POETRY
Los heraldos negros, 1918 (*The Black Heralds*, 1990)
Trilce, 1922 (English translation, 1973)
España, aparta de mí este cáliz, 1939 (*Spain, Take This Cup from Me*, 1974)
Poemas en prosa, 1939 (*Prose Poems*, 1978)
Poemas humanos, 1939 (*Human Poems*, 1968)
Obra poética completa, 1968
César Vallejo: The Complete Posthumous Poetry, 1978
Poesía completa, 1978
Selected Poems, 1981
The Complete Poetry: A Bilingual Edition, 2007 (Clayton Eshleman, editor)

OTHER LITERARY FORMS

César Vallejo (vah-YAY-hoh) wrote fiction, plays, and essays, as well as lyric poetry, although his achievement as a poet far outstrips that in any other genre. His short stories—many of them extremely brief—may be found in *Escalas melografiadas* (1923; musical scales). A longer short story, "Fabla salvaje" (1923; primitive parlance), is a tragic idyll of two rustic lovers, and *Hacia el reino de los Sciris* (1967; toward the kingdom of the Sciris) is set in the time of the Incas. *El tungsteno* (1931; *Tungsten*, 1988), is a proletarian novel with an Andean setting that was written in 1931, the year Vallejo joined the Communist Party. Another story, *Paco Yunque* (1969), is about the mistreatment of a servant's son by a classmate who happens to be the master's son.

Vallejo became interested in the theater around 1930, but he destroyed his first play, "Mampar." Three others, *Entre las dos orillas corre el río* (pb. 1979; the river flows between two banks); *Lock-Out* (pb. 1979), and *Colacho hermanos: O, presidentes de América* (pb. 1979; Colacho brothers), never published during the poet's lifetime, are now available in *Teatro completo* (1979; complete theatrical work). His long essay, *Rusia en 1931: Reflexiones al pie del Kremlin* (1931; reissued in 1965), was followed by *Rusia ante el segundo plan quinquenal* (1965); *Contra el secreto profesional* (1973); and *El arte y la revolución* (1973). His master's thesis, *El romanticismo en la poesía castellana*, was published in 1954.

ACHIEVEMENTS

Finding an authentic language in which to write has always represented a fundamental problem for Latin American writers, since it became evident that the language inherited from the Spanish conquerors could not match Latin American reality. The problem of finding such a language goes hand in hand with that of forging a separate cultural identity. An important attempt at renovating poetic language was made by the Spanish American *Modernistas* around the turn of the century, but their verse forms, imagery, and often exotic subject matter were also becoming obsolete by the time César Vallejo reached maturity. It was thus up to him and his contemporaries to find a language that could deal with contemporary concerns involving war, depression, isolation, and alienation. Although hardly recognized in his lifetime, Vallejo did more than perhaps any other poet of his generation to provide an idiom that would at once reflect the Spanish tradition, his own Peruvian heritage, and the contemporary world. Aware of his heritage from Spain's great writers of the past, he blended traditional poetic vocabulary and tropes with homely Peruvian idioms and even the language of children. Where the result was still inadequate, he made up new words, changed the function of old ones, and incorporated a lexicon never before seen in poetry, often savaging poetic convention.

Vallejo's gradual conversion to Marxism and Communism is of great interest to those attempting to understand how collectivist ideals may shape poetry. The evolution of his ideology continues to be studied intensively by many individuals committed to bettering the conditions of poverty and alienation about which Vallejo wrote so eloquently—conditions that still exist in Latin America and other parts of the world. His unflinchingly honest search for both linguistic and moral solutions to the existential anguish of modern human beings gives his poems universal validity, while their density and complexity challenge critics of the most antithetical modes.

Biography

César Abraham Vallejo was born in Santiago de Chuco, a primitive "city" of some fourteen thousand inhabitants in Peru's northern mountains that could only be reached by a rail trip and then several days ride on mule or horseback. Both of his grandfathers had been Spanish priests and both of his grandmothers native Peruvians of Chimu Indian stock. His parents were literate and of modest means; his father was a notary who became a subprefect in the district. Francisco de Paula Vallejo and María de los Santos Mendoza were an upright and religious pair whose marriage produced twelve offspring and who were already middle-aged when their youngest child, César, was born. In his writings, Vallejo was often to remember the security and warmth of his childhood home—games with three of his older siblings, and particularly with his mother, who might have been especially indulgent with her sensitive youngest child.

At age thirteen, Vallejo left Santiago de Chuco to attend high school in Huamachuco, another mountain village, where he received an introduction to literature and began scribbling verses. Economic difficulties prevented him from continuing the university studies that he had begun in the larger coastal cities of Trujillo and Lima in 1911. The young man first went to work in a nearby tungsten mine—an experience that he would later draw upon for his Socialist Realist novel *Tungsten*—and then on a coastal sugar plantation. While there, he observed the tightly structured hierarchy that kept workers in misery while the middle class, to which he himself belonged, served the needs of the elite. In 1913, he returned to the University of Trujillo and graduated two years later, having written a master's thesis titled *El romanticismo en la poesía castellana*. For the next few years, he studied law in Trujillo, supporting himself by becoming a first-grade teacher. One of his pupils, Ciro Alegría, later to become an important novelist, described Vallejo in those days as lean, sallow, solemn, and dark skinned, with abundant straight black hair worn somewhat long, brilliant dark eyes, a gentle manner, and an air of sadness.

During these years, Vallejo became familiar with the writings of Ralph Waldo Emerson, José Rodó, Friedrich Nietzsche, Miguel de Unamuno y Jugo, Walt Whitman, and Juan Ramón Jiménez. Vallejo also read the poems of two of the leading Spanish American *Modernistas*, Rubén Darío and Julio Herrera y Reissig, as well as those of Peruvian poets of the day. Vallejo declaimed his own poems—mostly occasional verse—at various public ceremonies, and some of them appeared in Trujillo's newspapers. Critical reception of them ranged from the cool to the hostile, since they were considered to be exaggerated and strange in that highly traditional ambience. Vallejo fell in love with a young Trujillo girl, Zoila Rosa Cuadro, the subject of several poems included in *The Black Heralds*. The breakup of this relationship provided one motive for his departure, after he had obtained a law degree, for Lima in 1918. There he found a position teaching in one of the best elementary schools and began to put the finishing touches on his first volume of poems.

Vallejo was soon in love with the sister-in-law of one of his colleagues, a woman identified only as "Otilia." A number of the *Trilce* poems, which he was writing at the time, deal with this affair. It ended when the poet refused to marry the woman, resulting in the loss of his job. This crisis was compounded by the death of his mother, a symbol of stability whose loss made him feel like an orphan. For some time, Vallejo had thought of going to Paris, but he decided to return first to his childhood home in Santiago de Chuco. During a national holiday, he was falsely accused of having been the instigator of a civil disturbance and was later seized and imprisoned for 112 days despite the public protests of many Peruvian intellectuals. The experience affected him profoundly, and the poems that he wrote about it (later published in *Trilce*) testify to the feeling of solidarity with the oppressed that he voiced for the first time. While in prison, he also wrote a number of the sketches to appear in *Escalas melografiadas*. In 1923, he sailed for Europe, never again to return to Peru.

While Vallejo's days in Lima had often been marked by personal problems, in Paris, he experienced actual penury, sometimes being forced to sleep in the subway. Eventually, he found employment in a press agency but only after a serious illness. He began to contribute articles to Lima newspapers, made friends with a number of avant-garde artists, and journeyed several times to Spain, where he was awarded a grant for further study. Increasingly concerned with injustice in the world, he made his first trip to Russia in 1928 with the intention of staying. Instead, he returned within three weeks, living soon afterward with a Frenchwoman, Georgette de Philippart, who was later to become his wife. With some money that had come to her, the pair set out on a tour by train through Eastern Europe, spending two weeks in Moscow and returning by way of Rome. As Vallejo's enthusiasm for Marxism became increasingly apparent in his newspaper articles, he found them no longer welcome in Lima, and in 1930, he was ordered to leave France because of his political activity. Once again in Spain, he wrote several plays and the novel *Tungsten* and published *Rusia en 1931*, the only one of his books to sell well. No publisher could be found for several other works. After a third and final visit to Russia as a delegate to the International Congress of Writers, he wrote *Rusia ante el segundo plan quinquenal* (Russia facing the second five-year plan) and officially joined the Communist Party.

In 1932, Vallejo was permitted to return to Paris, where he tried unsuccessfully to publish some new poems. In 1936, the Spanish Civil War broke out, and Vallejo became an active supporter of the Republic, traveling to Barcelona and Madrid to attend the Second International Congress for the Defense of Culture. He visited the battlefront and learned at first hand of the horrors suffered by the Spanish people in the war. Returning to Paris for the last time, he poured his feelings into his last work, *Spain, Take This Cup from Me*. In March, 1938, he became ill. Doctors were unable to diagnose his illness, and Vallejo died a month later on Good Friday, the day before the troops of Francisco Franco won a decisive victory in Spain.

Analysis

One of the unique qualities of César Vallejo's poetry—one that makes his work almost impossible to confuse with that of any other poet writing in the Spanish language—is his ability to speak with the voice and sensibility of a child, whether as an individual orphaned by the breakup of a family or as a symbol of deprived and alienated human beings everywhere. Always, however, this child's voice, full of expectation and hope, is implicitly counterposed by the adult's ironic awareness of change and despair. Inseparable from these elements is the poet's forging of a language capable of reflecting the register and the peculiarly elliptical reasoning of a child and, at the same time, revealing the Hermetic complexity of the adult intellectual's quest for security in the form of truth. The poetry that is Vallejo's own answer to these problems is some of the most poignant and original ever produced.

The Black Heralds

The lines of Vallejo's subsequent development are already evident in his first volume, *The Black Heralds*, a collection of sixty-nine poems grouped under various subtitles. As critics have observed, many of these poems reflect his involvement with

Romantic and *Modernista* poetry. They are conspicuous in many cases for their descriptions of idyllic scenes in a manner that juxtaposes words of the Peruvian Sierra and the vocabulary of Symbolism, including religious and erotic elements. Vallejo did not emphasize rhyme and rhythm to the extent that some *Modernistas* did, but most of these early poems are framed in verse forms favored by the latter, such as the Alexandrine sonnet and the *silva*. While demonstrating his impressive mastery of styles already worked out by others, he was also finding his own voice.

This originality is perhaps most evident in the last group of poems in *The Black Heralds*, titled "Canciones de Hogar" ("Home Songs"), poems dealing with the beginning of Vallejo's sense of orphanhood. In "A mi hermano Miguel in memoriam" ("To My Brother Miguel in Memoriam"), the poet relives a moment of the childhood game of hide-and-seek that he used to play with his "twin heart." Speaking to his brother, Vallejo announces his own presence in the part of the family home from which one of the two always ran away to hide from the other. He goes on to remind his playmate of one day on which the latter went away to hide, sad instead of laughing as he usually was, and could not be found again. The poem ends with a request to the brother to please come out so as not to worry "mama." It is remarkable in that past and present alternate from one line to the next. The language of childhood, as well as the poet's assumed presence at the site of the events, lends a dramatic immediacy to the scene. At the same time, the language used in the descriptive passages is clearly that of the adult who is now the poet. Yet in the last verse, the adult chooses to accept literally the explanation that the brother has remained in hiding and may finally respond and come out, which would presumably alleviate the mother's anxiety and make everything right once more. The knowledge that the poet is unable (or refuses) to face the permanent alteration of his past may elicit feelings of tragic pathos in the reader.

"Los pasos lejanos" ("The Distant Steps") recalls the poet's childhood home in which his parents, now aged, are alone—the father sleeping and the mother walking in the orchards. Here, the only bitterness is that of the poet himself, because he is now far away from them. He in turn is haunted by a vision of his parents as two old, white, and bent roads along which his heart walks. In "Enereida," he imagines that his father has died, leading to a regression in time so that the father can once again laugh at his small children, including the poet himself, who is again a schoolboy under the tutelage of the village priest.

Many of the poems in *The Black Heralds* deal with existential themes. While religious imagery is pervasive, it is apparent that the poet employs it to describe profane experiences. Jean Franco has shown that in speaking of "the soul's Christs" and "Marías who leave" and of Communions and Passions, Vallejo trivializes religious language rather than attempting to inflate the importance of his own experiences by describing them in religious terms. As well as having lost the security and plenitude of his childhood home, the poet has lost the childhood faith that enabled him to refer in words to the infinite.

In the title poem, "Los heraldos negros" ("The Black Heralds"), Vallejo laments life's hard blows, harder sometimes than humans can stand. He concludes that these blows come from the hatred of God, that they may be the black heralds sent by Death. In "Los dados eternos" ("The Eternal Dice"), God is a gambler throwing dice and may as easily cast death as life. In fact, Earth itself is his die. Now worn to roundness, it will come to rest only within the sepulchre. Profane love is all that is left; while the beloved may now be pure, she will not continue to be so if she yields to the poet's erotic impulses. Love thus becomes "a sinning Christ," because humankind's nature is irrevocably physical. Several poems allude to the poet's ideal of redeeming himself through brotherly love, a thematic constant in Vallejo's work, yet such redemption becomes difficult if not impossible if a person is lonely and alienated. In "Agape," the poet speaks of being alone and forgotten and of having been unable therefore to "die" for his brother. "La cena miserable" ("The Wretched Supper") tells of the enigma of existence in which humans are seen, as in "Agape," as waiting endlessly for spiritual nurture, or at least for some answer concerning the meaning of life. Here, God becomes no more than a "black spoon" full of bitter human essence, even less able than humans to provide needed answers. The lives of humans are thus meaningless, since they are always separated from what they most desire—whether this be the fullness of the past, physical love, God's love, or brotherly love.

Even in the poems most laden with the trappings of *Modernismo*, Vallejo provides unusual images. In "El poeta a su amada" ("The Poet to His Beloved"), he suggests that his kiss is "two curved branches" on which his beloved has been "crucified." Religious imagery is used with such frequency that it sometimes verges on parody, and critics agree that in playing with language in this way Vallejo is seeking to highlight its essential ambiguity, something he continues to do in *Trilce* and *Human Poems*, even while totally abandoning the imagery of *Modernismo*. Such stripping away of excess baggage is already visible in *The Black Heralds*. Antitheses, oxymorons, and occasional neologisms are also to be noted. While the great majority of the poems are elegantly correct in terms of syntax—in marked contrast to what is to become the norm in *Trilce*—there are some instances of linguistic experimentation, as when nouns are used as adjectives. In "The Distant Steps," for example, the mother is described as being "so soft, so wing, so departure, so love." Another device favored by the poet in all his later poems—enumeration—is also present. Finally, traditional patterns of meter and rhyme are abandoned in "Home Songs," with the poetic emotion being allowed to determine the form.

TRILCE

Despite these formal adumbrations and although *The Black Heralds* is not a particularly transparent work, there is little in it to prepare the reader for the destruction of language in the Hermetic density of *Trilce*, which came along only three years later. These were difficult years for the poet, in which he lost his mother, separated from Otilia, and spent what he was later to refer to as the gravest moments of his life in the Trujillo jail. All the anguish of these events was poured into the seventy-seven free-verse poems of his second major work. If he suffered existentially in *The Black Heralds* and expressed this suffering in writing, it was done with respect for traditional verse forms and sentence structure, which hinted at an order beyond the chaos of the poet's interior world. In *Trilce*, this order falls. Language, on which "logical assumptions" about the world are based, is used in such a way as to reveal its hollowness: It, too, is cut loose and orphaned. Abrupt shifts from one metaphorical sphere to another make the poems' internal logic often problematic.

A hint of what is to come is given in the title, a neologism usually taken to be a hybrid of *tres* (three) and *dulce* (sweet), an interpretation that is in accord with the poet's concern about the ideal number expressed in several poems. It is not known, however, what, if any, concrete meaning the poet had in mind when he coined the word; it has become a puzzle for readers and critics to solve. It is notable that in "interpreting" the *Trilce* poems, critics often work out explications that seem internally consistent but that turn out to be related to a system diametrically opposed to the explication and system of some other critic. It is possible, however, to say with certainty that these poems deal with a struggle to do something, bridge something, and say something. Physical limits such as the human body, time, space, and numbers often render the struggle futile.

Two of the thematic sets of *Trilce* for which it is easiest to establish concrete referents are those dealing with the poet-as-child and those dealing with his imprisonment. In poem III, the poet once again speaks in the voice of a child left at home by the adults of the family. It is getting dark, and he asks when the grown-ups will be back, adding that "Mama said she wouldn't be gone long." In the third stanza, an ironic double vision of years full of agonizing memories intrudes. As in "To My Brother Miguel in Memoriam," the poet chooses to retain the child's faith, urging his brothers and sisters to be good and obey in letter and spirit the instructions left by the mother. In the end, it is seen that the "leaving" is without remedy, a function of time itself; it eventually results in the poet's complete solitude without even the comfort of his siblings. In poem XXIII, the mother, the only symbol of total plenitude, is seen as the "warm oven" of the cookies described as "rich hosts of time." The nourishment provided by the mother was given freely and naturally, taken away from no one and given without the child's being obliged. Still, the process of nurturing leads to growing up and to individuation and alienation. Several poems mythicize the process of birth but shift so abruptly to demythicize human existence that the result is at first humorous. In poem XLVII, a candle is lighted to protect the mother while she gives birth, along with another for the babe who, God willing, will grow up to be bishop, pope, saint, "or perhaps only a columnary headache." Later, in *Human Poems*, there is a Word Incarnate whose bones agree in number and gender as it sinks into the bathtub ("Lomo de las sagradas escrituras"/ "Spine of the Scriptures").

In poem XVIII, the poet surveys the four walls of the cell, implacably closed. He calls up a vision of the "loving keeper of innumerable keys," the mother, who would liberate him if she could. He imagines the two longer walls as mothers and the shorter ones as the children each of them is leading by the hand. The poet is alone with only his two hands, struggling to find a third to help him in his useless adulthood. In poem LVIII, the solid walls of the cell seem to bend at the corners, suggesting that the poet is dozing as a series of jumbled thoughts produce scenes in his mind that follow no easy logical principle of association. The poet sees himself helping the naked and the ragged, then dismounting from a panting horse that he also attempts to help. The cell is now liquid, and he becomes aware of the companions who may be worse off than he. Guilt suddenly overwhelms him, and he is moved to promise to laugh no more when his mother arises early to pray for the sick, the poor, and the prisoners. He also promises to treat his little friends better at play, in both word and deed. The cell is now boundless gas, growing as it condenses. Ambiguously, at the end, he poses the question, "Who stumbles outside?" The openness of the poem is similar to that of many others in *Trilce*, and it is difficult to say what kind of threat to the poet's resolutions is posed by the figure outside. Again, the poetic voice has become that of a child seeking to make all that is wrong in the world right once more by promising to be "a good boy." Of course, he is not a child at all, as the figure outside may be intended to remind both him and the reader. The result is once again a remarkable note of pathos tinged with poignant irony.

Many of *Trilce*'s poems deal with physical love and even the sexual act itself. "Two" seems to be the ideal number, but "two" has "propensities of trinity." Clearly, the poet has no wish to bring a child into the world, and sex becomes merely an act of organs that provides no solution to anything. While the poet seems to appreciate the maternal acts performed by his lover, he fails to find any transcendental satisfaction in the physical relationship, even though he is sad when it is over.

An important theme that emerges in *Trilce* and is developed more fully in *Human Poems* and *Spain, Take This Cup from Me* is that of the body as text. In poem LXV, the house to which the poet returns in Santiago seems to be his mother's body. Parts of the body—the back, face, shoulder, eyes, hands, lips, eyelashes, bones, feet, knees, fingers, heart, arms, breasts, soles of the feet, eyelids, ears, ribs—appear in poem after poem, reminding the reader of human and earthly functions and the limitations of human beings.

In many ways, *Trilce* resembles the poetry of such avant-garde movements as Surrealism, Ultraism, and Creationism in the boldness of its images, its unconventional vocabulary, and its experimentation with graphics. Vallejo did have very limited exposure to some of this poetry after he reached Lima; his critics, however, generally agree that *Trilce* was produced independently. While Vallejo may have been encouraged to experiment by his knowledge of European literary currents, his work coincides with them as an original contribution.

Human Poems

As far as is known, the poems after *Trilce* were written in Europe; with very few exceptions, none was published until 1939, a year after the poet's death, when they appeared under the title *Human Poems*. While Vallejo's life in Peru was far from affluent, it must have seemed easy in comparison with the years in Paris, where he often barely subsisted and suffered several illnesses. In addition, while he did see a new edition of *Trilce* published through the intervention of friends in 1931 and his *Rusia en 1931* did go into three editions during his lifetime, he could never count on having his writings accepted for publication.

Human Poems, considered separately from *Spain, Take This Cup from Me*, is far from being a homogeneous volume, and its final configuration might have been different had it been Vallejo who prepared the final edition rather than his widow. Generally speaking, the poems that it includes deal with ontological anguish whose cause seems related to physical suffering, the passage of time, and the impossibility of believing that life has any meaning. In fact, *Human Poems* examines suffering and pain, with their corollaries, poverty, hunger, illness, and death, with a thoroughness that few other works can match. At times, the anguish seems to belong only to the poet, now not only the orphan of *Trilce* but alienated from other people as well. In "Altura y pelos" ("Height and Hair"), the poet poses questions: "Who doesn't own a blue suit?/ Who doesn't eat lunch and board the streetcar . . . ?/ Who is not called Carlos or any other thing?/ Who to the kitty doesn't say kitty kitty?" The final answer given is "Aie? I who alone was solely born." At least two kinds of irony seem to be involved here. The activities mentioned are obviously trivial, but neither is it easy to be alone. In the well-known "Los nueve monstruos" ("The Nine Monsters"), the poet laments the abundance of pain in the world: "Never, human men/ was there so *much* pain in the chest, in the lapel, in the wallet/ in the glass, in the butcher-shop, in arithmetic!" and "never/ . . . did the migraine extract so much forehead from the forehead!" Pain drives people crazy "in the movies,/ nails us into the gramophones,/ denails us in bed . . ." The poem concludes that the "Secretary of Health" can do nothing because there is simply "too much to do."

"The Nine Monsters" is representative of several features of *Human Poems*. The language is extremely concrete, denoting things that are inseparable from everyday existence. Much of the poem consists of lists, continuing a device for which the poet had already shown a disposition in his first work. Finally, the logic of the systems represented by the items named is hard to pin down, so that it is somewhat reminiscent of child logic in its eccentricity. Again and again, Vallejo's remarkable sensibility is demonstrated beyond any preciosity or mere posturing.

One reason for the poet's alienation is that he sees people as engaged in trivial occupations and as being hardly more advanced on the evolutionary scale than pachyderms or kangaroos, whereas he himself aspires to rise above his limitations. In "Intensidad y altura" ("Intensity and Height"), he tells of his desire to write being stifled by his feeling "like a puma," so that he might as well go and eat grass. He concludes, "let's go, raven, and fecundate your rook." He thus sees himself condemned not to rise above the purely mundane. Religion offers no hope at all. In "Acaba de pasar el que vendrá..." ("He Has Just Passed By, the One Who Will Come..."), the poet suggests that "the one who will come"—presumably the Messiah—has already passed by but has changed nothing, being as vague and ineffectually human as anyone else.

While the majority of these posthumously published poems convey utter despair, not all of them do. Although the exact dates of their composition are generally unknown, it is natural to associate those that demonstrate growing concern for others with Vallejo's conversion to Marxist thought and eventually to Communism. In "Considerando en frío..." ("Considering Coldly..."), speaking as an attorney at a trial, the poetic voice first summarizes the problems and weaknesses of humanity (he "is sad, coughs and, nevertheless,/ takes pleasure in his reddened chest/... he is a gloomy mammal and combs his hair...") Then, however, he announces his love for humanity. Denying it immediately, he nevertheless concludes, "I signal him,/ he comes,/ I embrace him, moved./ So what! Moved... Moved...." Compassion thus nullifies "objectivity." In "La rueda del hambriento" ("The Hungry Man's Wheel"), the poet speaks as a man so miserable that his own organs are pulled out of him through his mouth. He begs only for a stone on which to sit and a little bread. Apparently ignored, aware that he is being importunate, he continues to ask, disoriented and hardly able to recognize his own body. In "Traspié entre dos estrellas" ("Stumble Between Two Stars"), the poet expresses pity for the wretched but goes on to parody bitterly Christ's Sermon on the Mount ("Beloved be the one with bedbugs,/ the one who wears a torn shoe in the rain"), ending with a "beloved" for one thing and then for its opposite, as if calling special attention to the emptiness of mere words. It is possible to say that in these poems the orphan has finally recognized that he is not alone in his orphanhood.

SPAIN, TAKE THIS CUP FROM ME

Although first published as part of *Human Poems*, *Spain, Take This Cup from Me* actually forms a separate, unified work very different in tone from the majority of the other posthumous poems—a tone of hope, although, especially in the title poem, the poet seems to suspect that the cause he has believed in so passionately may be lost. In this poem, perhaps the last that Vallejo wrote, the orphan—now all human children—has found a mother. This mother is Spain, symbol of a new revolutionary order in which oppression may be ended. The children are urged not to let their mother die; nevertheless, even should this happen, they have a recourse: to continue struggling and to go out and find a new mother.

Another contrast is found in the odes to several heroes of the Civil War. Whereas, in *Human Poems*, humans are captives of their bodies and hardly more intelligent than the lower animals, *Spain, Take This Cup from Me* finds people capable of true transcendence through solidarity with others and the will to fight injustice. A number of poems commemorate the battles of the war: Talavera, Guernica, Málaga. Spain thus becomes a text—a book that sprouts from the bodies of an anonymous soldier. The poet insists again and again that he himself is nothing, that his stature is "tiny," and that his actions rather than his words constitute the real text. This may be seen to represent a greatly evolved negation of poetic authority, first seen in *The Black Heralds* with the repeated cry, "I don't know!"

Nevertheless, *Spain, Take This Cup from Me* rings with a biblical tone, and the poet sometimes sounds like a prophet. James Higgins has pointed out certain images that recall the Passion of Christ and the New Jerusalem, although religious terminology, as in all Vallejo's poetry, is applied to humans rather than to divinity. While Vallejo continues to use techniques of enumeration—which are often chaotic—and to use concrete nouns (including many referring to the body), he also employs abstract terms such as peace, hope, martyrdom, harmony, eternity, and greatness. The sense of garments, utensils, and the body's organs stifling the soul is gone and is replaced by limitless space. In Vallejo's longest poem, "Himno a los voluntarios de la República" ("Hymn to the Volunteers for the Republic"), a panegyric note is struck.

One of Vallejo's most immediately accessible poems, "Masa" ("Mass"), tells almost a parable of a dead combatant who was asked by one man not to die, then by two, and finally by millions. The corpse kept dying until surrounded by all the inhabitants of Earth. The corpse, moved, sat up and embraced the first man and then began to walk. The simplicity of the story and of its narration recalls the child's voice in *Trilce*, promising to cease tormenting his playmates in order to atone for the world's guilt. In this piece, as well as in all Vallejo's last group of poems, however, the irony is gone.

Poetic cycle

It is thus possible to see the completion of a cycle in the four works. Disillusionment grows in *The Black Heralds*, and then alienation works its way into the language itself in *Trilce*. *Human Poems* is somewhat less Hermetic than *Trilce*, but life is an anguished nightmare in which the soul is constrained by the ever-present body that seems to be always wracked with pain. Only in *Spain, Take This Cup from Me*, with the realization that men are brothers who can end their common alienation and suffering by collective action, does the poet regain his lost faith and embark upon a positive course. The orphan relocates the lost mother, whom he now sees to be the mother of all, since all men are brothers. The true significance of Vallejo's poetry, however, surely lies in his honesty in questioning all established rules of poetic expression, as well as the tradition of poetic authority, in order to put poetry fully in touch with the existential prison house of twentieth century humanity.

OTHER MAJOR WORKS

LONG FICTION: *Fábula salvaje*, 1923 (novella); *El tungsteno*, 1931 (*Tungsten*, 1988).

SHORT FICTION: *Escalas melografiadas*, 1923; *Hacia el reino de los Sciris*, 1967; *Paco Yunque*, 1969.

PLAYS: *Colacho hermanos: O, presidentes de América*, pb. 1979; *Entre las dos orillas corre el río*, pb. 1979; *La piedra cansada*, pb. 1979; *Lock-Out*, pb. 1979; *Teatro completo*, 1979.

NONFICTION: *Rusia en 1931: Reflexiones al pie del Kremlin*, 1931, 1965; *El romanticismo en la poesía castellana*, 1954; *Rusia ante el segundo plan quinquenal*, 1965; *Contra el secreto profesional*, 1973; *El arte y la revolución*, 1973.

BIBLIOGRAPHY

Britton, R. K. "Love, Alienation, and the Absurd: Three Principal Themes in César Vallejo's *Trilce*." *Modern Language Review* 87 (July, 1992): 603-615. Demonstrates how Vallejo's poetry expresses the anguished conviction that humankind is simply a form of animal life subject to the laws of a random, absurd universe.

Dove, Patrick. *The Catastrophe of Modernity: Tragedy and the Nation in Latin American Literature*. Lewisburg, Pa.: Bucknell University Press, 2004. This discussion of the theme of modernity as a catastrophe contains a chapter on Vallejo's *Trilce*.

Hart, Stephen M. *Stumbling Between Forty-six Stars: Essays on César Vallejo*. London: Centre of César Vallejo Studies, 2007. A collection of essays on various aspects of the poet.

Hart, Stephen M., and Jorge Cornejo Polar. *César Vallejo: A Critical Bibliography of Research*. Rochester, N.Y.: Boydell and Brewer, 2002. A bibliography collecting works of Vallejo. Invaluable for researchers.

Hedrick, Tace Megan. "Mi andina y dulce Rita: Women, Indigenism, and the Avant-Garde in César Vallejo." In *Primitivism and Identity in Latin America: Essays on Art, Literature, and Culture*, edited by Erik Camayd-Freixas and José Eduardo González. Tucson: University of Arizona Press, 2000. Relates the indigenism of "Dead Idylls" from *The Black Heralds* to the "avant-garde concerns and practices" of *Trilce*, often considered Vallejo's most brilliant work.

Higgins, James. *The Poet in Peru: Alienation and the Quest for a Super-Reality*. Liverpool, England: Cairns, 1982. Contains a good overview of the main themes of Vallejo's poetry.

Lambie, George. "Poetry and Politics: The Spanish Civil War Poetry of César Vallejo." *Bulletin of Hispanic Studies* 69, no. 2 (April, 1992): 153-170. Analyzes the presence of faith and Marxism in *Spain, Take This Cup from Me*.

Niebylski, Dianna C. *The Poem on the Edge of the Word: The Limits of Language and the Uses of Silence in the Poetry of Mallarmé, Rilke, and Vallejo*. New York: Peter

Lang, 1993. In the context of the language "crisis" of modern poetry and the poet's dilemma in choosing language or silence, Niebylski examines the themes of time and death in Vallejo's *Human Poems*.

Sharman, Adam, ed. *The Poetry and Poetics of César Vallejo: The Fourth Angle of the Circle*. Lewiston, N.Y.: Edwin Mellen Press, 1997. Collection of essays examining Vallejo's work from the perspectives of Marxism, history, the theme of the absent mother, and postcolonial theory.

Lee Hunt Dowling

LOPE DE VEGA CARPIO

Born: Madrid, Spain; November 25, 1562
Died: Madrid, Spain; August 27, 1635

PRINCIPAL POETRY
La Dragontea, 1598
El Isidro, 1599
La hermosura de Angélica, 1602
Rimas, 1602
El arte nuevo de hacer comedias en este tiempo, 1609 (*The New Art of Writing Plays*, 1914)
Jerusalén conquistada, 1609
Rimas sacras, 1614
La Circe, 1621
La filomena, 1621
Triunfos divinos, 1625
La corona trágica, 1627
Laurel de Apolo, 1630
Amarilis, 1633
La gatomaquia, 1634 (*Gatomachia*, 1843)
Rimas humanas y divinas del licenciado Tomé de Burguillos, 1634
Filis, 1635
La Vega del Parnaso, 1637
Desire's Experience: A Representative Anthology of Lope de Vega's Lyric Poetry, 1991

OTHER LITERARY FORMS

Lope de Vega Carpio (VAY-gah KAHR-pyoh), one of literature's most prolific writers, wrote several prose works, including *La Arcadia* (1598), a pastoral romance; *El peregrino en su patria* (1604; *The Pilgrim: Or, The Stranger in His Own Country*, 1621), a Byzantine romance; *Los pastores de Belén* (1612; the shepherds of Bethlehem), a pastoral romance; *Novelas a Marcia Leonarda* (1621; stories for Marcia Leonarda, four short novels dedicated to his last love, Marta de Nevares); and *La Dorotea* (1632), a highly autobiographical novel in dialogue. Both his prose and his poetic productions, however, are overshadowed by his plays. Lope de Vega himself claimed to have written about eighteen hundred plays, probably an exaggeration, but even the most conservative estimates place the total at about eight hundred. Some of the better known are *Peribáñez y el comendador de Ocaña* (pb. 1614; *Peribáñez*, 1936); *El*

Lope de Vega Carpio
(Library of Congress)

villano en su rincón (pb. 1617; *The King and the Farmer*, 1940); *La dama boba* (pb. 1617; *The Lady Nit-Wit*, 1958); *El perro del hortelano* (pb. 1618; *The Gardener's Dog*, 1903); *Fuenteovejuna* (pb. 1619; *The Sheep-Well*, 1936); *El mejor alcalde, el rey* (pb. 1635; *The King, the Greatest Alcalde*, 1918); and *El caballero de Olmedo* (pb. 1641; *The Knight from Olmedo*, 1961). He also wrote many *autos*, one-act Eucharist plays composed for religious celebrations.

Achievements

Lope de Vega Carpio lived during the most productive period of Spain's literary history, known as the Golden Age, and shone as its brightest light. He cultivated every literary form—succeeding in each one of them—and quickly gained popularity. A turbulent and charismatic personality, Lope de Vega participated passionately in every aspect of social life, including several scandalous love affairs, all of which he poeticized in one form or another. Writing was so much a part of him that, as some critics have said, his life was literature. He lived for, in, and through literature and was able to afford his carefree lifestyle because of literature; his numerous compositions brought him a steady flow of money. According to his first biographer, Pérez de Montalbán, Lope de Vega composed poems before he even knew how to write, and the author himself claimed that he wrote his first play at twelve. It is known that Lope de Vega was recognized as a good poet and playwright in his early twenties because Miguel de Cervantes praises him very highly in *La Galatea* (1585). Lope de Vega's first collection of lyric poetry appeared in 1602 and, with some alterations and additions was reprinted several times during his lifetime. New collections were published periodically, some of them incorporating long narrative poems that also appeared separately. In 1604, the first volume of his plays was published, and by the time of his death, twenty-two additional volumes (containing twelve dramas each) had appeared. With these plays, Lope de Vega created a new dramatic pattern that, although he felt a need to defend and justify it in *The New Art of Writing Plays*, was accepted and imitated by dramatists for more than a century. Lope de Vega influenced the theater to such an extent that he is considered the founder of the Spanish national drama. Because of this exuberant creativity, coupled with his outgoing personality, he was sought after to promote and to organize literary events when a celebration was in order. Thus, one sees him organizing poetic jousts for any event requiring celebration, from the birth of a prince to the canonization of a saint.

Lope de Vega's literary genius was recognized by all his contemporaries, although some of them resented his immense popularity. In a fitting tribute, Cervantes called him the king of playwrights, a prodigy of nature.

BIOGRAPHY

Lope Félix de Vega Carpio was the third child of Félix de Vega Carpio and Francisca Fernández Flores. Both parents were from Santander and moved first to Valladolid, where their first two children were born. Félix de Vega seems to have had the same passionate traits of character that his son would later show. Infatuated with another woman, Félix de Vega abandoned his family to follow her to Madrid, but Francisca followed her husband and managed to reunite the family. Out of this reconciliation came Lope de Vega, who would later poeticize the event in "Belardo' a Amarilis: Epístola séptima," inserted in *La filomena*, as he did with every aspect of his life.

Lope de Vega was taught Latin and Castilian by Vicente Espinel, a well-known poet and novelist, and soon was recognized as a child prodigy. After a few years at the Jesuit Imperial College—which emphasized the study of grammar and rhetoric—he entered the service of the bishop of Ávila, Don Jerónimo Manrique. Under Manrique's guidance, Lope de Vega studied for the priesthood at the University of Alcalá from 1577 to 1582 but abandoned his studies because of a love affair. It is possible, also, that he studied in Salamanca the next year before enlisting in the expedition to the Azores Islands. After returning from this expedition, Lope de Vega fell in love with Elena Osorio, thus beginning one of the most turbulent episodes of his life. Following a pattern that soon became a norm, pouring every event of his life into literature, Lope de Vega expressed his love for Elena in passionate verses that told everyone about their love affair. These poetic indiscretions jeopardized the reputation of Elena, a married woman, forcing her to end the relationship. Jealous and hurt, Lope de Vega wrote some compositions highly offensive to Elena and her family and disseminated them throughout Madrid. Elena's family took the case to court, and Lope de Vega was imprisoned while the trial took place and was later sentenced to exile—from the court for eight years and from the kingdom for two.

The court's sentence, not to be broken under penalty of death, did not have a marked effect on Lope de Vega, for soon after, he returned to Madrid and seduced Isabel de Urbina, a young woman from a prominent family. Trying to avoid the scandal, Isabel's father consented to the marriage of the two, and the wedding was done by proxy. A few months later, the poet went to Lisbon to enlist with the Spanish Armada. He was one of the lucky survivors of that disastrous expedition against England, which marked the decline of Spain as a world superpower. After his return, still under banishment from Castile, Lope de Vega went to Valencia with his wife. There, he saw several of his plays staged and seriously began to pursue his career as a playwright. In 1590, when his banishment from Castile was ended, Lope de Vega went to Toledo and entered the service of the marqués de Malpica. Later that year, he moved to Alba de Tormes in the province of Salamanca to work for the famous duke of Alba as one of his secretaries. There, the poet spent some of the most peaceful days of his life, alternating his duties with his literary activity and going frequently to Salamanca, whose university life he portrays so well in his plays. This restful existence ended in 1594 when Isabel died in childbirth, leaving the playwright in great grief.

In 1595, Lope de Vega returned to Madrid, where he was soon involved in another scandalous love affair, this time with a wealthy widow, Antonia Trillo de Armenta. Three years later, the poet married Doña Juana de Guardo, a daughter of a butcher/fishmonger, hoping to better his financial situation with her dowry. At the same time, however, he began another affair with Micaela de Luján, the beautiful wife of actor Diego Díaz de Castro. Lope de Vega spent the next several years sharing his time with the two women, establishing separate homes and families with each.

In 1605, Toledo entrusted him with the organization of a poetic joust to celebrate the birth of Prince Philip, later King Philip IV. Lope de Vega acted as the judge of this contest, contributed verses of his own, and even introduced a "Soneto de Lucinda Serrana" ("Sonnet by Lucinda Serrana"), the pet name of the illiterate Micaela. In 1607, Lope de Vega found yet another love: Jerónima de Burgos, with whom the poet would be involved intermittently for the next ten years. Greatly disappointed, Micaela went back to Madrid and quietly disappeared from his life. Three years later, the playwright returned to the capital, where for a time he led a quiet life dedicated to his family, his writing, and his garden.

Lope de Vega's marriage to Doña Juana marks the most productive period of his life.

During that time he published most of his long poems (*La Dragontea*, *El Isidro*, *La hermosura de Angélica*, *Jerusalén conquistada*, *The New Art of Writing Plays*) and romances (*La Arcadia*, *The Pilgrim*, *Los pastores de Belén*), two large collections of *rimas*, and three volumes of his collected plays. It was during this period, also, that the poet became acquainted with the duke of Sessa, starting a long epistolary friendship. Doña Juana died in 1613, leaving Lope de Vega in a state of spiritual crisis that he decided to resolve by becoming a priest. His motivation in taking this step is not completely clear, for the poet continued involving himself with women even when he was preparing for his ordination. Critic Juan Luis Alborg justifies Lope de Vega's actions by saying that he incarnated tragically both the most extreme passions and the most intense religious fervor, but one should not overlook the fact that Lope de Vega was going through financial difficulties and was possibly seeking a more comfortable situation; as a priest, it was easier to obtain some sort of permanent pension. Lope de Vega sought and obtained a chaplaincy in the Church of Saint Segundo in Ávila, with an annual income of 150 ducats.

The ecclesiastical habit did not take Lope de Vega away from women. He was involved with Lucia de Salcedo in 1616 and made a trip to Valencia simply to be with her. The poet soon ended this relationship, however, to attend exclusively to his last love, Marta de Nevares. In her, Lope de Vega found the ideal woman whom he had long been seeking. Marta was married, however, and her enraged husband, Roque Hernández, almost managed to have Lope de Vega killed. Marta began separation procedures, but Roque Hernández died in the midst of the litigation, leaving her free to live with Lope de Vega.

Marta entered Lope de Vega's life in his late years, and she rejuvenated him. She influenced his writing tremendously, and the poet enjoyed another period of intense productivity. In a few short years, he published several volumes of his plays and of his poems, wrote new ones, and, following Marta's encouragement, attempted new literary forms. His private life, however, might have annoyed some people, for he sought the position of royal chronicler but did not obtain it. On the other hand, his living arrangement was not an obstacle when it came to celebrating religious events, such as the 1620 and 1625 poetic contests organized by the city of Madrid to celebrate the beatification and canonization of Saint Isidro. For both occasions, Lope de Vega was in charge of the entire celebration.

The last years of the poet were full of misfortune and disaster. Marta lost her sight and her sanity, becoming extremely violent at times, until she finally died in 1632, leaving Lope de Vega in a state of deep depression. His son Lope drowned two years later while on a pearl-hunting expedition off the coast of the Island of Margarita. Finally, his beloved daughter Antonia Clara was abducted by Cristóbal Tenorio that same year, and Lope de Vega never saw her again. The playwright found himself accompanied by only his memories. Still, he kept poeticizing his emotions and the events of his life. Feeling that death was approaching, Lope de Vega repented daily for his sinful life and finally attained the office of priest. During this time he published *Rimas humanas y divinas del licenciado Tomé de Burguillos* (human and divine verses) under the pseudonym Tomé de Burguillos, as well as *Gatomachia*, a burlesque poem that ridicules the excesses of the Renaissance epic, and his autobiographical novel *La Dorotea*, considered by many to be one of the most beautiful examples of Spanish prose fiction.

Lope de Vega died in 1635, enjoying the greatest popularity of any living author, and so many people attended his funeral that, as Pérez de Montalbán recounted in *Fama póstuma* (1636), it looked like the funeral of a king.

Analysis

Lope de Vega Carpio reacted poetically to every event of his existence, always leading the true life of an artist. Everything became a poetic pretext for the author, from his passionate love for Elena Osorio to the bitter disappearance of his daughter, Antonia Clara, near the end of his life. As critic José F. Montesinos says, "Lope's biography constitutes the most attractive chapter of our literary history . . . because it shows the existence of the artist in every moment—converting real life facts into poetic creation."

Lope de Vega was conscious of this relationship between life and literature, and he left testimony of it in several of his works. The "Soneto a Lupercio Argensola" ("Sonnet to Lupercio Argensola"), published in the first edition of the *Rimas*, ends with these lines:

> You tell me not to write, or not to live?
> Make sure that my love will not feel,
> Then I will make my pen not to write.

In *La Dorotea*, one of his last works, he writes: "To love and to write verses is all one and the same."

Perhaps because of this intense vitalization of his poetry, Lope de Vega did not write great metaphysical poems, like Francisco Gómez de Quevedo y Villegas, nor did he adapt fully to the new poetic school headed by Luis de Góngora y Argote. He remained a poet of emotions, of feelings, of passions, of love. What is transparent in his poetry, says Dámaso Alonso, is "the life of a man in its turbulent plurality, day after day, in love and in hate, in his picaresque profile and in his periods of true repentance and sincere search for God." In this manner, continues the Spanish critic, Lope de Vega is profoundly original, anticipating the Romantics. Furthermore, these characteristics are not exclusive to his lyric poetry but are present in his objective compositions as well. As Karl Vossler has pointed out, Lope de Vega was able to write with the most lyric and intimate tones when he was poeticizing someone else's love. This does not mean, however, that Lope de Vega was only a poet of natural and simple spontaneity, a poet who cultivated exclusively the popular and traditional meters. He was also a poet full of curiosity who liked to experiment with new forms and poetic conventions. Together with the traditionalist, one finds in Lope de Vega a Petrarchist, a sophisticated poet able to produce very complicated compositions, perfectly assimilating Italian models; a Góngorist, trying to imitate his most vocal enemy in obscure linguistic games; and even a philosophical poet who, unable to imitate Góngora properly, adopts an austere style that is the polar opposite of Góngora's Baroque extravagance.

Lope de Vega published several books of poetry during his lifetime. Most of them were miscellaneous volumes containing short and long poems and, in some cases, prose works. Unlike Garcilaso de la Vega, Luis de León, and Góngora, Lope de Vega did not cultivate lyric poetry as an independent art. Many of his lyric poems were first incorporated in his plays or prose works, from which they were later taken so as to rescue them from oblivion.

LA DRAGONTEA AND EL ISIDRO

Lope de Vega's first publication was *La Dragontea* (Drake the pirate), an epic poem divided into ten cantos and written in royal octaves. As the title implies, this poetic composition narrates the forays of Sir Francis Drake to the Spanish possessions, concluding with his death in Portobelo at the hands of his own men. Full of patriotic fervor, the poem reveals the common sentiments of the Spaniards toward England in the years after the ill-fated Armada. *La Dragontea* has been criticized by some for its partiality, although it is important to mention that the events are narrated objectively. The poem is also distinguished by the vivid realism of its maritime descriptions, in which Lope de Vega shows his knowledge of nautical vocabulary.

A year later, the ten-thousand-line poem *El Isidro* appeared, written in the popular *quintilla* (five-line stanza) and divided into ten books. Of rather mediocre quality, this work was intended to popularize the figure of Saint Isidro the Ploughman, or the Farmer, as a plea for his canonization. A work of great simplicity, *El Isidro* is not an epic poem, but rather a familiar story poeticized with unusual naturalness. In spite of its poetic flaws, there were several editions published during the seventeenth century, certainly the result of the canonization of the saint, which occurred in 1622.

In 1602, the poet published a large volume containing *La hermosura de Angélica* (Angelica's beauty), *Rimas*, and *La Dragontea*. Lope de Vega started writing *La hermosura de Angélica* when he was at sea with the Armada. The poem was probably inspired by the success of Luis Barahona de Soto's *Primera parte de la Angélica* (1586; first part of Angélica), and it clearly shows Lope de Vega's intention of following the steps of Ludovico Ariosto's *Orlando Furioso* (1516, 1521, 1532; English translation, 1591). The poem, divided into twenty cantos and written in royal octaves, presents such a mixture of adventures and fantastic events that it ends up becoming a kind of Byzantine novel, wild and extravagant. The best parts of the poem are those that are based on Lope de Vega's personal experience, in which the passionate humanity of the poet reveals itself.

JERUSALÉN CONQUISTADA

Lope de Vega's next poetic effort, perhaps the greatest of all, was *Jerusalén conquistada* (Jerusalem regained), a rather long epic poem of six thousand stanzas divided into twenty cantos. He composed this work to emulate Torquato Tasso and also to correct Tasso's omission of the Spaniards in his *Gerusalemme liberata* (1581; *Jerusalem Delivered*, 1600). The poet incorporates here a legend that assumes that Alfonso VIII of Castile participated in the Third Crusade (1187-1192). Furthermore, Alfonso is presented in the foreground of the action after the fourth book, competing with and even overshadowing Richard the Lion-Hearted; thus, a disproportionate part of the poem is dedicated to someone who did not go to Palestine at all. Lope de Vega wrote this poem with unusual care, resulting in many beautiful passages. The author himself esteemed the work highly, as he told the duke of Sessa: ". . . it is something that I have written in my best age and with a different dedication from what I put into the writings of my youth, in which appetite prevailed over reason." In spite of this praise, Lope de Vega did not produce the great masterpiece he set forth to write. His intentions were to give Spain a national epic, doing for his country what Luís de Camões had done for Portugal with *Os Lusíadas* (1572; *The Lusíadas*, 1655). The poet, however, could not accommodate his genius to this enterprise, for, as Alborg says, "he was not able to sustain the solemnity and dignity of intonation that such a composition required." Instead, he assembled an amalgam of adventures, magicians, demons, and angels, much in the manner of a chivalric romance. In addition, he introduced material drawn from his personal life, portraying his mistress, Micaela de Luján, and their illegitimate children.

THE NEW ART OF WRITING PLAYS

In 1609, Lope de Vega published *The New Art of Writing Plays*, a didactic poem in which the playwright presents his formula for success in the theater. He had been writing plays for quite some time by then and had been involved in several controversies regarding his departure from the Aristotelian rules. A mature man of forty-seven, Lope de Vega expresses proudly what he considers to be the correct approach of his trade—that is, to please the common man. He advises playwrights to mix the tragic with the comic, as Nature does; to observe only the unity of action; to avoid an empty stage; to use a language appropriate to the speakers and to adjust the dialogue accordingly; to use different verse forms in accordance to the dramatic situation; to avoid obscure passages; to make the whole appear probable; and to use all the tricks of the trade.

Following the taste of the period, Lope de Vega also wrote several mythological poems, some of which appeared in 1621 with other short compositions. The nightingale in *La filomena* narrates the classical myth of Progne and Philomene in the first part, while the second part, written in *silvas*, portrays the poet, disguised as a nightingale, reciting a diatribe against the crow. "La Andrómeda" tells the fable of Andrómeda and Perseo, showing Gongoristic influences. In *La Circe*, Lope de Vega amplifies that episode of

Homer's *Odyssey* (c. 725 B.C.E.; English translation, 1614) with the arrival of Ulysses at the island of Circe, his voyage to Hell, and the love between Polifemo and Galatea.

LA CORONA TRÁGICA AND LAUREL DE APOLO

In 1627, Lope de Vega published *La corona trágica* (the tragic crown), a five-thousand-line poem written in memory of Mary Stuart, Queen of Scots. Here once again, Lope de Vega reflects Spain's hatred for England and Queen Elizabeth, whom the poet addresses with repulsive and offensive names and likens to infamous women from the Bible and from mythology. On the other hand, Mary Stuart is presented as a pure martyr of the Catholic Church. It is a rather dull poem, but, as critic George Ticknor claims, "it savors throughout of its author's sympathy with the religious spirit of his age and country; a spirit, it should be remembered, which made the Inquisition what it was." Lope de Vega dedicated this poem to Pope Urban VIII, who, in turn, gave the poet a degree of doctor of divinity and the Cross of the Order of Saint John.

If his desire to emulate Tasso and Ariosto resulted in the composition of *Jerusalén conquistada* and *La hermosura de Angélica* respectively, the example of Cervantes' *Viaje del Parnaso* (1614) inspired Lope de Vega to write his *Laurel de Apolo*. A seven-thousand-line poem divided into ten *silvas*, *Laurel de Apolo* is a catalog of nearly three hundred Spanish poets, as well as some Portuguese, Italian, and French authors and nine Spanish painters. Lope de Vega praises them all very freely, without much artistic discrimination; although he apologizes for possible unintentional omissions, there are some noticeable absences, such as Juan de la Cueva, Saint Teresa de Ávila, and Saint John of the Cross. The poem also presents Lope de Vega's ideas about writing poetry, discussing metrics, Italian influence and innovations, and many other topics. Following his well-established custom, the poet introduces some autobiographical notes.

GATOMACHIA

Near the end of his life, Lope de Vega wrote what is probably his best poetic composition, *Gatomachia*, a burlesque poem divided into seven *silvas* or *cantos*, which he published in 1634 in a miscellaneous volume under the pseudonym of Tomé de Burguillos. The work is a marvelous parody of the pedantic Renaissance epic, a genre that Lope de Vega himself had cultivated. It narrates the love affair of two cats, Micifuf and Zapaquilda, and the pretensions of a third one, Marramaquiz, who tries to seduce Zapaquilda with the help of the magician Garfiñanto. Marramaquiz fails, but during the wedding of the lovers, he kidnaps the bride and takes her to his castle. With the help of his friends, Micifuf captures the fortress, kills Zapaquilda's captor, and is reunited with his beloved; together, they live happily ever after. The tone of the poem is festive and light throughout, particularly the last two *silvas*, where Lope de Vega parodies both epic poets and traditional ballads, always with great success. Lope de Vega dedicated this work to his son, who would die before the book was published.

Lope de Vega used various verse forms in his poetic compositions, but he succeeded especially in two of them: the romance and the sonnet. The romances, or ballads, make up the first important group in Lope de Vega's poetic production. This traditional meter, derived from the epic, had become very popular during the poet's lifetime, as is attested by the publication of the anthology *Romancero general* in 1600 and 1604. Lope de Vega found the lightness of the romance very much in consonance with his vibrant poetic genius, and he used it to poeticize, for example, his love for Elena Osorio, his libels against her family, and his marriage to Isabel de Urbina. In the fashionable Moorish and pastoral romances, he found a vehicle to express his intimacy, and, disguising his identity under fictional Moorish lovers or shepherds, he wrote some of the best examples of the genre. When the poet suffered a spiritual crisis after the death of his wife Doña Juana de Guardo, he also expressed his most fervent religious sentiments in this poetic form. Lope de Vega's romances became very popular in his own time, a popularity that has endured, for they have a special freshness that makes them readable even today.

Lope de Vega was also a master of the sonnet. He used it frequently in his plays and even jokes about composing one in the well-known "Soneto a Violante" ("Sonnet to Violante"), included in *La niña de plata* (pb. 1617; the stunning beauty). Lope de Vega took many of these sonnets out of his plays and published them in different collections. The first such collection, *Rimas*, contained two hundred sonnets, the majority of which are dedicated to Micaela de Luján; in the refinements and subtleties of *Rimas*, one can clearly see the influence of Petrarch. Lope de Vega's humanity transcends the artificial structure of the form, however, giving these poems a genuine depth of feeling. As Montesinos says, these sonnets "combine literary motifs of two or three generations of poets with Lope's personal experience. In this sense, they are, perhaps, his most characteristic poetic collection." Lope de Vega cultivated the sonnet during his entire life, leaving other collections of different tones, such as those published in *Rimas sacras* (sacred verses), in which the poet fuses his most noble and spiritual feelings with a very refined poetic technique.

OTHER MAJOR WORKS

LONG FICTION: *La Arcadia*, 1598; *El peregrino en su patria*, 1604 (*The Pilgrim: Or, The Stranger in His Own Country*, 1621); *Los pastores de Belén*, 1612; *Novelas a Marcia Leonarda*, 1621; *La Dorotea*, 1632.

PLAYS: *Los comendadores de Córdoba*, pb. 1609 (wr. 1596-1598); *La noche toledana*, pb. 1612 (wr. 1605); *El nuevo mundo descubierto por Cristóbal Colón*, pb. 1614 (wr. 1596-1603; *The Discovery of the New World by Christopher Columbus*, 1950); *Peribáñez y el comendador de Ocaña*, pb. 1614 (wr. 1609-1612; *Peribáñez*, 1936); *El duque de Viseo*, pb. 1615 (wr. 1604-1610); *El anzuelo de Fenisa*, pb. 1617 (wr. 1602-1608); *La dama boba*, pb. 1617 (*The Lady Nit-Wit*, 1958); *Los melindres de Belisa*, pb. 1617 (wr. 1606-1608); *La niña de plata*, pb. 1617 (wr. 1607-1612);

El villano en su rincón, pb. 1617 (wr. 1611; *The King and the Farmer*, 1940); *El acero de Madrid*, pb. 1618 (wr. 1606-1612; *Madrid Steel*, 1935); *El mayordomo de la duquesa de Amalfi*, pb. 1618 (wr. 1599-1606; *The Majordomo of the Duchess of Amalfi*, 1951); *El perro del hortelano*, pb. 1618 (wr. 1613-1615; *The Gardener's Dog*, 1903); *Las flores de don Juan, y rico y pobre trocados*, pb. 1619 (wr. 1610-1615); *Fuenteovejuna*, pb. 1619 (wr. 1611-1618; *The Sheep-Well*, 1936); *La corona merecida*, pb. 1620 (wr. 1603); *El verdadero amante*, pb. 1620 (wr. before 1596); *La buena guarda*, pb. 1621 (wr. 1610); *La hermosa Ester*, pb. 1621 (wr. 1610); *Lo cierto por lo dudoso*, pb. 1625 (wr. 1612-1624; *A Certainty for a Doubt*, 1936); *Amar sin saber a quién*, pb. 1630 (wr. 1620-1622); *El castigo sin venganza*, pb. 1635 (based on Matteo Bandello's novella; *Justice Without Revenge*, 1936); *El mejor alcalde, el rey*, pb. 1635 (wr. 1620-1623; *The King, the Greatest Alcalde*, 1918); *Los Tellos de Meneses I*, pb. 1635 (wr. 1620-1628); *El premio del bien hablar*, pb. 1636 (wr. 1624-1625); *Las bizarrías de Belisa*, pb. 1637; *El guante de doña Blanca*, pb. 1637 (wr. 1627-1635); *El caballero de Olmedo*, pb. 1641 (wr. 1615-1626; *The Knight from Olmedo*, 1961); *La moza de cántaro*, pb. 1646? (wr. 1625-1626); *Castelvines y Monteses*, pb. 1647 (wr. 1606-1612; English translation, 1869); *Four Plays*, 1936; *Five Plays*, 1961.

NONFICTION: *Égloga a Claudio*, 1637.

BIBLIOGRAPHY

Fox, Diane. *Refiguring the Hero: From Peasant to Noble in Lope de Vega and Calderón*. University Park: Pennsylvania State University Press, 1991. Fox examines the image of the hero and class status in the works of Lope de Vega and Pedro Calderón de la Barca. Includes bibliography and index.

Heiple, Daniel L. "Political Posturing on the Jewish Question by Lope de Vega and Faria e Sousa." *Hispanic Review* 62, no. 2 (Spring, 1994): 217. During the Spanish Inquisition, Lope de Vega wrote a poem celebrating the persecution of Jews. Manuel de Faria e Sousa, who shared Vega's anti-Semitic views, also wrote a sonnet in tribute to Vega. Their writings are examined.

McKendrick, Melveena. *Playing the King: Lope de Vega and the Limits of Conformity*. Rochester, N.Y.: Tamesis, 2000. An examination of Lope de Vega's portrayal of the monarchy in his works. Includes bibliography and index.

Samson, Alexander, and Jonathan Thacker, eds. *A Companion to Lope de Vega*. Rochester, N.Y.: Tamesis, 2008. A comprehensive treatment of the life and writings of Lope de Vega.

Wright, Elizabeth R. *Pilgrimage to Patronage: Lope de Vega and the Court of Philip III, 1598-1621*. Lewisburg, Pa.: Bucknell University Press, 2001. This study focuses on the patronage system and the interactions between politics and the life and work of Lope de Vega. Includes bibliography and index.

Juan Fernández Jiménez

CHECKLIST FOR EXPLICATING A POEM

I. The Initial Readings

A. Before reading the poem, the reader should:
 1. Notice its form and length.
 2. Consider the title, determining, if possible, whether it might function as an allusion, symbol, or poetic image.
 3. Notice the date of composition or publication, and identify the general era of the poet.

B. The poem should be read intuitively and emotionally and be allowed to "happen" as much as possible.

C. In order to establish the rhythmic flow, the poem should be reread. A note should be made as to where the irregular spots (if any) are located.

II. Explicating the Poem

A. *Dramatic situation.* Studying the poem line by line helps the reader discover the dramatic situation. All elements of the dramatic situation are interrelated and should be viewed as reflecting and affecting one another. The dramatic situation serves a particular function in the poem, adding realism, surrealism, or absurdity; drawing attention to certain parts of the poem; and changing to reinforce other aspects of the poem. All points should be considered. The following questions are particularly helpful to ask in determining dramatic situation:
 1. What, if any, is the narrative action in the poem?
 2. How many personae appear in the poem? What part do they take in the action?
 3. What is the relationship between characters?
 4. What is the setting (time and location) of the poem?

B. *Point of view.* An understanding of the poem's point of view is a major step toward comprehending the poet's intended meaning. The reader should ask:
 1. Who is the speaker? Is he or she addressing someone else or the reader?
 2. Is the narrator able to understand or see everything happening to him or her, or does the reader know things that the narrator does not?
 3. Is the narrator reliable?
 4. Do point of view and dramatic situation seem consistent? If not, the inconsistencies may provide clues to the poem's meaning.

C. *Images and metaphors*. Images and metaphors are often the most intricately crafted vehicles of the poem for relaying the poet's message. Realizing that the images and metaphors work in harmony with the dramatic situation and point of view will help the reader to see the poem as a whole, rather than as disassociated elements.
   1. The reader should identify the concrete images (that is, those that are formed from objects that can be touched, smelled, seen, felt, or tasted). Is the image projected by the poet consistent with the physical object?
   2. If the image is abstract, or so different from natural imagery that it cannot be associated with a real object, then what are the properties of the image?
   3. To what extent is the reader asked to form his or her own images?
   4. Is any image repeated in the poem? If so, how has it been changed? Is there a controlling image?
   5. Are any images compared to each other? Do they reinforce one another?
   6. Is there any difference between the way the reader perceives the image and the way the narrator sees it?
   7. What seems to be the narrator's or persona's attitude toward the image?

D. *Words*. Every substantial word in a poem may have more than one intended meaning, as used by the author. Because of this, the reader should look up many of these words in the dictionary and:
   1. Note all definitions that have the slightest connection with the poem.
   2. Note any changes in syntactical patterns in the poem.
   3. In particular, note those words that could possibly function as symbols or allusions, and refer to any appropriate sources for further information.

E. *Meter, rhyme, structure, and tone*. In scanning the poem, all elements of prosody should be noted by the reader. These elements are often used by a poet to manipulate the reader's emotions, and therefore they should be examined closely to arrive at the poet's specific intention.
   1. Does the basic meter follow a traditional pattern such as those found in nursery rhymes or folk songs?
   2. Are there any variations in the base meter? Such changes or substitutions are important thematically and should be identified.
   3. Are the rhyme schemes traditional or innovative, and what might their form mean to the poem?
   4. What devices has the poet used to create sound patterns (such as assonance and alliteration)?
   5. Is the stanza form a traditional or innovative one?
   6. If the poem is composed of verse paragraphs rather than stanzas, how do they affect the progression of the poem?

7. After examining the above elements, is the resultant tone of the poem casual or formal, pleasant, harsh, emotional, authoritative?

F. *Historical context.* The reader should attempt to place the poem into historical context, checking on events at the time of composition. Archaic language, expressions, images, or symbols should also be looked up.

G. *Themes and motifs.* By seeing the poem as a composite of emotion, intellect, craftsmanship, and tradition, the reader should be able to determine the themes and motifs (smaller recurring ideas) presented in the work. He or she should ask the following questions to help pinpoint these main ideas:
   1. Is the poet trying to advocate social, moral, or religious change?
   2. Does the poet seem sure of his or her position?
   3. Does the poem appeal primarily to the emotions, to the intellect, or to both?
   4. Is the poem relying on any particular devices for effect (such as imagery, allusion, paradox, hyperbole, or irony)?

BIBLIOGRAPHY

GENERAL REFERENCE SOURCES

BIOGRAPHICAL SOURCES

Jackson, William T. H., ed. *European Writers.* 14 vols. New York: Scribner, 1983-1991.

Kunitz, Stanley, and Vineta Colby, eds. *European Authors, 1000-1900: A Biographical Dictionary of European Literature.* New York: Wilson, 1967.

Magill, Frank N., ed. *Critical Survey of Poetry: Foreign Language Series.* 5 vols. Englewood Cliffs, N.J.: Salem Press, 1984.

_____. *Critical Survey of Poetry: Supplement.* Englewood Cliffs, N.J.: Salem Press, 1987.

Serafin, Steven, ed. *Encyclopedia of World Literature in the Twentieth Century.* 3d ed. 4 vols. Detroit: St. James Press, 1999.

CRITICISM

Coleman, Arthur. *A Checklist of Interpretation, 1940-1973, of Classical and Continental Epics and Metrical Romances.* Vol. 2 in *Epic and Romance Criticism.* 2 vols. New York: Watermill, 1974.

Jason, Philip K., ed. *Masterplots II: Poetry Series, Revised Edition.* 8 vols. Pasadena, Calif.: Salem Press, 2002.

The Year's Work in Modern Language Studies. London: Oxford University Press, 1931.

DICTIONARIES, HISTORIES, AND HANDBOOKS

Auty, Robert, et al. *Traditions of Heroic and Epic Poetry.* 2 vols. Vol. 1, *The Traditions*; Vol. 2, *Characteristics and Techniques.* Publications of the Modern Humanities Research Association 9, 13. London: Modern Humanities Research Association, 1980, 1989.

Bede, Jean-Albert, and William B. Edgerton, eds. *Columbia Dictionary of Modern European Literature.* 2d ed. New York: Columbia University Press, 1980.

France, Peter, ed. *The Oxford Guide to Literature in English Translation.* New York: Oxford University Press, 2000.

Henderson, Lesley, ed. *Reference Guide to World Literature.* 2d ed. 2 vols. New York: St. James Press, 1995.

Oinas, Felix, ed. *Heroic Epic and Saga: An Introduction to the World's Great Folk Epics.* Bloomington: Indiana University Press, 1978.

Index of Primary Works

Hoffman, Herbert H. *Hoffman's Index to Poetry: European and Latin American Poetry in Anthologies*. Metuchen, N.J.: Scarecrow Press, 1985.

Poetics

Gasparov, M. L. *A History of European Versification*. Translated by G. S. Smith and Marina Tarlinskaja. New York: Oxford University Press, 1996.

Wimsatt, William K., ed. *Versification: Major Language Types: Sixteen Essays*. New York: Modern Language Association, 1972.

Spanish and Portuguese Poetry

General

Bleznick, Donald William. *A Sourcebook for Hispanic Literature and Language: A Selected, Annotated Guide to Spanish, Spanish-American, and United States Hispanic Bibliography, Literature, Linguistics, Journals, and Other Source Materials*. 3d ed. Lanham, Md.: Scarecrow Press, 1995.

Newmark, Maxim. *Dictionary of Spanish Literature*. Westport, Conn.: Greenwood Press, 1972.

Sefami, Jacobo, comp. *Contemporary Spanish American Poets: A Bibliography of Primary and Secondary Sources*. Bibliographies and Indexes in World Literature 33. Westport, Conn.: Greenwood Press, 1992.

Woodbridge, Hensley Charles. *Guide to Reference Works for the Study of the Spanish Language and Literature and Spanish American Literature*. 2d ed. New York: Modern Language Association of America, 1997.

Spain and Portugal

Bellver, Catherine G. *Absence and Presence: Spanish Women Poets of the Twenties and Thirties*. Lewisburg, Pa.: Bucknell University Press, 2001.

_____. *Dictionary of the Literature of the Iberian Peninsula*. Cranbury, N.J.: Associated University Presses, 2001.

Florit, Eugenio, ed. *Introduction to Spanish Poetry*. New York: Dover Publications, 1991.

Foster, David Williams, Daniel Altamiranda, and Carmen de Urioste, eds. *Spanish Literature: 1700 to the Present*. Spanish Literature 3. New York: Garland, 2000.

Fox, Gwyn. *Subtle Subversions: Reading Golden Age Sonnets by Iberian Women*. Washington, D.C.: Catholic University of America Press, 2008.

McNerny, Kathleen, and Cristina Enriques de Salamanca, eds. *Double Minorities of*

Spain: A Biobibliographic Guide to Women Writers of the Catalan, Galician, and Basque Countries. New York: Modern Language Association of America, 1994.

Merwin, W. S., ed. and trans. *Spanish Ballads*. Port Townsend, Wash.: Copper Canyon Press, 2008.

Mudrovic, W. Michael. *Mirror, Mirror on the Page: Identity and Subjectivity in Spanish Women's Poetry, 1975-2000*. Bethlehem, Pa.: Lehigh University Press, 2009.

Penna, Michael L., ed. *Twentieth-Century Spanish Poets: First Series*. Dictionary of Literary Biography 108. Detroit: Gale Research, 1991.

Pérez, Janet. *Modern and Contemporary Spanish Women Poets*. New York: Prentice Hall International, 1996.

St. Martin, Hardie, ed. *Roots and Wings: Poetry from Spain, 1900-1975*. Buffalo, N.Y.: White Pine Press, 2004.

Walters, Gareth. *The Cambridge Introduction to Spanish Poetry*. New York: Cambridge University Press, 2003.

West-Settle, Cecile, and Sylvia Sherno, eds. *Contemporary Spanish Poetry: The Word and the World*. Madison, N.J.: Fairleigh Dickinson University Press, 2005.

Wilcox, John. *Women Poets of Spain, 1860-1990: Toward a Gynocentric Vision*. Urbana: University of Illinois Press, 1997.

Winfield, Jerry Phillips. *Twentieth-Century Spanish Poets: Second Series*. Dictionary of Literary Biography 134. Detroit: Gale Research, 1994.

GUIDE TO ONLINE RESOURCES

Web Sites

The following sites were visited by the editors of Salem Press in 2010. Because URLs frequently change, the accuracy of these addresses cannot be guaranteed; however, long-standing sites, such as those of colleges and universities, national organizations, and government agencies, generally maintain links when their sites are moved.

LitWeb
http://litweb.net
 LitWeb provides biographies of hundreds of world authors throughout history that can be accessed through an alphabetical listing. The pages about each writer contain a list of his or her works, suggestions for further reading, and illustrations. The site also offers information about past and present winners of major literary prizes.

The Modern Word: Authors of the Libyrinth
http://www.themodernword.com/authors.html
 The Modern Word site, although somewhat haphazard in its organization, provides a great deal of critical information about writers. The "Authors of the Libyrinth" page is very useful, linking author names to essays about them and other resources. The section of the page headed "The Scriptorium" presents "an index of pages featuring writers who have pushed the edges of their medium, combining literary talent with a sense of experimentation to produce some remarkable works of modern literature."

Poetry Foundation
http://www.poetryfoundation.org
 The Poetry Foundation, publisher of *Poetry* magazine, is an independent literary organization. Its Web site offers links to essays; news; events; online poetry resources, such as blogs, organizations, publications, and references and research; a glossary of literary terms; and a Learning Lab that includes poem guides and essays on poetics.

Poetry in Translation
http://poetryintranslation.com
 This independent resource provides modern translations of classic texts by famous poets and also provides original poetry and critical works. Visitors can choose from several languages, including English, Spanish, Chinese, Russian, Italian, and Greek. Original text is available as well. Also includes links to further literary resources.

Poetry International Web

http://international.poetryinternationalweb.org

Poetry International Web features information on poets from countries such as Indonesia, Zimbabwe, Iceland, India, Slovenia, Morocco, Albania, Afghanistan, Russia, and Brazil. The site offers news, essays, interviews and discussion, and hundreds of poems, both in their original languages and in English translation.

Poet's Corner

http://theotherpages.org/poems

The Poet's Corner, one of the oldest text resources on the Web, provides access to about seven thousand works of poetry by several hundred different poets from around the world. Indexes are arranged and searchable by title, name of poet, or subject. The site also offers its own resources, including "Faces of the Poets"—a gallery of portraits—and "Lives of the Poets"—a growing collection of biographies.

Western European Studies

http://wess.lib.byu.edu

The Western European Studies Section of the Association of College and Research Libraries maintains this collection of resources useful to students of Western European history and culture. It also is a good place to find information about non-English-language literature. The site includes separate pages about the literatures and languages of the Netherlands, France, Germany, Iberia, Italy, and Scandinavia, in which users can find links to electronic texts, association Web sites, journals, and other materials, the majority of which are written in the languages of the respective countries.

ELECTRONIC DATABASES

Electronic databases usually do not have their own URLs. Instead, public, college, and university libraries subscribe to these databases, provide links to them on their Web sites, and make them available to library card holders or other specified patrons. Readers can visit library Web sites or ask reference librarians to check on availability.

Canadian Literary Centre

Produced by EBSCO, the Canadian Literary Centre database contains full-text content from ECW Press, a Toronto-based publisher, including the titles in the publisher's Canadian fiction studies, Canadian biography, and Canadian writers and their works series; *ECW's Biographical Guide to Canadian Novelists*; and *George Woodcock's Introduction to Canadian Fiction*. Author biographies, essays and literary criticism, and book reviews are among the database's offerings.

Literary Reference Center

EBSCO's Literary Reference Center (LRC) is a comprehensive full-text database designed primarily to help high school and undergraduate students in English and the humanities with homework and research assignments about literature. The database contains massive amounts of information from reference works, books, literary journals, and other materials, including more than 31,000 plot summaries, synopses, and overviews of literary works; almost 100,000 essays and articles of literary criticism; about 140,000 author biographies; more than 605,000 book reviews; and more than 5,200 author interviews. It contains the entire contents of Salem Press's MagillOnLiterature Plus. Users can retrieve information by browsing a list of authors' names or titles of literary works; they can also use an advanced search engine to access information by numerous categories, including author name, gender, cultural identity, national identity, and the years in which he or she lived, or by literary title, character, locale, genre, and publication date. The Literary Reference Center also features a literary-historical time line, an encyclopedia of literature, and a glossary of literary terms.

MagillOnLiterature Plus

MagillOnLiterature Plus is a comprehensive, integrated literature database produced by Salem Press and available on the EBSCOhost platform. The database contains the full text of essays in Salem's many literature-related reference works, including *Masterplots*, *Cyclopedia of World Authors*, *Cyclopedia of Literary Characters*, *Cyclopedia of Literary Places*, *Critical Survey of Poetry*, *Critical Survey of Long Fiction*, *Critical Survey of Short Fiction*, *World Philosophers and Their Works*, *Magill's Literary Annual*, and *Magill's Book Reviews*. Among its contents are articles on more than 35,000 literary works and more than 8,500 poets, writers, dramatists, essayists, and philosophers; more than 1,000 images; and a glossary of more than 1,300 literary terms. The biographical essays include lists of authors' works and secondary bibliographies, and hundreds of overview essays examine and discuss literary genres, time periods, and national literatures.

Rebecca Kuzins
Updated by Desiree Dreeuws

CATEGORY INDEX

AVANT-GARDE POETS
    Foix, J. V., 84
    Vallejo, César, 224

BALLADS
    García Lorca, Federico, 93
    Jiménez, Juan Ramón, 128

ELEGIES
    Garcilaso de la Vega, 104
    Jiménez, Juan Ramón, 128
    Manrique, Jorge, 185

EPICS
    Lucan, 167
    Vega Carpio, Lope de, 237

EPIGRAMS
    Machado, Antonio, 176
    Martial, 191

EXPERIMENTAL POETS
    Foix, J. V., 84
    García Lorca, Federico, 93

EXPRESSIONISM
    García Lorca, Federico, 93

GAY AND LESBIAN CULTURE
    Cernuda, Luis, 75

GENERATION OF '27
    Alberti, Rafael, 30
    Aleixandre, Vicente, 39
    Cernuda, Luis, 75
    García Lorca, Federico, 93
    Guillén, Jorge, 120
    Salinas, Pedro, 206

GENERATION OF '98
    Machado, Antonio, 176
    Unamuno y Jugo, Miguel de, 215

GHAZALS
    Judah ha-Levi, 152

GOLDEN AGE, SPANISH
    Calderón de la Barca, Pedro, 57
    Góngora y Argote, Luis de, 113
    John of the Cross, Saint, 139
    León, Luis de, 159
    Vega Carpio, Lope de, 237

HYMNS
    Judah ha-Levi, 152
    Unamuno y Jugo, Miguel de, 215

JEWISH CULTURE
    Judah ha-Levi, 152

LOVE POETRY
    Bécquer, Gustavo Adolfo, 48
    Guillén, Jorge, 120
    John of the Cross, Saint, 139
    Manrique, Jorge, 185
    Salinas, Pedro, 206
    Vallejo, César, 224

LYRIC POETRY
    Alberti, Rafael, 30
    Bécquer, Gustavo Adolfo, 48
    Cernuda, Luis, 75
    Foix, J. V., 84
    García Lorca, Federico, 93
    Góngora y Argote, Luis de, 113
    John of the Cross, Saint, 139
    Machado, Antonio, 176
    Otero, Blas de, 196
    Salinas, Pedro, 206
    Vallejo, César, 224
    Vega Carpio, Lope de, 237

MODERNISM
    Otero, Blas de, 196

MODERNISMO
    Castro, Rosalía de, 65
    García Lorca, Federico, 93
    Jiménez, Juan Ramón, 128
    Salinas, Pedro, 206

NARRATIVE POETRY
    Bega Carpio, Lope de, 237
    Lucan, 167
NATURE POETRY
    Aleixandre, Vicente, 39
    Castro, Rosalía de, 65
NEO-ROMANTICISM
    Jiménez, Juan Ramón, 128

OCCASIONAL VERSE
    Góngora y Argote, Luis de, 113

PASTORAL POETS
    Garcilaso de la Vega, 104
POLITICAL POETS
    Alberti, Rafael, 30
    Lucan, 167
    Otero, Blas de, 196
PROSE POETRY
    Cernuda, Luis, 75
    Jiménez, Juan Ramón, 128

RELIGIOUS POETRY
    Calderón de la Barca, Pedro, 57
    Castro, Rosalía de, 65
    John of the Cross, Saint, 139
    Judah ha-Levi, 152
    León, Luis de, 159
    Manrique, Jorge, 185
    Unamuno y Jugo, Miguel de, 215
    Vega Carpio, Lope de, 237
RENAISSANCE
    Garcilaso de la Vega, 104
    John of the Cross, Saint, 139

    León, Luis de, 159
    Manrique, Jorge, 185
ROMANTICISM
    Bécquer, Gustavo Adolfo, 48

SATIRIC POETRY
    Martial, 191
SONGS
    Garcilaso de la Vega, 104
    Machado, Antonio, 176
    Unamuno y Jugo, Miguel de, 215
SONNETS
    Calderón de la Barca, Pedro, 57
    Foix, J. V., 84
    Garcilaso de la Vega, 104
    Góngora y Argote, Luis de, 113
    Jiménez, Juan Ramón, 128
    Vega Carpio, Lope de, 237
SURREALIST POETS
    Alberti, Rafael, 30
    Aleixandre, Vicente, 39
    Cernuda, Luis, 75
    García Lorca, Federico, 93
    Salinas, Pedro, 206
    Vallejo, César, 224
SYMBOLIST POETS
    Jiménez, Juan Ramón, 128
    Salinas, Pedro, 206

ULTRAISM
    Vallejo, César, 224

VERSE DRAMATISTS
    Calderón de la Barca, Pedro, 57

WAR POETS
    Alberti, Rafael, 30
WOMEN POETS
    Castro, Rosalía de, 65

SUBJECT INDEX

"A la vida religiosa" (León), 165
"Adoration of the Magi, The" (Cernuda), 81
"Airiños, airiños, aires" (Castro), 70
Alberti, Rafael, 30-38
    "Ballad of the Lost Andalusian," 37
    Cal y canto, 33
    Concerning the Angels, 34
    "De los álamos y los sauces," 36
    Entre el clavel y la espada, 36
    Marinero en tierra, 33
    Retornos de lo vivo lejano, 36
    "Three Memories of Heaven," 34
    To Painting, 37
    To See You and Not to See You, 34
Aleixandre, Vicente, 25, 39-47
    Destruction or Love, 44
    Historia del corazón, 46
    Shadow of Paradise, 45
    Swords as if Lips, 44
    Ámbito, 43
Alonso, Dámaso, 25
Álvarez, Juan de Yepes y. *See* John of the Cross, Saint
Ámbito (Aleixandre), 43
Ancia (Otero), 202
Ángel fieramente humano (Otero), 202
Animal de fondo (Jiménez), 136
Annaeus Lucanus, Marcus. *See* Lucan
Arias tristes (Jiménez), 132
Ayala, Pedro López de, 12
Azorín, 23

Baladas de primavera (Jiménez), 133
"Ballad of the Little Square" (García Lorca), 98
"Ballad of the Lost Andalusian" (Alberti), 37

Beside the River Sar (Castro), 72
Black Heralds, The (Vallejo), 227
Book of Good Love, The (Juan Ruiz), 9
Boscán, Juan, 15
Bécquer, Gustavo Adolfo, 22, 48-56
    The Rhymes, 52
    "Rime of the Swallows," 55

Cal y canto (Alberti), 33
Calderón de la Barca, Pedro, 57-64
    "Decima," 62
    "Lágrimas que vierte un alma arrepentida," 62
    Psalle et sile, 62
Cancionero (Unamuno y Jugo), 220
Cantares gallegos (Castro), 70
Canticle (Guillén), 123
Cantigas (poetic form), 3
Castilian Camp, The (Machado), 181
Castro, Rosalía de, 65-74
    "Airiños, airiños, aires," 70
    Beside the River Sar, 72
    Cantares gallegos, 70
    Follas novas, 71
    "I Used to Have a Nail," 69
    "Saint Scholastica," 72
    "They Say That Plants Do Not Speak," 72
Cernuda, Luis, 75-83
    "The Adoration of the Magi," 81
    Donde habite el olvido, 80
    Egloga, elegía, oda, 79
    Las nubes, 81
    Perfil del aire, 79
    Los placeres prohibidos, 80
    Un río, un amor, 80

Christ of Velázquez, The (Unamuno y Jugo), 219
Clamor (Guillén), 123
Conceptismo, 16
Concerning the Angels (Alberti), 34
Confianza (Salinas), 213
Coplas on the Death of His Father (Manrique), 187
Corona trágica, La (Vega Carpio), 245
Costumbrismo, 22
Cruz, Sor Juana Inés de la, 18
Culteranismo, 16
Cántico espiritual (Otero), 201

"Dark Night, The" (John), 147
"De los álamos y los sauces" (Alberti), 36
De un cancionero apócrifo (Machado), 183
"Decima" (Calderón de la Barca), 62
"Déjame" (Otero), 200
Destruction or Love (Aleixandre), 44
Diary of a Newlywed Poet (Jiménez), 134
Diego, Gerardo, 26
Donde habite el olvido (Cernuda), 80
Dragontea, La (Vega Carpio), 243
"Dwelling Place in Heaven" (León), 165

Egloga, elegía, oda (Cernuda), 79
"Elegía a doña Juana la Loca" (García Lorca), 97
En Castellano (Otero), 203
Entre el clavel y la espada (Alberti), 36
Epigrams (Martial), 193
Espronceda, José de, 21
Esto no es un libro (Otero), 203
Estío (Jiménez), 134

Fable of Polyphemus and Galatea (Góngora y Argote), 117
"Fable of Pyramus and Thisbe, The" (Góngora y Argote), 116

Fables, 19
"Farewell, Go with God!" (Unamuno y Jugo), 219
"First Eclogue" (Garcilaso de la Vega), 109
Foix, J. V., 84-92
    "I Was Riding at Full Gallop Around the City Walls, Pursued by a Throng of Superstitious Coalmongers," 91
    "The Partisans of the Sun," 90
    Sol, i de dol, 91
    "Without Symbolism," 89
Follas novas (Castro), 71
Fray Luis. *See* León, Luis de

Garcilaso de la Vega, 15, 104-112
    "First Eclogue," 109
    "Second Eclogue," 107
García Lorca, Federico, 25, 93-103
    "Ballad of the Little Square," 98
    "Elegía a doña Juana la Loca," 97
    The Gypsy Ballads of García Lorca, 99
    Lament for the Death of a Bullfighter, 100
    Poet in New York, 100
    "Somnambule Ballad," 99
    "The Song of the Horseman," 98
Gatomachia (Vega Carpio), 245
Generation of '27, 22
Generation of '98, 22
Gongorism, 16
Gonzalo de Berceo, 6
Guillén, Jorge, 120-127
    Canticle, 123
    Clamor, 123
    Homage, 124
Gypsy Ballads of García Lorca, The (García Lorca), 99
Góngora y Argote, Luis de, 16, 113-119
    Fable of Polyphemus and Galatea, 117
    "The Fable of Pyramus and Thisbe," 116
    The Solitudes, 118

Ha-Levi, Judah. *See* Judah ha-Levi
Heine, Heinrich, 51
"Here" (Salinas), 210
Hernández, Miguel, 26
Historia del corazón (Aleixandre), 46
Homage (Guillén), 124
Human Poems (Vallejo), 232
Humanism, 14
Hymns, 6

"I Used to Have a Nail" (Castro), 69
"I Was Riding at Full Gallop Around the City Walls" (Foix), 91
Isidro, El (Vega Carpio), 243

Jardines lejanos (Jiménez), 132
Jerusalén conquistada (Vega Carpio), 244
Jiménez, Juan Ramón, 23, 128-138
    Animal de fondo, 136
    Arias tristes, 132
    Baladas de primavera, 133
    Diary of a Newlywed Poet, 134
    Estío, 134
    Jardines lejanos, 132
    Pastorales, 132
    La Soledad sonora, 133
    Spiritual Sonnets, 134
John of the Cross, Saint, 139-151
    "The Dark Night," 147
    "The Living Flame of Love," 149
    "The Spiritual Canticle," 148
Judah ha-Levi, 152-158
    "Ode to Zion," 156

Kharjas (poetic form), 2

"Lágrimas que vierte un alma arrepentida" (Calderón de la Barca), 62
Lament for the Death of a Bullfighter (García Lorca), 100

Laurel de Apolo (Vega Carpio), 245
Levi, Judah ha-. *See* Judah ha-Levi
León, Luis de, 159-166
    "A la vida religiosa," 165
    "Dwelling Place in Heaven," 165
    The Perfect Wife, 164
    "To Christ Crucified," 163
    "To Santiago," 164
"Living Flame of Love, The" (John), 149
Lucan, 167-175
    Pharsalia, 169
Luzán, Ignacio de, 18

Machado, Antonio, 23, 176-184
    The Castilian Camp, 181
    De un cancionero apócrifo, 183
    Nuevas canciones, 181
    Proverbios y canciones, 182
    Soledades, 181
Manrique, Jorge, 185-190
    Coplas on the Death of His Father, 187
Marinero en tierra (Alberti), 33
Martial, 191-195
    Epigrams, 193
Mientras (Otero), 204
Modernismo, 22
Moratín, Nicolás Fernández de, 19
"My Religion" (Unamuno y Jugo), 218
My Voice Because of You (Salinas), 211

New Art of Writing Plays, The (Vega Carpio), 244
Novísimos, 27
Nubes, Las (Cernuda), 81
Nuevas canciones (Machado), 181

"Ode to Zion" (Judah ha-Levi), 156
Ortega y Gasset, José, 24
Otero, Blas de, 196-205
    Ancia, 202

Cántico espiritual, 201
"Déjame," 200
En Castellano, 203
Esto no es un libro, 203
Mientras, 204
Pido la paz y la palabra, 202
Que trata de España, 203
Redoble de consciencia, 202
Ángel fieramente humano, 202

"Partisans of the Sun, The" (Foix), 90
Pastorales (Jiménez), 132
Perfect Wife, The (León), 164
Perfil del aire (Cernuda), 79
Pharsalia (Lucan), 169
Pido la paz y la palabra (Otero), 202
Placeres prohibidos, Los (Cernuda), 80
Poem of the Cid (anonymous), 3
Poema de Fernán González (anonymous), 8
Poet in New York (García Lorca), 100
Poetics, 18
Proverbios y canciones (Machado), 182
Psalle et sile (Calderón de la Barca), 62

Que trata de España (Otero), 203
Quevedo y Villegas, Francisco Gómez de, 17

Redoble de consciencia (Otero), 202
Retornos de lo vivo lejano (Alberti), 36
Rhymes, The (Bécquer), 52
Rimado de palaçio (Ayala), 12
"Rime of the Swallows" (Bécquer), 55
Romanticism, 20
Río, un amor, Un (Cernuda), 80

Saavedra, Ángel de, 21
Saint John of the Cross. *See* John of the Cross, Saint
"Saint Scholastica" (Castro), 72
Salamancan poets, 15

Salinas, Pedro, 25, 206-214
 Confianza, 213
 "Here," 210
 My Voice Because of You, 211
 The Sea of San Juan, 212
 "Sheet of Paper," 210
 Todo más claro, y otros poemas, 213
 "Yes, Too Much of Everything," 211
Sea of San Juan, The (Salinas), 212
"Second Eclogue" (Garcilaso de la Vega), 107
Sem Tov, Rabbi, 11
Sevillan poets, 15
Shadow of Paradise (Aleixandre), 45
"Sheet of Paper" (Salinas), 210
Shemuel ha-Levi, Yehuda ben. *See* Judah ha-Levi
Sol, i de dol (Foix), 91
Soledad sonora, La (Jiménez), 133
Soledades (Machado), 181
Solitudes, The (Góngora y Argote), 118
Solitudes, The (Góngora), 17
"Somnambule Ballad" (García Lorca), 99
"Song of the Horseman, The" (García Lorca), 98
Spain, Take This Cup from Me (Vallejo), 233
Spanish poetry
 origins to fifteenth century, 1-13
 fifteenth century to present, 14-29
"Spiritual Canticle, The" (John), 148
Spiritual Sonnets (Jiménez), 134
Swords as if Lips (Aleixandre), 44

"They Say That Plants Do Not Speak" (Castro), 72
"Three Memories of Heaven" (Alberti), 34
"To Christ Crucified" (León), 163
To Painting (Alberti), 37
"To Santiago" (León), 164
To See You and Not to See You (Alberti), 34

Todo más claro, y otros poemas (Salinas), 213
Trilce (Vallejo), 229

Unamuno y Jugo, Miguel de, 23, 215-223
    Cancionero, 220
    The Christ of Velázquez, 219
    "Farewell, Go with God!," 219
    "My Religion," 218

Vallejo, César, 224-236
    The Black Heralds, 227
    Human Poems, 232
    Spain, Take This Cup from Me, 233
    Trilce, 229

Vega Carpio, Lope de, 17, 237-247
    La corona trágica, 245
    La Dragontea, 243
    Gatomachia, 245
    El Isidro, 243
    Jerusalén conquistada, 244
    Laurel de Apolo, 245
    The New Art of Writing Plays, 244
Villancicos (poetic form), 3

"Without Symbolism" (Foix), 89

"Yes, Too Much of Everything" (Salinas), 211